LITTLE ENGLANDERS

LITTLE ENGLANDERS

Britain in the Edwardian Era

ALWYN TURNER

Profile Books

First published in Great Britain in 2024 by
Profile Books Ltd
29 Cloth Fair
London
ECIA 7JQ
www.profilebooks.com

Copyright © Alwyn Turner, 2024

All images reproduced with permission from Alamy.

1 3 5 7 9 10 8 6 4 2

Typeset in Garamond by MacGuru Ltd
Printed and bound in Great Britain by
Clays Ltd, Elcograf S.p.A.

A CIP catalogue record for this book is available from the British Library.

ISBN 978 1 80081 530 8
eISBN 978 1 80081 532 2

FSC
www.fsc.org
MIX
Paper | Supporting
responsible forestry
FSC® C018072

This book is dedicated to Sam Harrison,
with all the usual thanks.

In each century since the beginning of the world wonderful things have been discovered. In the last century more amazing things were found out than in any century before. In this new century hundreds of things still more astounding will be brought to light.

Frances Burnett, *The Secret Garden*, 1911

It was a land where it seemed as if it must be always summer and generally afternoon, a land where bees hummed among the wild thyme and in the flower beds of cottage gardens, where the harvest-mice rustled amid the corn and nettles, and the mill-race flowed cool and silent through water-weeds and dark tunnelled sluices, and made soft droning music with the wooden mill-wheel. And the music carried with it the wording of old undying rhymes.

Saki, *When William Came*, 1913

CONTENTS

NOTE ON CURRENCY AND INCOME

The UK's pre-decimal currency was a little convoluted. There were twelve pennies to a shilling, and twenty shillings to the pound, so a pound was the equivalent of 240 pence. Prices tended to be written in the form £2 12s 6d, representing two pounds, twelve shillings and sixpence. To confuse matters, there were also standard units of a crown (five shillings) and half a crown (two shillings and sixpence). And some payments were made not in pounds but in guineas, with a guinea being one pound and one shilling.

The average annual income of a household in this period was around £100. This would sustain, say, a working father and older son, along with a non-working mother, two other children and perhaps an elderly relative. An annual household income of £50 meant absolute poverty. This did not, though, apply to domestic servants, who were provided with food and board in addition to wages; servants' pay ranged from £100 per annum for a butler down to £8 for an in-between maid. The division between the working and middle classes – the gentility line, as it's sometimes known – can be seen as an annual income of £160, which was the threshold for paying income tax. Five and a half million people lived in households above that level, including 1.4 million with an income of over £700 a year.[1]

TWO DEATHS

We seem to be standing at the end of one era, and our hearts are filled with wonder what shall come next.

The Reverend R. G. Matthew, Rector of Wigan, 1901[1]

'Fact one: News is not news unless confirmed by the papers. Fact two: Print is necessary to national thought.'

Edgar Wallace, *Private Selby*, 1912[2]

King Edward VII (1841–1910), who succeeded his mother Queen Victoria on her death in 1901, pictured by cartoonist Spy in *Vanity Fair* magazine.

THE ROOM OCCUPIED BY SEBASTIAN MELMOTH was on the first floor of a run-down hotel in a poor quarter of Paris, the small windows looking out on to a claustrophobic, unswept court-yard. The furniture was sparse and soiled, the bed too short for his six-foot frame. By his own account, the place was dirty, depressing and devoid of hope, a squalid setting for a man whose life had been devoted to the pursuit of beauty and amusement. 'I used to live entirely for pleasure,' he wrote. 'I shunned suffering and sorrow of every kind.'[3] Now, riddled with debt and disease, seldom rising from bed until the afternoon, he was drinking heavily – champagne in the daytime, absinthe and brandy in the evening – and receiving injections of morphine, until even that proved insufficient to ease his pain and was replaced by opium and chloral. He had lost an alarming amount of weight and his skin was covered in angry red blotches. It was November 1900 and he was just forty-six years old.

In his day, not long ago, he had been the literary sensation of London. He was still known as Oscar Wilde back then, when his play *An Ideal Husband* opened at the Haymarket Theatre in January 1895, its immediate and sensational success eclipsed only by the premiere of *The Importance of Being Earnest* at the St James's the following month. After fifteen years of writing poetry and plays, stories, essays and journalism, he had finally found the true expres-sion of his talent, the artistic and commercial triumphs justifying at last all the promise he'd shown and all the promises he'd made. In particular, *Earnest* was a masterpiece, a social comedy so perfect that the only question was what he could possibly do to top it.

The opportunity never arose. By the end of May 1895, he was utterly disgraced and beginning a sentence of two years' hard labour, having been convicted of gross indecency with young work-ing-class men. When he emerged from prison, his health broken, he had fled into exile in France, assuming the identity of Melmoth from the doomed hero of *Melmoth the Wanderer* (1820), a Gothic novel written by his great-uncle Charles Maturin.

'When my plays were on, I drew a hundred pounds a week,' he reflected, though even then he'd lived beyond his means.[4] Now he was trying, and failing, to live on a £150 annual allowance from his estranged wife, together with what he could beg from friends and from friends of friends. Most ignored his pleas for money, for though some remained loyal, more did not. The British tourists and residents he encountered in his exile – as well as many locals he met – snubbed him, and he was constantly at risk of being refused service by restaurateurs, bar keepers and shop owners.

Wilde dealt with those last years of poverty-blighted misery by embracing the shame. His work, beneath the layers of wit, had always been rooted in a simplicity of structure and morality, having something in common with fable and something with cheap periodicals. And since he had always seen himself as his finest creation, he painted his decline in similarly bold colours, the parable of a giant brought low. 'I have been a king, and now I want to be a beggar,' he declared.[5] This was to be his last great role, emulating the defeated Napoleon Bonaparte after Waterloo, exiled on a remote island in the South Atlantic: 'St Helena was the greatest theme of all – for an artist, the most completely significant in the whole of modern history.'[6]

It was a hard pose to maintain, though, and he knew he couldn't keep it up for long. 'I will never outlive the century,' he told friends in the autumn of 1900. 'The English people would not stand for it.'[7] And on 30 November he duly died.*

The British papers covered his demise, but not always in great depth. One press report read, in its entirety, 'An eccentric career, sadly beclouded of late years, ended in Paris yesterday with the death of Oscar Wilde.'[8] Others ran along the same lines in varying shades of condemnation: 'one of the most brilliant and one of the most notorious men of our time';[9] 'no career was ever more absurdly ruined';[10] 'a life of wretchedness and unavailing regret'.[11]

---

* In those more Christian, more literal times, the new century was deemed to start on 1 January 1901 rather than 1900.

His sins were unforgiven and, said London's *Evening News*, 'the most charitable thing that one can hope for is that he should be forgotten'.[12]

For the first few years of the new century, he was indeed shut out of the public memory, his creed of art for art's sake having become deeply unfashionable. Not that it had really taken hold in the first place, for modern Britain did not pride itself on its cultural appreciation. The ideal picture for the wall of a decent middle-class house, according to the playwright J. M. Barrie, was something 'of which you may say "Jolly thing that," without losing caste as knowing too much'.[13] The writer Max Beerbohm – a former friend of Wilde – once met in Florence an Englishman he knew, standing in front of Botticelli's *Primavera* and looking bored. 'Have you no sense of beauty?' Max demanded, to which the man replied simply, 'No,' and walked away.[14]

The fall of Wilde amplified that attitude; so toxic was his name that he was felt to have contaminated art itself. This was to be a great era for writers who sought social reform – George Bernard Shaw, H. G. Wells, John Galsworthy* – but one in which non-utilitarian culture was viewed with some suspicion. The publisher John Lane said in 1905 that it had been almost impossible to sell poetry since Wilde's arrest,[15] and A. E. Housman resorted to self-financing his book of verse, *A Shropshire Lad* (1896). Novelist George Meredith was thoroughly respectable by the time he died in 1909 – he was a member of the Order of Merit and president of the Society of Authors – but memories of his scandalous first novel, *The Ordeal of Richard Feverel*, all of fifty years earlier, meant that, though there was a memorial service in Westminster Abbey, the dean refused permission for him to be buried there. Thus was the page turned on the disreputable, decadent excesses of the old century.

---

* Beerbohm said of Galsworthy: 'He has sold his literary birthright for a pot of message.'

ii

A bigger break with the past was to come a few weeks later, when the celebrations for the new century were immediately followed by the death on 22 January 1901 of Queen Victoria. This truly was the end of an era, and everyone was conscious of the fact. Her reign had been so long – more than six decades – that generations had been born, grown up and died. The population of England, Scotland and Wales had doubled during those years, to stand at 36 million people.* Of these multitudes, few could remember a time before Victoria: only one in twenty had even been alive in 1837 when she ascended to the throne. If no one had actually expected her to live forever, still it had been hard to envisage her absence. She was, said the newspapers, 'the Mother Queen of a people who have grown up under her rule of gentleness and love'.[16] So of course it felt like a major turning point. 'The end of a great epoch has come upon us,' said future prime minister Arthur Balfour in the House of Commons.[17]

Over those years the look and feel of the country had been completely transformed. Victoria's reign had seen the arrival of photographs, gramophone records and motion pictures; telegraphs, telephones and typewriters; the penny post, paperback novels and mass-circulation newspapers; bicycles, motor cars, underground railways and electric trams; the Manchester Ship Canal, the Great Western Railway, the London sewerage system. Abroad, the Empire had grown wider still and wider, with the acquisition of vast swathes of Africa, stretching from Cairo to the Cape. Intellectually, Charles Darwin had revolutionised humanity's view of itself to a degree unmatched by any other individual in history. And through all the decades of frenetic activity – industrial, scientific and financial, though seldom military – the queen empress had been the one fixed point. Now she was gone, and the new century looked less reassuring as a result.

Perhaps, too, the Empire – of which Victoria had been the

---

* Though that of Ireland had halved, with over three million lost.

talisman, more fetish than figurehead – was now less secure. The scale of the imperial enterprise had been impressed upon the nation in June 1897 (a month after Oscar Wilde's release from Reading Gaol), when London had staged its greatest ever parade, to mark the queen's Diamond Jubilee. Delegations and deputations had come from all the colonies, dependencies and dominions to pay tribute, and the British people saw – for the first time in many cases – just what it was that had been accumulated so slowly, so haphazardly over the course of centuries. 'Not even Rome in her proudest days could ever show such an assemblage of Emperors, Kings, Princes and Potentates – European, Indian, African – as were included in that memorable procession,' marvelled the obituary writers as they looked back.[18] 'She has remade the Empire in her own image, and her virtues have breathed into it the breath of a noble life.'[19]

How would the imperial family fare without the guiding hand of its mother? Certainly, her eldest son, now Edward VII, was a very different proposition, a well upholstered yet less weighty figure, more cavalier and more public, like a latter-day Henry VIII, though with multiple mistresses rather than wives. 'Edward the Caresser' American novelist Henry James called him.[20] He could play the banjo, having been taught by the black Canadian James Bohee,* he'd invited music-hall stars to perform for him at Windsor and Sandringham, and there was a story that he owned a golf bag made from the skin of an elephant's penis, given to him by an Indian prince. In his world, 'Diamond Jubilee' tended to refer to a racehorse that he owned, winner of the Triple Crown in 1900, having been ridden to victory by nineteen-year-old Herbert Jones in the 2,000 Guineas, the Derby and the St Leger. If that augured well for the reign of a new merry monarch, it was also noted that the horse had a 'villainous temper' and a tendency to 'fractious behaviour at the post'; it had attacked its jockey and spectators, earning a reputation as a 'chicken-hearted coward'.[21]

---

* James and his younger brother George subsequently billed themselves as the 'Famous Royal Bohee Brothers, Banjoists to H.R.H. the Prince of Wales'.

The period to which Edward VII lent his name, the years between his mother's death and the outbreak of the Great War in the summer of 1914, was to be a less innovative time for Britain than the Victorian era, 'rather an empty patch',[22] as John Buchan later reflected. There were no technological inventions to rival those of the previous decades, and the most significant development – heavier-than-air powered flight – was pioneered in America.* The only major expansion of the Empire came with the protracted and painful annexation of the Transvaal and the Orange Free State in the Boer War. At home – and in the home – life was more stable than it had been. The birth rate had fallen by nearly a third in the last five decades, but the death rate was also down, and the result was an older population and smaller households; by 1914 families averaged 2.3 children, compared to 6.2 a half-century earlier.[23]

These developments were, of course, more marked among the wealthy than the poor, but there was a new determination that such social divisions should be, if not removed altogether, then at least softened. The hope in many quarters was that this would be an era of greater equality. The Conservative peer Lord George Hamilton, who chaired a royal commission on the Poor Laws, wrote, 'The object and incitement of the nineteenth century was to accumulate wealth, while the duty of the twentieth century is the far more diffi-cult task of securing its better distribution.'[24] From the other side of politics, Henry Campbell-Bannerman, leader of the Liberal Party, said that his aim was to make Britain 'less of a pleasure ground for the rich and more of a treasure house for the nation'.[25]

This democratic impulse wasn't simply a question of the redis-tribution of wealth; it was also about recognising the demand that ordinary people be heard, not merely the great and the good. It could be seen in a new breed of politician. When Herbert Asquith

---

* What was potentially Britain's greatest invention was never developed. In the summer of 1914, Archibald Low unveiled TeleVista, 'his new telephone, which enables you to see the face of the person you are talking to'. The project was shelved with the outbreak of war, and Low turned his attention to inventing the drone.

became prime minister in 1908, he was the first premier not to have a country estate. The man he appointed chancellor of the exchequer, David Lloyd George, had risen from the humblest of origins, a fact which proved, said the *Tatler*, that 'nothing is impossible to anyone who has application, ability and a moderate amount of luck'.[26]

The same spirit could be seen in the spate of Boer War memorials. There had always been monuments in the aftermath of conflict, but there was a difference now, an emphasis on recording the names of the fallen of all ranks, not just those of commanders and generals. In the first years of the century, more than 600 memorials were unveiled across the country, listing the dead of regiments, of schools, of towns and cities – and all honoured the private soldier alongside the officer.

Above all, the new mood of democratic expression could be seen in the rise of the popular press. When a future historian 'comes to reckon up the new factors in British civilisation that have altered the whole constitution of life for this generation,' mused the *Bystander* magazine in 1903, 'he will put in the foremost place, above motor-cars, tariff reform, appendicitis, radium, George Edwardes and india-rubber heel-pads, that portentous thing that we call, with irreverent curtness, the *Mail*.'[27] Maybe that was overstating the case a little, but not by much; in the early twentieth century newspapers were indeed altering the whole constitution of public life, and the *Daily Mail* was in the vanguard of the change.

The newspaper was launched in 1896 by Alfred Harmsworth, a thirty-year-old entrepreneur who already had a couple of papers to his name – London's *Evening News* and the *Edinburgh Daily Record* – as well as a string of magazines, largely aimed at women and children. It was the *Mail* that counted, though. Priced at a halfpenny, half the standard price of a newspaper, it was an instant success, and reached a circulation of a million early in the new century.* Aimed at the newly literate white-collar classes, it had

---

* At the time of the *Mail*'s launch, the entire circulation of the national morning titles only amounted to a million.

sharper headlines and shorter stories than its rivals; it revelled in real crime – especially murders – and in tales of family life, particularly if they involved divorces, mothers and children. 'Life, passion, drama, the human heart. That is what makes a newspaper circulation,' wrote journalist Philip Gibbs in his novel *The Street of Adventure* (1909), and it was the *Daily Mail* that discovered the formula.

The *Mail* changed the nature of journalism. 'The old notion in regard to a newspaper was that it was a responsible adviser of the public,' observed a contemporary. 'Its first duty was to provide the news, uncoloured by any motive, private or public; its second to present a certain view of public policy which it believed to be for the good of the state and the community.'[28] Harmsworth was different. He was very definitely coloured by motive, and his concept of what was good for the community was never disinterested. His detractors alleged that he was irresponsible in his pursuit of sensation, that – in the words of H. G. Wells – he displayed 'an entire disregard of good taste, good value, educational influence, social consequences or political responsibility'.[29] But there was something more important than bad taste going on, a democratic drive that overturned previous assumptions.

Unlike existing titles, the *Daily Mail* had little interest in lengthy, detailed pieces about the wealthy and powerful. It wasn't concerned with the sober recording of official business; rather the emphasis was on articulating the concerns of its readers. Harmsworth was an idiosyncratic mess of contradictions – a pragmatic sentimentalist, a radical Conservative, a traditionalist obsessed with new technology – and his titles were made in his image. 'Most of the ordinary man's prejudices are my prejudices and are therefore the prejudices of my newspapers,' he explained. 'We don't direct the ordinary man's opinion. We reflect it.'[30] In the process, he changed the nature of democracy, making the press primarily a conduit for public opinion, articulating the concerns of a large swathe of the nation and shaping the debate to a degree that no other proprietor had managed.

Harmsworth's one big misstep was the decision to launch the *Daily Mirror* in 1903 as a penny paper not merely aimed at women, but written and edited by women as well. 'Feminine, but not effeminate,' was the slogan.[31] The experiment didn't work, largely because of a lack of sufficiently experienced female journalists, and was swiftly terminated. Undaunted, Harmsworth revamped the *Mirror* as an illustrated paper – the first of its kind – with a heavy emphasis on photographs, and dropped the price to a halfpenny; its circulation rose to become second only to that of the *Mail*. He then bought *The Times* in 1908, and although he didn't interfere too much with the existing style, it too became more popular, its price falling from threepence to a penny by early 1914. He now owned nearly half the daily newspaper circulation in the country.

Harmsworth's hands-on approach to ownership meant he exerted considerable social power and political influence, often to the distaste of politicians. Lord Salisbury, the veteran Conservative leader who was still prime minister as the new century dawned, sniffed that Harmsworth had 'invented a paper for those who could read but not think'.[32] But the *Mail* was too important to be ignored, and in 1905 Salisbury's successor, Arthur Balfour, raised Harmsworth to the peerage as Lord Northcliffe. While not quite the first press baron – Edward Levy-Lawson of the *Daily Telegraph*, Lord Burnham, had got there two years earlier – he was certainly the most successful and powerful there had ever been.

iii

In the weeks between the arrest of Oscar Wilde and the commencement of his trial, the newspapers had been almost uniformly hostile to him, and some feared that he would struggle to get a fair hearing. In desperation, his friend Frank Harris, a writer himself, visited the then-proprietor of *The Times*, Arthur Walter, asking that the paper might publish an article calling for judgement to be suspended and for due respect to be given to Wilde's stature and accomplishments as an artist.

Walter did not agree. 'A man who had written a great poem or a great play did not rank in his esteem with a man who had won a skirmish against a handful of unarmed savages, or one who had stolen a piece of land from some barbarians,' wrote Harris scornfully. 'In his heart he held the view of the English landed aristocracy, that the ordinary successful general or admiral or statesman was infinitely more important than a Shakespeare or a Browning.'

Harris was convinced that this was a mistaken assessment of who and what really mattered. Wilde would be remembered, he insisted, while 'the names of Gladstone, Disraeli, Wolseley, Roberts, and Wood, would diminish and fade from day to day till in a hundred years they would scarcely be known, even to the educated'.[33] He was wrong about the names of William Gladstone and Benjamin Disraeli, but he was surely right about that trio of field marshals. Garnet Wolseley, Frederick Roberts and Evelyn Wood have long since ceded top billing to the author of *The Importance of Being Earnest*.

This book is more inclined to the view of Frank Harris than that of Arthur Walter. It is an attempt to take the temperature of the nation as it emerged from a century when it had dominated the world and was beginning – whether it knew it or not – a long process of decline. It draws heavily on popular literature, on the songs of the music hall and on the newspapers. Consequently, it might sometimes seem trivial: the administrators of Empire feature less than the headliners at the Empire, Leicester Square, and the politicians that appear are those who were embraced by the public. Trivial, but not insignificant, for these were the stories the country told itself at a time when it was re-evaluating what Britain meant, and the notes struck here were to echo through the whole of the twentieth century and beyond.

For despite the apparent tranquillity, serious changes were happening. The relationship between the state and the family was being recast. So too the nature of party politics, with splits in Conservative and Unionist ranks, the reinvention of the Liberals and the birth of the Labour Party. It was also a period of escalating crisis. Increasingly violent disputes over the role of women, the rights of trade unions and the status of Ireland disrupted the political system, threatening to derail it entirely. And questions of Britain's trade and diplomatic relationship with the Empire and the wider world grew ever more pressing, while tensions in Europe became dangerously strained.

Through it all ran some sense of an ending, though none knew quite what was coming to a close. The death of the queen empress had seemed so definite a break in its own right, but over the ensuing decade or so, there was a rumbling unease, pre-tremors of a still greater rupture. There was much talk of anarchists and revolutionaries, of foreign invasions and enemies within, of ancient gods and future fears, of national decline and of complacency in the face of that decline. Surely an ending was in sight. In Wilde's *The Picture of Dorian Gray* (1891) the phrase *'fin de siècle'* is mentioned, and Dorian sighs. 'I wish it were *fin du globe*,' he says. 'Life is a great disappointment.' It was a characteristically self-dramatising pose, but it was not out of tune with the new century.

Actual predictions of doomsday were largely confined to obscure cults such as the Israelites of the House of David – 'Lunatics from America', according to the press, though they were now ensconced on the Romford Road in east London[34] – or the Brighton-based Army of the Lord, whose leader King Solomon (born James Wood) announced in 1906 that the world would end 'any day in the next fortnight'.[35] But even in more mainstream society, the language of the Last Days was becoming commonplace. ARMAGEDDON! screamed one headline, as early as 1905 – the result 'if Britain and Germany Went to War'.[36] A few years later, a series of industrial disputes provoked similar horror: 'Ruin hangs, like a dark pall, over the nation itself. It threatens a cataclysm of disaster.'[37] And when J. L. Garvin, editor of the *Observer*,* surveyed the situation in Ulster, he compared it 'to a political apocalypse'.[38]

Where there had been confidence, now there was doubt. One

---

* Alfred Harmsworth bought the *Observer* in 1905.

of the coming men was Winston Churchill, a former cavalry officer who had already seen action on three continents by the time he was elected in 1900 as a Conservative MP. Many were to vest their hopes for the future in him, and he exuded optimism. Yet even he sometimes displayed gloom on a grand scale. The most memorable passage in his first – and only – novel, *Savrola* (1900), envisaged the slow death of the planet: 'The cooling process would continue; the perfect development of life would end in death; the whole solar system, the whole universe itself, would one day be cold and lifeless as a burned-out firework.'

1

MONEY AND MUSIC HALL

'Money, my dear Jessie, is the main thing. Money is, in fact, the hub of everything; only fools try to fight the world without it.'

Alice Maud Meadows, *A Million of Money*, 1903[1]

Why, if I was to try and sing highly moral songs, they would fire ginger beer bottles and beer mugs at me. They don't pay their sixpences and shillings at a music hall to hear the Salvation Army.

Marie Lloyd, 1897[2]

Singer Marie Lloyd (1870–1922), the Queen of the Music Halls, from a programme for the Oxford Music Hall, Oxford Street, London. Also on the bill that week was Dan Leno.

ON A COLD, MOONLIT NIGHT IN JANUARY 1909, a car skidded on a dangerous curve at Penmaenmawr, on the coast of Caernarfonshire, crashing into the sea wall and throwing its driver, a young woman named Violet Charlesworth, through the windscreen to fall forty feet into the waters below. Happily, the other occupants of the car – her sister, Lilian, and their chauffeur, who she had persuaded to take a back seat while she drove – survived, but for Violet it was a tragically premature end to a life of great prospects. She was just short of her twenty-fifth birthday, when she would have come into an inheritance of £75,000, a legacy from her fiancé, who had died abroad.

In anticipation of this fortune, she and Lilian, together with their mother, had been living very well – hence the chauffeur-driven car – with a rented villa at St Asaph, thirty miles east of the fatal scene, as well as houses in Wiltshire and Ross-shire. It had been a spectacular rise for the daughter of a mechanic from Stafford, but she was unaffected by it all. 'The character of the simple village maiden became her admirably,' it was reported. 'She had a habit of dropping her eyelids and speaking, half shyly, in a low, gentle voice.'[3]

The police were satisfied with the account of the accident given by the survivors, but there were things that didn't quite add up. Most strikingly, there was no body, and it seemed unlikely that it could have been washed out to sea in the shallow waters at Penmaenmawr. Nor was there any blood at the scene, and the car was surprisingly undamaged from its encounter with the stone wall.

The press – attracted initially by the tragedy of the heiress and by the slightly exotic world of motoring – sniffed an even better story and swiftly discovered that the Charlesworths were heavily in debt to tradesmen, jewellers, landlords and motor dealers. There was thirty pounds in unpaid wages for the kennelman employed by Violet to look after her beloved St Bernard dogs and, at the other extreme, more than £10,000 owing to a London stockbroker. Then came a report that a young woman in a crimson motoring-cloak had been spotted boarding an express train at Bangor, ten miles down the coast, on the night of the accident. Had the death been faked? asked the papers, and for two weeks their pages were full of pursuits and sightings of crimson-cloaked women, until finally a reporter ran Violet Charlesworth to ground in a small temperance hotel in Oban, Argyllshire.

The story that emerged was one of fraud, initiated by the mother and taken up with enthusiasm by Violet. There was, it transpired, no dead fiancé and no inheritance. It had all been a fiction, enabling the family to live on credit and to borrow substantial sums of money. The biggest victim was one Dr Edward Hughes Jones, who met Violet in Rhyl, proposed to her, and was fleeced for £4,000. Charged with obtaining money on false pretences, mother and daughter were sentenced to five years' penal servitude, though two days later the judge reduced their sentences to three years each.

It was all rather squalid – one of the fraud victims was an elderly neighbour who lost her lifetime savings – yet such was the public's fascination with getting rich quick that Charlesworth enjoyed a brief period as a celebrity.* She was a young, pretty scoundrel; in recognition of her fame, the curve in the road became known as Violet's Leap, while a nearby rock was named Violet's Thumb.

ii

The story of Violet Charlesworth was a short-lived sensation, a manifestation of the power of the popular press, both positively – the papers exposed the crime that the police had overlooked – and negatively: the glamorising of a fraudster. While it was entirely

---

* A newspaper editor in Edith Nesbit's novel *The Story of the Treasure Seekers* (1899) explained who were to be considered celebrities: 'The Queen and the Princes, and people with titles, and people who write, or sing, or act – or do something clever or wicked.'

typical of its time, it wasn't how Edwardian Britain wanted to see itself. For that, one might look to the readers of the magazine *Leisure Hour*, who were asked in 1901 to nominate the Greatest Living Englishman, the person who represented the best of the country. The people's verdict was split, a tie for first place between two soldiers, one secular, the other spiritual.[4]

There was Field Marshal Frederick Roberts, the sixty-nine-year-old commander-in-chief of the British Army. Bobs, as he was universally known, was a veteran of the Indian Mutiny, had seen active service in Abyssinia and Afghanistan, and had most recently led the imperial forces in the Boer War. And there was General William Booth, the teetotal, vegetarian co-founder – with his wife, Catherine – of the Salvation Army, which had grown in twenty-five years from a single evangelical mission in the East End of London to an international church working in nearly fifty countries. In its early days, Booth's crusading church had faced much opposition, from the intellectual scorn of scientist Thomas Henry Huxley – Darwin's Bulldog, as he was known – to the physical assaults of gangs of youths calling themselves the Skeleton Army. But it had persevered, and these days Booth was received with respect by the Governor General of Australia, the President of the United States, the Emperor of Japan, even by King Edward VII himself.

Together, Bobs and Booth presented a familiar self-image for the country: mighty in arms, committed to the Empire, devoted to service and duty, the exemplar of a practical and charitable Christianity. Perhaps, however, they also reflected the lowered aspirations of the times. Because the truth was that, in the pantheon of British military commanders, Earl Roberts was hardly on the level of Wellington or Marlborough, Nelson or Blake. And Booth, despite his mighty work in fighting alcohol and prostitution, didn't change the nation to the same degree as the social-reforming evangelicals who preceded him: John Wesley, William Wilberforce, the Earl of Shaftesbury. The country's contemporary heroes were still impressive, admirable men, of course, but they were somehow on a smaller scale than the giants of the past. Maybe this was not to be an age fit for heroes. 'Life is too easy and mannered,' wrote John Buchan in 1900; 'the field for a man's courage is in petty and recondite things.'[5]

Some believed the same was true of the governing class, grown fat on peace and prosperity. The larger part of a century had passed since Napoleon had been defeated in 1815, and though there had been wars in that time, they were remote affairs; the country itself had not been threatened. The long, comfortable peace seemed to have changed Britain and, the frontier days of imperialism having passed, the leading actors in the national drama were more concerned with administration than adventure. 'Lords without anger or honour, who dare not carry their swords,' scoffed G. K. Chesterton. 'They fight by shuffling papers.'[6]

Similarly, the great leaps forward of the Industrial Revolution were long gone, replaced by the less productive, if more profitable, accumulation of money in the City of London. There was still room for an entrepreneur, as Alfred Harmsworth and others showed, but for the most part the man of enterprise was being supplanted by the managing director. Cecil Rhodes – described as 'the greatest Englishman of our time' by the *Globe*[7] – remarked that, in a hundred years' time, 'when I look down from the sky at this little planet, I shall find that it has passed into the hands of a Hebrew financier'. And veteran journalist W. T. Stead* largely agreed, though without the anti-Semitism: 'Money is the coming king, and the American dollar will be the emperor of the world.' He added, though, that such a development would not be welcomed. 'If the money king is to be the potentate of the future, he will not owe his elevation to supreme power to any intrinsic popularity which he enjoys with the public.'[8]

Perhaps. But it seemed that the rise of money provoked not so

---

* Stead's high point had come in 1885 with a sensationalist series of articles, 'The Maiden Tribute of Modern Babylon', which exposed child prostitution, saw him sent to jail and helped raise the age of sexual consent from thirteen to sixteen.

much resentment as a wish to join in, as the case of Violet Charles-worth illustrated. At the respectable end of society, there was a growing number of shareholders – estimated at a million by 1911 – seeking to ride on the frock-coat-tails of the financiers. They were satirised in Hilaire Belloc's novel *Mr Clutterbuck's Election* (1908), the fable of a small-time City broker nursing the capital he inherit-ed from his father until, in a slightly shady deal, he invests £750 in buying a million eggs that are destined for British forces in the Boer War. When the conflict ends, with the eggs unshipped, he fears that his money is lost, but the government has other ideas: it wouldn't want patriotic businessmen to be out of pocket, so it promises compensation. 'Within a week of the cessation of hostilities, offers had been made to all the owners at the rate, less carriage, of one shilling for each egg,' and Clutterbuck's £750 is instantly converted to £45,000. Within a decade he's doubled this, and then – thanks to an error by his clerk – he becomes a very rich man indeed, able 'to pass from ease to affluence'.

Even for those without disposable income to invest, there was still the dream of unearned, unexpected money. The idea of coming into a substantial legacy, for example, was a recurrent subject in popular songs, from Bessie Wentworth's 'Good Old Uncle Brown' (1894) to Fred Lincoln's 'A Matrimonial Chase' (1904) and George Robey's 'Bang Went the Chance of a Lifetime' (1908); it was also parodied in Harry Champion's 'Any Old Iron' (1911), in which the inheritor of a gold watch and chain discovers that they're made of base metal. Popular literature was even more fascinated by fanta-sies of sudden, implausible riches. Alice Maud Meadows' *A Million of Money* (1903) hinges on a woman assuming a fake identity to secure a massive inheritance, while in Louis Tracy's *The King of Diamonds* (1904), a meteorite made of extraterrestrial diamonds lands in the backyard of an East End slum, bringing enormous wealth to the orphan boy who finds it.

This acquisitive tone was found in the unlikeliest of places. Sherlock Holmes, the biggest fictional hero of the early 1890s, had always prided himself on being uninterested in material gain. 'I play the game for the game's own sake,' he insisted. And yet, as his career drew towards its close in the early years of Edward's reign, the great detective became ever more mercenary.* In 1901 he accepted a cheque for £6,000 from Lord Holdernesse – 'I am a poor man,' he shrugs – and the following year he took on an investigation into a woman's disappearance for pecuniary motives: 'The family are anxious, and as they are exceedingly wealthy no sum will be spared if we can clear the matter up,' he tells Dr Watson. Whether by coincidence or otherwise, this new-found interest in financial reward occurred at a time when Holmes's creator, Sir Arthur Conan Doyle, had become the highest-paid author in the world.[†] In 1893, having tired of the character, he'd documented Sherlock's death, killed in a struggle with his nemesis Professor Moriarty at the Reichenbach Falls. The reading public, however, were far from tired, and their clamour for more adventures became irresistible. A decade on from Holmes's supposed demise came the sensational revelation that he had survived after all, and magazines in America and Britain were so excited by the news that they were prepared to stump up $8,000 for each short story, with book royalties and licensing rights to be added. Money mattered, and Sherlock put behind him the Wildean 1990s, by this time no longer a 'man who loves art for its own sake'.

Even team sport – that great gift of English public schools to the world, on which manhood and Empire relied – was being corrupted by cash. Association football was long since lost; that had been evident when the Old Etonians were beaten in the 1883 FA Cup Final by Blackburn Olympic, the first professional (and the first northern) team to win the trophy. As money flowed into the game, players began to be sold from club to club, and in 1905

---

* The exact chronology of Holmes's career has been the subject of much Sherlockian debate, but the dates given here are generally agreed.
† He also inspired the name of comedy double act Conan and Doyle, who went in for eccentric dancing but never made the big time.

Middlesbrough FC bought England international Alf Common from Sunderland for a world-record price of £1,000.*

There was also the creation of the Northern Rugby Football Union in 1895, which split rugby into two codes, one amateur, the other professional, with similar fractures following in Australia and New Zealand. Cricket still maintained its dignified distinction between Gentlemen and Players, but the latter were becoming more numerous by the season, and anyway the rules could always be bent: the sport's most celebrated figure, W. G. Grace, was in the habit of over-claiming expenses to an extent that belied his amateur status.

The revived Olympic Games – staged at the Great Stadium in London's Shepherd's Bush in 1908† – jealously guarded their spirit of amateurism, yet there was leeway here. George Larner won two gold medals in the walking events that year, and testified in adverts that appeared immediately afterwards that his success was 'in no small measure due to my consistent training on Bovril'.[9] Meanwhile, Oxo was boasting that it had signed up 'sixty-eight of the competitors chosen to represent Great Britain'. Photographs of these were included in Oxo's own 'Games Souvenir', available free on written request.[10]

Thus was competition on the athletics field mirrored by commercial rivalry between meat products. That in itself was largely driven by an advertising industry enjoying a golden age, its rapid growth aided by literacy and by the popular press. Intellectual types read books such as *The Psychology of Advertising* (1908) by American psychologist Walter Dill Scott, who promised to bring scientific theory to the art of persuasion, but most advertisers settled for excessive puffery. 'Everybody who does a large advertised trade is selling something common on the strength of saying

* By 1914 this record had risen to £2,500.
† London lost out to Rome in the bidding process, but the need to repair the damage done by Mount Vesuvius erupting in 1906 meant Italy lacked the funds to build the infrastructure, and London got the games by default.

it's uncommon,' says a businessman dismissively in H. G. Wells's novel *Tono-Bungay* (1909). He himself is selling what is essentially coloured water as a supposed health tonic. And at this time that was fine, because the industry was virtually unregulated. A spate of treatments for sexually transmitted diseases had prompted the Indecent Advertisements Act 1889,* and the following year the various trade associations of billposters had come together to police their business, launching the Joint Censorship Committee. Beyond those minimal restrictions, though, advertising was a free-for-all with a lot of room for fanciful, sometimes startling copy.

'Why eat when you can live on Mal-Kah cigarettes?' demanded one 1906 advert.[11] It cited the example of Sacco the Fasting Champion, an Austrian endurance artist who was then touring the country with an act that saw him lying in a glass cabinet for up to fifty-two days without eating. He did, however, drink sparkling mineral water and, as Mal-Kah were proud to announce, he also smoked twenty-five of their cigarettes a day.† In 1912 the makers of Nestor went a stage further, with the boast that their product had been smoked by 'the late Mr Henry Labouchère'. The point was that, since the recently deceased MP and journalist had lived to the age of eighty, this proved that 'cigarette smoking is not prejudicial to longevity – if you smoke the best'. Still, it wasn't entirely reassuring to have a dead man proclaim the health benefits of smoking.[12] Those supposed benefits saw Grimault's Indian Cigarettes advertised as a cure for 'asthma, nervous coughs, catarrh, sleeplessness and oppression'.[13]

Cigarette smoking had been the preserve of the privileged,

---

* In 1977 this legislation would be used to prosecute (unsuccessfully) a record shop in Nottingham that had a window display featuring the album *Never Mind the Bollocks, Here's the Sex Pistols*.

† In addition to suppressing his appetite, the cigarettes yielded ash that Sacco rubbed into his skin to give an appropriately gaunt pallor. (The fasting, incidentally, was not genuine; he smuggled food – concentrated meat paste – into the cabinet, sewn into his bedding.)

but it was now moving rapidly down the social scale, the market crowded with brands whose names created an aura of aspiration and a return to nature: Albany, Ariston and Lobby; Brave Saxon, Butterfly and Welsh Flower.* Which cigarettes you smoked could even proclaim your politics. Red Flag cigarettes, available from Lewis Lyons & Sons of Bethnal Green, London, were sold as being 'made by socialists for socialists, from pure tobacco, free from dust, under best working conditions', and cost just two shillings per hundred ('as cheap as the cheapest capitalist cigarettes').[14] Or there was Green Box, as advertised in the *Suffragette*: 'hand made by skilled women makers, who work in unusually favourable conditions'. They were more expensive, though, at three shillings for a hundred.[15]

Ever-present advertising helped to create a society that offered temptation at every turn, and the story of Violet Charlesworth was part of that world, which gave her a certain allure. There were limits, though. During the period between her arrest and her trial, Charlesworth was booked to appear at a London music hall, telling her story in an act entitled 'A Clever Woman'. She came on stage in her famous crimson cloak, but the winning manner that had enabled her to commit fraud was not matched by her stage presence; the audience was unimpressed, hissing and booing her off, and she lost the booking after just two days.[16] Perhaps that reception said more about public values than did the relish of the popular press in recounting her tale. For if one truly wanted to gauge the mood of the nation, a visit to a music hall, the most popular cultural expression of the time, was the best option.

---

* Other Edwardian cigarette brands included: Black Cat, Call of the East, Country Life, Chairman, Columbine, Craven, Cropper, Crown Virginia, Donore Castle, Front Bench, Gold Bond, Gold Plate, Golden Dawn, Infant Plant, Isherwood's, Matinee, Mitcham Cricket Green, Myrtle Grove, Navy Cut, Nutcracker, Orbit, Park Drive, Perfectos, Pioneer, Pirate, Polo, Private, Quo Vadis, Regal Oval, Richmond Gem, Royal Navy, Savoy, State Express, Sweet Caporal, Tabs, Teofani's, Three Castles, Three Nuns, Tintern Abbey, Waverley.

iii

'Historians, when they come to deal with the opening years of the twentieth century, will probably call this the Music-Hall Age,' wrote P. G. Wodehouse in 1909.[17] But he was a young man then, and some with longer memories thought that the age of which he spoke had already passed. 'The music hall proper has been nigh obliterated, and its music is being snubbed out of existence,' complained a correspondent to the theatrical paper the *Era*.[18] Both perspectives were probably right.

Music hall grew out of taverns in the mid-nineteenth century, with the Canterbury, opened by Charles Morton in Lambeth, south London, in 1852 generally seen as the first purpose-built hall. The format was simple: a succession of live acts appeared on stage over the course of an evening. A small admission fee was charged, with the real money coming from sales of drink and food. It was an essentially urban phenomenon, a product of the population explosion in British cities – London grew from one to six million inhabitants over the course of the nineteenth century – and of greater leisure time. As the radical economist J. A. Hobson wrote in 1901, music hall came from 'a gradual debasement of popular art attending the new industrial era of congested, ugly, manufacturing towns'. He didn't approve, but he did recognise the importance of the institution: 'a more potent educator than the church, the school, the political meeting or even the press'.[19]

The layout of music halls reflected their origins in public houses; seats weren't arranged in rows facing the front, but at tables placed at a right angle to the stage. As this layout suggested, these were places for eating, drinking and socialising as much as for performance. Consequently, audiences were rowdy, seldom sober, and not shy of expressing their opinion if an act failed to satisfy. In some of the rougher halls the orchestra pit was covered with an iron grille, so that the musicians might be spared the impact of any missiles thrown in disapproval. In some venues balconies overhung the stage, giving disgruntled members of the audience the opportunity to urinate from a great height on unfortunate performers.

The bar was at the rear of the hall, with waiters servicing the tables (sometimes with the bottles chained to their trays, to prevent them being used as weapons), and it was at the back that prostitutes tended to ply their trade. Their presence attracted a thrill-seeking type of upper-class young men,* but for the most part the music hall was a working-class world. It was also, in the audience, a very male world, though on stage it was a different matter, with near-parity between the sexes: the 1878 edition of the *Era*'s 'Almanack' listed 384 female comic singers and 357 male.[20]

This was not a milieu for subtlety of artistic expression. It required a performer to reach above and across the band into a fog of cigar and cigarette smoke, to engage with a drunken audience that, in the bigger halls, could be a couple of thousand strong. And then it might be on to the next engagement, for in London, where there were hundreds of halls, it was not unusual for a big name to play three or four, even five venues a night. In 1905 Sam Mayo, a deadpan comic known as the Immobile One, made a record fifty-eight appearances in just six days. It was an unforgiving environment that did little for artists' health, and many music-hall performers died prematurely, most of them through drink; the greatest of them all, Dan Leno, who invented modern stand-up comedy, was just forty-three when he died in 1904.

Yet the demands of music-hall performing also ensured that anyone who made it to the top of the bill was genuinely a popular favourite; these were not audiences easily seduced by hype, and the biggest stars were those who articulated best the imagination and the concerns of the crowd. In return they were well remunerated; male impersonator Vesta Tilley was said to be Britain's highest-paid woman in the last years of the nineteenth century.

---

* Max Beerbohm first visited a hall in 1891: 'I was filled with an awful, but pleasant, sense of audacity in venturing into such a place, so plebeian and unhallowed a den, as a music hall.'

The music-hall stage was one of the few places a working-class man or woman might make a fortune.*

As the format evolved, there was a growing demand for novelty and variety to fill bills that might, in the larger halls, consist of up to a couple of dozen acts. By the turn of the century, there were acrobats and jugglers, magicians and mind readers, sharpshooters, trick cyclists, ventriloquists and clog dancers. There were animal acts, the likes of Velanche and His Wonderful Football Dogs,† as well as performing seals, goats, monkeys and elephants, and – most famously – the boxing kangaroo at the London Aquarium, who was stuffed in 1894 after his death and displayed in a glass cabinet, still wearing his gloves.‡ There was a brief fad for one-legged dancers, and a strong vein of sensationalist acts: Charles Noissee, the Living Skeleton; Andrew Hull, the Man with the Iron Cranium; Antoine Menier, the Human Ostrich, who ate 'coal, candles, stones, broken glass, brass, wood, paper and bricks, washed down with train-oil, ink and methylated spirits';[21] and Unthan the Armless Wonder, 'who does everything with his feet that another man would with his hands, such as writing a letter, using a pocket handkerchief, peeling an orange, firing a pistol &c'.[22]

As the phrase implied, though, music hall was dominated by songs. They might be comic or melodramatic, sentimental or just silly, but they all tended to feature big choruses that encouraged the audience to join in. That was the easiest way of getting the crowd onside, and communal singing was intrinsic to the

---

* Or, in the case of women, where one might marry a fortune. Singer Belle Bilton married the 5th Earl of Clancarty in 1889; Connie Gilchrist, best known for a skipping-rope dance, married the 7th Earl of Orkney in 1892; and chorus girl Rosie Boote married the 4th Marquess of Headfort in 1901.

† Even more gimmicky, there was a troupe called the Football Girls, who used to play a game against male members of the audience.

‡ When the Aquarium was sold to the Methodist church in 1903 (the Methodist Central Hall, Westminster was built on the site), the fixtures and fittings were auctioned off; the stuffed kangaroo failed to meet its guide price of fifty pounds, going for just two guineas.

entertainment. 'It makes a lot of difference to a singer if she (or he) feels that the audience is with her,' said Bessie Bonehill, another of the male impersonators. 'It does one good to hear them joining in and singing with you.'[23]

A relatively small number of professional writers poured out thousands of songs every year, seeking to sell them to individual performers for their exclusive use. The vast majority of this material left little trace, but there were those that stayed the course; by the time he retired, singer George Chirgwin calculated that he'd performed his biggest hit, 'The Blind Boy' (1883), more than 20,000 times.[24] Some songs burned themselves so deep into the public consciousness that they would far outlive their performers: the likes of Lottie Collins's 'Ta-ra-ra Boom-de-ay' (1891), Katie Lawrence's 'Daisy Bell (Bicycle Made for Two)' (1892),* Florrie Forde's 'Down at the Old Bull and Bush' (1904),† Mark Sheridan's 'I Do Like to Be Beside the Seaside' (1909) and Jack Judge's 'It's a Long Way to Tipperary' (1912).

Songs were also the comedian's stock in trade – the transition to patter was only just emerging – and it was the comics who really drew the crowds; those with harsh lives tend to seek entertainment in laughter rather than lamentation. Many documented working-class life, but they wore the hardships lightly. Gus Elen, born in a Pimlico slum, adopted the look and persona of the costermongers who traded in the London streets, and his song 'The Coster's Mansion' (1899) praised with considerable irony the convenience of a family occupying a single room; if you want to see his dining room, parlour, office or bedroom: 'You've only got to stop just

---

* According to one international traveller in 1902, 'Daisy Bell' was an international hit, heard 'in the streets of France and Germany, Spain, Portugal and Italy' and 'equally popular among the natives of Madagascar, New Guinea and the islands of the South Sea'.

† The original version, in 1903, was an American advert for the Anheuser-Busch brewery in St Louis, Missouri: 'Come, come, drink some Budweis with me, under the Anheuser Bush.'

where you is.' The same theme was found in his best song, 'The Cockney's Garden' (1894). He's occupying a house this time, and the views from the backyard are tremendous:

> Wiv a ladder and some glasses
> You could see the 'Ackney Marshes,
> If it wasn't for the 'ouses in between.

There's no suggestion that these conditions might ever change. All one could do was accept the situation with fortitude, resignation and good humour. And, of course, with alcohol. One of Gus Elen's other songs, 'Arf a Pint of Ale' (1905), makes clear his dislike of tea, coffee and cocoa, and his attachment to beer: his drinking day starts with a half-pint at breakfast and culminates in a barrel and a half for supper. There were plenty of other tributes to alcohol. 'Kind friends, I do implore you all, teetotallers to be,' sang Sam Mayo. 'Don't touch the drink, oh, touch it not! Then there'll be more for me.'

Generally, food was less important, although Harry Champion, of 'Any Old Iron' fame, had a strong line in songs about fantasy feasts: 'Boiled Beef and Carrots', 'Good Old Yorkshire Pudden', 'Home-Made Sausages', 'Hot Meat Pies, Saveloys and Trotters', 'I Want Meat', 'A Little Bit of Cucumber', 'Oh! That Gorgonzola Cheese', 'Put a Bit of Treacle on My Pudden' Mary Ann'.* There was, of course, an element of double entendre in much of this. In her song 'Girls, Study Your Cookery Books' (1908) Florrie Forde advised that a 'man's appetite is the way to reach his heart', and urged women to 'give him the tender part'. Evidently, there was more than one appetite that needed satisfying: 'A nice rice pudding reminds him of the day that he was wed.'

The queen of innuendo, indeed 'the queen of our variety stage',

---

* If the diet seems a little light on healthy foods, that only reflected the real world; when the first official index of the cost of living was drawn up in 1914, no one saw the need to include fresh fruit or green vegetables in the typical basket of goods.

as the *Music Hall and Theatre Review* called her,[25] was Marie Lloyd. Born Matilda Wood in 1870 in the East End of London, Lloyd didn't make her professional debut until she was fifteen,* but she found success almost immediately and by the start of the new century was the leading light of the London halls and an international star. Her enduring appeal lay in her ability to communicate pleasure: life was to be enjoyed, and human failings were inherently funny and forgivable. She exuded warmth, wisdom and tolerance. Above all, she celebrated sex. Her song titles gave the broad picture: 'Among my Knick-Knacks', 'Are You Looking for a Girl Like Me?', 'He Knows a Good Thing When He Sees It', 'Naughty, Naughty, Naughty', 'What's This For, Eh?'. All were delivered with a generous helping of winks and gestures to ensure that the meaning was not missed.

Then there were her railway songs, also laced with sexual subtexts. In 'Oh, Mr Porter' (1892) a woman on her way home from London finds herself going further than she intended. 'Oh, Mr Porter, what shall I do? I want to go to Birmingham and they're taking me on to Crewe,' she frets. Happily an 'old gentleman' in her carriage is there to sympathise – or at least to 'declare that it was hard'. And in 'What Did She Know About Railways?' (1897) a country girl gets the train to London, but is innocent of modern ways, even when it comes to the basics of travelling: 'The guards and porters came round her by the score, and she told them all she'd never had her ticket punched before.' Despite her naivety, however, our heroine is capable of looking after herself; as the men become more persistent, she resists their advances, and finds herself in court the next morning, facing 'twelve black-eyed porters'.

Lloyd's self-assertiveness was not confined to the songs. On her first visit to Sheffield, famous for its steel, she interrupted her act to harangue a hostile audience. 'You know what you can do with

---

* Many of the biggest stars were born into performing families and were on stage early: Vesta Tilley at three years, Dan Leno at four, Hetty King at five, while Vesta Victoria was just six weeks old when she first appeared.

your stainless knives and your scissors and your circular saws?' she challenged. 'You can stick 'em up your arse.' She stalked off, and the manager had to persuade her to go back out to an audience that had been won over: 'They'll do what you say with the knives and scissors, but can they be spared the circular saws?'[26] Her response when asked to sing for the other first-class passengers on a ship home from South Africa was similarly blunt; she felt that they'd snubbed her throughout the journey, so she declined. 'They wouldn't recognise me,' she said. 'I'm buggered if I'll recognise them.' She did, however, perform for those travelling in second class and steerage.[27]

Lloyd's refusal to compromise was a large part of her appeal. She earned a fortune but remained resolutely working class in her tastes, attitudes and culture, and she was adored for it. Anyway, her accumulation of money was more than matched by her open-handed generosity to friends, colleagues and strangers. She was Britain's biggest star in the Edwardian years. Serious critics, including George Bernard Shaw, Max Beerbohm and James Agate, paid tribute. 'She knew that the great English public will open its arms to vice, provided it is presented as a frolic,' wrote the latter.[28] Or, in the words of the world's most famous actress, Sarah Bernhardt: 'No other country in this world has got an artist equal to your Marie Lloyd'.[29]

iv

The coarseness of the music hall, the offensive material on stage, and the drinking and prostitution off it – these things had long been the target of moral reformers. The Salvation Army, in particular, was largely built on its battle against music hall in the East End, cheerfully appropriating the enemy's tricks to pull in the crowds. The melodies of popular songs were stolen, for example, but had new lyrics attached, so that George Leybourne's 'Champagne Charlie' (1866) became 'Bless His Name, He Sets Me Free'. 'I rather enjoy robbing the Devil of his choice tunes,' crowed General William Booth.[30]

Meanwhile the evangelical tradition of reformed sinners testifying to their deliverance through Jesus became more sensationalist, giving prominence to speakers who resembled music-hall acts. Fanny Burt of Chatteris, Cambridgeshire – a forty-year-old woman who stood forty inches tall and weighed just forty pounds – was billed as the Salvation Midget,* while at the other end of the scale was the Hallelujah Giant, who weighed thirty-two stone. 'People go to see the Hallelujah Giant,' noted one observer, 'with the same feeling that they go to see Tom Thumb and the Siamese Twins.'[31] Others included Emmerson Davison, the Hallelujah Wrestler, and Thomas Darkin of Colchester, the Hallelujah Darkie.

As the Salvation Army grew, it also began acquiring premises previously used for entertainment. By 1879, it was boasting that it had taken over a hundred 'music halls, penny gaffs, dancing rooms and the like' in the East End, turning these 'fortresses of Beelzebub' into 'places of divine service'.[32] Three years later came a great coup – converting the Eagle Tavern in Hoxton, the very place where Marie Lloyd had first made her name.† This symbolic transformation was celebrated in a new song, performed at the first Salvationist meeting there: 'The Devil's mad and we are glad, because he's lost this trap he had.' At the end of each chorus, the soloist leaped in the air, gyrating wildly, and General Booth apologised for his high spirits:[33] 'You must excuse him; he's a converted trapeze man, and some of his old notions cling to him.'‡

As with so much in society, however, the wild days were passing into history, and music hall was becoming more respectable. The London County Council (LCC) had been created in 1889, and

---

* There were other Salvation Midgets, including a forty-year-old milliner named Miss Crabtree of Ravensthorpe, West Yorkshire, who was confined to a lunatic asylum in 1884 after attempting suicide.

† The pub was also mentioned in the nursery rhyme 'Pop Goes the Weasel': 'Up and down the City Road, in and out the Eagle'.

‡ The music hall retaliated with songs mocking the Salvation Army, including: Nellie L'Estrange's 'No Fear' (1887), Lizzie Fletcher's 'Sister Ria' (1895), and Rosie D'Alberg's 'Obadiah Walked Behind the Drum' (1897).

established a Theatres and Music Halls Committee to grant entertainment licences. The result, regretted humorist Barry Pain, was 'a County-Council-inspected music-hall, with both its eyes on its licence'.[34] Proprietors became much more careful, even censorious, when booking acts, for fear of the regulators.

And those proprietors were acquiring ever-greater power with the establishment of chains of halls. Most notably, at the end of the nineteenth century, the promoter Edward Moss joined forces with two others – Oswald Stoll and Richard Thornton – to form the Moss Empires group, building new venues constructed like conventional theatres, with rows of seats. They 'must not be confused with the old-time music halls', said the press,[35] with adverts emphasising that they were places for family entertainment. When the Shepherd's Bush Empire opened in 1903, it was sold as being 'scientifically ventilated', as having 'luxurious seats' and 'charming surroundings', and of allowing only inoffensive material on stage: 'the entertainment is refined and the audience always select'. Consequently, gentlemen were advised, 'there really is no excuse for not giving your wife or sister a pleasant evening'.[36] The Moss Empires became the biggest circuit of variety theatres in the country, with dozens of venues, and did much to clean up the reputation of music hall. 'The vicar goes – you may go', promised the Chiswick Empire.[37] Edward Moss was knighted in 1905.

The changing tone was one of the features of the period and spread to other halls. 'All these places are nowadays family resorts to a vastly greater degree than of old', read a 1909 report. 'The organisers, the performers, now consider what will suit the taste of the family circle rather than the more boisterous desires of an audience of men.'[38] In 1913 it was reported that a young woman was told off by a uniformed attendant for laughing loudly at a comedy troupe. 'Good gracious!' she said. 'Can't we laugh?' And he replied, 'Yes, but not so loud.'[39]

The suffocation of the old raucous spirit was regretted by some, for whom it was another manifestation of the commercialising, corrupting influence of money. The big chains were squeezing out the independent proprietors, and there were fears that new talent was also being stifled by an over-reliance on proven old favourites who went down well across the entire national circuit. The industry was becoming monolithic, the entertainment sanitised; it was a homogenous business. 'The music hall is dominated by not more than five men', complained the *Clarion* in 1902, and the managers employed by those men to run their venues were risk-averse pen-pushers: 'essentially "of good appearance", dependable accountants, competent to discipline clerks and janitors, civil to reporters, tactful in dealing with exuberant undergraduates'.[40]

One consequence was that there was a decline in complaints from Christian groups about the halls' baleful influence. Indeed, there were those, such as Liberal MP Samuel Smith, who saw the LCC's committee as a model for how the 'moral evils' of the legitimate theatre could be curbed.[41] There were still controversies, though. The appearance of Violet Charlesworth at the Canterbury music hall was unpopular not only with her inebriated audience, but with those who felt it was wrong for a criminal – even if she were not yet convicted – to appear on stage as entertainment. And Charlesworth was not an isolated case; she was just one of many freak turns, as they were known, celebrities booked for newsworthiness rather than talent, who were a growing presence in the halls. When the artist Robert Wood was acquitted of the murder of prostitute Emily Dimmock in 1907 (the Camden Town Murder, as it was known), he was offered a contract at a music hall in Woolwich, though in this case the Variety Artistes' Federation, a union with some 9,000 members, objected sufficiently strongly for the engagement to be cancelled.

One freak turn who did appear on stage, if only briefly, was Carrie Nation, a militant temperance campaigner from America who gained the nickname the Kansas Smasher by attacking bars with an axe, smashing up their stock and fittings in what she liked to call hatchetations. She was sixty-two by the time she came to Britain in 1908, axeless but still formidable. Booked into the Canterbury, she was received by a drunken crowd with a torrent of abuse and missiles, hit in the face by a rotten egg, but she stood her ground and eventually had to be dragged off stage by the manager. Many found the spectacle deeply distasteful, a reminder that the sometimes cruel spirit of the old music hall was not entirely extinct. 'To see a woman standing in the limelight with a Bible in her hand before a mocking crowd, hardly accords with our insular notion of the fitness of things,' lamented one newspaper.[42]

Freak turns were provocative enough, but the greatest storm came over a different kind of act, the living statue. In 1906 Australian performer Pansy Montague, twenty-two years old and known professionally as La Milo, arrived on the London stage, dressed in a sheer, close-fitting body stocking, and striking a set of poses based on classical statuary. It was artistic, she said, but as the papers pointed out, she was 'so nearly naked that you can't tell the difference'.[43] She was 'the sensation of the London season', maybe even 'the most talked-of woman in the world',[44] and there was at least one documented case of a man committing suicide when she spurned his advances.* Rivals soon proliferated, including the Modern Venus and Galatea (born Maud Odell), and as the craze spread, it attracted the attention of the LCC's Theatres and Music Halls Committee.

When Captain George Swinton, the committee chairman,† went to see what all the excitement was about, he was sufficiently horrified to resolve that no one else should be exposed to such a spectacle as he'd had to endure. He recommended that music halls

---

* In April 1907 Richard Lucas of Byfleet, Surrey, killed himself in the lavatory of Kingsway Tube station by inhaling prussic acid fumes through a complicated apparatus of his own making. A forty-six-year-old correspondent for the *Auto-Motor Journal*, who had a classics degree from Cambridge – and had once been involved in revolutionary Finnish politics, before becoming an ardent Spiritualist – he thought La Milo was 'the most perfect being upon earth' and developed what the papers called an 'extravagant and embarrassing interest in the artiste'. At the time of his death, he had a bushy red beard, which turned out to be fake, a disguise he'd adopted to follow her in the streets. 'He was a very good husband, and I cannot express my feelings and my love for him,' wept his wife at the inquest.
† George Swinton was the great-grandfather of actress Tilda Swinton.

be prohibited from featuring living statues because, he insisted, this really wasn't art – and he spoke from a position of authority: 'for three years he had drawn from the nude himself'.[45] A meeting of the full LCC saw sixty-six members vote for a ban, most of them Progressives, and forty-three against, all but two of whom were Moderates.* Councils in other cities – Manchester, Liverpool, Hull – followed suit, and the living statues were driven from the halls.

The fact that this was a Liberal, rather than Conservative, cause was revealing. Similarly, when La Milo was booked to appear as Lady Godiva in Coventry's annual street procession, it was women's rights campaigner Millicent Fawcett who spoke most loudly against it, saying La Milo would 'degrade the beautiful Godiva legend'.[46] There was a new line of attack emerging, one that was concerned for the mental, rather than the moral, well-being of audiences. Instead of Christian campaigners, it was now radicals and social reformers who most loudly denounced the halls, and the charge was not spiritual corruption but stupidity.

In 1900 the *Contemporary Review*, a liberal, intellectual journal, shuddered at 'the really mournful exhibitions of inanity to which the so-called "knockabout" comedians treat their patrons'.[47] W. T. Stead likewise despaired of the 'inane drivel' he saw on his first-ever visit to a hall in 1906. 'It was not the immorality of the thing that roused me so much as the imbecility of it all,' he wrote. 'It was difficult to realise that the well-dressed "ladies and gentlemen", who had paid four and five shillings to occupy these stalls, and who appreciatively applauded vulgarities which might have shamed a costermonger, were citizens of an Empire on which the sun never sets, arbiters of the destinies of a quarter of the human race.'[48] (He did make an exception for La Milo, however: 'it was a great pleasure to see her'.[49])

In response to such critics, eighty-year-old Charles Morton, the man who had started the music-hall business with the Canterbury

---

* In the early days of the LCC, Liberals went under the name of Progressives, while Conservatives were known as Moderates.

back in 1852, suggested that audience tastes hadn't really changed that much, whatever Edward Moss liked to think. 'There is no doubt that the public enjoy innuendos and double entendres,' he shrugged. 'However praiseworthy any attempts by managers at reform may be, they will have no effect. The people go out to be amused, not to be educated, and they won't be educated by managers or anyone else.'[50]

v

Music hall provided a stepping stone for some who would achieve fame in other fields. Richard Freeman was born in Greenwich, south London, in 1875. The illegitimate son of an actress, he was adopted by a Billingsgate fishmonger and his wife, who already had ten children of their own. Largely uneducated, he drifted through various jobs and casual work; at one point he was being paid a shilling a time by the Rotherhithe Liberal and Radical Association to disrupt Conservative Party meetings. Then he tried the merchant navy, before joining the army, signing on in the name that he would retain for the rest of his life: Edgar Wallace.

He had higher aspirations than this, though, fancying himself as a versifier; in 1896, while still in uniform, he scored his first success when the music-hall star Arthur Roberts bought a song from him, 'A Sort of a Kind of a —'. Wallace asked ten shillings for the song and (at least in Roberts' account) was instead paid ten pounds.[51] Stationed in Aldershot, he went AWOL for five days to watch it performed in a musical comedy, *Biarritz*, at the Prince of Wales Theatre in London's West End; in return, he got four days' detention with hard labour.

Posted to South Africa, where there were fewer opportunities for songwriters, he began writing verses that were heavily indebted to Rudyard Kipling's poems of military life in *Barrack-Room Ballads*:

> Out 'ere, they've got a notion that Tommy isn't class;
> 'E's a sort of brainless animal, or wuss!

Vicious cuss!

No, they don't expect intelligence from us.[52]

It wasn't particularly good poetry, but his work was published in the *Cape Times*, where it attracted the attention of the great man himself, then on a visit to the country.* 'Mr Kipling strongly advised him to stick to the army for the present – and also to his verse writing,' it was reported.[53] He did neither. He bought himself out of the army and then, when the Boer War started five months later, became a war correspondent.

Wallace began by filing copy for the Reuters news agency, before he stumbled into working for the *Daily Mail*. He compensated for his lack of conventional journalistic skills with a newly discovered gift for storytelling, and alongside accounts of British heroism, he happily spun tales of enemy war crimes. 'The Boers murder wounded men,' he told shocked readers in July 1901, sensationally claiming that British troops had been shot dead in the aftermath of an encounter at Vlakfontein.[54] Appearing at a sensitive time in negotiations, the report caused outrage at the War Office. There was an official denial, and the *Daily Mail* was banned from receiving official bulletins; further, warned St John Broderick, the war secretary, any agency supplying the paper would also be boycotted by the government. 'Never before has such a shameless, if clumsy, attempt been made to muzzle the British press in the interests of one minister,' thundered the *Mail*.[55] The stand-off between government and press attracted enough attention to make Wallace a big name – and to obscure the original issue of whether the report was actually true.†

---

* Kipling was himself inspired to write *Barrack-Room Ballads* (1892) by the material he heard amid 'the smoke, the roar and the good fellowship of relaxed humanity at Gatti's' Music Hall in Charing Cross, London. (*Something of Myself*)

† Lord Kitchener, who had succeeded Lord Roberts as commander-in-chief of Empire forces in South Africa, later confirmed that wounded British soldiers had indeed been shot at Vlakfontein, though others present that day denied it. The truth is unknown.

Returning home, Wallace became one of the *Daily Mail*'s star writers, still refusing to let the facts get in the way of a good story. He was convinced that he was destined for bigger things. 'We were the poor who were not satisfied with our poverty,' he wrote later,[56] and he lived beyond his means while constantly seeking the get-rich scheme that would pay the bills. Stumbling upon the eternal truth that publishers make more money than their authors, he self-published *Smithy* (1905), a collection of tales about a philosophical soldier. It sold 15,000 copies and made a decent profit, but not enough to clear his debts, let alone keep him in the profligate lifestyle to which he aspired. Thinking further on the subject, he concluded that the key to making money out of literature lay entirely in marketing. 'I shall be glad to have the book finished,' he wrote to his wife, as he worked on his first novel, 'for I am most anxious to get on with the advertising part of it. This latter is really the most important part.'[57]

The novel in question was *The Four Just Men* (1905), again self-published, and he spent huge sums on a promotional campaign that included posters on buses, Tube trains and 2,000 hoardings across London. The campaign featured wonderfully hyperbolic copy – 'The book stamps Mr Edgar Wallace as a master of the dramatic art,' he wrote of himself[58] – while a half-page advert in the *Daily Mirror* claimed it had gone through three print-runs of 5,000 copies each in its first three days.[59] To seal the deal, he offered, via the pages of the *Daily Mail*, a £250 top prize to anyone who could solve the locked-room mystery that he left incomplete at the end of the story – without specifying that there was just one top prize.

The book did well, selling 38,000 copies on publication, but the promotional costs meant that Wallace was still £1,400 down on his investment, and that was without allowing for the hordes of readers who correctly guessed the solution. Alfred Harmsworth was prevailed upon to compensate the disappointed winners – his papers having pushed the competition – and Wallace declared himself bankrupt, selling the rights to the novel to George Newnes (publisher of the *Strand* magazine) for seventy-five pounds.*

Harmsworth grudgingly forgave Wallace, but worse was to come. When the *Mail*'s proprietor launched a crusade against the rising cost of soap (which, he believed, was the result of a cartel of manufacturers), Wallace was one of those charged with finding copy. He turned in a typically colourful account of a washerwoman driven into penury by rapacious capitalists, a story riddled with unchecked and exaggerated claims. It prompted legal action against the paper by soap manufacturers Lever Brothers and, represented by Edward Carson (the barrister whose dogged cross-examination had brought about Oscar Wilde's downfall), the company won £50,000 damages, the highest libel award yet handed down by a British court. This time Wallace was sacked from the *Mail*.

This was 1907, and the desperate state of his finances prompted Wallace to begin his writing career in earnest. Over the next six years, he wrote twelve books (published by others) and then increased his output further, turning himself from a celebrated journalist into the country's most popular writer of fiction.[†] Like Harmsworth, he discovered that his taste chimed with a large swathe of the public, even if it was sneered at in literary circles. 'I like actions, murderings, abductions,' he said, 'dark passages and secret trapdoors and the dull, slimy waters of the moat, pallid in the moonlight.'[60] So did his readers.

Edgar Wallace was entirely a product of his times, a man who rose from nothing by a combination of good luck, the ruthless exploitation of his talent and the indulgence of the popular press. All the while, he retained an affinity with the people he sprang from, sharing their fads and fantasies. He was seduced by the superstitious fringes, consulting palmists and practising bibliomancy. He was an extravagant gambler on both cards and horses.

---

* It went on to sell over three million copies and spawned five sequels, two films and a television series.

† At the peak of his success, in the years before his death in 1932, it was calculated that one in every four books read in Britain was written by Edgar Wallace.

And, above all, he had one driving ambition: 'It's money I want,' he said. 'Lots of money.'[61]

vi

Edgar Wallace doesn't quite work, though, as the spirit of the age. For that there needs to be an element of the City of London, of the financial industries that were growing faster than manufacturing. And there is one person who fits the bill: the ebullient, excessive Horatio Bottomley, a man who was acclaimed by the masses and ridiculed by polite society. (Even his 'remarkable conjunction of names is quite enough to create mirth,' mocked one newspaper.[62])

Born in 1860, the only son of a tailor's cutter in Bethnal Green, London, Horatio Bottomley lost both parents before he was five, and was placed in a Birmingham orphanage, from which he ran away at the age of fourteen. A succession of casual and clerical jobs led to him becoming a shorthand writer in the law courts at the age of twenty, a three-year stint that furnished him with sufficient legal knowledge and self-confidence that in his future court cases – of which there were to be very, very many – he liked to defend himself. He tended to win these cases, for he turned out to be a persuasive advocate, charming and disarming, swinging between passionate outrage and jovial self-deprecation.

It was that same manner that enabled him to make his fortune in the frenzied speculation of the Australian goldrush in the last years of the nineteenth century. London was awash with investors in search of profits, and Bottomley reinvented himself as a financier, launching companies that were forever just about to strike gold but never quite did, and which in the meantime had no assets beyond the funds he raised. When his reserves ran low, largely untroubled by moral qualms, he went back to the same investors and convinced them to throw good money after bad. 'If I were asked to describe the square mile which constitutes the City,' he declared, 'I should say that it represents that portion of the earth upon which are daily gathered together the worst types of the human race from a physical, moral and intellectual standpoint. It is the centralised and concentrated essence of primaeval man – and top hat.'[63] Generally, the City liked to emphasise top hat rather than primaeval nature, seeing itself as a place for civilised gentlemen. P. G. Wodehouse, who worked for the Hongkong and Shanghai Banking Corporation for two years from 1900, said there was 'a distinct flavour of a school republic' about such institutions.[64] But Bottomley didn't care about such niceties; he revelled in being an outsider, living off his wits.

He raised tens of millions of pounds from investors who were as greedy and gullible as he was unscrupulous. 'People who invest under his magic wand and expert guidance are not such as would be content with 3 or 4 per cent,' noted the press; 'they want to become rich in a hurry, and they sometimes do so.'[65] Mostly, though, they didn't. But Bottomley did. Much of the money – an estimated £3 million in ten years – found its way into his pocket, and he was so brazen about his misappropriations that he got away with them. Challenged once at a shareholders' meeting about what had happened to £700,000 that had gone missing from the accounts, he came clean: 'I have not the faintest idea.' And he sat down to cheers.[66] Cartoonist H. M. Bateman caricatured him for the *Tatler* in 1906, wearing racing silks and flogging a panting nag that could barely carry his weight; the horse was labelled Shareholder, and the picture was captioned 'The Last Ounce'.[67]

In short, Bottomley was a 'barefaced swindler' who 'deliberately planned schemes to rob the public', as one contemporary put it (Bottomley sued for libel and won), or 'the cleverest thief in the Empire', as a prosecuting lawyer in yet another case suggested.[68] He was also a popular hero, seen by the non-investing classes as one of their own; he was the East End boy who'd made good, thoroughly relishing a life of champagne, racehorses and chorus girls. Bottomley lived on the scale that Edgar Wallace dreamed of, whether losing £40,000 on a musical comedy starring one of his mistresses or winning £70,000 when one of his horses won the

Stewards' Cup at Goodwood. He had style. When an office boy was caught stealing stamps, he shrugged: 'We've all got to start in a small way.'[69] He saw himself as 'England's Superman',[70] though the chorus girls called him Botty.

In keeping with the times, Bottomley used some of his wealth to launch himself as a newspaper proprietor, buying a London title, the *Sun*, in 1902. His big gimmick was to get celebrities to spend a week as guest editor, including music-hall star Dan Leno,* the dockers' leader Ben Tillett, and Sussex and England cricketer Prince Ranjitsinhji. Not all were a success. The Congregationalist minister Joseph Parker stipulated that there would be no betting, gambling or speculative finance on his editorial watch, and he replaced the paper's racing tips with scriptural texts; the result was a complete collapse in sales. 'If Joe's editorship had lasted another week, the *Sun* would have set in the west,' chuckled Bottomley.[71]

He also had political ambitions, and indeed relations. His maternal uncle was the leading radical George Holyoake,† and he claimed a connection with the Liberal MP and atheist Charles Bradlaugh. 'You know that Bradlaugh was my father,' Bottomley would say, right up to his own death,[72] though there was no evidence for this, save for a physical resemblance.‡ He himself was not really a radical, but he did have genuine sympathy for, as one paper noted, 'the despised, the rejected and the downtrodden';[73] that went a long way when he was adopted as Liberal candidate for slum-ridden Hackney South.

He nursed his constituency with a devotion that bordered on

---

* Showing an admirable grasp of advertising and new technology, Bottomley had a promotional film made of the event: 'Mr Dan Leno, Assisted by Mr Herbert Campbell, Editing "The Sun"' (1902).

† Holyoake is the man credited with coining the word secularism.

‡ Not that that was necessarily much of a boast, as the music-hall star G. H. 'the Great' MacDermott had sung back in 1881, 'Young Bradlaugh who is clever (you'd not think so by his looks) . . .'

bribery, setting up soup kitchens, giving Christmas parties for hundreds of local children (naturally, he appeared as Santa Claus), and providing free entertainments: there was, for example, an excursion to White City for as many residents as could fit in the fifty carriages he'd hired. He was also said to be a ready source of racing tips. Consequently, in the 1906 general election he achieved a swing from the Conservatives of 16.7 per cent (the national average was 5.4 per cent) and secured the largest Liberal majority for a London constituency.

He had, however, received no support from the party leadership during the campaign, and he found no welcome in the Commons. His business reputation preceded him in Westminster, ensuring a frosty reception; other Liberal MPs 'tried to ignore Mr Bottomley by conversing in loud tones to one another while he was addressing the House'.[74] He responded by simply pretending that nothing untoward was happening. He 'is in the Liberal Party but not of it', marvelled one commentator; he 'outfaces the cold displeasure with which his interpositions are received with the most sublime effrontery'.[75] The self-assurance was unshakeable and, to compound his crimes, he was a good speaker, witty and engaging. Some were won over, but much of the hostility remained. Three years into his parliamentary career it was still being noted that 'the Liberal Party in the House are not very fond of him, for he is always attacking them; the Labour Party are still less fond of him, for, although politically a disciple of Bradlaugh, he has no reverence for the fustian jacket'.[76]

And that lack of self-righteousness, ultimately, was the key to his popularity in the world beyond Parliament. Though he was unencumbered by party allegiance (he 'is really a Bottomleyite', it was noted[77]), his political instincts were sound. He was generous to the ordinary folk he met, kind to children, courteous to women. He remembered not only people's names but those of their families. And unlike many who sought to improve the lives of the working class, he had not the faintest trace of puritanism about him. Many of his parliamentary colleagues were in favour of temperance; he most emphatically was not.* He proposed abolishing the duty on ale and replacing it with a tax on 'ginger beer and other horrible gaseous liquids'.[78] When he ran the country, he said, the state would stay out of people's lives. 'Molesting and restrictive legislation will be kept for the nursery. What people eat, what they drink, and what they play at will be a matter entirely for themselves to determine'.[79] Like Marie Lloyd and Edgar Wallace, he knew how to enjoy himself, and people enjoyed him in return. It was probably not too much to say that he was loved.

Shortly after his election, Bottomley launched a weekly paper, *John Bull*, much of which he wrote himself. This was an entertaining mix of salacious gossip, investigative journalism, highly opinionated comment and shock exposés of 'the vilest habits of sexual depravity and degradation', such as massage dens where 'Lesbian and other vices are regularly indulged in'.[80] There were also some very dubious competitions. One asked readers to predict the scores of twenty football matches, an almost impossible task; there were, though, seventeen winners one week, a refutation of the laws of probability that only made sense when it emerged they were all employees of Bottomley, their names appearing only in order to lure in more entrants.

There was also a print equivalent of a protection racket: a company that was repeatedly targeted in the pages of *John Bull* would be told that the attacks would stop in return for a financial consideration. At one stage Bottomley was being paid a retainer by Harrods department store to investigate complaints by former staff – complaints for which he was the only source. By 1909, the year he published his memoirs under the cheerfully self-advertising

---

* The war against drink derived largely from the Nonconformist roots of the Liberal Party, where teetotalism was strong. In 1903 it was reported that 700 congregations in Scotland alone were using non-alcoholic wine for Holy Communion, though care had to be taken: worshippers at a Nonconformist church in Sunderland in 1906 had suspicions of the 'non-alcoholic wine' they'd been sold and sent it off for analysis – it turned out to be double the strength of a claret.

title of *Bottomley's Book*, the paper claimed to be selling 300,000 copies a week. It made money and kept him in the public eye.

Although he was never to be a significant actor in Westminster politics, Bottomley was one of the best-known figures in the country. Short and stocky, with a figure that was destined to run to fat, he had a large head and a soft, round face, his chin already starting to slide into his neck. He exuded a perpetual air of bonhomie and he partially inspired Toad of Toad Hall in Kenneth Grahame's *The Wind in the Willows* (1908), the boisterous, boastful, irresponsible Mr Toad, who shared Violet Charlesworth's love of motor cars and who was similarly sent to jail.[81] In Horatio Bottomley – financier, politician, press baron, crook – the old Victorian values of self-help were transmuted into a creed of helping yourself. Where Bobs and Booth represented an idealised vision of the nation, Bottomley was the real thing, the self-advertising, self-satisfied embodiment of Edwardian Britain, a music-hall turn posing as a man of importance. The title of his newspaper was almost right: he wasn't John Bull but he could have been a disreputable cousin.

2

WAR AND IMPERIALISM

Sons of old England, marching off to war
With our brave colonials from a distant shore;
We're going to fight and conquer as we've done before,
For the love of our country and our queen.

Leo Stormont, 'Sons of Our Empire', 1899[1]

At the time when the Boer War commenced, Linden was
an enthusiastic jingo: his enthusiasm had been somewhat
damped when his youngest son, a reservist, had to go to the
front, where he died of fever and exposure.

Robert Tressell, *The Ragged-Trousered Philanthropists*, 1914[2]

Imperialist Cecil Rhodes (1853–1902), pictured holding
a telegraph wire that stretches from Cairo to the Cape
in an illustration titled 'The Rhodes Colossus'.

THE TELEGRAM ARRIVED ON 11 MAY 1897: 'See Mr Maturin's advertisement Daily Mail – might suit you.' The message made little sense to its recipient, Bunny Manders, but it seemed to hold out the prospect of employment, and that was desperately welcome to a man only recently released from jail, having served eighteen months for burglary. Not that Bunny had ever been much of a criminal; he'd just been led into bad ways by an old friend, A. J. Raffles, who he'd idolised since schooldays ('he was captain of the eleven, and I his fag').

That was all behind him now. Raffles had been missing these past two years, presumed drowned after he leaped from a ship into the open waters of the Mediterranean to escape the law. Bunny had been left behind, left to pay his debt to society in the new prison at Wormwood Scrubs. Then came the telegram, swiftly followed, when Bunny answered the mysterious advert in the *Daily Mail*, by the startling, joyous revelation that Raffles was not dead after all. Against all the odds, he'd managed to get to shore ('it was the very devil of a swim'), and he'd been lying low in Europe until his return to London in the guise of Mr Maturin.

So begins *The Black Mask* (1901), the second volume of Raffles stories. They were written by E. W. Hornung, brother-in-law of Arthur Conan Doyle, and the character was created as a kind of criminal inversion of Sherlock Holmes. Raffles leads a dangerous double life: carefree gentleman and amateur cricketer by day, sneak thief by night. He's a master of disguise and accent, and he shares Sherlock's aestheticism. ('Art for art's sake is a vile catchword, but I confess it appeals to me.') And now here he was, back from the dead, having escaped a watery grave in a manner that pre-empted Sherlock's own return.

Raffles's choice of pseudonym added a new dimension to the tales. For those who recognised the reference, it could only evoke Charles Maturin, author of *Melmoth the Wanderer*, the very book that had inspired Oscar Wilde to name himself Sebastian

Melmoth when going into exile. The connection was no coincidence, as the date made clear: May 1897, when Raffles re-emerges, was also the month Wilde was released from jail and adopted his alter ego. Hornung was a friend of Wilde, had even named his son Oscar, and was now deliberately identifying his best-known creation with the disgraced playwright, another who had led a double life. 'Raffles had the subtle power of making himself irresistible at will,' writes Bunny. 'He was beyond comparison the most masterful man whom I have ever known.' Their relationship was always depicted as more emotionally charged than that of Holmes and Watson; now it was as overtly homosexual as it could be, while remaining publishable.*

Reunited, Raffles and Bunny resume their life of crime, but it's more febrile, less playful. They've each suffered great hardship in the two years apart, and in London they're social outcasts, their sordid, secret lives having been exposed to the world. There's no doubt where Hornung's sympathies lie, but no doubt either that this existence can't be sustained. Apart from anything else, the gentlemanly code to which Raffles sometimes paid allegiance was clear: dishonour should be followed by an honourable, redemptive death.

Their opportunity came in 1899, when war broke out in South Africa. The two men were gripped by war fever, eagerly devouring the newspapers and too busy studying the strategic options even to go out robbing. But reading the reports was not enough. 'Old school-fellows had fallen, and I know Raffles envied them; he spoke so wistfully of such an end.' In February 1900 they sailed for the Cape, disguised, with false names, and enlisted in an irregular cavalry regiment.

It's there, on the African veldt, sheltering behind a rock from

---

* Bunny Manders's name is echoed in Bunny Mathers, a character in Eden Phillpotts' school stories *The Human Boy Again* (1908). Mathers is 'a chap who is like a girl in some ways', who has a theatrical bent – 'the artistic temperament,' as one teacher says – and who joins the cadet corps 'chiefly that he might wear the red bags with black stripes, and drill once a week under the sergeant'.

a hail of Boer bullets, having rescued a wounded Bunny, that A. J. Raffles gives his life for queen and country. Despite his charm, he had been in his time a thief who often resorted to violence – but when the Empire was in need, when the news became 'more than Englishmen could endure', he knew where his duty lay.

ii

The Boer War had been a long time in the making. The Cape of Good Hope, on the far south-west tip of Africa, had first been colonised by the Dutch East India Company in the seventeenth century for use as a staging post on the trade route to Asia. Its location made the settlement equally desirable for other European nations, and in the fallout from the Napoleonic Wars, control of the post and adjacent territory passed to Britain.

The Dutch-descended settlers remained, however, subject to a foreign power, culturally separate and dreaming of being politically separate too. A generation on, and Britain's abolition of slavery in 1833 proved the last straw for some, prompting thousands of Cape Dutch to push north-east into the interior, beyond British rule, a migration called the Great Trek. These were the Boers, as they became known (the word means farmer in Afrikaans), and they established two independent states: the South African Republic – commonly referred to as the Transvaal – and the Orange Free State.

For so long as the Boer territories were of little interest to the British, a wary co-existence was possible in the region. But the discovery, first, of diamond deposits at Kimberley, just outside the Free State, and then, in the 1880s, of gold in the Transvaal, transformed the economy of southern Africa. The demography changed as well, as an influx of outsiders, many of them Indian or Chinese, came to work the mines. More difficult to handle were the British new-comers, since their presence raised political questions. Citizenship of the Boer republics was already restricted to white people,* but if

* This was not the case in the British-ruled territories of Cape Colony and Natal,

it were granted to these British *uitlanders* (foreigners), the ethnic identity of the state would be compromised. And so the right to representation was denied, even though the *uitlanders* comprised half the white male population of the Transvaal. The outraged British, both in southern Africa and in Westminster, took up their cause, arguing passionately for equality while eying enviously the mineral reserves over the border.

As the nineteenth century came towards its close, with no progress being made in negotiations, and with both sides strengthening their military, conflict grew inevitable. And in October 1899, after a summer of headlines – THE TRANSVAAL CRISIS, OMINOUS RUMOURS and BOER WAR PREPARATIONS[3] – the storm finally broke, when Paul Kruger, president of the Transvaal, declared war on Britain in the name of the two Boer republics.

In Britain there was widespread support for the imperial cause, including among the vast majority of newspapers. The most notable exception was the *Daily Chronicle*, whose editor, the Liberal Henry Massingham, argued that this was a British war of annexation. That did neither the paper nor Massingham himself any good; sales collapsed, and a month into the conflict he was obliged to resign, unable to comply with the instructions of his proprietor. 'I was peremptorily required to maintain absolute silence on the policy of the government in South Africa until after the conclusion of the war,' he explained. 'That was impossible.'[4]

There was even less dissent in the music halls, where audiences sang along to newly written patriotic songs, some boastful, some sentimental: 'A Hot Time in the Transvaal Tonight,'* 'Off to the War', 'Our Sons Across the Sea', 'Stand by Your Country, Stand by Your Queen', 'Up with the Old Flag', 'We Will Never Give In'. Charles Coborn – best known for 'The Man Who Broke the Bank

---

where there was a property requirement for voting that excluded most non-whites, but no official colour bar.

* Taken from 'A Hot Time in the Old Town Tonight' (1896), an American song first performed by the McIntyre and Heath Minstrels.

at Monte Carlo' (1891) – sang 'To Pretoria', and Marie Lloyd joined in with 'The Red and the White and the Blue', which spoke of how 'Mr Kruger and his Boers imagined England's flag was white' and how:

> We'll shortly put an end to all their bluster and their brag,
> When above them at Pretoria we hoist the good old flag.

Gus Elen, meanwhile, simply incorporated events into his coster comedy with 'His Nibs, the Boer of Bethnal Green'. There was a simultaneous spate of war songs that celebrated Irish loyalty, at a time when Fenian violence was fresh in the collective memory. 'You used to call us traitors because of agitators, but you can't call us traitors now!' declared Pat Rafferty in 'What Do You Think of the Irish Now?', while Pat Carey's 'The Irish Are Always in Front' similarly distanced loyal troops from 'vile agitators'.

The most durable of all the Boer War hits, though, was 'Goodbye, Dolly Gray', which tells the story of a soldier going to war and leaving his girl behind, complete with a fine singalong chorus. It was originally written for the Spanish–American War of 1898, but that conflict was so brief that the song was shipped over to Britain, where it went down very well. American songs specifically about the conflict, on the other hand, tended not to cross the Atlantic, being almost entirely pro-Boer in tone, the likes of 'When Kruger Spanked the Queen'.

For much of the world, this was a case of David and Goliath, the fearless little Boer nation taking on the world's greatest power. Further, it was a David with whom it was easy for Americans and Europeans to identify. The Boers were not 'a different race of mankind to ourselves', observed Henry Campbell-Bannerman, leader of the opposition Liberal Party; they were 'a European people of a race akin to our own, a Christian people, a Protestant people'.[5]

Most assumed a swift British victory, but some doubted whether the country had sufficient resolve for the conflict. 'The

Boers fight for homes and liberties,' wrote Emma Hardy, estranged wife of novelist Thomas, 'we fight for the Transvaal Funds, diamonds and gold!'[6] That was eight months before war was declared, and her prediction was, at least initially, borne out. In the early stages the Boers had the upper hand; their troops were more readily mobilised, more familiar with the terrain, more numerous; and they inflicted several heavy defeats on the British, most notably three battles in mid-December 1899 ('that Black Week across which the names of three African villages are written forever in letters of blood', mourned Bunny Manders). It was in response to these calamities that Lord 'Bobs' Roberts was sent to take over command in South Africa.

He did not come alone. Troops arrived in South Africa from all over the Empire to crush the Boers, and it seemed increasingly certain that might would ultimately triumph, even if the news reaching Britain remained grim and depressing, a long litany of setbacks and defeats. Nonetheless, there were some stories in that first, bad winter to stir the blood and to inspire the civilian population at home.

There was, for example, twenty-four-year-old Winston Churchill, who attracted publicity without seeming to try. He'd recently resigned his commission in the 4th Hussars for a much-heralded political career – his father, Randolph, was a former chancellor of the exchequer – though he started poorly, losing a Conservative parliamentary seat to the Liberals in a by-election in Oldham. When war broke out, he headed straight for South Africa to report for the *Morning Post*, arriving at the end of October. He was already a name and, at £250 a month, he didn't come cheap, but he was worthy of his hire: barely a fortnight after landing, he was making the news, coming under enemy fire as he helped rescue a train derailed by Boer artillery. The train got away, carrying news of his 'bravery and coolness'[7] (the train driver said he 'deserved the Victoria Cross'[8]), though he and others were taken prisoner. To cement his reputation, he then escaped from a detention centre in Pretoria and – hiding in a mineshaft, jumping freight trains and aided by English residents – he managed to reach the safety of Portuguese East Africa, some 280 miles away. His resolve, said the patriotic press, showed 'that when a Briton makes up his mind to escape, he will do so, and that as a rule he does not find the task of eluding his pursuers so very difficult'.[9]

Churchill was acclaimed a hero. So too was 'plucky little Bugler Dunne',[10] who made his name at the Battle of Colenso, one of the disastrous encounters of Black Week.* Under fire as the Dublin Fusiliers tried to cross a river, John Dunne was shot in the arm but, undaunted, switched the bugle over to his other hand and continued to sound the Advance until he fell, losing his instrument in the water. He was fourteen years old, and it was already his third taste of action. Brought back to recuperate at the military hospital in Netley, Hampshire, he found himself a darling of the press, greeted by cheering crowds when he ventured out in public and deluged with charitable donations and gifts (including a gold watch, a writing desk and a goat). He even got to meet the queen, who presented him with a silver-mounted bugle to replace the one he'd lost; he gave her a large photograph of himself. Celebrity, though, wasn't what he really wanted. 'I like the army life, and have no desire to leave it,' he told the press.[11] Sadly, it didn't work out. Bedevilled by bad luck, on returning to Cape Town, he broke his leg when a horse fell on him, and then he developed heart disease. By the time he was sixteen, he'd been invalided out of the service and was on the music-hall stage as part of a military sketch, 'During the Siege', in which he sounded calls on his silver bugle.

The siege depicted in that sketch was what really gripped the public imagination. The small town of Mafeking – some 180 miles west of Pretoria – was surrounded by Boer troops early on, in October 1899, but the garrison refused to surrender and held out for months, despite being outnumbered four to one. Under the command of Colonel Robert Baden-Powell, the defenders built

---

* British losses at Colenso were over 1,100 dead, wounded or captured; the Boer losses were 38. Among the British fatalities was Lieutenant Roberts, only son of Bobs.

networks of trenches and bomb-shelters to protect the population from enemy shelling, and showed great ingenuity in the deployment of their limited resources. Among those trapped in the town were Lord Edward Cecil, son of prime minister Lord Salisbury, and Lady Sarah Wilson, daughter of the Duke of Marlborough, whose colourful accounts of the siege, published in the *Daily Mail*, kept the story in the public eye. Despite the dismal news elsewhere, here was true British heroism: the brave few, isolated and defiant, standing strong against all the odds.

Being Christians, the two sides at Mafeking agreed to suspend hostilities on Sundays, though religious differences remained: the Boers, as strict Calvinists, took a dim view of the British profaning the Sabbath with sporting competitions. There were cultural differences too. The 200th day of the siege happened to fall on a Sunday, and Baden-Powell was playing cricket when a Boer envoy arrived to suggest that this might be an appropriate day to surrender. 'I am batting,' he replied. 'I am 200, not out – and I mean to stay at the wicket.' As George Tighe of the Town Guard later wrote, 'How could you fail to have faith in a leader like that?'[12]

The siege finally ended soon after, on 17 May 1900, the 217th day, when a British force arrived to relieve the town. Word arrived in London on a Friday evening, and rapidly spread outwards from Fleet Street, people spilling into the streets to share the good news in an impromptu display of pride and joy.[13] Managers of theatres and music halls interrupted proceedings to make announcements from the stage, and the jubilant throngs grew still greater, while the railways and the telephone ensured that by midnight every corner of the kingdom had the news.

The partying started again the next morning, with huge crowds in streets and parks across the country, and lasted all day and through most of the night. One focus was St George's Place bordering Hyde Park, where Baden-Powell's mother lived; another was the house of his half-brother in Oxford. Much of the country took the day off work and shops closed at midday. 'No officially proclaimed holiday was ever celebrated with more gusto,' it was said of Glasgow, and the crowds in Liverpool were bigger than anyone could remember. Union Jacks and bunting adorned buildings and buses, bicycles and horses in every town and village, the red, white and blue worn by men, women and babies (even by dogs, it was noted in Hastings). Effigies of Kruger were burned in Dorchester, Oxford and Ramsgate; another was fired from a howitzer in Peterborough.* Those towns, such as Shaftesbury in Dorset, that had old Russian cannon, spoils of the Crimean War, fired salutes. And in Dockwray Square, North Shields, theatre manager Arthur Jefferson staged a show that featured a re-enactment of the siege and depictions of the major figures of the war, with his nine-year-old son, also named Arthur, playing Bugler Dunne.† As the jubilant week went on, there were firework displays and torchlight processions, which meant injuries from accidental explosions and fires. Other casualties of the celebrations were those robbed by pickpockets or by gangs of roughs, and those believed to be pro-Boer: premises in Dover, Harlesden, Leeds and elsewhere were attacked by crowds.

There was genuine delight. It was a patriotic outpouring, but it was not at heart triumphalist, more a release of tension after months of strain. There was no great victory to glory in, rather a celebration of survival against the odds. Baden-Powell was a recognisably British hero, honoured for his defiance and duty in the face of adversity. Many noted echoes of General Gordon, similarly besieged at Khartoum in 1885, but killed two days before a relief force reached him.

Despite the revelries, the relief of Mafeking was of no great military significance, but it was seen by the public as a decisive moment because it accompanied a change in British fortunes. The army of the Empire in South Africa had swelled to a quarter

---

* Camberwell in south London had been ahead of the game in this regard, burning an effigy of Kruger as early as October 1899.

† A statue of the younger Arthur Jefferson – who became better known as Britain's greatest film comedian, Stan Laurel – would be erected in Dockwray Square in 1989.

of a million, the largest British force that had ever been assembled abroad, and the overwhelming numbers were beginning to tell. Kimberley and Ladysmith, where British garrisons had also been under siege, were relieved, the Boer centres of Bloemfontein, Johannesburg and Pretoria all fell, and the Transvaal and Orange Free State were formally annexed. By June 1900 the British had, it seemed, won.

iii

'A war in South Africa would be one of the most serious wars that could possibly be waged,' the MP Joseph Chamberlain had warned the House of Commons back in 1896. 'It would be a long war, a bitter war, and a costly war.'[14] Yet three years later, as secretary of state for the colonies, Chamberlain did more than any other Westminster politician to provoke the Boers until conflict became inevitable. The issue, he now said, was 'whether there should be equality for all the white races of South Africa, or the corrupt and tyrannical domination of the Boers'.[15] In response, his enemies furiously threw back at him those earlier words, evidence, they said, of his fickle, self-contradictory career. But then consistency had never been his strong suit.

Joseph Chamberlain was born in Highbury, London in 1836, moving to Birmingham when he was eighteen to work for his uncle's screw-making firm. Soon taking over the management of the company, his intelligence and enterprise built it to such an extent that he made a good deal of money on its sale, enabling him to retire from business in his middle age. Switching his attention to a political career, he became mayor of Birmingham in 1873. He was at the radical end of the Liberal Party – 'an ultra-radical,'[16] according to his critics, with 'severely Republican opinions'[17] – and his three reforming years in office, which included a huge programme of public works and slum clearance, became known locally as the Great Mayoralty.[18] Elected to Parliament in 1876, he arrived in a flurry of excitement, a new kind of politician, a Nonconformist representative of the industrial classes, a man with a populist's disdain for privilege and an immensely loyal power base in and around his constituency. He became known simply as Joe, accorded a mononym like Benjamin 'Dizzy' Disraeli, Lord 'Pam' Palmerston and very few others, while Birmingham City Football Club gained the nickname Joe's Town. Despite his public criticism of the party leader, William Gladstone, he was too big a figure to be passed over for promotion, and in 1880, after just four years in Westminster, he entered the cabinet as president of the board of trade.

Then came the great upheaval of 1886. Gladstone's Home Rule Bill, which was intended to provide Ireland with a degree of devolution, met with serious opposition, even in his own party. A dissenting group of Liberals, including Chamberlain, blocked the bill, brought down the government and split off, naming themselves the Liberal Unionists and drifting towards the Tories. In the 1895 general election the Conservative and Liberal Unionist grouping won a 152-seat majority in the House of Commons, and Joe Chamberlain found himself back in government, this time as colonial secretary under a Tory prime minister, a former radical prosecuting an imperialist war in South Africa. The part he played in conducting the conflict completed his transformation in the eyes of radicals from folk hero to folk devil. The public, though, was on his side, particularly in his heartland around Birmingham.*

By the time of the Mafeking celebrations, when he needed a police escort to protect him from the crowds of well-wishers, Chamberlain was the most recognisable and influential politician in the country. He was in his sixties but looked younger, a slim, smartly dressed figure, clad in a long black overcoat with an astrakhan collar,† always with an orchid in his buttonhole and a monocle

---

* Music-hall star Wilkie Bard had a song, 'Limerick Mad', which included the story of a man who had the temerity to say 'Down with Joe Chamberlain' in Aston. It doesn't end well: 'He was buried at Witton today.'
† 'This coat I wear belonged, I declare, to Joe Chamberlain once on a time,' sang Harry Bedford in 'A Second-Hand Aristocrat'.

in his right eye. The image was memorable, a strong personal brand appropriate for this age of advertisement. He 'keeps as little in the background as possible', noted the *Yorkshire Evening Post* drily.[19] His speeches attracted big audiences, drawn by the contemptuous invective he threw at his opponents and by the relish with which he squashed hecklers.*

Away from politics, he took no exercise, he had no hobbies – save for growing orchids in his greenhouse – and if there was anything behind the public facade, he allowed no one to see it. He was 'morally pachydermatous, habitually cynical', according to a judge who knew him in Birmingham, and that verdict was not unusual.[20] 'His soul never rises above barter', wrote trade unionist Ben Tillett. 'No feeling or passion; a ton of coal, a human life, are equally measurable quantities, assets of marketable values.' Further, Tillett said, he lacked courtesy and grace: 'He is not only the least kindly of the ministers I have met, but he is the least gentlemanly.'[21] Lord Rosmead, a long-serving colonial administrator, similarly deplored Chamberlain's manners: 'No gentleman would act as he does to his subordinates.' It was assumed that such a man would be a terror to his staff in Whitehall, though a senior civil servant in the Colonial Office was unperturbed by his appointment: 'He'll be too busy intriguing against his colleagues in the cabinet to give us much trouble.'[22]

Chamberlain's progress – and he had further yet to go – was symptomatic of a realignment of the parties that was still not complete. On the right, Chamberlain's defection from the Liberals accelerated the migration of new money away from the party, so that by the end of the century it was the Tories who were the voice of business; after the 1900 election more than half of Conservative MPs came from commerce and industry, replacing the formerly

---

* Ever the optimist, Edgar Wallace sent Chamberlain a copy of *The Four Just Men*, suggesting that 'if by any chance he could find some way of dragging in the *F.J.M.* into a political speech I should everlastingly be obliged to him'. The request went unanswered.

dominant landed interest. The Liberals were also in danger of losing support to their left with the emergence of working-class parties: the Social Democratic Federation (SDF), a Marxist grouping founded in 1881, the Independent Labour Party (ILP, 1893) and the Labour Representation Committee (LRC, 1900). After the election defeat of 1895, Gladstone's successor, Lord Rosebery, expressed his concern for the future, fearing 'the elimination of Liberalism, leaving the two forces of Socialism and Reaction face to face'.[23]

The Boer War illuminated the state of politics. The Conservative Party was a broad alliance spanning squirearchy to manufacturing, but it still had a recognisable identity, rooted in the monarchy, Church and Empire. 'It is a party shackled by tradition,' wrote its leader Lord Salisbury. 'It stumbles slowly and painfully from precedent to precedent with its eyes fixed on the ground. Yet the Conservative Party is the Imperial Party.'[24] When confronted with war in the colonies, it remained solid.

The same was not true of the Liberals, now in the throes of an identity crisis. Although there were radicals in the party who opposed the war, an equally large faction was supportive. In a 1900 Commons vote on the South African war, the party's MPs divided into three roughly equal groups, voting for the motion, voting against it and abstaining. Each of these groups included a current or future Liberal leader: Henry Campbell-Bannerman and his successors, Herbert Asquith and David Lloyd George. This was a deeply divided party.

The socialist Left outside Parliament was similarly split. 'I am for peace and for international brotherhood,' declared Robert Blatchford, editor of the influential *Clarion*. 'But when England is at war I'm English. I have no politics and no party.'[25] This went down badly with his erstwhile comrades. Harry Quelch, editor of the SDF paper *Justice*, said he couldn't agree with, or even understand, Blatchford's position. 'I am neither pro-British nor anti-British,' he wrote, though 'what I desire most heartily is that the Boers should be overwhelmingly successful.'[26] Dissent was also heard in Blatchford's own paper, where Scottish socialist John Morrison Davidson argued that 'this is a dirty Semitic gold-grabbers' raid – a war of capitalists, by capitalists, for capitalists'.[27]

With the opposition split, and with good news coming from South Africa, Salisbury's government called an election in September 1900 – the Khaki Election as it was known, since peace had not yet been declared.* Chamberlain led the government campaign, focusing so heavily on the war that it became virtually a single-issue election: 'A seat lost to the government is a seat won by the Boers,' he declared.[28] He relentlessly mocked the 'many leaders of the Liberal opposition', suggesting that they were unpatriotic, pro-Boer and, in the case of 'the Little Englanders section of the Liberal Party', against the Empire itself.[29]

In the end, it felt a little like kicking a lame dog. The Liberals' disarray was such that they could field just 402 candidates in the election, 167 fewer than the Conservatives and Liberal Unionists. The result was another big victory for the government; its majority was cut slightly to 134, but it was still a huge endorsement. Of little immediate significance, two candidates from the Labour Representation Committee were elected. One of them was Lanarkshire-born ex-miner Keir Hardie, the new MP for Merthyr Tydfil.

iv

In later years, after the war was over, the noisy enthusiasm of the populace came to be widely condemned. 'Music-hall jingoism was a degrading symptom of very subordinate patriotism during the Boer War,' said those who knew best; it had all been 'cheap and contemptible'; love of one's country demanded more than 'shouting in music halls about England's might'.[30] W. T. Stead added another offence to his charge sheet against the halls: 'Jingoism is

---

* Although khaki had been introduced to the British Army in the 1860s, it was the Boer War that fixed in the public's mind the image of the khaki-clad, as opposed to scarlet-tunicked, soldier.

the ultimate product of the drivelling brain of the dregs of our people.'[31] Things were not, though, quite as clear-cut as these judgements suggested.*

It was striking, for example, that the first major novel of the Boer War was *Boy* (1900) by Marie Corelli, the most popular novelist of the 1890s. Corelli was sneered at by the literary estab-lishment for her gaudy, ill-disciplined prose and her sentimental spirituality, but her work was read across the social spectrum, including by monarchs and prime ministers. 'She is doted on in the drawing-room as well as in the servants' hall,' conceded one paper, gritting its teeth.[32] And doted on too by the army; there was a story that a copy of her novel *The Soul of Lilith* (1892) was shared on the march during the Boer War; pages were torn out and read individually, with each soldier, as he finished his page, passing it on to the man next to him, so that sixty men were simultaneously reading the same volume.

Boy, however, did not return the army's affection. The title char-acter, Robert D'Arcy-Muir, is the only child of a violently alcoholic father and an indolent, self-indulgent mother, and despite material privileges he is neglected and unloved. Consequently, he grows up a weak, selfish wastrel who falls into drunkenness and gambling before a sudden revelation shows him his errors. Then, like Raffles in *The Black Mask*, he joins the army as a private and sails for South Africa, seeking to redeem himself. It doesn't work out like that, and he dies a meaningless death at Colenso, the encounter that made a hero of Bugler Dunne.

As ever with Corelli, the message is not hard to find. 'If the politicians who work up wars could only realize the true horror of

---

* The word 'jingoism' came out of music hall, taken from the chorus of an 1877 song by the Great MacDermott, written for a conflict that didn't happen: 'We don't want to fight, but by Jingo if we do, we've got the ships, we've got the men, we've got the money too.' That gung-ho enthusiasm wasn't universal; the following year came Herbert Campbell's parody: 'I don't want to fight, I'll be slaughtered if I do. I'll change my togs, I'll sell my kit, and pop my rifle too.'

bloodshed they would surely be more careful!' exclaims a nurse, talking to a surgeon as they await the first casualties from the battlefield, and he can only agree: 'The proper way for civilized nations to behave in a difficulty is to submit to peaceful arbitration. War – especially nowadays – is a mere slaughter-house.'

Corelli is equally harsh on military discipline; the way it crushes the individual is an extension of British society, where the aim is 'to check all natural emotion – kill enthusiasm – and let the wonders of the world pass by, while you stand in the place where fortune or circumstance has thrown you.'* The same condemnation of the army was seen in one of the other big hits of the war years, A. E. W. Mason's *The Four Feathers* (1902). The boy here, Harry Feversham, grows up beneath the portraits of soldier ancestors: 'men of courage and resolution, no doubt, but without subtleties, or nerves, or that burdensome gift of imagination', who are 'hardly conspicuous for intellect; to put it frankly, rather stupid – all of them, in a word, first-class fighting men, but not one of them a first-class soldier'. Our hero tries to reject this world, but ultimately he too ends up in Africa, seeking absolution in the Sudan campaign of the 1880s.

The Black Mask, Boy, The Four Feathers – all express that long-held belief that death on the battlefield is a matter not just of glory and honour but of penance. There's no conviction, however. A. J. Raffles does indeed die as he intended, but he leaves Bunny Manders behind, lonely and lame. 'I used to think of a wound received in one's country's service as the proudest trophy a man could acquire,' reflects Bunny. 'But the sight of mine depresses me every morning of my life.' Similarly, Harry Feversham's best friend is blinded by the African sun, condemned to 'dragging, profitless years alone'.

---

* Corelli was generally unimpressed by the British. 'They have some very fine qualities,' she once conceded. 'But they are materialists. Beef and money! Money, money, money!' Despite such sentiments, and despite her Italianate pen name, she was herself British, born in London as Mary Mackay.

Not all popular culture was mindlessly jingoistic, then. There was even subtlety to be found in the much-maligned music halls, for the tone there began to change as the news coming from South Africa failed to meet the bellicose triumphalism of the early songs. Why was the army performing so poorly? Tommy could not be blamed, so the explanation must be that he was unprepared, under-resourced, betrayed by incompetent bureaucrats in White-hall. A song by Will Evans in 1900 sarcastically took aim at the War Office:

When they were wanted, they acted so dense,
Knew nothing of fighting and less of defence.
Where is their intelligence? Where is their sense?
You don't know, they don't know, and I don't know!

Some noticed that audience allegiances were shifting. 'The music hall patriot is a contemptible creature,' said the *Irish News*, 'but he is certainly a barometer of public feeling.' That was in October 1901, the comment being prompted by reports that when a picture of Lord Roberts was shown on screen in a Guildford hall, it was met by 'a storm of hissing, groaning and hooting.'[33] The same phenomenon was noted elsewhere. Yet this was just a few months after the readers of *Leisure Hour* had voted Bobs joint-Greatest Living Englishman. What had gone wrong?

v

Lord Roberts' abrupt fall from public favour reflected develop-ments in South Africa. By any conventional measure, the British had won by the summer of 1900 – everyone knew that – but still the war wasn't over, because the Boers refused to accept their defeat on the battlefield and continued to wage a guerrilla cam-paign against the occupying forces.

'My pal, the Boer, ain't used to proper war,' Edgar Wallace had written in one of his better poems, but irregular war was another matter. The ponderous British army, with its long, vulnerable supply lines, encumbered by equipment and stores, struggled to deal with the small groups of self-sufficient, self-disciplined and mobile Boer irregulars who fought on in their now-occupied lands. For the British soldiers, it was demoralising work. 'Start in the early morning in the high and burning hope of meeting your enemy, who has been reported in front of you, and halt at night, utterly worried and discouraged, only to learn that he has vanished and is probably somewhere in your rear, ready for a swoop in the darkness,' remembered Private James Dunning, of the Northumberland Fusiliers. 'I would rather fight a score of pitched battles than go again through the pursuit of a phantom army.'[34]

The insurgents were sustained by support from the civilian population and, as the months wore on, the British adopted extreme tactics to isolate their enemy. The land was divided by barbed wire, farms and settlements were burned down, and civilians were rounded up into what were called (in established army jargon) concentration camps. It was these latter that became the story of 1901, further damaging Britain's image abroad and providing a focal point for the anti-war faction within the country.

The camps – there were forty-five of them eventually – were intended to provide temporary accommodation to those whose homes had been destroyed. 'We have relaxed the customs of war, and made for ourselves new duties,' said the *Spectator*.[35] Some senior officers attacked the policy for precisely that reason. 'There is too much "law", not enough of the rough and ready justice in this land,' grumbled Lieutenant Colonel Douglas Haig, one of those struggling to suppress the Boer resistance.[36] Mostly, though, the complaints came from the other direction. Because the reality was that, even if well intentioned, the camps were overcrowded, ill-supplied and lacking in adequate water and sanitation. Consequently, they were prey to disease and infection, with the young especially vulnerable: government figures showed that in May 1901 the Transvaal camps saw the deaths of 39 men, 47 women and 250 children.[37]

The following month, the anti-war campaigner Emily Hobhouse was allowed to visit some of the camps, and she reported back on the horrific scenes she had witnessed: 'a six months' baby gasping its life out on its mother's knee'; a child with measles 'stretched on the ground, white and wan'; a man kneeling by his dying daughter, 'while, next tent, his wife was watching a child of six, also dying, and one of about five drooping'.[38] Food was so scarce that the soldiers guarding the camps often gave some of their rations to the inmates, 'half-starved themselves in order that the Boer women and children might be fed'.[39]

There was a concerted effort to shoot the messenger. Hobhouse was vilified in the patriotic press – she was 'pro-Boer', seethed the *Scotsman*, having 'gushed on platforms in this country on the iniquity of the war'[40] – and on a subsequent visit to South Africa she was detained and deported to stop her doing further damage. But by then it was too late; the camps had become an international scandal, and growing numbers at home were speaking out. This was 'a war of infanticide', said one Irish MP,[41] a 'holocaust of child-life', in the words of John Percival, Bishop of Hereford.[42] Following a meeting with Hobhouse, Henry Campbell-Bannerman – a man, she said, 'in whom wisdom and humanity were paramount'[43] – spoke on the issue in the Commons. 'When is a war not a war?' he asked acerbically. 'When it is carried on by methods of barbarism in South Africa.' This was a question of who we were as a people, he insisted: 'The character of our nation is at stake in this matter.'[44]

Then there was David Lloyd George, a Liberal MP who had frequently appeared at meetings alongside Hobhouse over the past year and who spoke most persistently in Parliament.

As with Edgar Wallace, the Boer War was to be the making of Lloyd George, establishing him as a national figure and laying the ground for future achievements. He'd been born in 1863, his father a teacher who died the following year. His mother took the boy back to her home village in north-west Wales, where he was brought up in the ways of his uncle, a shoemaker who was radical in politics, Baptist in faith. By the age of twenty-two, David had set up in practice as a solicitor and become active in Liberal politics, inspired by the crusading example of Joe Chamberlain; in 1890 he was elected MP for Caernarvon Boroughs.

Like Chamberlain, Lloyd George's natural environment was on stage. He was a brilliant speaker, with all the emotive showmanship of the dissenting minister. Physically, he was unimposing, but in front of a 5,000-strong crowd it was a different story. 'The small, slight figure grows and expands to the eye, as the ear listens to the musical voice, and the mind is impressed by the passion of the words. Mr Lloyd George on a great occasion, stirred by genuine emotions, is a tragic poem. He is the hero of his own epic.'[45]

He was outraged by everything to do with the war: by the claim that it was in pursuit of democracy, by its conduct, by its cost. His speeches against the conflict brought him national attention and a great deal of hatred, most notably in December 1901 when he was invited to speak at Birmingham Town Hall. The city was still Chamberlain's great stronghold, and the two men were now on opposite sides. For Lloyd George to take his anti-war message into such hostile territory was a deliberately provocative act and, duly provoked, a huge crowd – 30,000 strong, by one estimate – gathered in the streets outside to protest. As *Punch* magazine summarised the events:

> Taffy is a Welshman – Bannerman's his chief;
> Taffy went to Joe's town and there he came to grief.[46]

As the meeting got underway, a hail of stones and bricks smashed the windows and gunfire was heard, before the mob gained access to the hall. The ensuing riot saw some thirty people hospitalised, one of them subsequently dying, and several arrests made. Lloyd George had to be smuggled out of the hall, disguised as a policeman and in genuine fear of his life. He had, however, made his mark; even if Chamberlain wasn't inclined to pass on the baton of Liberal populism, he was prepared to seize it.

And Lloyd George had a following every bit as devoted as

that of Chamberlain. He was, wrote *Daily News* editor A. G. Gardiner, a man who aroused 'fierce enthusiasms and fierce hates'. His unswerving opposition to the war may have alienated many, but he 'came out of the battle-smoke victorious – the one reputation made by the war, the one fortune born on the battlefield where so many were buried'.[47]

He was, though, never a darling of the music halls. As with so many Liberals, Lloyd George came from the temperance movement, where he had learned his oratorical craft; that counted against him with the patrons of drinking establishments. Nor was his anti-war stance popular. The halls were sentimental, loving the underdog, and would have backed the Boers against any other imperial power, but their patriotism trumped other considerations. Nonetheless, although they never turned their back on the Tommies, they did become hostile to the conduct of the war, to the scorched-earth policy and the concentration camps. They blamed Lord Roberts for these things and for the military humiliations, for the fact that, in H. G. Wells's words, 'Our Empire was nearly beaten by a handful of farmers amidst the jeering contempt of the whole world.'[48]

The protracted conflict finally staggered to a halt with the Treaty of Vereeniging in May 1902,* and novelist Hilaire Belloc offered ironic applause to the generals, 'who, in less than three years from the decisive victory of Paardeberg, imposed peace upon the enemy'.[49] The Transvaal and the Orange Free State were brought under British rule, with the promise of self-government in the future, and, in a highly unusual move, the victors agreed to pay the losers: a substantial sum was allocated for reconstruction and for compensating those whose properties had been destroyed.

It had been, just as Joseph Chamberlain had predicted it would be, 'a long war, a bitter war, and a costly war'. More than 26,000 Boer civilians had died in the camps, the vast majority of them

---

* Edgar Wallace got the scoop on the successful outcome of the negotiations, having bribed an informant inside the sealed-off camp where they were taking place.

children, along with an estimated 20,000 black internees, housed separately. The conflict had cost Britain the lives of 22,000 soldiers and around £200 million, nearly as much as total government expenditure in 1898, the last year before the war. Liberal MP John Burns suggested that it be paid for by 'a £10 poll-tax on the head of every music-hall patriot who shouted for war, and £20 on the heads of those who didn't enlist'.[50]

vi

In March 1902, towards the end of the war, almost as a footnote to it, the death was announced of Cecil Rhodes at the age of forty-eight. A vicar's son who'd been sent to Natal for his health when he was seventeen, Rhodes had become the richest man in southern Africa, thanks to the diamonds of Kimberley – he founded the De Beers company – and then the most politically powerful, serving as prime minister of the Cape Colony 1890–96. He also created the British South Africa Company (BSAC), which, furnished with a royal charter, brought an extensive area north of the Limpopo River under British control to form a new country, named Rhodesia in his honour.*

His ambition was greater still. 'I contend that we are the first race in the world, and that the more of the world we inhabit the better it is for the human race,' he wrote in his mid-twenties, dreaming that a reunion of America and Britain could make 'the Anglo-Saxon race but one Empire'.[51] On a good day he could even be heard fantasising about the colonisation of other planets.

Rhodes's extraordinary domination of southern Africa had come to an abrupt end shortly before the Boer War, with an 1896 attempt to engineer an uprising of the *uitlanders* in Transvaal. As part of the plot, his associate Leander Starr Jameson had taken a small armed force to the border, ready to sweep in on the pretext of

* Later split into Northern and Southern Rhodesia, and later still renamed Zambia and Zimbabwe.

restoring order; the insurrection failed to materialise, but even so Jameson unilaterally led an incursion into the Transvaal. With no local support, the enterprise ended in ignominious failure. While Rhodes was not directly responsible for the Jameson Raid, he had initiated the project, and he was badly tarnished by the fiasco, forced to resign as prime minister of the Cape and as a director of the BSAC.* His last years saw him fade to the margins, but he remained a charismatic presence. 'He impressed me greatly, the sense he gave one of huge but crippled power, the reedy voice and the banal words in which he tried to express ideas which represented for him a whole world of incoherent poetry,' wrote novelist John Buchan, who met him at this time. 'I felt him as one feels the imminence of a thunderstorm.'[52]

Admired, if not liked, Rhodes was a divisive figure. 'He is as cordially respected by some as he is frankly loathed by others,' observed the press as he lay dying,[53] and even the positive obituaries that followed acknowledged the controversy that surrounded him. 'With all his faults, and they were neither few nor small, Cecil John Rhodes was a great Empire-maker and a great Englander,' wrote the *Daily Telegraph*.[54] 'He has many enemies, he has made mistakes, perhaps even worse,' agreed *Queen* ('the Lady's Newspaper'), 'but he is one of the greatest Englishmen born in the nineteenth century.'[55] Others were more hostile: 'His famous and much-quoted remark that "territory is everything" goes far to explain his colossal failure,' observed the *Daily News*. 'It is not only profoundly false. It shows an incurable blindness to all that makes the nation really great.'[56]

W. T. Stead, a friend of Rhodes who edited his *Last Will and Testament*† for publication, saw him as a pioneer of the coming

---

* Questions were also asked about whether Joseph Chamberlain had prior knowledge of the Jameson Raid, but an enquiry by a House of Commons committee exonerated him. It helped that Chamberlain himself was one of the committee members.
† Rhodes bequeathed a substantial piece of land to South Africa, on which the University of Cape Town was built, and left money to establish the Rhodes

age, 'the first of the new Dynasty of Money Kings which has been evolved in these later days as the real rulers of the modern world'.[57] But the money was merely the means to the end, a way of exerting power and influence. As Rhodes once observed, 'It is no use for us to have big ideas if we have not got the money to carry them out.'[58] And for much of the public, it was not the money that made him so difficult, so much as those big ideas, that dream of an ever-expanding empire.

There was one image to which the obituarists kept returning. 'Like Napoleon, he seemed not to recognise there is such a word as "Impossible"'; 'With a Napoleonic vagueness Mr Rhodes combined Napoleonic paganism'; Rhodes was 'The Modern Napoleon.'[59] In this formulation, the Jameson Raid was his equivalent of the 1812 invasion of Russia, the overreach that saw the beginning of the end.[60] Even notices in the foreign press used the same reference point. He was 'the Napoleon of South Africa', said *Petit Temps* in France,[61] while the Belgian *Petit Bleu* called him 'the genial Napoleon of a practical unidealistic age'.[62]

Therein lay the problem with Cecil Rhodes – because Napoleon was such a profoundly un-British figure with whom to be compared. G. K. Chesterton expressed it best in 'The Rolling English Road' (1913):

> I knew no harm of Bonaparte and plenty of the Squire,
> And for to fight the Frenchman I did not much desire;
> But I did bash their baggonets because they came arrayed
> To straighten out the crooked road an English drunkard made.[63]

Napoleon's imperialism was seen as the grandiose expression of one man's will, born of an egotism and a pride that attempted to impose rational order on the world: 'empire-making Lust and personal

---

Scholarship scheme, funding postgraduate students from the Empire, the USA and Germany to attend Oxford University. 'They will read that after I am gone,' he said of his will, 'and will do me justice when I am dead.'

Gain', as Thomas Hardy put it.[64] By contrast, the British Empire had been built piecemeal over centuries, in a disjointed series of often random, unpremeditated acquisitions. It had no logic, no coherent structure, and consequently it was seen as organic and evolving with nature. 'You call our civilisation a machine, but it is something far more flexible,' one of John Buchan's heroes says. 'It has the power of adaptation of a living organism.'[65] He's talking to an evil criminal mastermind (the disappointingly named Andrew Lumley), who boasts of himself, 'No man since Napoleon has tasted such power.'

The model for Lumley was Sherlock Holmes's nemesis Professor Moriarty, who was referred to as 'the Napoleon of Crime', and there were any number of fictional variations on this theme, from 'the Napoleon of Wall Street' in E. C. Bentley's *Trent's Last Case* (1913) down to the bathetic paper-manufacturing hero of Frank Danby's novel *An Incompleat Etonian* (1909): '"The Napoleon of the Paper Trade" they'll call me. See if they don't!' Real life offered its own versions. Edward Moss, of Moss Empires, was 'the Napoleon of music halls'; Horatio Bottomley 'the Napoleon of finance'; Joe Chamberlain 'the Napoleon of Birmingham'; Alfred Harmsworth 'the Napoleon of journalism'.[66] (The latter idolised Bonaparte, and on a visit to Versailles was delighted to find that the hat of his great hero fitted his own head perfectly.) Not even spiritual leaders were exempt from comparison: 'William Booth is, in his way, as great a general as Napoleon Bonaparte.'[67]

'The real mischief of Napoleon's immensely disastrous and accidental career began only when he was dead and the romantic type of mind was free to elaborate his character,' observes the narrator of H. G. Wells's semi-autobiographical novel *Tono-Bungay*. 'When in doubt between decent conduct and a base advantage, that cult came in more and more influentially: "think of Napoleon; think what the inflexibly wilful Napoleon would have done with such scruples as yours;" that was the rule, and the end was invariably a new step in dishonour.'[68]

There was a semi-admiring, semi-horrified fascination with the legend of the ultimate self-made man, the Little Corporal who rose to rule a continent. 'The fear of that man hung like a black shadow over all Europe,' wrote Arthur Conan Doyle.[69] That was in one of his historical novels, but he could easily have been talking about the modern day, so ubiquitous did Bonaparte's name become in Edwardian Britain, every mention a nervous reassurance of how solid by contrast was the Empire.

It was inevitable, then, that Cecil Rhodes would be seen as Napoleonic, but it wasn't the whole truth. Rather he was a transitional figure. On the one hand, he seemed a throwback to the pioneering days of Clive of India, in a way that jarred with modern bureaucratic politics; on the other, he represented a new world of money. There was little orthodoxy of religion in his endeavours; his faith was in an almost mystical veneration of the Anglo-Saxon race. Rhodes was 'a Darwinian rather than a Christian', wrote Stead; he believed in 'the gospel of evolution, of the survival of the fittest, of progress by natural selection'.[70] But it was an inverted Darwinism, assuming that the present was the predestined end of the evolutionary process. Britain's dominant position in the world was the result not of favourable conditions, but of natural superiority.

Rhodes gave the impression that he believed himself to be the finest expression of that superiority, and in that at least he justified his billing as the modern Napoleon. It is also why the public never took him to its heart; a Bonapartist in pursuit of power was too alien a figure to be a British hero. The Empire was about institutions not individuals these days. The people's imagination could still be stirred, of course, by a Robert Baden-Powell or by someone like Mary Slessor, a former mill-worker turned missionary, acclaimed as 'one of the most remarkable women of our time'.[71] These people made sense in the popular image of the colonies; they were Bobs and Booth again, glory and compassion. But Rhodes was an austere businessman, and he didn't fit. Further, he died at a time when the Boer War was unresolved and the concentration camps still in the news, undermining Britain's self-proclaimed position on the moral high ground. Everyone agreed that he was an extraordinary, exceptional man – and that was largely why the public were so ambivalent towards him: he was so atypical in his imperialism.

The most savage obituary of Rhodes came in the liberal *Morning Leader*, which saw him as being without glamour or even true vision. 'His insensibility to moral ideas, his carelessness of human sufferings, his rough handling of the delicacies and scruples of honourable men were not even the calculated callousness of the Napoleonic person, the "overman", who overrides ethics like a natural force. These things betrayed rather a coarseness of fibre and a deficient imagination.' And then the final twist of the knife: 'Napoleon, at least, rose by his personal force; Mr Rhodes mounted to power on a cheque-book.'[72]

3

PAST AND FUTURE

For men were men in the olden time
Not money making schemers.
We had less poverty, want and crime
And socialistic dreamers.
Life was worth living, for England's wealth
Was shared with justice sincere
More equally 'twixt the masters and men
In the days of the Cavalier.

Vesta Tilley, 'In the Days of the Cavalier', 1897[1]

In my hot and silly brain, Jesus and Pan held sway together,
as in a wayside chapel discordantly and impishly consecrated
to Pagan and to Christian rites.

Edmund Gosse, *Father and Son*, 1907[2]

Postcard advertising the National Pageant of Wales in 1909.

WORD OF THE MUTOSCOPE first reached Britain in 1897, provoking much excitement. This was the 'latest invention in animated photography',[3] a system that took hundreds of photographs a minute, which were then mounted on boards and loaded on to a reel in a cylindrical metal machine. You put a coin in the slot, turned a handle and, through a pane of glass at the top of the machine, watched the pictures flick rapidly through, recreating the movement of the original scene. The mutoscope was, suggested the British press, an invaluable tool for 'the anatomist, or student of quick locomotive forms'.[4]

It was also a commercial opportunity. The machines cost twenty pounds each, and although only one person could be accommodated at a time, the minute-long scenes allowed a rapid turnover of patrons. When the technology was first exhibited in Britain, at Edward Moss's Waverley Market Carnival in Edinburgh, each machine drew an average of 372 customers a day, paying a penny each, a total of thirty-one shillings, so an entrepreneur would earn back his investment in under a fortnight. The other great advantage was that solo viewing made this a semi-private experience, and it could therefore be promoted with the promise of risqué content. Never mind the anatomist or the student of locomotion, the real money was to be made with pictures such as *Four Frivolous Girls*, *A Mouse in a Girl's Bedroom*, *Should Ladies Wear Bloomers?*, *Where Ignorance Is Bliss* and *How to Serve the Salad Undressed*. And then there was the most famous of them all, the title that became the generic name for the mutoscope in Britain: *What the Butler Saw*.*

The craze spread rapidly around the country. At one end of the business there were the pleasure grounds at Earl's Court in London, with hundreds of machines; at the other was the gentlemen's lavatory on Rhyl seafront, where their presence caused much

---

* Release dates for these pictures are seldom known, but *What the Butler Saw* was no later than 1907, when it first appeared in a British court case.

overcrowding, to the annoyance of those wishing to use the conventional facilities. The more normal practice, though, was for an exhibitor to rent a shop and install a dozen or so of the things. Some of these proprietors were colourful showmen, characters such as W. G. Smith, aka Captain Texas, who dressed in a cowboy costume and ran a company called Fanning's Irish-American Marionette Company on Great Britain Street in Dublin.* His stock of mutoscope pictures was seized by the police in 1902 under the Obscene Publications Act, and denounced as 'leprous pictures' by the press, 'immoral garbage' that 'should not be tolerated for a single instant'.[5]

Smith was not the only businessman to fall foul of the law, as moralists rushed to condemn this new cultural phenomenon. The Liberal MP William Caine worried that 'tens of thousands of young people were every day polluted and degraded by the pictures'.[6] Dr Rawlings of Swansea Council said that 'most of the pictures are lewd and obscene, and calculated to excite evil passions'.[7] And the Reverend J. S. Balmer, a noisy Nonconformist minister from Blackpool, said having inspected the machines for himself, he had 'looked through the gateway to perdition'.[8] Amid a wave of outrage, it took political nerve to remain calm, but the home secretary Charles Ritchie managed to do so; challenged in 1901 about obscene pictures being shown on Hampstead Heath, he sounded amused and faintly disappointed as he reported that he'd been there recently 'but failed to find anything objectionable, though he spent several pennies on his investigation'.[9]

Ritchie's estimation was correct; the reality was far less shocking than the campaigners claimed. A series titled *Life in Paris* included a sequence of 'a lady getting out of bed'.[10] Elsewhere, Liberal MP Samuel Smith described images of 'girls engaged in kicking at a hat which was held above their heads, there being at each attempt a liberal display of underclothing'.[11] And magistrates in Folkestone heard that a seized picture showed 'a young lady

---

* Renamed Parnell Street in 1911, in honour of Charles Stewart Parnell.

looking out of the window, and as she did so she showed her legs'. None of this was anything more than one could see in the music halls and theatres, and the defence in the Folkestone case argued that police raids on mutoscopes revealed a double standard: 'The poor people went and paid a penny to see that exhibition because they could not afford to pay two shillings and have it at the Pleasure Gardens Theatre.' If this material was found obscene, it would show that 'there was a law for the rich and one for the poor'. The magistrates, however, were unpersuaded and ordered the pictures to be destroyed.[12]

The real concern was about boys gathering around the mutoscopes, egging each other on. Even worse, sometimes it wasn't just boys. There was a report from one Midlands city of 'a group of girls ranging in age from ten to fifteen years' crowded around a machine. 'An outer circle was formed by youths and men, who, with leering eyes and base language, supplemented any vicious suggestions these pictures had already made.'[13]

Despite the seizures and the prosecutions, and despite the emergence of far better moving-pictures technology, the mutoscope proved remarkably durable. Long after the initial craze faded away, the machines remained commonplace, primarily in seaside resorts. Proprietors elsewhere found they had to diversify a little. William and Maud Barron, the married owners of Funland, an establishment in Kingston upon Thames, were prosecuted in 1912 for showing 'absolutely obscene and indecent' pictures on machines that were labelled 'For girls only – Spicy' and 'For gentlemen only'.[14] Two months later, the Barrons were back in court on charges related to Funland's other attraction, penny-in-the-slot gaming machines. In both cases it was noted that the customers were mostly children.[15]

ii

The mutoscope symbolised for some the ugliness of the modern world. It wasn't just the tawdry content of the pictures, it was the machines themselves, each with a young person attached, passively absorbing uncensored material. It didn't augur well for the next generation, nor for the future of society. At least the music halls offered shared, flesh-and-blood entertainment, however debased it might be; this, on the other hand, was the triumph of a mechanised age, devoid of community.

In a trend that was deplored in civilised circles, machines were becoming part of everyday life, a technological revolution that, if not as dramatic in its impact as that of the mills and mines on earlier generations, was nonetheless profound. At home, the telephone – described by writer Saki as having 'undermined almost every fastness of human privacy'[16] – was changing communication; the National Telephone Company* announced in 1900 that 640 million calls had been made that year, compared to the 90 million telegrams that had been sent.[17] At work, the rise of the typewriter, joined by the newly invented Dictaphone and calculating machines, was transforming the office and bringing new employment opportunities; by 1911 there were nearly 140,000 female clerical workers. Worst of all, there was the noisy, intrusive presence of the motor car, beloved of Violet Charlesworth and Toad of Toad Hall.

The first horseless carriage on British roads was manufactured by Panhard et Levassor of Paris and imported by the Honourable Evelyn Ellis in 1895. It was 'a very neat and compact four-wheeled dog-cart, with accommodation for four persons and two good-sized portmanteaus', marvelled the press. 'It can travel at a speed of fifteen to twenty miles an hour.'[18] The following year, Walter Arnold of East Peckham in Kent became the first person to be fined for speeding, travelling four times the legal limit (two miles per hour in towns); a few months later, Bridget Driscoll, a forty-four-year-old labourer's wife from Croydon, became the first fatality of a motorised vehicle, run over and killed at the Crystal Palace. By

---

* The National Telephone Company ran the phone network until 1911, when it was taken over by the Post Office.

1900 there were reckoned to be up to 800 cars in the country, with ownership already becoming a passion for some wealthy owners; Lady Wimborne and her son had a fleet of nine cars: Daimlers, Darracqs, Mercedes and Napiers.

That first car of Evelyn Ellis was said to have been 'conspicuous by the absence of either smoke, heat or smell', but that wasn't the common experience of those who came into contact with 'this modern monster'.[19] There were a great many complaints about the smoke, the smell, the noise, the speed, the vibration, the glare of headlights, and – above all – the dirt that was raised on roads that had been built for horses. 'As it flew, it gathered the deep white dust, and hurled it thirty feet into the air,' wrote John Finnemore in *The Wolf Patrol* (1908), 'leaving the road in the wake of the car one utterly blinding, choking mass of eddying dust.' In 1902 the Highway Protection League was founded to counter what it called 'the terrorism of the flying machine'.[20] It fought a losing battle, of course, for the advantages of a car to its owner were so great, in terms of convenience and efficiency, as well as pride and ostentation. (As novelist Arnold Bennett noted, 'It remains the supreme symbol of swagger.'[21]) Even the high initial price was partially offset by a long-term saving: retaining a single driver-mechanic was a cheaper option than maintaining a stable of horses.

There was no turning back. The Motor Car Act of 1903 introduced vehicle registration and driving licences, and in 1905 there were just under 16,000 holders of the five-shilling licence; five years later, there were nearly 90,000. The 1911 census showed grooms and coachmen outnumbering chauffeurs by around three to one, but the trend was clear. The car was, some found, a necessity in modern life, particularly if one lived beyond the railway network. 'Surely this means a little revolution in rural life,' the *Tablet* had suggested in 1895. 'What will it matter being six miles from a station when you can travel in your carriage without horses twelve miles an hour at the cost of one penny?'[22] A decade or so later and a character in one of Frank Danby's novels was convinced: 'You can't live in the country without the motor.'[23] They were still less than reliable, though, prone to breakdowns and punctures, and hostesses learned not to hold dinner if guests were travelling by motor car.

By now, ownership had become affordable to those further down the social scale, as prices began to fall. Domestic firms were not the chief beneficiaries, however. British car manufacturers tended to concentrate on the top end of the market, where demand was already established, and they largely failed to recognise the potential of cheaper models for the middle classes. That left the field open for more enterprising foreigners, and in 1911 the American industrialist Henry Ford bought a disused carriage works in Trafford Park, Manchester; Model T cars were soon coming off the production line. In 1913 some 12,000 cars were sold in Britain at a price under £200, and two thirds of them were Fords. As was increasingly the way in much of British industry, the quality of the product couldn't be faulted, only the lack of commercial vision.

There was no doubting, either, the country's enthusiasm for motorsport. In 1902 Britain won the third annual staging of the Gordon Bennett Cup, when the businessman Selwyn Edge, driving a Napier, was the only entrant to complete the 350-mile course from Paris to Innsbruck; the following year, in recognition of his achievement, the race left France, and special legislation was passed to allow it to be held on the roads of County Kildare, the first such contest in the United Kingdom.* The public was smitten, for this sport was unlike anything anyone had seen, with a thrilling level of danger. In a race on the Isle of Man in 1904 the British driver Clifford Earp was hospitalised when he smashed into a stone wall, but he was back the next year to win the Flying Start Race at Brighton's first Motor Race Week, reaching a speed of 97.2 miles per hour.[24] This surely was a harbinger of the future of consumer technology, a world of shiny, mechanised haste.

---

* In honour of the location, the British team wore shamrock green, henceforth to be known as British racing green.

iii

Seemingly in another country, another century, the reality for many lacked any such sense of modernity. The 1901 census showed that 77 per cent of the population of England and Wales were living in urban areas and, despite the millions of pounds spent in recent years on slum clearance, there remained a great deal of contemporary life that was as squalid and foul as it had been when documented by Charles Dickens, Friedrich Engels and others fifty years earlier.

A new era of campaigning on social conditions was launched by General William Booth, as he took the Salvation Army from saving individuals to advocating social reform. His book *In Darkest England, and the Way Out* (1890) popularised the expression 'the submerged tenth' as a description for the estimated three million people who were either homeless, destitute, criminal, insane, in workhouses or otherwise excluded from mainstream society. The desperation of their lives was a stain on the nation. 'England emancipated her negroes sixty years ago,' wrote Booth, 'and has never ceased boasting about it since. But at our own doors, from Plymouth to Peterhead, stretches this waste continent of humanity.'[25]

In Booth's wake there was a spate of sociological and economic studies: Benjamin Seebohm Rowntree, *Poverty, A Study of Town Life* (1901); Jack London, *On the Edge of the Abyss* (1901); Charles Booth (no relation), *Life and Labour of the People of London* (1902); Leo Chiozza Money, *Riches and Poverty* (1905);* Beatrice Webb, *Minority Report of the Poor Law Commission* (1909); Will Reason, *Poverty* (1909); Philip Snowden, *The Living Wage* (1912); Maud Pember Reeves, *Round About a Pound a Week* (1913). The title of the latter came from an assessment of the poverty line, identified by Rowntree as being a household income of 21s 8d a week, or £56 a year; by that measure, he said, around a third of the population lived in poverty. This barrage of books collectively reframed an argument that had been raging since the Industrial Revolution;

---

* Born Leone Chiozza, he was an economist who added Money to his name in an act of reverse nominative-determinism.

poverty was increasingly seen not in moral terms, but as a function of social inequality.

Life was still appallingly harsh at the bottom of society. The death rate in Liverpool slums was four times the national average. The Reverend J. W. Horsley, who had worked in deprived London parishes in Woolwich and Walworth, said conditions there 'were bleaching and enfeebling, attenuating and dwarfing, sickening and slaying the proletariat'.[26] Public health inspectors in Bradford reported in 1909 on a world that sounded little different to that of the concentration camps in South Africa: 'In one overcrowded house, there was no bedstead of any description, the only bedding being an old straw mattress, on which slept two parents and seven children, whose only covering were the old clothes worn during the day.' In another property, housing two married couples and their children, it was hard to wake anyone at 11.30 in the morning, until eventually 'A slatternly woman crawled down the staircase, which reminded one of the entrance to a hen-roost. There was very little furniture and only one bed. Altogether, one wondered whether this was a human habitation or a piggery.'[27]

There were similar scenes in many English cities. 'The room was nearly empty, with nothing but a rickety table and two bacon boxes to relieve the plastered floor and the crumbling walls,' reported the Reverend Thomas Bass, vicar of St Lawrence's in Birmingham.* 'On the table lay a dead child, looking fearful in the candlelight, and by it stood the father and mother, gazing painfully at the body. They were sitting up all night to keep the rats off their dead child!' It was said that 'a clergyman who had lost his sense of smell for two years recovered it on going down a street in this parish of Birmingham'.[28]

The situation was no better in the cities of the other home nations. There were six-storey tenements in Glasgow that housed

---

* According to the *Llandudno Courier*, Birmingham's slums were 'worse than any in England', but that probably required a pinch of salt; this was a paper loyal to Lloyd George taking aim at Joe Chamberlain's heartland.

up to seventy families, with a single tap providing the entire water supply, while up to a quarter of Dublin's population lived in one-room tenements. 'The dirt, the overcrowding, the defective sanitation, the impure air, the misery and squalor, poverty and drink!' lamented the *Irish Times*. 'The cry of the slum dweller goes up to Heaven for vengeance night and day!'[29]

Improving such areas was a lengthy undertaking. One of the first proposals approved by the London County Council on its formation in 1889 had concerned a district between Drury Lane, the Strand and Lincoln's Inn Fields, a random, slovenly patchwork of alleys, lanes and courts, but it took until 1901 to complete the largest urban planning project in the capital since the building of the Thames Embankment.* The result was impressive, with the widening of the Strand and the construction of Kingsway, running from Holborn in the north down to the magnificent new crescent of Aldwych. Some, though, regretted the loss of history. In particular, there was the destruction of Holywell Street, famous a generation earlier for radical politics and pornographic bookshops, and one of the few surviving remnants of Elizabethan London: 'The architectural features of the quaint old houses and shops carry us back to Tudor time,' reflected the *Pall Mall Gazette*.[30] Now it was demolished, and the chaotic mess replaced by broad thoroughfares with coherent planning and architecture. Certainly it was more appropriate for the capital of the Empire, but maybe it was also a little soulless.

Soulless was an accusation also directed at the suburbs that had grown up to house the ever more numerous ranks of the middle class. By the start of Edward's reign, there were 25,200 clergymen, 23,000 doctors and 5,300 dentists, 21,000 lawyers and 12,500 accountants. There were also 230,000 teachers, though apart from those at the major public schools, their social standing was not

---

* In keeping with normal practice for major public works, the cost had risen dramatically in the meantime, from an estimated £1.5 million to more than £6 million.

high.[31] Altogether, the number of men and women employed in the professions and in commerce had grown by 65 per cent in twenty years to stand at 2.8 million. The number of domestic servants, however, had shown a more modest 10 per cent increase to 2 million over the same period; many of those rising into respectability made do with just one servant, or even none at all.[32]

To accommodate this expanding section of society, small towns and villages in the vicinity of cities were swallowed up in a sprawl of new housing that seemed to some to embody this unheroic age. Stranded between city and country, between society and slum, suburbia was seen as prim, small-minded, unadventurous. It was all too easy, wrote Ford Madox Hueffer,* to 'sniff at the "Suburbs" as a place of small houses and dreary lives',[33] a world where, in the words of the Reverend J. A. Grant of the Church Socialist League, 'narrowed interests ruled and were extolled into virtues'.[34]

This dismissive attitude didn't go unremarked by those who lived in such places. Novelist James Hilton, born in 1900, grew up in Walthamstow, 'a suburb which people from Hampstead or Chelsea would think entirely characterless, but which, if one lived in it for twenty years as I did, revealed a delicate and by no means unlikeable quality of its own'.[35] This town, north-west of London, was typical of many, with a population that leaped from 10,000 to 130,000 in the forty years to 1910. With land available for new development, such places responded rapidly to new cultural initiatives – in the case of Walthamstow, it was roller-skating[†] at 'the largest, finest and best-equipped rink around London'[36] and the cinematograph films at the Prince's Pavilion and the Arcadia Electric Theatre. Despite their bland reputation, there was colour in these streets. 'It was fun to step out of the classroom on winter evenings and search a book-barrow lit by naphtha-flares, or listen to a Hindu peddling a corn-cure,' remembered Hilton. 'And there

---

* Later, and better, known as Ford Madox Ford.
† 'Don't fail to see the football match upon skates on Saturday evening,' urged the adverts.

was a roaring music-hall nearby, with jugglers and Little Tich and Gertie Gitana; and on Friday nights outside the municipal baths a strange-eyed long haired soap-boxer talked anarchism.'[37]

The best chronicler of the suburbs was humorist Barry Pain in a saga that started with *Eliza* (1900) and ran for another four volumes. We never learn the name of Eliza's husband (our narrator), but he's cut from the same cloth as Charles Pooter in George and Weedon Grossmith's *Diary of a Nobody* (1892), a pompous, ignorant, socially awkward bumbler who believes himself to be the embodiment of common sense and moral rectitude. He's concerned, above all, with the appearance of respectability, disapproving of such things as 'betting on horse-races, check trousers on Sundays, the wash hung out in the front garden, whisky and soda, front steps not properly whitened, and the door-handle not up to the mark'. And he tries very hard, if not always successfully, to get his wife to conform to his standards. 'She has lost the silly playfulness which was rather a mark of her character during the period of our engagement,' he notes approvingly, though he also admits that 'her temper is more easily ruffled now than then when I point out things to her'.

Despite his myriad faults, Eliza's husband is at heart a decent sort of chap. Not so his son. Physically, the boy Ernest cuts an unimpressive figure: 'even ma says that I do not photograph well', he admits. He's stout, bespectacled and useless at games, but he's also intelligent, the recipient of all the academic prizes at school, and he never gets into trouble. As a result, he's bullied relentlessly, and his unsympathetic parents despair of him ever becoming 'an ordinary human being'. His greatest offence is to identify at an early age with the force that was driving society. 'I always like to know the price of everything,' he explains. Or, as his father sees it, he has a 'love of money, amounting almost to avarice'. And so he finds a role for himself. He buys pens wholesale and sells them at a huge mark-up to fellow pupils who have lost their own; he lends money at an interest rate of 50 per cent per week; and he turns a handsome profit when he makes a book on the Epsom Derby (with the sanctimonious justification that his aim is 'to show other boys the folly of betting'). The pre-conversion Scrooge would have approved of the way he keeps a profit-and-loss ledger for Christmas presents given and received. He is rootless, amoral, an embryonic Horatio Bottomley without the *joie de vivre*, his soulless materialism presented as suburbia's contribution to building the future.

The era's other great treatment of the suburbs was G. K. Chesterton's novel *The Napoleon of Notting Hill* (1904), set in 1984, when the capricious King Auberon decides on a whim that the new districts should have their own ceremonial and chivalrous identities. 'A revival of the arrogance of the old mediaeval cities applied to our glorious suburbs,' he rhapsodises. 'Clapham with a city guard. Wimbledon with a city wall. Surbiton tolling a bell to raise its citizens. West Hampstead going into battle with its own banner.'

His vision appeals to one idealist, Adam Wayne, who becomes provost of Notting Hill. 'Terribly quiet; that is in two words the spirit of this age,' reflects Wayne. 'I see blank well-ordered streets and men in black moving about inoffensively, sullenly. It goes on day after day, day after day, and nothing happens; but to me it is like a dream from which I might wake screaming.' When a major new road threatens to cut through his territory, he rouses his people to armed resistance, awakening the pride and passion that lurks in their suburban hearts. The area might look banal to outsiders, but humanity can vest an emotional charge in the least prepossessing places: 'These little gardens where we told our loves. These streets where we brought out our dead. Why should they be commonplace? Why should they be absurd?'

Some reviewers saw the novel as 'a satire on the Boer War',[38] but it was equally possible to see it as a defiant assertion of community in a world of machines and slums.

iv

Louis Napoleon Parker was born in France to an English mother and an American father. He was a schoolteacher, a composer and a playwright, but he became best known as 'the father of modern pageantry'.[39] His concept, first manifest in a historical pageant in Sherborne, Dorset, in 1905, was of an outdoor spectacle that depicted centuries of local history, 'a Festival of Thanksgiving, in which a great city or a little hamlet celebrates its glorious past, its prosperous present, and its hopes and aspirations for the future'.[40] There was to be no scenery in these performances, just the judicious use of existing locations, and they were to be created and performed by members of the community, who, in the interests of equality and inclusion, should be anonymous.

Parker's pageants had two intentions: they were 'designed to kill' the 'modernising spirit' which 'destroys all loveliness and has no loveliness of its own to put in its place',[41] and they should foster patriotism. Those who participated in a pageant would learn 'that the grand story of Britain is written chapter by chapter in her green villages,' with the result that 'local pride will gradually blossom into the larger sense of glory in being British – in being part of the Empire upon which the sun never sets.' Nonetheless, Parker insisted, 'This is not the gospel of a noisy jingoism, kept alive by doggerel ditties in music halls.'[42]

The idea was an instant success, so popular that a new word was coined to express the phenomenon. 'An epidemic of "pageantitis" is threatened as a result of the Sherborne folk-play,' reported the press,[43] and there were outbreaks all over the country, including, in the summer of 1907, in Allendale, Bury St Edmunds, Cardiff, Chelsea, Dudley, Felixstowe, Ilford, the Isle of Wight, Liverpool, Newlyn, Oxford, Potter Heigham, Romsey, St Albans, Stratford-on-Avon and Winchester. The contagion was even reported to have spread to America. Not all the pageants were as spectacular or as well organised as those that managed to secure the services of Parker himself, but there was an energy and enthusiasm that swept away even the doubters. An account in the *Labour Leader** of the

---

* Founded by Keir Hardie in 1888, the *Labour Leader* was now owned by the Independent Labour Party.

Bury St Edmunds Pageant, with 'two thousand performers drawn from all classes of the community', concluded that it was evidence of socialist truth: 'a magnificent triumph of collective effort' that was 'infinitely greater than would be inspired by all the incentives of competition'. Particularly winning was the depiction of Tudor times, in which 'all classes met upon equal terms' and 'everyone was perfectly happy'.[44]

This romanticised view of the past was not uncommon in the world of British radicalism, where there had long been a strand of utopian nostalgia for a lost pastoral paradise. It had been articulated most recently in the title of Robert Blatchford's two-million-selling book *Merrie England* (1893),* and although Blatchford's support of the Boer War cost him some standing in socialist circles, his patriotic, heart-over-head brand of politics resonated with tens of thousands. 'English Socialism is not Marxian, it is humanitarian,' he wrote. 'It does not depend upon any theory of "economic justice", but upon humanity and common-sense.'[45]

The same title was used by composer Edward German for his best-known opera, first staged in 1902, with a libretto by Basil Hood that centred on the court of Queen Elizabeth. In this instance, it also referenced Arthur Sullivan's ballet *Victoria and Merrie England*, written for the Diamond Jubilee in 1897, and the two long-reigning queens were now linked in British culture; the memory of Good Queen Bess was often invoked in the years after Victoria's death. 'Not only thoroughly English, but thoroughly joyous,' as the critics said of German's opera.[46]

Elsewhere, the imagery of a pre-industrial country was seen as an excuse to dress up and have a good time, on occasions such as Ye Olde Englishe Fayre, a week-long Mayday festival in the London suburb of Edmonton in 1900. Held to raise funds for the Lower Edmonton Independent Church, it offered 'an attractive programme of music, concerts and village revels' together with an

---

* He was also the author of *Britain for the British* (1902), which he described as 'a successor' to *Merrie England*.

historically themed bazaar featuring the likes of Ye Olde Booke Shoppe, Ye Olde Lollipop Shoppe, Ye Puritan Shoppe, Ye Queen Elizabeth Shoppe and Ye Shamrock Inn.[47] Similarly playful was an event staged that year in Brixham, Devon, with what was advertised as a 'Fancy Fair' under the title Ye Olde Englyshe Garden. 'The attendants' dresses depicted the Stuart period and placed a picturesque finish to the fair,' reported the local press. 'The elder attendants wore Court dresses, and the younger ones white or pink dresses and garden hats. The Puritan maidens were dressed in the sad Puritanical colours of the Stuart age and wore neatly made white caps.'[48] There was no agenda to any of this: Elizabethans, Cavaliers, Puritans were just images pulled out of the ragbag of history, to be adopted for a bit of fun.* The attitude, however, the sense of play and make-believe, was entirely characteristic of British cultural traditions. The past was not there to be venerated.

At a more elevated level, though, there was a growing wish to preserve the physical heritage of the nation, seen in a series of Ancient Monuments Protection Acts (in 1882, 1900, 1910 and 1913) and in the foundation in 1895 of the National Trust for Places of Historic Interest or Natural Beauty. The National Trust's report for the year 1901–2 illustrated the breadth of its field of interest, recording its involvement in 'the enclosure of Stonehenge, the preservation of the view from Richmond Hill, and the preservation of Croxden Abbey, Launceston Castle and the Bartlemas Hospital at Oxford'.[49] That year the organisation also made its first major purchase, the 108-acre Brandlehow estate on the west shore of Derwentwater, Cumbria, which came on the market amid fears it would be built upon. The Trust launched a public appeal and bought the land for £7,000,[50] promising to 'leave the property as far as possible in its present condition, relying upon the good taste

---

* A more sober reminder of the past came with the death of a Mrs Bug in Suffolk in 1913, the last known fatality in Britain from the Black Death.

of the public to respect the natural amenities of such a desirable spot'.*

One of the pioneers of preservation was designer, writer and socialist William Morris, who had died in 1896 and since been canonised as the patron saint of pre-industrialism. The Arts and Crafts Movement that he popularised had begun as a reaction against mechanisation and the consequent decline of craftsmen, and reached its peak in the Edwardian years. Certainly, architectural fashion was now dominated by Arts and Crafts, with strong elements of Tudor. At the top end of the market were the country houses created by architects Charles Voysey and Edwin Lutyens, preferably with gardens by Gertrude Jekyll. (Lutyens also designed the offices of *Country Life* magazine, which launched in 1897.) For adventurous city workers who wanted something more progressive than a suburb like Walthamstow, there was the garden city movement, which advocated logically planned, self-contained communities; its first manifestations were in Brentham Garden Suburb (started 1901), Letchworth (1903) and Hampstead Garden Suburb (1906). And further down the social scale still, there were the model villages of Bournville in Birmingham (1893) and Port Sunlight on Merseyside (1899), founded by manufacturers George Cadbury and William Lever respectively, to house their workers. All to various degrees looked to the past as a model of the future.

The celebration of heritage extended into a defence of high culture, with the building of artistic encampments that defined what was to be protected. There was the National Gallery of British Art in Pimlico, London, founded in 1897.† There was the anthology *The Oxford Book of English Verse 1250–1900*, edited by Arthur Quiller-Couch, which was published in 1900, sold half a million

---

* The wish to protect history was not confined to beauty spots and the remote past. In 1903, just a generation after his death, the Corporation of Portsmouth paid £1,125 to buy the house in which Charles Dickens had been born, an otherwise nondescript property.

† Later renamed the Tate Gallery, and later still Tate Britain.

copies, and fixed the poetic canon for generations of Britons. And there was the renewed reverence for William Shakespeare that saw the launch in 1902 of the London Shakespeare League, a group that campaigned for a national theatre dedicated to the country's greatest writer; there had been many such campaigns before, all unsuccessful, and though this one came close, it too ended in failure.

Even without his own theatre, however, Shakespeare was still the dominant presence on the London stage. Actor-managers Herbert Beerbohm Tree and Henry Irving staged productions with spectacular scenery and elaborate costumes that were supposedly faithful to the historical settings of the plays, while William Poel's Elizabethan Stage Society specialised in recreating the stripped-down style of the original productions. Both were, in their own ways, harking back. Related was the rise of the drama school, a modern take on the Elizabethan stage apprenticeship, with the establishment of the Royal Academy of Dramatic Art (1904), the Central School of Speech and Drama (1906) and the Italia Conti Academy of Theatre Arts (1911), all centred on Shakespearean acting and elocution.

Perhaps the most fruitful aspect of the revivalist tendency was symbolised by the creation of the Folk Song Society in 1898.* Its members roamed the countryside, seeking out amateur singers and transcribing what remained of oral folk traditions. And since those members included some of the more notable composers of the younger generation – George Butterworth, Percy Grainger, Ralph Vaughan Williams – this had a wider impact than might have been the case. For it was not intended to be just a scholarly exercise. 'If the folksong has nothing to say to us *as we are now* without a sham return to an imaginary (probably quite illusory) arcadia of several centuries ago,' wrote Vaughan Williams, 'then I would burn all the collections I could lay hands on and their singers with them.'[51]

---

* The closely related English Folk Dance Society was founded by Cecil Sharp in 1911 and ensured the survival of morris dancing.

Some of the results filtered through in *The English Hymnal* (1906), a collection of which Vaughan Williams was music editor, most famously in the carol 'O Little Town of Bethlehem'; the melody was taken from a song, 'The Ploughboy's Dream', that he'd learned from an old Sussex-born labourer. Beyond that, he and others sought to create a distinctively British orchestral sound, drawing on folk song and on Tudor music, with a strong focus on local, pastoral identity. By the end of the Edwardian period, the geographical repertoire was so extensive that one could tour the British Isles without leaving the concert hall: Rutland Boughton, *The Chilterns* (1900); Charles Villiers Stanford, *Irish Rhapsody* (1901); Havergal Brian, *English Suite* (1904); Edward German, *A Welsh Rhapsody* (1904); Vaughan Williams, *In the Fen Country* (1904) and *Two Norfolk Rhapsodies* (1906); Gustav Holst, *A Somerset Rhapsody* (1906); Cecil Coles, *From the Scottish Highlands* (1907); Ethyl Smyth, *On the Cliffs of Cornwall* (1908); George Butterworth, *A Shropshire Lad* (1911); Edgar Bainton, *Celtic Sketches* (1912); Henry Balfour Gardiner, *A Berkshire Idyll* (1913); Frederick Delius, *North Country Sketches* (1914).*

This was not the sum total of the serious music being written, of course, and even the pieces evoking a sense of place weren't always rural: Edward Elgar's *Cockaigne Overture* (1901) and Vaughan Williams's *A London Symphony* (1914) both depicted the contemporary world of the capital. Nor were these pastoral works the most popular music of the day. In 1904 a bandmaster on the south coast polled his audience asking what they wanted to hear, and the 532 responses suggested that the contemporary musical comedies staged by impresario George Edwardes were the people's choice; Sidney Jones's *The Geisha* (1896), Lionel Monckton's *A Country Girl* (1902) and Ivan Caryll's *The Girl from Kays* (1902) topped the list, though Richard Wagner's *Tannhäuser* did make the top five.

Nonetheless, something was happening here, with the pageants

---

* In a similar spirit was Samuel Coleridge-Taylor's greatest work, *Symphonic Variations on an African Air* (1906).

and Olde Englishe Fayres, the conservationists and traditionalists, Shakespeareans and composers. It was as if the new century, in search of its own identity, was casting aside the violent social upheavals of the last hundred years, drawing instead on a nostalgic vision of a pre-industrial Britain to reinvigorate a culture under attack from mass consumption.

The fightback was necessary because, it was feared, regional variations and characteristics were being flattened out. To combat this, there were attempts to win over the next generation: a 1903 collection, *British Songs for British Boys*, grouped its material in nine themed sections, with the second-largest (after 'English Songs') being 'Songs of Country Life'. But the homogenisation continued. The music hall, particularly in its modern form, played a part in this. Popular songs were no longer the spontaneous expression of the people, but 'have become material for commerce, and represent no one's soul at all', argued journalist Filson Young. 'They are a pattern article, turned out to the designs of a department of the great Cosmopolitan Amusement Industry, Unlimited.'[52]

Worse still was the rise of recorded music, which – like the mutoscope and the cinematograph – was incapable of responding to an audience, further stripping culture of its geographical ties as it mechanically repeated the same performance all over the country. There were two formats for this new technology: the disc and the cylinder. Gramophones, machines for playing discs, were very definitely a status symbol: the Trump Graphophone from the Columbia Phonograph Company, which in 1908 cost two guineas, was housed in an 'oak cabinet, beautifully polished' with a 'flower horn, assorted colours'.[53] Machines for playing cylinders, though, were cheaper, a fact that proved to be the downfall of the format; when the economy began to stutter in the middle of the decade, the wealthy continued to buy gramophones, but those further down the income scale cut back on such luxuries.

Some argued that sound recording was an important step in democratising culture. 'It is a means to music which was before unattainable except to the wealthy and leisured classes,' enthused the trade journal, *Talking Machine News*. 'It has brought the treasures of song within the reach of all. The best artists sing for you; the finest bands play for you at your own fireside.'[54] Others feared its impact on young people. Time was when parents used to engage their children's minds by reading aloud to them, argued Dr W. H. D. Rouse, headmaster of the Perse School in Cambridge, but not any more. 'Children take their amusements passively now. The gramophone is in the home.'[55]

And that encapsulated the problem. These innovations came at a price. Even progressive political measures could add to the destruction of culture; the *Globe* worried 'that a uniform elementary educational system throughout the country tends to destroy local accent, and that cheap transit is weakening the territorial feeling.'[56] The point about transport was indisputable. Siegfried Sassoon wrote of a country-dwelling aunt whose world 'extended no further than the eight or ten miles which she could cover in a four-wheeled dog-cart.'[57] Railways and the telegram had already made the country a smaller place; now the motor car and the telephone were hastening the process.

In response came assertions of local pride and, by extension, of patriotic spirit. If this pastoral idyll was largely a fantasy, it was nonetheless powerful. And if it all sometimes seemed a little defensive of national identity, perhaps that was understandable too when the threat of further mechanisation was increasingly seen as foreign, associated with the inexorable rise of America. One couldn't imagine anything further from Arts and Crafts than the mutoscope or that Ford factory at Trafford Park.

v

Of all the deities of ancient Greece, Pan is the only one whose death was recorded. The historian Plutarch told the story of a ship on the Ionian Sea whose captain was instructed by a mysterious, disembodied voice to call out as he passed the next island, 'Great Pan is dead.' When he did so, 'there was a great cry of lamentation, not of one person, but of many, mingled with exclamations of amazement'.[58]

This happened, Plutarch noted, during the reign of Tiberius Caesar, and although none could make sense of the mysterious episode at the time, the dating of the incident was later considered to be of great significance. For Tiberius was Emperor of Rome at the time of Christ's ministry, and those who came after felt there was great symbolism in the simultaneous announcement that the ancient goat-god of wild places was dead. As G. K. Chesterton wrote, 'Pan died because Christ was born.'[59] *The Death of Pan* (1903), a woodcut by London artist Louise Glazier, showed the god as a witness to the Nativity.

But Pan was not dead. He lived on, subsumed into the form of the Devil, the tempter of humanity, luring the unwary to their destruction with his blasphemous celebration of fertility and sexual abandon. He lurked still in the darkest, thickest undergrowth, a perpetual threat to the rule of the Christian god.

As Britain began to drift from Christianity* and to embrace a pastoral past, Pan seized his moment. It started with the over-wrought fantasy of Arthur Machen's *The Great God Pan* (1894), in which a decadent, dilettante scientist embarks on a horrific research project, performing brain surgery on an unwilling work-ing-class girl so that she might behold 'the most awful, most secret forces which lie at the heart of all things; forces before which the souls of men must wither and die and blacken'. The experiment succeeds too well, and his victim looks upon the face of Pan. Nine months later, now an incurable lunatic, she gives birth to the god's offspring, a girl who embarks on a career of sex and destruction.

Having been thus summoned, the 'goat-foot God of Arcady' – to use Oscar Wilde's phrase[60] – was now loose in the modern world, and for at least two decades he stalked the literature of the

---

* Although a quarter of the adult population, predominantly women, attended church on a weekly basis, congregations were already in decline by the start of the century.

land, seeking whom he might devour. 'The worship of Pan never has died out,' warns a character in a short story by Saki. 'He is the Nature-God to whom all must come back at last.'[61] Seldom seen directly, Pan's presence is attested by the marks he leaves behind, 'as if caused by the hoofs of some monstrous goat', in E. F. Benson's words.[62] Those hoofprints were to be found all over Edwardian writing, from Edward Elgar's setting of Andrew Ross's poem 'The Pipes of Pan' (1900) to the purple prose of magician Aleister Crowley's *Liber Liberi vel Lapidis Lazuli* (1907), a book he claimed had been dictated to him by Aiwass, messenger of the ancient Egyptian god Horus. The traces were evident even in the pages of the children's classics of the era, with J. M. Barrie's Peter Pan, the leader of the tribe of Lost Boys (1904), and with Kenneth Grahame's *The Wind in the Willows* (1908), in which the Rat and the Mole are drawn down the river at dawn by 'dance-music, the lilting sort that runs on without a stop' and encounter the god himself.

In 'The Story of a Panic' (1904) E. M. Forster recounted the experiences of upper-middle-class English picnickers in southern Italy. Among their number was a 'taciturn and moody' fourteen-year-old boy named Eustace who, in the absence of any parents, is being cared for by two indulgent maiden aunts. On the picnic Eustace makes himself a whistle from a piece of wood and, blowing on it, appears to summon dark forces, perhaps the ancient spirits of the woods. His adult companions are plunged into a state of abject terror, 'not the spiritual fear that one has known at other times, but brutal overmastering physical fear'. The only one who responds positively to the moment of panic is Eustace, who turns into a wild spirit 'whooping down on us as a wild Indian', pretending to be a dog and 'scurrying in front of us like a goat'. As the adults endeavour to control the boy, hoofprints are seen in the moist earth, and a clergyman in the party concludes solemnly, 'The Evil One has been very near us in bodily form.'

After the Rat and the Mole have encountered Pan on the river in *The Wind in the Willows*, they are granted 'instant oblivion, lest the awful remembrance should remain and grow, and overshadow mirth and pleasure'. Similarly, the adults in Forster's tale conspire to forget their moment of panic in Italy, agreeing 'that we should say nothing, either there or in our letters home'. But it wasn't possible to draw a discreet veil over such manifestations, and the tales of Pan kept coming.*

The best of them was James Stephens's bewitching novel *The Crock of Gold* (1912).† Set in rural Ireland, this is a magical world of 'banshees and cluricauns', where the ancient Gaelic gods are still to be found, where animals talk to each other and where worldly rank doesn't count for very much at all. 'A Leprecaun is of more value to the Earth than is a prime minister or a stockbroker, because a Leprecaun dances and makes merry, while a prime minister knows nothing of these natural virtues.'

Into this pastoral paradise comes the Great God Pan, a stranger to the land. 'There is no record of his ever having journeyed to Ireland,' explains the Philosopher, the story's central character. Pan reveals himself to a young goatherd named Cáitilin Ni Murrachu, who is attracted by his flute playing and is then repulsed when he strides out of the bracken towards her: 'The upper part of his body was beautiful, but the lower part . . .' He talks to her 'in a strange voice, coming like a wind from distant places', but she is still uncertain. 'I don't know what you want me to do,' she says. 'I want you to want me,' replies Pan. 'I want you to forget right and wrong; to be as happy as the beasts, as careless as the flowers and the birds. To live to the depths of your nature as well as to the heights.'

She follows him, though later, when Pan and the 'desolate'

---

* Including Henry Nevinson's collection of essays, *The Plea of Pan* (1901), Richard Garnett's short story 'Pan's Wand' (1903), Forrest Reid's novel *The Garden God* (1905), Algernon Blackwood's *Pan's Garden* (1912), and poetry collections *Pan-Worship* (1908) by Eleanor Farjeon and *The Triumph of Pan* (1910) by Victor Neuberg.

† 'What sort of book is it?' wondered a reviewer, before concluding that it was 'a prose poem, a fairy legend, a series of essays, a theory of the universe, an allegory, and an exercise in humour all at once'.

Gaelic deity Angus Óg* vie for her loyalty, she chooses the latter. This time 'she did not go with him because she had understood his words, nor because he was naked and unashamed, but only because his need of her was very great, and, therefore, she loved him'. She finds fulfilment with Angus Óg, and Pan disappears from the story. Whatever threat he presented has been overcome by her embrace of 'the terrible sadness of the gods'.

The insistent presence of Pan through these years spoke of fears that civilisation was more fragile than it appeared, that Christianity had not fully supplanted pagan faiths, that progress was not inevitable. Pan was the shadow cast by the spirit of a more primitive, more natural past, but how that might manifest in the modern world was entirely unclear; he was an elusive, intangible atmosphere more than a physical presence. The only thing that seemed certain, as the Philosopher says in *The Crock of Gold*, was that 'his coming intends no good to this country'.

In a less primal form, the same anxiety could be seen in the carnival of ghost stories by writers such as W. W. Jacobs, M. R. James, William Hope Hodgson and Violet Hunt. All told of the past erupting into the present, revealing that what is dead is not necessarily gone. Algernon Blackwood's psychic detective John Silence investigates the case of a man who has been experimenting with cannabis oil. 'I am a writer of humorous tales, and I wished to increase my own sense of laughter,' he explains, 'to see the ludicrous from an abnormal point of view.' It transpires that the drug opens a door to 'ancient forces', allowing the evil of the past to break through into the modern world.

Pan is the ultimate embodiment of such dread. And there's something else, a subsidiary theme that hints at Pan awakening female sexuality. It's seen most explicitly in *The Great God Pan* and *The Crock of Gold*, but even Peter Pan – the least-sexual incarnation there is – finds himself the object of erotic attraction for Wendy, Tinker Bell and Tiger Lily. What is it that these girls want from

---

* Now more commonly known as Aengus.

him, wonders Peter, and Wendy retorts in frustration, 'That isn't for a lady to tell.'[63] But she knew.

Meanwhile Arthur Machen, having summoned up Pan, was struggling. He'd been considered part of the decadent movement of the 1890s – 'a literary Aubrey Beardsley', some said[64] – and his reputation was hit by the fall of Oscar Wilde; his novel *The Hill of Dreams* was only published in 1907, a decade after he wrote it. Similarly, 'The White People' (1904), an unsettling vision of ancient sorceries and adolescent sexuality, struggled to find a publisher. In this hallucinatory fragment – more a tone poem than a short story – a sixteen-year-old girl remembers her early experiences of a countryside teeming with magic and myth, fairies and 'dead heathen gods'. 'I must not say who the Nymphs are, or the Dôls, or Jeelo, or what voolas mean,' she writes in her journal. 'All these are most secret secrets, and I am glad when I remember what they are, and how many wonderful languages I know, but there are some things that I call the secrets of the secrets of the secrets that I dare not think of unless I am quite alone.'

vi

At the moment of death, when the monstrous offspring of the pagan deity is finally killed in *The Great God Pan*, she sheds her human form, sliding back through evolution. 'I saw the body descend to the beasts whence it ascended,' says a witness.* This was a modern addition to the mythology of Pan and, perhaps, it was part of the reason for his re-emergence. In a world whose thinking had been reshaped by Charles Darwin, he was the missing link, his body – half-goat half-man, as though frozen in the act of evolution – a symbol of humanity's brutish heritage, a reminder of the beast within.

---

* The same de-evolutionary fate met the Beast Folk, the pitiful creatures manufactured by another mad scientist in H. G. Wells's *The Island of Doctor Moreau* (1896).

Darwin himself was now acclaimed as the only serious rival to Isaac Newton as Britain's greatest-ever scientist. The mid-Victorian controversies were long gone, and in 1909 the centenary of his birth – and the fiftieth anniversary of the publication of *On the Origin of Species* – was marked with an international conference in Cambridge, celebrations in Oxford, London and Shrewsbury (his birthplace), and an exhibition at the Natural History Museum, while a 'library of literature' was published.[65] 'The evolution theory has become generally, if not entirely, accepted,' was the settled view.[66] Darwin had 'completely revolutionised the average man's conception of life and nature in science, philosophy, religion and literature' wrote Walter Spencer, the town librarian of Bingley, Yorkshire.[67] Nowadays, even the church 'openly flirts with Charles Darwin'.[68]

It was all still a bit jokey, though, in the public mind. One of the hits at the London Hippodrome in 1904 was Consul, a monkey trained to mimic various human activities, and billed as evidence 'in support of the theory of the evolution of mankind from the apes'.[69] As an editorial in the *Daily Mirror* pointed out, this was as much as most people knew of Darwin, that 'we are all descended from monkeys'. Yet even that, however simplistic, however wrong, was an extraordinary leap: 'From a gorilla to Goethe – what a distance!' Which prompted a further reflection, that nature had not yet finished with evolution: 'Some day she may produce the Overman who shall be to Goethe what he was to the gorilla.'[70]

For some this was a source of hope and inspiration. Darwin having revealed the mechanism, it was now possible that humanity could consciously make its own evolutionary destiny. That was the intention of eugenics, a science that sought to shape the future of the race, to improve the quality of human stock by excluding those deemed unfit to reproduce, a social application of evolution.* The human body was unlikely to change much further, argued Dr

---

* The word eugenics was coined by Darwin's cousin Francis Galton.

Caleb Saleeby, a respected physician, author and eugenicist,* but the scope for intellectual and spiritual growth was vast. He looked forward to 'the making of a new race that so transcends ourselves as we transcend the chimpanzee and the worm'. That, of course, meant that legislation would be needed to ensure that 'defective persons should not contribute to the future of the race'.[71]

This was a strand of thinking that informed much early science fiction, most obviously the works of H. G. Wells and his imitators and detractors. (Chief among the latter was E. M. Forster's 1909 dystopian short story 'The Machine Stops'.) There were also those who warned of how transient and unsatisfactory the society of today would look to those of the future.

In John Davys Beresford's *The Hampdenshire Wonder* (1911)† a child is born possessed of exceptional abilities, a superman from humanity's far evolution. At the age of four he reads and memorises the entirety of the *Encyclopaedia Britannica* in three weeks, and he isn't overly impressed by the sum of human knowledge. 'Is this all?' he asks, gesturing at the books. 'Elementary, inchoate, a disjunctive patchwork.' He reads further and becomes more despairing still. 'Is there none of my kind?'

There is not. 'He is too many thousands of years ahead of us,' says the local squire, himself 'a man of some scholarship', who takes the boy under his wing. In exchange, the Wonder tries to explain some of what he knows, but it is so far beyond contemporary comprehension that the man is fearful, refusing to speak of the experience because it 'would have revived many memories he wished to obliterate'. As in the encounters with Pan, there are mysteries best forgotten.

This terrifying awareness of the inadequacy of humanity is expressed specifically in terms of Britain's claim to cultural

---

* Saleeby was also a believer in a racial hierarchy, heliotherapy, teetotalism and nudism, and served during the Great War as an adviser to the Ministry of Food.
† Beresford's fame was later eclipsed by that of his daughter Elizabeth, creator in 1968 of the Wombles of Wimbledon Common.

supremacy. 'Think of the gap which separates your intellectual powers from those of a Polynesian savage,' says the squire. 'Why, after all, should it be impossible that this child's powers should equally transcend our own?'* Even so, he concludes, one can only marvel at humanity's successor: 'I rather admire the spirit; there is something Napoleonic about him.'

Similarly, in their collaborative novel *The Inheritors* (1901) Joseph Conrad and Ford Madox Hueffer depicted the coming into our world of creatures from the Fourth Dimension. They look just like human beings but are uncontaminated by such weaknesses as 'beliefs, traditions; fears; ideas of pity, of love'. The Dimensionists are 'a race clear-sighted, eminently practical, incredible; with no ideals, prejudices, or remorse; with no feeling for art and no reverence for life; free from any ethical tradition; callous to pain, weakness, suffering and death'.

They will inevitably overwhelm human society, because they are stronger and purer. 'As to methods,' reflects our human narrator, 'we should be treated as we ourselves treat the inferior races.' He is among the first to encounter one of these beings, and he resents, while recognising, their superiority: 'I was not a negro – not even relatively a Hindoo. I was somebody, confound it, I was somebody.'

As the first Dimensionists stealthily infiltrate human society, a parallel is being played out in British politics. There's a project afoot to colonise the wastes of Greenland. This is a grand enterprise of moral imperialism, the building of a 'model state' where 'perfect equality shall obtain for all races, all creeds, and all colours'. For this to work, says the financier who's floating the venture, Britain needs to back the proposed Trans-Greenland Railway. It won't be cheap, but 'it was our duty not to count the cost of humanising a lower

---

* Winston Churchill made the same point in reverse when praising British colonial administrators. 'In Uganda,' he wrote in *My African Journey* (1908), 'a class of rulers is provided by an outside power as remote from and, in all that constitutes fitness to direct, as superior to the Baganda as Mr Wells's Martians would have been to us.'

race'. More cynically, it's also an investment that will reap handsome rewards; in due course, 'the thing would pay like another Suez Canal'.

Part of the aim of the Dimensionists is to undermine existing social structures, to reveal how corrupt and rotten they have become. And so they leak the 'real horrors' that lie behind this high-flown talk of equality and freedom in Greenland: the 'flogged, butchered, miserable natives, the famines, the vices, diseases, and the crimes'. And as the reality of imperial rule is uncovered, so too is the hypocrisy that has allowed violence to flourish under cover of a supposed morality: 'there were greed and self-seeking, stripped naked; but more revolting to see without a mask was that falsehood which had been hiding under the words that for ages had spurred men to noble deeds, to self-sacrifice, to heroism'.

The Inheritors was neither a commercial success nor a critics' favourite. 'Incomprehensible,' said the *St James's Gazette*, 'hopelessly insane'.[72] Even those who approved of the novel did so with little enthusiasm: 'a notable, if not a wholly satisfactory, piece of work'.[73] But it articulated the fear that a world which seemed so solid now was not destined to last. If Cecil Rhodes's social-Darwinian faith were accepted, then Britain could scarcely complain that the country's rule would be superseded by others. 'We inherit the earth,' one of the Dimensionists declares flatly, 'and you, your day is over.'

4

HOME AND ABROAD

'Happy is the country that has no geography.'

Saki, *The Unbearable Bassington*, 1912[1]

Don't be gulled by Yankee bluff.
Support John Bull with every puff.

Advertisement for British-made Guinea Gold cigarettes, 1901[2]

Cabinet minister Joseph Chamberlain (1836–1914), drawn by
Hubert von Herkomer for *Black & White* magazine, 1906.

THOMAS 'DADDY' RICE FIRST CAME TO BRITAIN IN 1836, three years after the Slavery Abolition Act was passed. He was an American entertainer and a pioneer of blackface minstrelsy, in which white artists used make-up made from burned cork to darken their face and hands, before performing caricatures of what was believed to be black culture, particularly that found on the slave plantations of the American South. Rice was the first such performer to be seen on a London stage, and his theme song 'Jump Jim Crow' was an instant hit.*

The following decade came the first minstrel group – Dan Emmett and his Virginia Minstrels – a four-man act who wore blackface and provided a full programme of song, dance and comedy. They too proved highly popular, and for the rest of the nineteenth century a succession of troupes visited Britain, playing to packed houses. The appeal was largely to middle-class audiences; the simple humour and catchy melodies were seen as essentially clean, so if the music hall was too crude and vulgar, you could still take the family to a minstrel show.

The popularity of the minstrels inspired the creation of British troupes, but there was a difference. In 1846 the Ethiopian Serenaders crossed the Atlantic, bringing with them letters of recommendation from President James Polk and other white Americans who, reported the press, were 'better able to appreciate the accuracy of their African delineations than Europeans are'.[3] Whether Polk's judgement was to be trusted or not, the point was that it was felt to be necessary. Britons, it was correctly assumed, would have no cultural knowledge of the world the minstrels were purporting to portray.

So the British troupes – copying white Americans, who were themselves parodying black Americans – were at least two stages

---

* In America, Rice's Jim Crow character was so famous that the name was used as a generic term for the laws enforcing racial segregation in the South after the Civil War.

removed from reality. Sometimes more, for there were also troupes with gimmicks. Montague Roby's Midget Minstrels were child performers, and Andy Merrilee's Armour Clad Female Christys had little connection with Southern plantations: 'A bevy of beauty in a great and glorious Amazonian scene,' ran the advertising copy. 'Armour-clad Amazons from the Silver City of Atlantis.'[4]

Some of these minstrel shows were spectacular events. For the Christmas of 1879, the sixty-strong company of impresario Sam Hague took up residence at the Bingley Hall in Birmingham, putting on a twice-daily show for an audience of 10,000 a time, with a supporting bill that included a strongman (the Australian Samson), Cuban violinist Claudi Brindis de Salas (the Black Paganini), the A'La Baby Elephants, trick cyclists Stirk and Allo, and Lulu the Beautiful Girl Acrobat.*

Those had been the glory days, but by the Edwardian era the new respectability of the music halls, together with their business efficiency, was making the big minstrel shows redundant. Sam Hague died in 1901, and although his troupe continued briefly under his name, it didn't last much longer; nor did rivals such as the Livermore Brothers' Court Minstrels, the Mohawk Minstrels and the Moore & Burgess Minstrels. 'The popular demand for burnt-cork minstrelsy seems to have abated,' observed the *Graphic* as the latter troupe gave their final performance in 1904.[5] One of the few which survived were the Metropolitan Police Minstrels, an institution in London since the 1870s, fundraising amateurs who continued to put on a complete evening's entertainment with songs, dancing and sketches.†

---

* Lulu wasn't actually a girl, but a young boy named Samuel Wasgate, wearing a girl's outfit and a blonde wig. He was the adopted son of William Hunt, better known as the Great Farini, tightrope-walker, showman and deviser of the human-cannonball act. In 1885 father and son crossed the Kalahari Desert on foot, claiming to be the first white men to do so.

† The Metropolitan Police Minstrels were still playing into the mid-1930s, the last representatives of the nineteenth-century troupes.

What did endure, though, was the music-hall adaptation of blackface, with solo acts rather than troupes. There was, as one newspaper put it, a 'rage for coon songs',[6] material drawing on the minstrel tradition,* but that was only part of the story. There were also blackface strongmen and jugglers, eccentric comedians and trick cyclists. Little Tich, whose Big Boot Dance was the most celebrated comedy routine of the Edwardian music hall, had started out as a blackface clog-dancer, while other stars also used the make-up early in their careers including Alfred 'the Great' Vance, Lottie Collins, Harry Champion and Gus Elen. Just as Britain had taken the conventions of the Italian *commedia dell'arte* (filtered through France) and transformed them into Punch and Judy shows and pantomime, so the American blackface tradition was appropriated and adjusted by the music hall. The make-up became a licence to experiment, liberating the performer from any pretence of reality.

The greatest British exponent of the form was George Chirgwin. The son of a circus clown, born in London in 1854, he was seven when he first appeared on stage as part of the Chirgwin Family, and by the turn of the century he was as popular as any music-hall star in the land, save for Dan Leno and Marie Lloyd. He used to wear straight blackface until – in his own account – a fly flew in his eye just as he was about to go on stage; he rubbed his eye, removing a patch of make-up, and got a big laugh from the audience just for his appearance. Adopting that as his gimmick, he henceforth painted a white diamond over his right eye, with the rest of his face black. Dressed in a black body stocking, with a frock coat and enormously tall stovepipe hat, he was billed as the White-Eyed Kaffir.

---

* The biggest British song in the style – and one of the best of all music-hall hits – was 'Lily of Laguna' (1898), written by Leslie Stuart (a former church organist from Southport) and performed by Eugene Stratton and then G. H. Elliott. An adapted version, removing the racial references, became popular in America, most famously in a duet by Bing Crosby and Mary Martin in 1942.

Chirgwin's act comprised songs, topical and political jokes, 'atrocious puns and more or less inane patter'.[7] He had an impressive vocal range, singing bass, tenor and falsetto, interspersed with the occasional spell of yodelling, and he played a diverse collection of instruments, including violin, cello, banjo and trombone, as well as some of his own devising, including the phono-fiddle, which crossed a violin with a gramophone horn. As time went on, his visual style became more elaborate. He'd reverse the colours, with white clothes and white face, except for a black diamond over his eye. Or he'd divide himself vertically: left side white, right side black (but still with the white diamond). Meanwhile, his hats got taller, his shoes longer, and the black body stocking acquired a white handprint on the left buttock.

The term blackface scarcely does justice to Chirgwin's act. Far from minstrelsy, it was a thoroughly theatrical creation, a set of masks that allowed him to explore his artistry. Like Olde English dressing up, it was artificial, make-believe. He did have some material that drew on minstrelsy, but when he performed 'The Cockney Coon' (1899), accompanying himself on a one-string fiddle to which he'd added a metal sounding board, he was a long way from Thomas 'Daddy' Rice. Particularly when he switched into a Scottish character and played the bagpipes.

ii

'He thinks that Allybama is as far off as the moon,' George Chirgwin sang of Harry, 'The Cockney Coon', and the same was true of his audiences. Detailed knowledge of foreign places was not a feature of music hall. 'I'm an Indian, I come from Timbuktu,' declared Sam Mayo in 'Wallah, Wallah, Wallaperoo' (1910). In another song, 'The Chinaman' (1906), Mayo gave the name of his character:

It's Ching Chang, Wing Wang, Bing Bang Boo –
Known from Piccadilly up to Timbuktu.

This song is ridiculous, the worst that's in the land,
But it's marvellous the trash that the public stand.

As those lines made clear, the audience was in on the joke. They knew this stuff was silly, that Timbuktu wasn't really where Indian or Chinese people came from. It was a form of nonsense, akin to Edward Lear's 'The land where the Bong tree grows'.[8] Timbuktu was a delightfully memorable collection of sounds, cherished for the same reason that the story of Nebuchadnezzar casting Shadrach, Meshach and Abednego into the fiery furnace* was such a firm favourite in Sunday schools; what child could resist the rhythm of those names? In 'Wide, Wide World Man' (1898) T. E. Dunville boasted of sailing on the Amazon, the Damazon, the Congo and the Pongo, and declared that 'at the Matabele ballet, I'm a bally hot 'un'. The actual words signified nothing; it was just tongue-twisting joy for an audience of drinkers.

As for what Africa was actually like, music hall was really not interested. 'It's Very, Very Warm Round There,' observed Mark Sheridan, adding that 'the nice black belles dress in leaves and shells', which didn't entirely ring true. In the same vein, Marie Lloyd's earlier 'She Wore a Little Safety-Pin Behind' (1896) suggested that the 'damsels of the tropics were by Nature dressed in black, and for artificial clothing disinclined'. She also confirmed that 'it's rather warm', but that was about as much as her audience needed to know.

Nor was this cheerful ignorance confined to Africa. The great cultural divide was between home and abroad: 'you know how different we are from foreigners', says the hero of Erskine Childers's novel *The Riddle of the Sands* (1903). Few worried much about the details of foreignness, as the Bulgarian wrestler Ivan Offtharoff discovered when he adopted the guise of a Turk named Kara 'the Silent' Suliman. Likewise the American-born William Robinson, alias Chinese magician Chung Ling Soo, who first visited Britain

---

* Daniel 3:12–30

in 1900 and became a star in music hall.* Ernest Bramah's short-story collection *The Wallet of Kai Lung* (1900) was set in China, but the cover design was Japanese. 'Perhaps in those youthful days I did not know the difference,' the publisher, Grant Richards, later admitted; 'today the error makes me hot under the collar'.[9] Some appreciated the anonymity they were thus afforded. 'All foreigners look alike to English people,' wrote the Russian revolutionary Nadezhda Krupskaya, who arrived in London in 1902 with her husband, Vladimir Lenin; 'our landlady took us for Germans all the time we were there'.[10] As a station porter in Edith Nesbit's *The Railway Children* (1906) says, 'You can't be sure with foreigners. My own belief is they're all tarred with the same brush.'

Nearer to home, there was a general perception that Europeans were mostly amusing curios, sometimes untrustworthy and deceitful, always melodramatic. They were also a little unmanly: when the eponymous Four Just Men in Edgar Wallace's novel send a letter to the British government, 'the handwriting was of the flourishing effeminate variety that is characteristic of the Latin races'. Thrillers revelled in Italian political secret societies, with their spine-chilling oaths of loyalty, their obsession with bloody revenge, and their networks of undercover agents.† Meanwhile detective fiction had a fashion for French sleuths who displayed an excess of vanity. Scotland Yard was all very well, said Robert Barr's Eugène Valmont, but 'for intellectuality, mental acumen, finesse – ah, well! I am the most modest of men, and will say nothing'.[11] A. E. W. Mason's detective Monsieur Hanaud referred to himself in the third person as 'the great, the incomparable Hanaud'.[12]

Other prejudices abounded in the literature of the times. The

---

* Chung Ling Soo spoke in English only once on stage. 'Oh my God!' he said in 1918, as his trick of catching a bullet with his bare hands went very wrong. 'Something's happened.' He died the next day in Passmore Edwards Cottage Hospital in Acton, West London.

† As encountered by both A. J. Raffles (in 'The Last Laugh', 1901) and Sherlock Holmes ('The Adventure of the Red Circle', 1911).

upper-middle-class Forsyte family in John Galsworthy's *The Man of Property* (1906) 'did not like telling lies, having an impression that only Frenchmen and Russians told them'.[13] One of Arnold Bennett's characters summed up Russia in six words: 'Plots! Nihilism! Secret police! Marble palaces!'[14] And when a character in a Saki story asks, 'Are the Russians really such a gloomy people?' another replies, 'Gloom-loving but not in the least gloomy. They merely take their sadness pleasurably, just as we are accused of taking our pleasures sadly.'[15]

Then there were the Japanese, and no one understood them at all. When Prince Fushimi Sadanaru visited Britain in 1907, the government ordered that there was to be no public production of Gilbert and Sullivan's opera *The Mikado* (1885) during his trip, lest its Japanese setting prove offensive to their guest. Military bands were also forbidden to play music from the show. It was an absurd act of censorship – as virtually everyone agreed – since W. S. Gilbert's satire was directed very clearly at British, not Japanese, society. Further, there had been no complaint from Japan; any potential insult was entirely in the minds of the bystanders. One of the few who approved of the ban confessed, 'It may be that I am supersensitive – for other people.'[16] There was no need. Indeed, the prince himself said that he was disappointed not to see a performance of *The Mikado*, and the restrictions became untenable after a Japanese naval band was heard playing a selection from the opera.* But maybe the incident raised bigger questions. If drama was to be banned in case it offended other nations, where would it all end? Would Shakespeare be at risk, asked *Truth* magazine, because 'he's always sneering at the foreigners somewhere'? The Danes would object to *Hamlet*, the Italians to *Romeo and Juliet*, the Jews to *The Merchant of Venice*,

---

* To add to the absurdity, it was while his words were considered too dangerous to be heard on the London stage that Gilbert was awarded a knighthood. Despite this appallingly insensitive provocation, reported the *Bystander* sarcastically, 'we understand that the Japanese people are keeping calm'.

and the French to 'nearly all the historical plays, because they're always being beaten in them'.[17]

None of which meant that Britons were completely incurious about other lands. The arrival of the cinematograph revealed an appetite for travelogues that gave a glimpse of, say, Athens or India, films such as *Along the Nile* or *Religious Fetes at Tiber* or *Seal Catching off Tasmania* (all 1910).* But as those titles indicate, the public taste was for glamour, adventure, the exotic; reality wasn't high on the agenda of either the working-class or suburban audience. On a typical night in 1911 the audience at the Theatre Royal Cinema in Stockton-on-Tees could see a programme that featured *The Sacking of Rome*, *Apache Gold* and 'a most beautiful scenic picture of Venice'.[18] That was what went down well, and if there was no truth in the pictures, who would know?

The reason the popular perception of other peoples was shaped by stereotypes was that so few were ever encountered. For all the pride in its maritime history, Britain was not a nation of travellers, and nor was it a land of immigrants. The 1901 census showed that 96 per cent of the population of England and Wales had been born there. Most of the remainder came from Scotland or Ireland, with just one in every 250 people born in the colonies. The average Briton was unlikely to know anyone from outside these islands, and even more unlikely to have visited – let alone lived – anywhere beyond them. A 1911 cartoon in the *Graphic* by the Irish artist David Wilson showed John Bull surrounded by caricatures of Germans, Spaniards, Russians, Americans, Chinese and others; it was titled 'People We Have Heard Of – But Never Met'.[19]

The exceptions often illustrated the prevailing note of insularity. When in 1901 the twenty-five-year-old John Buchan was offered an administrative post in South Africa, he accepted, even though

---

* In some parts of the kingdom, more mundane material was sufficient: an adventure film that featured a train provoked gasps of wonder on Guernsey, which didn't have its own railway. (Jersey, on the other hand, did have a small railway, much to the annoyance of its neighbours.)

'I had never been out of Britain – indeed I had never wanted to.'[20] Julius Salter Elias, chairman of the publishing company Odhams Press,* only went abroad twice in his life: once to Le Touquet to play golf, and once to Boulogne for a day trip – and on the latter occasion he remained on the boat. Even Sir Edward Grey, who spent eleven years as foreign secretary, made just one trip abroad in that time. And the hero of Arnold Bennett's *The Card* (1911) is a Staffordshire man who 'had once been to Dieppe, and had come back as though from Timbuctoo with a traveller's renown'.

iii

It was one of the more striking business launches of the time. Twenty-two bright yellow wagons, accompanied by Chinese men on foot, were sent on to the streets of London in September 1900 to advertise the opening of the Chinese Hand Laundry. The main premises of the firm – also painted bright yellow – were in Great Portland Street, with three subsidiary laundries across the West End, promising 'pure sweet linen of snowy whiteness'. As the company's name promised, they washed by hand, which meant there was no risk of items being torn, as they so often were in the primitive steam machines used elsewhere.

This was intended to be a big enterprise. Later that year, the company bought seventeen acres of land off the Edgware Road in Hendon to build a new facility, complete with housing for its workers. It was not, however, Chinese-owned. The proprietors were a pair of laundry owners from New York, Leo Scheff and Charles Radcliffe Benjamin, looking to replicate their business in Britain. 'We have already brought 167 Chinamen to London,' Scheff told the press, but that was just the start.[21] 'We shall import more and more Chinese – thousands of them – and extend our operations all over England and Wales, and even Ireland and Scotland.'[22] Those remarks revealed the reason for the presence of the

---

* Later ennobled as Lord Southwood.

company in London: cheap migrant labour. Britain at this stage had no immigration restrictions, but the US did, with the explicitly targeted Chinese Exclusion Act of 1882; consequently, there was limited room for further expansion in the States.

Not everyone was thrilled by the new venture. The National Laundry Trade Protection Association complained bitterly about the interlopers, warning the public of the unhygienic habits prevalent in these establishments. Instead of using a sprinkler when ironing, the association's secretary said, the workers would spit on the linen, and that was 'only one of a hundred filthy tricks in which Chinese washermen are prone to indulge'.[23] Beyond these dark allegations, the real concern was with the undercutting of wages, and therefore of prices. It was unfair competition, it was argued, since the Chinese 'can live and thrive with half the pay and half the food'.[24]

Deeper still was the fear of cultural invasion. The expression Yellow Peril was already in common use, and there were those who wished to follow the American lead of curbing Chinese migration, however much it went against the principles of free trade and free movement. 'The Chinese are a race of lower civilisation and morale to our own,' wrote a columnist in the *St James's Gazette*; 'and if we allow them to come among us in large numbers the inevitable result must be a woeful deterioration, physical and moral, of the inhabitants of these islands.'[25] Was this, though, not simply a case of the biter bit? Some suggested that Britain, having insisted on its businesses having free access to China, could hardly complain when the principle was reciprocated. To which the counter-argument was that the cases were very different: the British presence was good for China, its example inspiring its people to improve their lot. 'The balance is, of course, enormously on the Englishman's side,' the *Western Daily Press* breezily declared, though it did concede, 'it is very difficult to induce the inhabitants of China to believe that'.[26]

The controversy prompted music-hall star George Robey (the Prime Minister of Mirth) to introduce a new song, 'The Chinese

Laundry Man': his wife takes in washing, but her business is suffering from Chinese competition, causing him to pretend to be Chinese himself in order to drum up trade. It didn't stay long in his repertoire, because the Hand Laundry was little more than a nine-days wonder. 'The Chinese invasion of London does not appear to be the immediate success that was anticipated,' announced the press gleefully in November 1900.[27] Some thirty-nine employees took Benjamin and Scheff to court, claiming that their wages hadn't been paid for several weeks, and in December, less than three months after the launch, the two businessmen made a hurried departure from the country, leaving their debts behind them and the wages still unpaid.

Perhaps it was the scale that was wrong. When Chinese laundries did begin to establish themselves a few years later, they were smaller, less grandiose concerns, initially set up by Chinese people relocating from America. In 1906 it was reported that there were seventy or eighty such enterprises in Liverpool, the primary port for transatlantic trade, and that the industry was moving further inland: 'About one hundred yellow men are now washing clothes in Manchester.'[28] Again, there were protests about unfair competition, and there was a brief spate of attacks on some premises, but their customers seemed pleased: the service was not only cheaper but better than the competition.

By then, the position on immigration had changed. The Aliens Act 1905 was in force, and the process of obtaining labour for these establishments was illustrated by the case of a ship carrying a group of forty Chinese men which arrived in London in 1906. Immigration officials established that eight of the men had sufficient means to support themselves (at least five pounds each, which was the official guideline) and were permitted to land, but the other thirty-two were detained. They were, they said, on their way to Liverpool 'where they were to be cooks, laundrymen and grocers' assistants'. At a hearing before the Alien Immigration Board, a Liverpool grocer, Kwong Sing Ling, explained that the men he employed had borrowed money for their passage from Hong

Kong and were repaying it from their wages; those working in his shop were paid eight shillings a week and given their keep, while laundries started workers on 5s 6d. As the chairman of the board observed, 'That sounds very much like Chinese slavery.' However, a missionary who worked at the Strangers' Rest in Liverpool gave evidence that the Chinese in the city 'lived decently, were law-abiding, not immoral' and there was no problem with overcrowding. After several days of deliberation, the men were permitted to land and to go on to north-west England.[29]

Others were less sanguine about the situation. Liverpool had 'the largest Chinatown in this country',[30] augmented by the presence of around a thousand Chinese sailors at any one time, and in 1906, following press stories of criminality and violence, the city council set up a commission of enquiry. Young English girls were said to have been 'lured from their homes in the suburbs of Liverpool through the medium of the Chinese laundries scattered all over the city, and taken to the dens of Chinatown, where they were induced to smoke opium and lead a life of unspeakable degradation'. In one case, it was said, 'a police sergeant took the law in his own hands by breaking into a Chinese laundry and thoroughly thrashing half-a-dozen Chinamen in order to rescue his fifteen-year-old daughter from shame'.[31] There was nothing more than anecdotal evidence to support these claims, but the commission was convinced. 'Evidence of seduction of girls by Chinamen is conclusive,' it reported, adding, 'the Chinese appear to much prefer having intercourse with young girls, more especially those of undue precocity'.[32]

If that were true, it was not evident elsewhere. 'Most of the Chinese in England are sober and industrious,' said the *Daily Mirror*,[33] and reports from London were far more positive. There were accounts of Chinese boarding houses in Poplar where the parlours had pictures of the king and queen on the walls, while 'on the mantelshelf are the usual chimney ornaments of a modest English home, and the furniture is as English as English can be'. There were also stories of a younger generation embracing the local culture:

'Cockney butcher-boys arm-in-arm with young coolies stroll into public houses, rows of grinning Chinese fill the best seats of Poplar music halls, and slant-eyed cabin boys, triumphantly smiling, have their boots blacked by white men.' Even interracial marriage was acceptable in London's docks, where 'almond-eyed little children prattle in the Cockney English to a father who wields chopsticks,' and where the white wife of tobacconist Tsang Wah, a woman 'comely of face and sweet of voice', regularly performed in the music halls.[34]

There remained, however, the opium dens in London's docklands for which the Chinese had long been notorious. The sale and consumption of opium was legal, but its non-medicinal use was disapproved of, confined to places where the only Britishers who dared to tread were the decadent and the desperate.* The remnants of that dark reputation were still just about visible. 'I am credibly informed,' wrote one breathless journalist, 'that if "a foreign devil" had the temerity to go alone into a Chinese opium den, I should in all probability never come out alive.'[35] But it wasn't the same as it had been. Not once Madame Tussaud's wax museum added an opium den to the attractions in its Chamber of Horrors in 1906: 'the recumbent figures of the doomed smokers are shown, their dreams represented by shadowy, unearthly figures in the background'.[36] That fed again the public's taste for the exotic. It was much more glamorous than the shabby, down-at-heel reality of most such places, catering largely for Chinese sailors rather than debauched tourists from the upper classes.

Yet the Edwardian pursuit of profitable respectability was such that, even in this world, a new, more businesslike approach was occasionally to be glimpsed. Just off London's Tottenham Court Road, Emily Mitcham ran what she said was 'the only West End opium den' (though others disputed the claim). It wasn't cheap, at a pound a visit, and its clientele seemed mainly to be American.

---

* As depicted in Oscar Wilde's *The Picture of Dorian Gray* and Arthur Conan Doyle's 'The Man with the Twisted Lip' (both 1891).

'You people in England don't use opium, though England produces about all the opium that is used,' one customer explained. 'Over here people seem to be afraid of it; they've heard false accounts of opium smoking.'[37]

Meanwhile, Ah Wong, formerly of San Francisco, opened a restaurant in Limehouse, serving chop suey to a clientele of 'army officers who have been in China, society people, popular jockeys and sometimes politicians'. Not all of them were aware that upstairs was a high-class opium den. Compared to neighbouring establishments such as the Dream Shop (five shillings a pipe) or Chick's (half a crown), Ah Wong's was pricey: it cost a guinea a pipe, plus another five shillings if you needed assistance. But you did get a private room with thick carpet, silk drapes and a beautifully upholstered couch; Wong claimed to have spent £2,000 on the furnishings.[38]

iv

'China's all the rage,' sang Albert Chevalier (the Costers' Laureate) in 1896, reflecting its growing presence in popular culture. At its lightest, this was seen in a fashion for musical comedies with a Chinese theme, from *San Toy* in 1899 to *See-See* and *The New Aladdin** in 1906, all of which enjoyed long runs and none of which was seen as anything but fantasy. 'I should not expect anyone who knows his Far East,' wrote one reviewer of *San Toy*, 'to be hypnotised by the glamour of Mr [George] Edwardes's *mise en scène*.'[39] Such comments were common: 'a sprinkling of quaint, even if imaginary, Chinese customs', 'the effect is not always convincingly out and out Chinese'.[40] The biggest of these shows was *A Chinese Honeymoon* (1899), which played for nearly three years in London from 1901. One of the storylines saw Hang Chow, ruler of Ylang Ylang, sending an emissary to find him a bride; the envoy knows he'll face a protracted, painful death if he fails in his quest,

---

* The 'original' *Aladdin* had been a pantomime favourite for decades.

and in that simple plot were elements that were already familiar and would become more so: romance, social hierarchy, cruelty.

The show inspired a music-hall song by Vesta Tilley, 'I Want to Have a Chinese Honeymoon' (1904), about a young lady who's 'mashed upon a fellow whose skin's a brilliant yellow'. This was a different angle. The musical comedies tended to revolve around interracial romances between Englishmen and Chinese women, but the music hall presented the more subversive idea that Chinese men were sexually attractive to British women: 'He is so jiggy-jiggy, look at his piggy-piggy,' sang Tilley. The same was true of Ella Retford's 'Have You Seen My Chinee-man?' (1908), while even George Robey, having adopted his Chinese laundryman's outfit and pigtail, finds that 'the girls throw me sly glances'.*

Guy Boothby's *A Bid for Fortune*, which began serialisation in the first edition of the *Windsor Magazine* in 1894, introduced a new stereotype. This being just a year on from the death of Professor Moriarty, there was room in the market for a supervillain, and Dr Nikola was the first to try to fill that gap. He's not Chinese himself – he's originally Italian – but he's travelled extensively in the Far East, and his fiendish pursuit of immortality and world domination takes him to an occult society that founded a Tibetan monastery in pre-Christian times and also controls the Triads. It's a confused story that never resolves across five volumes, but despite critical disapproval it was wildly popular, painting China in lurid colours of mystery, violence and conspiracy.†

Ernest Bramah's *The Wallet of Kai Lung* (1900) centred on a

---

* There was also Jock Lorimer, who wore a tam o' shanter with an attached pigtail, and was billed as the Chinese Scotsman. His son, Max Wall, became one of the greatest of all British comedians.

† Only the title of the final book in the series, *Farewell, Nikola* (1901) received praise from reviewers: 'We are very glad to bid Dr Nikola farewell.' In a twelve-year writing career – he died of influenza in 1905 at the age of thirty-eight – Boothby produced over fifty books, so perhaps it wasn't entirely surprising that the quality sometimes faltered. Before creating Dr Nikola, he had written the libretti for three light operas by folk-song collector Cecil Sharp.

storyteller who spins fanciful yarns in which excessive courtliness and ceremony co-exist with omens, superstition and magic. The best-known of the tales, 'The Transmutation of Ling', hinges on a young man drinking an alchemical elixir that changes his body so that when pieces of him are cut off – hair, fingernail clippings – they turn instantly to solid gold. This presents Ling with a conundrum: how to monetise this attribute without compromising his bodily integrity. He considers having a limb amputated, but a business syndicate make him a better offer: they'll give him a signing-on fee, an annuity, and substantial life cover to look after his dependants, all in exchange for his body when he dies. He agrees, before realising the horror of what he's done. In a culture of ancestor worship, this 'mercenary-souled' contract is an abomination: instead of leaving his bones for the family graveyard, he'll be cut up and used as currency or turned into ornaments and jewellery. The clash between traditional morals and modern business practice is – as one reviewer pointed out – 'rather after the manner of our Western stock markets'.[41]

Indeed, *The Wallet of Kai Lung* is more a satire on contemporary Britain than the 'Chinese *Arabian Nights*' that was advertised.[42] It depicts a society that proclaims recognisably Victorian values: 'the Five General Principles of Fidelity to the Emperor, Respect for Parents, Harmony between Husband and Wife, Agreement among Brothers, and Constancy in Friendship'. Yet it's populated by corrupt officials, self-serving politicians and grasping businessmen, all of whom blight the lives of honest men and beautiful maidens. The humour – and it was one of the funniest books of its time – lies partly in the mock-formality of the writing, and partly in its targets, from the advertising and publishing industries to the authorship of Shakespeare's plays.* Perhaps the Chinese trappings

---

* 'Friends, Chinamen, labourers who are engaged in agricultural pursuits, entrust to this person your acute and well-educated ears,' runs one line. Another: 'A sedan-chair! A sedan-chair! This person will unhesitatingly exchange his entire and well-regulated Empire for such an article.'

were too elaborate, however, for it was to take more than two decades for *The Wallet* to become a success. It did have its early supporters, though: the literary critic Arthur Quiller-Couch was a devotee, while Hilaire Belloc, himself a fine satirist, said it was one of the six books he couldn't live without.

A less subtle character, and one far more to the popular taste, made his debut in Sax Rohmer's novel *The Mystery of Dr Fu-Manchu* (1913).* Again in imitation of Professor Moriarty, and with more than a nod to Dr Nikola, Fu Manchu is a Chinese supervillain with a striking physical presence: 'tall, lean and feline, high-shouldered, with a brow like Shakespeare and a face like Satan, a close-shaven skull, and long, magnetic eyes of the true cat-green'. He is also 'a phenomenon such as occurs but once in many generations' according to his arch-enemy, Sir Denis Nayland Smith, 'the greatest genius which the powers of evil have put on earth for centuries'. He's a gifted linguist, a brilliant scientist, an adept in the occult arts. He thinks highly of himself as well. 'I am the lord of the fires,' he boasts. 'I am the god of destruction!'

Fu Manchu has little time for simply shooting his enemies. Instead, he devises trap doors that drop unsuspecting victims into death traps; he develops drugs that can simulate death and induce madness; his 'fiendish armoury' includes snakes, spiders and scorpions as well as 'my tiny allies, the bacilli', and he grows giant mutations of the toxic amanita mushroom. His army of human accomplices comprises not only Chinese, but also Arabs and Africans, bandits from Burma and Thugs from India. In short, 'Fu Manchu is omnipresent; his tentacles embrace everything.' So great is his reputed power that when a man is found dead next to an Egyptian sarcophagus, there is a very real fear that he might have control over mummies as well.

---

* Like Edgar Wallace, Sax Rohmer came out of music hall, having previously written songs for George Robey and ghosted Little Tich's autobiography. Fu Manchu was his greatest success; a further twelve books were published in Rohmer's lifetime, and there have been dozens of print, film, radio and television spin-offs.

This 'archangel of evil' is 'the head of the great Yellow Movement', part of a 'secret society which sought to upset the balance of the world'. Fu Manchu is 'the evil of the East incarnate' and 'his existence is a danger to the entire white race'. All that stands between him and 'the triumph of the yellow races' is Nayland Smith, formerly a senior police office in Burma. He lacks Fu Manchu's genius and charisma but instead embodies 'clean British efficiency', and he holds himself to the highest moral standards: 'A servant of the Crown in the East makes his motto: "Keep your word, though it break your neck!"'

The ultimate message of *The Mystery of Dr Fu-Manchu* is spelled out by the narrator, Dr Petrie: 'East and West may not intermingle.' And perhaps that was the core of the British attitude to China; the Celestial Empire was so old, so established and evolved, and yet so utterly alien, that it passed European understanding. It was ancient and modern, glamorous and horrifying. Despite the jokes and the silly names, and even despite the confusion with Japan, there was an underlying respect for China, in a way that wasn't really true for India and certainly not for Africa. This couldn't be seen as a primitive culture, as Britain had been before it embarked on its journey from savagery to civilisation. China had clearly taken another path altogether and yet travelled just as far. If anything, the intrusion of modern elements into the old China of *The Wallet of Kai Lung* implied that Britain was trailing in its wake.

There was something unfathomable about China, something perhaps to do with a fundamentally different moral code. After all, despite the best efforts of an army of missionaries, these people weren't Christian, and they didn't seem to observe basic principles of social behaviour. In a public-school story by Eden Phillpotts, a Chinese pupil, Tin Lin Chow, fits in perfectly well in the classroom and on the playing fields, but there are still cultural problems because 'Chinese chaps have quite different ideas to English chaps, owing to their bringing-up.' He tries to bribe a teacher to give him better marks in an arithmetic exam; he's an inveterate liar (though 'his knowledge of English wasn't up to lying without being found out'); and worst of all, he sneaks to the headmaster on a fellow pupil. The latter is the single greatest sin any schoolboy can commit; it offends against a code of honour so ingrained that it doesn't need teaching, and even the headmaster regrets the way Chow 'has relapsed upon the degraded and barbaric customs of a great but benighted country'.*

Dr Petrie's comment in *The Mystery of Dr Fu-Manchu* about the impossibility of East and West intermingling had deliberate echoes of Rudyard Kipling's 'East is East, and West is West, and never the twain shall meet.'[43] The point of that poem was that divisions of race and class can be overcome 'when two strong men stand face to face', but Rohmer's novel – and popular culture more generally – were less optimistic. Nayland Smith's Britain and Fu Manchu's China are completely dissimilar in morality and honour and caste, in everything save the pursuit of power. At heart, they are simply two very different civilisations. And in a world that was being shrunk by technology, that meant they were also irreconcilable rivals.

So if there is respect, there is also fear. A fear that British – European – cultural dominance might only be temporary. As *St James's Gazette* put it, when criticising the Chinese Hand Laundry, 'We assert that we are a superior race, and we must, so long as we have the power, simply act upon that assertion.'[44] That phrase 'so long as we have the power' was laden with doubt.

v

China had a unique standing in relation to Britain. It wasn't part of the Empire, but it wasn't entirely outside, either. Hong Kong had been gradually ceded between 1842 and 1898 (when a ninety-nine-year lease on the New Territories was signed), Britain retained

---

* This dastardly act also costs him the love of the headteacher's daughter, who has been sweet on him until then, and in his misery – with a familiar confusion of oriental customs – he tries to commit hara-kiri..

certain trading rights in Canton and Shanghai, and British interests were integral to the Chinese economy. Politically, the country was seen as peripheral, not a major power in a region where Russia and Japan were the big players. But as the fiction and the fascination illustrated, it was capable of exerting a strong grip on British public consciousness, a fact seen most starkly in the outcry over Chinese labour in South Africa.

When stability returned to that country following the Boer War, the owners of the Transvaal mines discovered that there was a labour shortage. The solution, approved by the British government, was to import indentured Chinese workers, who were without rights of citizenship and who lived in compounds rife with disease and violence. The first men arrived in 1904 and by the following year, there were 47,000 of them. In Britain, there was outrage at what a *Daily News* headline called YELLOW SLAVES FOR THE RAND.[45] A demonstration in Hyde Park attracted 70,000 people, the trade unions objected, and churchmen were thunderous. 'They are serfs or slaves,' said the Bishop of Hereford, who had earlier spoken against the concentration camps; 'the conditions of their employment are little different from those which characterised the West Indian slavery'.[46]

Cheap Chinese labour also had an impact on local employment. A poster for the Liberals in the run-up to the 1906 general election showed a line of Chinese men with the caption 'What Toryism Means – South Africa for the Chinese.' This ensured that the policy went down badly in other parts of the Empire, in Australia, Canada and New Zealand. All three nations had sent troops to South Africa, and the Boer War had been a joint enterprise, the colonies coming together to defend the interests of one of their own. What they certainly hadn't been fighting for was the importation and exploitation of foreign workers, to the inevitable detriment of the colonial population.

The standing of the Conservative and Unionist government was heavily damaged by the affair, and the unity of the Empire was weakened at a moment when Britain was already paying the financial and reputational price of the Boer War. Further, this was a time when its global pre-eminence was starting to fade, only partially concealed by the expansion of the City of London. Although British manufacturing and exports were still growing, the country was being outstripped by America and Germany. Britain's production of steel, for example – essential in the dawning era of machines and mechanised warfare – had increased sevenfold in the last three decades of the nineteenth century, but others were growing faster; ten years on, British steel production was less than half that of Germany and less than a quarter of America's. More significant still was the population growth in the three nations: in the thirty years to 1911, the British population grew by 13.5 million, but that of Germany by 23.9 million and that of the US by 53.2 million.

If the Empire was going to respond to this unaccustomed competition, it needed, some felt, a new approach, something to reverse the slow downwards drift. At the 1897 Colonial Conference, called to mark the Diamond Jubilee, Joseph Chamberlain advocated closer political union within the Empire, working towards a federal council that would replace the Westminster government for key imperial decisions, such as the declaration of war. His proposals, however, were rejected, as they were again at the 1902 Colonial Conference.* And so, thwarted on the political front, his attention turned instead to greater economic integration.

'Imperial Preference' was the slogan launched by Chamberlain in the spring of 1903, subsequently becoming 'Tariff Reform'. In essence, he argued that Britain should rewrite its relationship with the world: goods imported into the Empire would be subject to tariffs, but internal trade would be favourably treated. This would strengthen imperial ties and fortify the British economy against its rivals. There would still be trade with America, Germany and

---

* The 1897 conference was attended by the premiers of the eleven colonies that had a measure of self-government: Cape Colony, Canada, Natal, Newfoundland, New Zealand and the six territories of Australia. By 1902 the Commonwealth of Australia Constitution Act had brought the latter together into a federated nation.

elsewhere, but it would be much reduced in scope. Just as importantly, the tariffs would raise money for the government. This mattered because although Chamberlain had largely moved away from the radicalism of his younger self, he remained a social reformer by instinct, and among the causes he championed was the introduction of an old-age pension as a way of 'providing for the declining days of the poorer class'.[47] The cost of the Boer War had prevented any progress being made on the issue, but now he argued that a scheme could be funded by the Imperial Customs Union he advocated.

Chamberlain's proposal was not an original idea. Other countries, including Germany, had imposed tariffs on imports, and Canada had a system of imperial preference. Nor were selected tariffs unknown in Britain. Yet the scale of the policy made it controversial, as it flew in the face of the prevailing British philosophy of free trade, and Chamberlain failed to win over all his colleagues in the Conservative and Unionist government.

There had by now been a change in prime minister. Lord Salisbury had stepped down in 1902, after thirteen and a half years in office, and been replaced by his less impressive nephew, Arthur Balfour. 'Nothing leonine, masterful or strenuous could be introduced in any description of his character,' observed union leader Ben Tillett. 'Languorous almost to effeminacy, long, attenuated arms, limply dragging by side, or helmed by thumbs to arm hole of waistcoat, an almost rueful look, which regrets being disturbed into consideration of the mundane.'[48] Even John Buchan, a friend of Balfour, had to concede that 'he had none of the gifts which attract an easy popularity', though he did claim that he was 'the best talker I have ever known'.[49] ('He says nothing so beautifully, I could listen to him for hours,' was the verdict of one trade unionist.[50])

Chamberlain himself had a reasonable claim to the succession by virtue of his seniority, but he would have been too discordant a choice, and anyway he was out of circulation at the crucial moment, injured in a cab accident. He remained, though, the dominant force in British politics, and was attacked by Liberal politicians on precisely those grounds. Horace Mansfield, MP for Spalding, criticised 'the nominal, child-like prime minister' who was obliged 'to obey the commands of his dictator, Mr Joseph Chamberlain,'[51] while Lord Tweedmouth compared Balfour to the Mechanical Turk, the chess-playing automaton of a century earlier that was ultimately revealed as a hoax: 'Chamberlain was the man inside moving the pieces.'[52] The *Graphic* newspaper summed it up: 'Mr Arthur Balfour reigns; Mr Joseph Chamberlain rules.'[53] And indeed the prime minister proved unable to contain his older and more ruthless colleague. Over the summer of 1903 Balfour tried to procrastinate on the question of tariff reform, but Chamberlain forced the issue, and in September he resigned from the government in order to pursue his cause.

Joe Chamberlain was sixty-seven years old by now, but still capable of disruption and division like no one else. Four others – all free traders – left the cabinet at the same time as him, including the Duke of Devonshire, who had led the great Liberal schism of 1886 and was the leader of Chamberlain's own party. And so the splitters split, with a sizeable chunk of the Liberal Unionists returning to their Liberal home, and with Chamberlain left in control of the rump. Nor was that all. Eleven free-trade Conservative MPs also crossed the floor to join the Liberals, including Winston Churchill, who'd only been elected in 1900 but was already tipped for high office. He was described by H. H. Asquith – then a political opponent – as 'brilliant,'[54] and his oratory was attracting positive notices: 'the tones are those of a Napoleonic leader of men.'[55]

It was Churchill who, while still a Tory MP, asked Chamberlain the critical question about tariff reform in a Commons debate: how was it actually going to work? The slogans were good, but if we were unilaterally to change our trading arrangements, where was the detail that would allow for an informed decision, rather than just a leap in the dark?* 'How can we discuss the question,' he asked, 'unless we know, at any rate, the outlines of his scheme?'

---

* Asquith said that it was not so much a leap in the dark as 'political plunging'.

Chamberlain blustered. 'Nothing in the nature of a complete plan can be put before the country,' he said. 'But it does not require much acumen to see what are the general lines which any arrangement of this kind must follow.' He did, however, concede that it would raise prices. 'If you are to give a preference to the Colonies,' he admitted, 'you must put a tax on food.'[56]

That was the central problem when it came to selling the policy: repudiating free trade would hurt people's living standards. The Harmsworth newspapers dubbed tariff reform the Stomach Tax; it would raise the food bills of middle-class households, for whom 'the increase of even a few pounds a year will mean further pinching and squeezing to keep up appearances.'[57] Harmsworth later changed his mind and backed the idea, but there were plenty of others ready to talk about the cost of a loaf to the working class.

David Lloyd George mocked the tariff reformers on the platform at one of Chamberlain's meetings: 'There were three dukes, two marquises, three or four earls, and as many lords as there were ministerial resignations.' And what did these distinguished gentlemen want? 'To help the workman to tax his own bread.'[58] Meanwhile, hostile newspapers alleged that Chamberlain was trying 'to distract popular attention' from his inept handling of the Boer War and from the government's 'policy of aggressiveness and jingoism'.[59] And the Bishop of Hereford was – as ever – outraged: Chamberlain's trade policy appealed 'to the lower and baser motives', he thundered; it represented 'those elements in our materialistic civilisation which are pre-eminently unchristian, or, it might even be said, anti-Christian'.[60]

The reply to the objection over the cost of living was that British industry would be so stimulated by the reduction in imports that there would be 'Work for All'.* Again there was a lack of precision about the process, but precision wasn't necessary. Chamberlain

---

* It might as well have been 'Games for All, Pianos for All, Bicycles for All and Cheaper Wool,' scoffed A. A. Milne, a young writer whose work was just starting to appear in *Punch* magazine.

wished to establish a clear dividing line that would reshape politics, just as Irish Home Rule and the Boer War had defined earlier stages of his career. 'I believe in a British Empire,' he declared. 'I do not believe in a Little England.'[61]

He had, some years earlier, defined this term: 'A Little Englander is a man who honestly believes that the expansion of this country carries with it obligations which are out of proportion to its advantages.'[62] So, it was someone who didn't wish the Empire to grow any further. But that was before the Boer War had ratcheted up Chamberlain's rhetoric. During the conflict he'd repeatedly referred in dismissive scorn to 'Little Englanders and pro-Boers' as though the two positions were synonymous and tantamount to treason. He now portrayed Little Englanders as being not just opposed to imperial expansion, but also to his proposal for tariff reform and to the Empire itself. The expression had become little more than a term of abuse, encompassing both anti-imperialists and free traders. All of them, he suggested, were lacking 'that broader patriotism by which alone our Empire can be held together'.[63] Though Chamberlain's policy to erect trade barriers against three quarters of the world was essentially defensive, he painted his opponents as being the ones with limited vision and aspiration.

He was playing to an audience that understood the basic division of home and abroad, that recognised the fundamental conflict between Nayland Smith and Fu Manchu. However vague the British public's perception of foreign cultures, there was a sense of an imperial family, an emotional bond that extended at least to the white colonies. Being concerned with the world beyond that family was disloyal and somehow small-minded. This was something 'that Little Englanders do not understand', said Chamberlain. 'They care more for the opinion of foreign nations than for that of their own countrymen, or for their kith and kin across the sea.'[64] But he understood, he cared. He would speak for the people, and the message would be taken to them.

vi

The point of Chamberlain's resignation from the cabinet was that, freed from collective responsibility, he might campaign out in the country and win over the people to tariff reform.* The fact that he made any headway at all with the public was tribute to what the papers called 'the mere force of his character'.[65]

He spoke at a series of mass rallies, selling out venues such as the 5,000-seater Olympia in Newcastle, with tickets ranging from five shillings to a sovereign, but changing hands at many times their face value. To accommodate some of the disappointed, the nearby Drill Hall was pressed into service as an overflow room, the seats oversubscribed five times over, with people listening as he spoke in front of 'a row of electrophone receivers to convey the speaker's words in his own tone of voice'.[66] For those parts of the country that he couldn't get to in person, gramophone records were made of his speeches and were played to audiences.

This innovative use of new technology was matched by the campaign's exploitation of popular culture, with a big push to get the subject of tariff reform raised in the music halls. The first recruit to the cause was Leo Stormont, originally an opera singer from Dundee who had studied in Milan and appeared at La Scala before turning to the halls. A performer who specialised in patriotic songs, he was an obvious choice: he'd had a trio of Boer War hits with 'Sons of the Empire', 'Brave Boys' and 'Take the Lion's Muzzle Off'. In November 1903 he debuted a new song, 'No Fear', at the London Pavilion, which did at least refer to the problem of food prices, though the message wasn't cheerful:

> Giving in is not the policy of Saxons or of Celts,
> It was not the way in days gone by.
> For if food then was not plenty, soldiers tightened up their belts

---

* He took care, though, to maintain a family presence in government; on his resignation, his son, Austen Chamberlain, was appointed chancellor of the exchequer.

When they went to lift the old flag high.

The position on tariffs was unequivocal – 'if our trade is foreign-fettered, let us knock those fetters off' – and the song had a rousing chorus with the repeated line 'Shall we take it lying down?' to which the audience returned a resounding 'No fear!'

Running alongside this invocation of the past was a promise that Britain's glory could be reclaimed by Chamberlain, now being portrayed as the leader in internal exile, the once and future king. The hit musical comedy *A Country Girl* (1902) added a topical song to the show, tongue-in-cheek but still admiring:

It will all come out right in the future,
Though at present we cannot see how.
But it's bound to be so, our wonderful Joe
Is at work on the problem now.
He is bound to get back, for he never will lack
The support we give him now.

Similarly, Arthur Reece's song 'The Trainer' (1904) offered an insider's tip that Chamberlain would become prime minister: 'Joe's the one!'

There was at times the appearance of a personality cult. Cora Urquhart Brown-Potter, an American socialite who'd become an actress in Britain, was engaged by the Imperial Tariff League to deliver a poem, 'The Pledge of the British', at the Hippodrome music hall in Birmingham. Wearing 'a beautiful clinging gown of soft white crêpe de Chine, made up under silver tissue, and a large white picture hat of tulle', she recited the poem accompanied by slow music.[67] And when it came to the chorus, 'no fewer than one hundred working men, all exposing their shirt sleeves'[68] stepped forward to sing:

I pledge my word the Empire needs protection!
I pledge my word that through protection we will gain!

I pledge my word that this will benefit the nation!
These are the words of Joseph Chamberlain.

In case there were any mistake, a huge portrait of Chamberlain was used as a backdrop. The act went down a storm in Birmingham (where a simple mention of the great man's name in a pantomime could stop the show), and Brown-Potter took it on to the Canterbury, Tivoli and Euston halls in London.

The most successful song to emerge from tariff reform was 'The John Bull Store' (1903), which brought all the themes together.* It began by recalling the good old days 'When our Nelson kept the British flag a-flying, When we hammered Boney on the shore'. Now, as 'the Empire's glory seems to fade,' foreigners are overtaking us, but 'our Joe' (he 'is straight and square, and he's always played us fair') will restore our fortunes with his 'plan to draw our lads together'. The chorus was a stirring call for action:

Buy! Buy! Buy! At the John Bull Store.
The Deutscher and the Yank we shall want no more.
And the money that we gain will in British hands remain
If we buy at the John Bull Store.

Initially sung by George Whitehead at the Alhambra and the Canterbury in London, it was 'reputed to be the biggest hit of the season'.[69] Again this was a personalised message: 'A portrait of Mr Chamberlain was shown on the screen after the song, and was enthusiastically received without a dissentient voice.'[70] Over the Christmas of 1903, it was said that 'no fewer than 247 pantomimes

---

* The words were by Bertram Fletcher Robinson, who had reported on the Boer War for the *Daily Express* and later edited the paper. He also supplied Arthur Conan Doyle with much of the background material for *The Hound of the Baskervilles* (1902), in return for which he received a lucrative share of the royalties. He didn't live to enjoy the full fruits, however, dying of typhoid fever in 1907 at the age of thirty-five.

in the country' included songs in favour of Chamberlain and tariff reform,[71] of which 'The John Bull Shop' was the most popular.

Audiences were not always of one voice: when Herbert Campbell sang 'Good Old Joe' in the Drury Lane production of *Humpty Dumpty*, 'there was a sturdy minority who hissed disapproval'.[72] For the most part, though, the songs were at least moderately well received, much to the fury of Chamberlain's opponents, who saw such appeals to the masses as trivialising politics. Liberals said the tariff reformers represented 'the unthinking part of the population who visit music halls'.[73] Winston Churchill described Chamberlain's politics as 'music-hall imperialism and pantomime finance'.[74] And Henry Campbell-Bannerman shuddered at the insubstantiality of the entire enterprise: 'No amount of theatrical vulgarity would give bone and sinew to these promises.'[75]

This was the familiar complaint about jingoism in the halls, though this time it was focused on the one politician who chose to mine that seam. The outbreak of songs about 'Our Joe' and tariff reform was not entirely spontaneous. A substantial budget had, in fact, been allocated to the propaganda effort: 'The cost of arranging Mr Chamberlain's fiscal songs at the pantomimes and music halls is given as between £6,000 and £7,000,' it was reported.[76]

No other British politician had harnessed the power of popular culture in this way, and there was some truth in that charge of music-hall imperialism. The bright primary-coloured world of the halls was not the place for political analysis, but it did potentially lend itself to Chamberlain's populist dividing lines. A couple of years ago, it had been Patriots versus Pro-Boers, now it was Tariff Reformers versus Little Englanders, but the message was the same: the country was split into two camps, and Chamberlain was ready to ride to the rescue.

The music-hall offensive was not intended to have a decisive electoral impact. Some 7.25 million property-owning men were eligible to vote, around six in ten of all men, but the proportion was much lower for working-class music-hall audiences. This wasn't where elections would be won and lost. Instead the aim was to set the agenda, to get tariff reform talked about in every corner of the kingdom, such that it couldn't be ignored.

The problem, though, was that economic patriotism wasn't as simple as the call for loyalty during war; buying at the John Bull Store involved a conflict of interests. In 'Serves You Right' (1908) Billy Williams (The Man in the Velvet Suit) remonstrated with the British worker:

> A German cut out the clothes you wear,
> A Russian barber has cut your hair,
> Matches cut in Sweden too, you use if you want a light.
> Now a foreigner's cut you out of a job
> And it jolly well serves you right.

Even if it were true that British workmen were losing their jobs because the market was flooded with cheap foreign goods, the low prices were still a temptation. Consequently, all such appeals failed. In 1905 Conservative MP William Evans Gordon launched the British-Made League 'to promote the demand for, and the sale of, goods manufactured in any part of the British Empire'.[77] The initiative attracted considerable press attention, but it fizzled out within a month.

It was also the case that the economic arguments weren't quite as simple as the slogans suggested, and some were puzzled when Campbell-Bannerman and Chamberlain extrapolated such very different outcomes from the same premise. As Albert Chevalier sang, in the character of a contrary old labourer:

> Never mind what C. B. sez, or Chamberlain is at,
> Let's git dahn to the bed-rock fust. Who's talking tommy-rot?
> Can both on 'em be right I arst?
> An' hif not, why not?

The result, said the *Daily News*, was that Chamberlain's campaign wasn't as successful as he had hoped: 'Music hall jingoism was uproariously successful. Music hall protectionism falls rather flat.'[78] But it did get Chamberlain talked about, and his carefully cultivated image became unavoidable. Over the course of 1905, it was recorded, he was caricatured by cartoonists in a bewildering array of garbs, as 'a pirate, a carrot, a boat, a missionary, a Salvation Army officer, a juggler, William Pitt, a coster, Napoleon, a ballet-girl, a terrier, a candlestick, a Chinaman, Mr Mantalini, Mr Turveydrop, a clock, Betsy Prig, a nigger minstrel, a Pierrot, a bishop, a Red Indian, a Roman Emperor, a Turkish pasha, a snake, a swordfish, a king, a snowman, a trapeze artist, a dead baby, a champion walker, a mad hatter, Brer Fox, a settee, a blind beggar, a prize-fighter'.[79] Whether any of this was ultimately of benefit to him was another matter, but it transformed politics. Having already helped split the Liberals in 1886, he'd now done the same to the Liberal Unionists, while setting Tory against Tory. The government ranks looked divided, confused and chaotic.

The impact of Chamberlain's campaign on the Liberals, by contrast, was entirely positive. The divisions of the Boer War days were put behind them in a rush of unity; defending the principle of free trade was the one thing that could bring the whole party together, at least in public. 'We hear no more of great Liberals living in solitary tents or ploughing lonely furrows,' noted the *Manchester Evening News* approvingly.[80]

The internal strife over tariff reform finally finished off a government that was already beleaguered and weary. In December 1905 the Tory prime minister Arthur Balfour resigned and handed the premiership to Liberal leader Henry Campbell-Bannerman, who promptly called a general election.

As in the Khaki Election of 1900, the campaign in January 1906 was largely fought on a single issue chosen by Chamberlain, but now the dividing line split the government, leaving the opposition intact. And this time the Liberals took the initiative, making food prices the centre of their campaign. A poster showed a large loaf of bread marked 'Free Trade' and a much smaller one inscribed 'Protection'. 'We plead for the women and children,' implored the caption; 'Which will <u>you</u> have?' The electorate knew the answer to that, and the cause of tariff reform was comprehensively rejected. The Liberals won a landslide majority, emerging with 397 MPs (a gain of 214 on the last general election), while the Unionists collapsed to 156 (down 246). Balfour was one of those who lost his seat, and until he returned to the Commons at the end of February 1906, Chamberlain was acting leader of the parliamentary rump of the Conservative and Unionist party.

It was virtually the last act of his public life. In July 1906 he had a massive stroke, and although he recovered a little, he was unable to attend Parliament, let alone return to his barnstorming. He died in July 1914. With him removed from front-line politics, the cause of tariff reform struggled to be heard beyond the ranks of the Conservative faithful, though many continued to see it as a badge of political identity. At one point Balfour proposed holding a referendum on the subject of Britain's trading relationship with the rest of the world, but there was very little public interest in the idea.

5

CHILDREN AND YOUTHS

If modern writers for the young have done nothing else, I think they have done much in the way of ridding children's books of the large amount of forced morals which was often nothing but unadulterated cant

Novelist Harold Avery, 1906[1]

Chairman of Magistrates: What are Peaky Blinders?
Supt. Evans: The roughs of Birmingham, sir!

Proceedings in Nuneaton Magistrates' Court, 1901[2]

John Trundley (1898–1944), billed as the Fat Boy of Peckham, pictured in the *Tatler* at the age of five, lifting a grown man off the floor.

THE FIRST REPORTS APPEARED in November 1903: a boy from Peckham, south London, had just turned five years old and was growing at a remarkable rate.[3] At nearly 4 feet tall, John Trundley already had a 42-inch waist, and weighed 10 stone 4 pounds. His bulk meant that he was unable to walk far and was too heavy to be pushed in a pram, but apart from that, he was in good health and strong enough to lift his father off the ground. He was also, said his mother, an intelligent child: 'Johnnie knows his alphabet, can add two and two, can say "Little Jack Horner" and "Little Miss Muffet".'

By chance, the same month saw the publication in *Pearson's Magazine* of the first instalment of H. G. Wells's new novel, *The Food of the Gods*, which told of scientists developing Boomfood, a substance that accelerates animal growth; wasps swell to the size of owls, earwigs to the size of lobsters, and when it's fed to infant humans, it produces giants.* Oversized children were clearly newsworthy; within weeks John Trundley had been signed up by two music halls in south London at ten pounds a week each, followed by an offer from Edward Moss to appear at the Edinburgh Empire for forty pounds a week. These were riches too great to be resisted by Trundley's father, a dustman who suffered badly from rheumatism (an occupational hazard); by the end of the year, the Fat Boy of Peckham, as he was billed, was earning the family's living on stage.

It wasn't much of an act, for Trundley had no talents beyond his size. So he came on in a sailor suit and stood in the middle of the stage, holding his father's hand, while a lecturer hired for the occasion displayed an enlarged copy of his birth certificate and

---

* These infants have to be trained not to use their strength, which leads to a psychologically intriguing relationship between child and guardian: 'For Lady Wondershoot, in these early days, he displayed the profoundest awe. She found she could talk to him best when she was in short skirts and had her dog-whip, and she gesticulated with that and was always a little contemptuous and shrill.'

expounded upon his vital statistics. After a couple of minutes, the sailor suit was removed, to reveal a close-fitting pink body stocking. He was asked his name ('Sunny Jim') and what he wanted to be when he grew up ('a policeman') and that was all there was. It was sufficient. His appearance provoked great laughter and, it was reported, he brought in the crowds, 'especially ladies'.

How the Fat Boy felt about these proceedings was unclear. 'Johnny showed no symptoms of mirth,' noted the papers. 'He simply gazed at the footlights as if not quite comprehending their use.' He was no simpleton, though. There was also the story of a medical examination, during which, evidently bored, he failed to respond to questions. 'That boy is mentally deficient,' the doctor said, and received a sharp retort: 'I've got more brains than you.' But on stage, confronted by a chortling crowd, he simply froze.[4]

The press made great play of the Fat Boy's career, while simultaneously professing themselves outraged. 'The mere exhibition of monstrosity is degrading to the spectators, and doubly degrading to the unfortunate object of their so-called amusement,' fumed the *Daily Mirror*. He had been 'trained to exhibit his fat as the beggars of old exhibited their deformities, trained to appeal to some low instinct of curiosity, which it is difficult for cultured people to understand'.[5] So great was the outcry that a prosecution was brought against the proprietors of the halls and against Trundley's father under the Prevention of Cruelty to, and Protection of, Children Act 1889. The case collapsed, however, when the magistrate ruled that the law did not apply. 'The act provides that no child under the age of eleven years, unless licensed, should appear upon a stage for the purpose of singing, playing or performing for profit,' he ruled. 'In this case the child was not on the stage for the purpose of singing or playing or performing for profit, but was there as a freak of nature and nothing else.'[6]

It wasn't exactly a ringing endorsement of the morality of the halls, but it did declare open season in the search for other outsized children. Charles Watts of Woodchurch, Kent – twelve years old and nineteen stone in weight – was offered the opportunity to be similarly exhibited, but his parents declined the offer. So too the parents of newspaper discoveries Harold Bishop of Birmingham (10 stone 7 pounds at the age of twelve) and nine-year-old Elizabeth Daltrey, weighing in at 8 stone 6 pounds. But there were bookings for fifteen-year-old Miss Lucie, the Russian Fat Child, who was claimed to top them all, at twenty-five stone. 'Miss Lucie, who appears as a ballet dancer, is as graceful as a fairy,' read the reports.[7]

Meanwhile, the Fat Boy of Peckham was discovering a hard truth of modern celebrity: that the only thing worse than being forgotten about is not being forgotten about. When it came time for John Trundley to go to school, there was much excitement that a special chair and desk had to be constructed to accommodate him. More sensational still, a tramline had to be extended by 400 yards because he couldn't walk to the nearest stop. The *Daily Mail* led the thunderous attack on this waste of council money, and from being a figure of fun, Trundley found himself recast as a burden on the public purse. It didn't end his career, though, and he continued to be exhibited by his father into his teenage years.* He also came to symbolise the depths of journalistic triviality: in 1905 the Socialist Labour Party† mocked the likes of Henry Hyndman and Keir Hardie – leaders of the Social Democratic Federation and Labour Party respectively – for chasing publicity, seeking 'to get into the papers, along with the Fat Boy of Peckham'.[8]

ii

The fact that the local council was responsible for getting John Trundley to school was the consequence of the Education Act 1902, the greatest domestic achievement of Arthur Balfour's government. School attendance had been compulsory since 1880 (the

---

* In later life, John Trundley found some work as a comic actor, before retiring from the stage to become a watchmaker. He died in 1944 at the age of forty-five.
† The Socialist Labour Party was a splinter of the Independent Labour Party.

leaving age was initially set at ten, later raised to twelve), but the administration of education was a confused patchwork, with local councils responsible for some institutions and school boards for others; there was also a large voluntary sector, dominated by the Church of England, together with a smaller Catholic presence. The 1902 act brought all these under the authority of councils. The independent, fee-paying sector remained separate, but there was now a uniformity of state provision across the country.

It proved to be a sensible and successful measure, but it was deeply contentious at the time, seen as an extension of state power. In particular, it was opposed by Nonconformists who saw it as a way of giving public funds to faith schools, but only those that were run by specific churches. David Lloyd George was vociferous in his denunciations, as was Joseph Chamberlain. The Education Act was passed but, along with the controversy over indentured Chinese labour in South Africa and the Licensing Act of 1904 (seen as a 'brewers' Bill'[9]), it allowed opponents to paint Balfour's administration as 'a retrograde and immoral government'.[10] That perception – articulated by 'every reverend occupier of a Free Church pulpit', according to furious Tories[11] – did considerable damage, helping to ensure the election defeat of 1906.

The Education Act was partly a recognition that this was another area in which Britain was falling behind its competitors. A 1900 report showed that only around a quarter of British children remained at school after the age of twelve, compared to three quarters in Germany. Attendance was also lower, not helped by the arrangement called half-time, which allowed older children to attend school for only half the day, with the remainder spent at work; in 1907 there were some 37,000 half-timers, mostly in northern mill towns.

Meanwhile, a separate campaign was calling for schools to provide meals for pupils. As things stood, this was the territory of charity. In 1890 the London School Dinners Association (LSDA), in conjunction with the London Vegetarian Society, had begun providing subsidised lunches of vegetable soup and wheatmeal bread to 25,000 children in the capital, charging a halfpenny each. Thomas Spalding, the LSDA secretary, explained: 'Our idea of an underfed child is of a child attending school in such a condition as makes it a real cruelty to expect it to learn.' He recognised, though, that this initiative would achieve little in isolation. 'Meals are not a remedy; they merely relieve actual suffering. For remedies, one must go much deeper down and get better conditions of life for the people, more regular employment, less drinking, and so on.'[12]

By 1905 the LSDA was supplying 122,000 meals a week, and some councils were beginning to introduce free lunches. That early vegetarian menu was still being followed; in Walworth 200 dinners a day were being provided, comprising 'a pint of soup – made from lentils, peas, haricot beans, rice, pearl barley and substitutes for animal fats – a piece of wholemeal bread and a piece of currant bread'.[13]

This use of public funds was actually illegal, and it came at a time when voices were being raised about council expenditure. London was in the grip of 'Progressive-Socialist wastrels', thundered the *Daily Telegraph*. Spending to assist the capital's poor was twice as high per head of population as the national average, and while some of the recipients were probably in genuine distress, many were thought to be 'pampered paupers'.[14] School meals only compounded the offence. Nonetheless, argued campaigners, they were the way forward. 'The vision of a child with a brain crammed and a stomach empty' was 'our national sin', declared F. W. Barnes, a school attendance officer from Leigh, Lancashire, and while voluntary provision was commendable, it failed to reach many of those for whom it was intended. 'Charity hurts,' he said; it was felt as a humiliation, and 'the poor are proverbially proud'.[15]

The pressure for state action came mainly from the Left, and one of the first measures of the new Liberal government in 1906 was the Education (Provision of School Meals) Act, which allowed local authorities to levy a special halfpenny rate in order to provide lunches for poor children. By 1910 the London County Council was providing 7.7 million meals a year at 808 of the 1,005 schools under its control, 'the remainder being in the richer districts where there was not the demand for feeding'.[16]

Beyond the poor, though, there was a wider problem. Even some of those who could afford to feed their children were woefully careless of nutritional standards. There were 'neglectful mothers', complained Monsignor William Brown of Lambeth,* who sent children to school 'with bags of biscuits or cakes' and didn't prepare dinner, settling instead for buying 'fried fish and potatoes'.[17] Furthermore, children could be their own worst enemies; expenditure on sweets, said Helen Bosanquet of the Charity Organisation Society, 'is analogous to that upon drink, and in its incessant indulgence of an unwholesome craving is a fitting prelude to the continual "boozing" of later years'.[18]

These things played into wider concerns about the health of the young. In 1901 Dr Middleton Connon, medical officer of health for Montrose, warned that cigarettes, particularly cheap ones, 'caused premature decay of the teeth, and seriously affected the eyesight'. The problems were not just physical but moral: youths would smoke in ice-cream parlours, drinking 'lemonade and other sweet rubbish sold in such shops, but acquiring habits which might lead to the tavern and the more potent liquors to be got there'.[19] A few years later, Dr Herbert Tidswell of Torquay presented a paper to the British Medical Association claiming that, by smoking cigarettes, 'boys were killing themselves by hundreds and thousands'. He conceded that the trail of cause and effect was obscure, but 'the connection between smoking and insanity was closer than was generally believed'.[20] There was greater danger yet from foreign cigarettes, many of which – a parliamentary select committee was told – were made 'in filthy surroundings, and "doped" with belladonna, opium and cocaine, and were often composed of such refuse as cigar and cigarette ends, and "quids of tobacco" picked up in the streets or from the floors of drinking saloons by low-class Italians'.[21]

---

* Brown was to be consecrated as a bishop in 1924.

Poor diet, smoking, children's health – such issues would previously have been seen as private matters, but attitudes were changing, partly in response to what the Boer War had revealed about the country. That conflict saw a flood of recruits to the army, but if working-class patriotism was in fine fettle, the same could not be said of working-class health. Around three in ten who applied to join were rejected on medical grounds; even one in five of those employed in heavy manual work was deemed unfit for service. Demands grew that the state should take action, for the future defence of the realm if for no other reason.

It was in this context that the Children's Act of 1908 made it illegal to sell alcohol or tobacco products to anyone under the age of sixteen. Publicans were banned from having children in the bar while they were open; it became an offence to give alcohol to a child under five years of age, except under medical advice; and policemen and park keepers were authorised to confiscate tobacco, cigarettes and cigarette papers from underage smokers and to search boys (though, for reasons of delicacy and decency, not girls) for such items.

If that represented an intrusion of the state into people's private lives, the Children's Act also expanded the duties of parents, making it a requirement for them to accompany their children to court and to be responsible for paying any fines they received. Cruelty to children was already a crime; now it was joined by negligence. Other measures saw the formal abolition of capital punishment for those aged under sixteen, and the greater separation of young offenders from the judicial and penal system that applied to adults.

Whether this latter worked in practice was doubted by some. A youth detention centre had been opened in the village of Borstal, Kent in 1902, giving its name to other such institutions, and one of its graduates was distinctly unimpressed. 'Borstal is nothing more or less than a complete failure', declared 'Gentleman' George Smithson, a thief who got a three-year sentence as a juvenile in 1910.[22] Borstal was 'the Academy of Crime', he said, and it was there, while 'serving my apprenticeship in prison-craft', that he met the boy who would become his business partner. On their release, they began to burgle the country houses of the wealthy and the titled, selecting their victims from *Debrett's* and the society pages of *The Times*. It was a moral as well as a pragmatic decision, reasoned Smithson: 'The rich have it to lose, and the poorer people do not.'*

iii

At the beginning of the 1880s a new phenomenon had been observed on Sunday evenings in east London: youths promenading in the streets, swaggering around in their best clothes. 'Well-dressed roughs were pushing people about in the Bow Road and throwing stones and gravel at each other, and anyone else who happened to be passing,' it was reported. 'They also caught hold of one or two young girls who were passing quietly along, hugged them round the waist, and behaved towards them in a scandalous manner.'[23]

This weekly ritual became known locally as the monkey parade, and the name – as well as the practice – caught on across the city and beyond. 'These twilight parades of young people, youngsters chiefly of the lower middle-class, are one of the odd social developments of the great suburban growths,' wrote H. G. Wells; 'the shop apprentices, the young work girls, the boy clerks and so forth, stirred by mysterious intimations, spend their first-earned money upon collars and ties, chiffon hats, smart lace collars, walking-sticks, sunshades or cigarettes, and come valiantly into the vague transfiguring mingling of gaslight and evening.'[24]

The sight was sufficiently familiar that when a Patriotic Pageant was staged in Brixton in 1900, amid the floats celebrating the army's endeavours in South Africa there was one titled Brixton

---

* In later life, having completed a six-year stretch in Dartmoor for the theft of two Gainsborough paintings, Smithson was to retire from crime and write his memoirs, *Raffles in Real Life* (1930).

Monkey Paraders Caged. As that indicated, the problem wasn't taken too seriously. 'Boys will be boys,' shrugged a Manchester paper, 'and even girls will be girls.'[25] When a new chief constable was appointed in Brighton, his priorities were said to be swearing in the street, spitting in the street, and then the monkey parade.[26] It was generally understood that these 'crowds of young men and maidens, all bent on the tender dalliance of love,'[27] were engaged in a courtship dance that at worst might result in a detour to a nearby park or cemetery.

Like so much else, the Edwardian version of the monkey parade was less rough and rowdy than it had once been. When 'two well-dressed young fellows' in north London were charged with 'disorderly conduct by pushing people off the pavement in Holloway Road' in 1905, the magistrate noted that such prosecutions had become a rarity. 'I remember the monkeys' parade,' he mused. 'When I sat at this court some years ago it was not uncommon for fifteen or twenty boys to be charged each Monday morning with this kind of conduct.'[28] This time, he fined the offenders one pound each.

Any offences committed tended to be of a very minor nature. Apart from anything else, youths who had spent good money on clothes were disinclined to risk damaging their finery. And the clothes were becoming very fine indeed, reflecting a change in youth employment. The growth in non-manual labour was bringing a swathe of men into the world of semi-respectability, with all the demands that entailed. 'The clerk has to appear like a gentleman, to pretend to live like a gentleman, and to have the manners of a gentleman,' said the National Union of Clerks, as it pursued a pay claim in 1909.[29] There were also the shopworkers, who in the larger establishments often lived on the premises; by the time deductions had been made for accommodation, food and sundries, there was little left save for status. 'They had their pride,' remembered one. 'If the wages was light and the work was heavy, the frock-coat at least was highly esteemed and satisfyingly genteel.'[30]

From this world emerged a generation of lower-middle-class

youths who obsessed over clothes. Thus was created the masher, otherwise known as the swell or the fop ('the "dude" as our American cousins call him', added one paper[31]). In his pomp, he wore a morning coat with tails, tight trousers, a wide coloured tie with socks to match, kid gloves and a collar so high and so stiff that it was hard to turn one's head.* These things were subject to fashion, though. A few years earlier collars had been wide and low, exposing the top of the chest, and in 1908 there was excited talk of zebra patterns: 'The cloth is marked with alternate wide stripes in two colours; the shades are in no way vivid, but delicate.'[32]

The greatest fictional masher was the eponymous hero of H. G. Wells's novel *Kipps* (1905), an apprentice in a draper's emporium who engages in 'grave discussions about collars, ties, the cut of trouser legs, and the proper shape of a boot-toe'. When he comes into an entirely unexpected inheritance (a familiar plot line), Artie Kipps indulges himself with 'a new suit of drab flannels, a Panama hat and a red tie' accessorised with 'a silver-mounted stick with a tortoise shell handle' and 'a magnificent gold-decorated pigskin cigarette case'. Later, his genteel fiancée explains that his new outfit is too flash for his new social position. 'You mustn't be too – too dressy. It's possible to be over-conventional, over-elaborate,' she tells him. 'A real gentleman looks right, without looking as though he had tried to be right.' To the masher, such niceties smacked rather of hiding one's light under a very dull bushel.

The working-class dandy was not a new phenomenon – 'We keep no horse, but a clothes-horse,' Charles Dickens had written back in the 1830s[33] – and he had been satirised in the music hall for decades, in a succession of songs about poseurs from deprived areas: Arthur Lloyd's Shoreditch toff (in his 1868 song 'Immenseikoff'), T. W. Barrett's 'The Marquis of Camberwell Green' (1884), Tom Leamore's 'Percy from Pimlico' (1898). Those characters had been isolated individuals, though, rather than the massed ranks of the

---

* A circus act in 1904 featured a giraffe dressed as a parody of a masher, wearing the highest collar of all.

monkey paraders, and a different note was now being struck in the cultural portrayal, still mocking but with a touch of pathos. Ella Shields's 'Burlington Bertie from Bow' (1914) was in the same tradition, but he sounded desperate (he's been 'so long without food, I forgot where my face is'). And then there was George Formby.*

Born the illegitimate son of an alcoholic prostitute in Ashton-under-Lyne, Lancashire, the young Formby (or James Booth, as he then was) spent long nights sleeping out on the streets while his mother worked at home. That was when he developed the lung condition that would scar his career. By the time he was topping bills at the start of the century, aged just twenty-five, he had to have oxygen tubes on the side of the stage in case he collapsed. Billed as the Wigan Nightingale, his mournful voice sounding as if he'd known nothing but defeat all his life, he'd come on stage in a shabby outfit, far too large for his scrawny frame, and implausibly claim to be a swell:

It must be the clothes that I'm wearing,
That sets all the pretty girls staring.
It must be my smile, my best Sunday tile,
That makes all the other swells copy my style.

As the orchestra vamped between verses, he would soliloquise on his status: 'Oh, I'm a swell all right. I have been called other names, but of course that doesn't matter. Young lads like us, we don't care ...'

If music hall was inclined to laugh at the affectations of its audience members – for the halls were very much the masher's natural habitat – sterner voices were also heard, condemning the obsession with dressing up. 'The time spent by some men, as well as women, at the looking-glass is reprehensible, alike as a waste of

---

* After Formby died in 1921, his identically named son embarked on his own career, becoming Britain's biggest movie star; thereafter the music-hall artist tended to be referred to as George Formby Senior.

precious moments and as indicative of a vain and frivolous character,' pronounced the Reverend A. F. Forrest of the United Free Church in Kirkintilloch, Dunbartonshire. 'The mind grows in the contemplation of great subjects, but is dwarfed by absorption with trifles.'[34]

This was another dimension to the problems revealed by recruitment for the Boer War. It wasn't just the physical ill-health of the young that was concerning; it was also their moral condition. 'One of the great needs of the world today is manliness in its young men,' pronounced the Cornish writer and Methodist minister the Reverend Silas K. Hocking in a lecture entitled 'There's Now't So Queer as Folk'. 'So many young men are destitute of the most elementary principles of manliness; they are weak, flabby, back-boneless and jelly-kind of creatures that drift hither and thither on the waves and before every wind that blows.'[35]

Unfortunately, the mashers, at whom these tirades were aimed, tended to miss pulpit denunciations, being too busy spending their Sundays displaying and disporting themselves on the streets. Music-hall comedian Charlie Chaplin, who came from extreme poverty in south London, remembered 'the doleful clang of reprimanding bells that accompanied carousing youths and giggling wenches parading the darkened high streets and back alleys. It was their only Sunday evening diversion.'[36]

There was no real harm in the masher or the monkey parader. A couple of steps further down the social ladder, though, the feral youths said to infest large parts of the towns and cities caused real concern. They went by different names in different places: Hooligans in London, Scuttlers in Manchester, High Rippers in Liverpool, Peaky Blinders in Birmingham.* Whatever they were called, they were all of a piece: wild, uncontrollable street gangs, whose members attacked the police, each other and sometimes

---

* The BBC television series *Peaky Blinders* (2013) was set in the post-war years – by which time the phenomenon had passed – and depicted gangsters rather than street gangs.

members of the public. They didn't care much about the names they were given; territorial identity was the important thing. For a working-class youth in Chelsea it mattered only whether you belonged to the Oakum Bay Faction or their fierce rivals the Sandsend Faction. Glasgow gangs included the Hi Hi's, the Tim Molloys, the San Toys, the Village Boys and the Wellingtonia, and the differences between them were more important than the similarities.

There were established fashions that amounted to a uniform – cap worn forwards over the eyes, no collar, a muffler or neckerchief instead of a tie, bell-bottom trousers, hobnailed boots – but there were also identifying marks to signal allegiance: the Silver Hatchet Gang in London, for example, wore a badge on their lapel, showing an axe with the motto 'Tried, Tested and True.'[37] In some quarters there was a fashion for the Newgate fringe: a shaved face with a beard running below the jawline, in imitation of where the hangman's noose would be placed. 'The most characteristic part of their uniform,' read one report, 'is the substantial leather belt heavily mounted with metal. It is not ornamental, but then it is not intended for ornament.'[38] Other weapons in the arsenal included knuckledusters, sticks, knives and occasionally guns.

This wasn't an exclusively male preserve. 'There are girls as well as boys,' said Liberal MP and educationalist Thomas Macnamara. 'Dirty, ragged, unwashed, unkempt, foul-mouthed girls, with tempers like tigers and habits like wild beasts, are roaming about the streets, preying on society every day.'[39] It was reported in 1906 that Glasgow was 'experiencing a modified reign of terror', with gangs that included 'young girls of ages averaging from fourteen to seventeen, with very long draggled skirt and hair in tightly twisted pigtail'.[40]

The rhetoric was sometimes exaggerated, but the violence was real. Even restricting the examples to assaults on the police by Birmingham's Peaky Blinders, the charge sheet was serious. In 1900 eighteen-year-old Henry Attwood and sixteen-year-old Percy Langridge were convicted of 'stabbing two policemen who arrested a couple of their friends for disorderly conduct.'[41] The following year PC Charles Gunter died after being struck on the head with a brick, and three men were given fifteen years' penal servitude for manslaughter.[42] And the year after that, two brothers, aged twenty-eight and nineteen, were convicted of the attempted murder of PC Blinko and sentenced to penal servitude for life; the policeman had served a summons on the older brother, and in retaliation they 'smashed in his skull with a chopper. This was in open daylight and in a crowded street.'[43]

Not even the football pitch provided protection. During one match in Birmingham a gang of Peaky Blinders attacked and robbed a goalkeeper, while the rest of his team was in the opponents' half. Passing sentences of hard labour, 'Mr Justice Lawrence said he thought the football field was safe for all except the referee, but in Birmingham it was not so for either a player or goalkeeper, if his comrades were away from him.'[44]

iv

Fear of the gangs led some to take precautionary measures. 'Citizens are arming themselves with weapons of defence,' it was reported of Glasgow in 1906, 'and the revolver is becoming a popular adjunct to one's evening outfit.'[45] Such extreme measures weren't necessary, according to John Burns, Liberal MP for Battersea. He was cycling through Tooting in 1900 when he saw 'four young ruffians molesting a couple of ladies', so he dismounted and laid about him with his fists, dispersing the gang. 'If every self-respecting man did likewise,' he observed, 'hooliganism would be extinct in a few hours.'[46] Similarly, when the Reverend Wilson Carlile, founder of the Church Army, was struck by a drunken youth, he followed the Lord's teaching and turned the other cheek. Having received a blow on that side as well, he 'stripped off his black coat and gave the hooligan one of the soundest thrashings he had ever had'.[47]

This kind of citizens' action addressed the symptoms, not

the root cause. But what was the root cause? Many theories were offered. It was a problem of poverty, overcrowded homes and neglectful parents, argued some; insufficient numbers of police carrying inadequate equipment, said others, regretting the fact that since 1902 officers were no longer armed with cutlasses when patrolling the more dangerous parts of towns.

Truancy was perhaps a factor. There were six and a half million working-class children of school age, a meeting of the Bristol and District Teachers' Association was told in 1900, but three quarters of a million of those were not on a school register. 'What chance had they? Theirs was a boyhood of misery and vice.'[48] Elsewhere, a meeting of the National Union of Teachers in the Midlands suggested that those who did attend school were being betrayed by a lack of chastisement. 'This resulted in the production of the Hooligans and Peaky Blinders, who were not properly disciplined at school because the Board were afraid of the parents.'[49] It was a common complaint. 'The schoolmaster hardly dare correct a pupil,' grumbled the *Sheffield Daily Telegraph*, 'lest he be assaulted by an indignant parent, or dragged into the police-court to justify his conduct before a bench of magistrates.' It was regarded as evidence of 'a pseudo-humanitarianism which is sapping our manliness.'[50]

Other theorists blamed the lack of proper apprenticeships; many children left school at twelve and were employed in short-term unskilled jobs rather than learning a trade. And sociologist Sir Joshua Fitch put it down to imperialism, arguing that the celebration of 'the might and majesty of the British Empire' during the Boer War promoted violence at home. 'We are training up a nation of hooligans by glorifying war.'[51]

The latter seemed unlikely, if only because, however violent the streets were now, things weren't as bad as they had been during the long years of peace. When James Scotson retired in 1904 after a fifty-six-year teaching career in Manchester, he reflected that the Scuttlers of today weren't as numerous or as vicious as they had been: 'The moral tone is infinitely superior in these latter days.'[52]

Even the Peaky Blinder was in decline: 'The time has passed away, happily, when he was a familiar institution,' noted a 1901 report; though the violence remained, the numbers involved had reduced.[53]

Those inclined to optimism about the moral health of the younger generation could point to the vigorous work of the Sunday school movement, founded before the advent of compulsory school attendance, which remained a powerful cultural and moral presence. Indeed it was reaching record numbers; the interdenominational National Sunday School Union (NSSU), which celebrated its centenary in 1903, had around 15,000 affiliates with over two million scholars,[54] and there were many more in unaffiliated groups.[55] It was estimated that nine in ten children attended, even if not for very long. Sunday schools, said the Reverend F. B. Meyer of the Baptist Union in Glasgow, were the antidote to 'the deadly poison' of 'the low music-hall, the suggestive cinematograph, and the tons of filthy literature provided for growing lads and girls'.[56] They were, according to David Lloyd George, 'the university of the people'.[57]

Sunday schools often ran small libraries. The Wesleyans in Totnes, for example, had a collection of 100 books, with a further 85 donated after an appeal in 1905; the Baptists in Enfield, north London had 360. The NSSU had its own imprint, producing wholesome fiction, often with school settings: W. E. Cule's *The Captain's Fags* (1901), Eleanora Stooke's *Tom Tufton's Loyalty* (1906), Robert Leighton's *A Bit of a Bounder* (1907). Beyond the school stories there were also novels such as Florence Witts' *In the Day of His Power* (1902), 'a story of strife between manufacturers and their "hands", beginning with a constitutional strike and proceeding to starvation and violence', after which the local Christian Endeavour Society negotiates a settlement.[58] Also popular were biographical studies of inspiring figures from the past, great heroes ranging from the Anglo-Saxon rebel Hereward the Wake to the Tory politician and social reformer Lord Shaftesbury. The aim was to foster Christian, British principles in children, values of selflessness and steadfastness, decency and determination, resolution, hard work and enterprise.

Reinforcing the moral tone was the Scouting movement, launched in 1907 by Robert Baden-Powell, hero of Mafeking. By 1910 there were 100,000 Scouts, including several thousand girls. The latter had not originally been expected to participate, and that year Baden-Powell and his younger sister, Agnes, created the Girl Guides to build on the development. Scouting and Guiding was a uniformed – though deliberately non-military – movement dedicated to public service, not public disorder. 'The idea is to inculcate the spirit of good citizenship and patriotism,' approved the *Army and Navy Gazette*. 'If the tendency of drift towards hooliganism can be checked by this scholarly means, General Baden-Powell will have done good work.'[59]

Joining the Scouts was intended to provide excitement, a liberation from the drabness of the everyday. The emphasis on woodcraft also reflected the contemporary interest in pre-industrial skills, and the movement even invoked old concepts of chivalry. 'Their ideals,' said Baden-Powell, 'should be exactly the same as those of the knights of King Arthur – to serve their country, to be fearless and unselfish, to help the weak, to keep their honour absolutely unstained, and, if need be, to die in its defence.'[60] There was instruction in colonial history and geography and in citizenship, which sought to achieve reform across the social spectrum: 'To help the lowest from drifting into hooliganism and to give them health, character and aims; to teach the better class how to work well, and to be patriotic first and political second; to teach the wealthier to be chivalrous and sympathetic with their less-favoured brothers.'[61]

The need for action across the classes was also articulated by others. Because while, of course, the primary focus was on the state of working-class youth, there was a further concern that bad behaviour was spreading up the social ladder.

There was, for instance, the Slade Coster Gang, a group of students at the Slade School of Art that included C. R. W. Nevinson, Stanley Spencer, Mark Gertler, Edward Wadsworth, Maxwell

Gordon Lightfoot* and others. Dressing in the style of London costermongers – caps, corduroy waistcoats, neckerchiefs and boots – they took their recreation in drinking and fighting. They frequented the Café Royal in Piccadilly until a brawl that was bad enough for all artists to be banned from the premises; after that, they patronised the Petit Savoyard, a French restaurant on Greek Street. 'We were the terror of Soho,' Nevinson recalled later. 'Fortunately we were well known to the police, who in those days treated "college lads" with an amazing tolerance.' Among other exploits, he said, they had been 'violent participants, for the mere love of a row, at such places as the anti-vivisectionist demonstrations at the Little Brown Dog at Battersea.'[62]

The story of the Brown Dog Riots began in 1903 when two Swedish anti-vivisectionists brought to public attention the experiments performed on animals at University College London, in particular on a small brown dog that was killed after being used in a lecture demonstration. Their account, published as *The Shambles of Science* (1903), led to a libel trial and a royal commission on vivisection, though not the prosecution of the scientists involved, despite clear breaches of the Cruelty to Animals Act.

The dead dog came to symbolise the anti-vivisection movement, and in 1906 campaigners erected in Battersea a memorial fountain in red granite, surmounted by a bronze statue of the animal, accompanied by a deliberately provocative inscription: 'In Memory of the Brown Terrier Dog Done to Death in the Laboratories of University College in February 1903'. For months the statue was the site of protests, as medical students, seeking to smash it or throw it in the Thames, clashed with the police and fought with the Slade Coster Gang and others. Dozens of students were brought up in unsympathetic magistrates' courts, and protecting the memorial required

---

* Perhaps the most talented of the young artists who emerged in the Edwardian years, Lightfoot committed suicide in 1911, cutting his throat with a razor, apparently after learning that his fiancée, who he'd met when she was working as a life model, was as promiscuous as artists' models were widely reputed to be.

two policemen during the day and four at night, at an estimated cost of £700 a year – more than five times the value of the statue. In 1910, after elections to Battersea Council saw a landslide victory for the Conservative-allied Municipal Reform Party at the expense of the Progressives, the statue was quietly removed.*

The participants in the Brown Dog Riots were mostly students, the future of respectable society. Whatever explanations were offered for the behaviour of the Scuttlers, Hooligans and Peaky Blinders, they did not apply here.

Less violent, but also less excusable still, were the Hughligans, a small faction in Parliament led by Lord Hugh Cecil, described by the *Liverpool Daily Post* as 'an enthusiastic reactionary, a medi-aevalist both in politics and in theology, an aristocrat in the narrowest sense of the term'.[63] The name of his group was invented by Cecil's exasperated father, the prime minister Lord Salisbury, and was intended humorously, though the papers picked up on it as an apposite description. 'Their interruptions, their disregard for authority, and their attacks on innocent passers-by who do not see eye to eye with them on Church matters are sufficiently akin to the habits of the street Hooligan to make the joke pass even outside the family circle.'[64]

It seemed to some that violence had become endemic among the young, whatever their class. Even the pastoral idyll of Olde England was not exempt. The Berkshire village of Cookham was located on a delightful part of the Thames – 'perhaps the sweetest stretch of all the river', wrote Jerome K. Jerome in *Three Men in a Boat* (1889) – but outside the pubs in the village there were signs telling the customers 'All fighting to be over by 10 o'clock.'[65]

v

The 1902 edition of *Old Moore's Almanack* included a cartoon of imps throwing books at the heads of small boys. In case the

---

* A new Brown Dog memorial was erected on a nearby site in 1985.

message wasn't clear, a caption explained that it represented 'the irresponsible demons dealing out this trash to the greedy group of hungry readers, with the result that we have bred up our gang of youthful Jack Sheppards,* and cultivated that terrible form of ruffian, the Hooligan'.[66]

Of all the alleged causes of delinquent youth, this was perhaps the most widely voiced. 'We teach the young people to read, but not how and what to read,' argued John Ballinger of the Cardiff Free Library. 'The half-educated boy reads sensational and harmful trash or nothing, and his education is practically wasted.'[67] The target of such complaints was spelled out in 1905 by former Royal Navy doctor W. Gordon Stables, a man whose improving books included Jules Verne-inspired novels such as *From Pole to Pole* (1886); he called for penny dreadfuls to be banned, because they 'help to fill our gaols and increase the great army of hooligans and burglars'.[68]

In fact, the penny dreadfuls – cheap serial magazines filled with lurid tales of highwaymen, murderers and thieves, which had dominated boys' reading for generations – were already in retreat, struggling against a counter-offensive led by the *Boy's Own Paper*, for which Stables himself wrote. Launched in 1879 by the Religious Tract Society, the *BOP* followed the Salvation Army's example by engaging the enemy on his own ground. It offered a nutritious alternative to the unhealthy dreadfuls, and inspired a slew of papers with inspiring material to stiffen the sinews of the younger generation: the *Union Jack* (launched 1880), *Chums* (1892), *Pluck* (1894), *The Boys' Friend* (1895), *British Boys* (1897), *The Captain* (1899), *The Boys' Realm* (1902), *The Boys' Herald* (1903), *The Gem* (1907), *Vanguard* (1907), *The Magnet* (1908), *The Dreadnought* (1912),

---

* The thief Jack Sheppard was one of Britain's greatest popular heroes, famed for his escapes from prison. When he was hanged in 1724, at the age of twenty-two, around 200,000 people, a third of London's population, turned out to witness his execution. He inspired novels, plays and penny dreadfuls, as well as the character Macheath in John Gay's *The Beggar's Opera* (1728).

The Popular (1912).* Mostly, these were story-papers with tales that, said *Every Boy's Favorite* [*sic*] *Journal* (1892), were morally uplifting: 'right will triumph over might, virtue and innocence will be triumphant in the end'.[69] As *The Halfpenny Marvel* (1893) proclaimed, 'No more penny dreadfuls! These healthy stories of mystery adventure etc will kill them.'[70]

They said they were for boys, but the advertising inside these papers suggested a broader age range than that; a typical copy of *The Boys' Friend* from 1910 included adverts for a gramophone and a suit, as well as for air rifles, spring-grip dumb-bells – as endorsed by music-hall strongman Eugen Sandow – and a treatment that 'positively guaranteed' you would grow a moustache.[71] Similarly, the readership spanned classes, despite the fact that the world depicted was alien to many; an editorial recommending the virtues of cold baths urged, 'Do not make more splash than you can help so as to give the servant trouble.'[72]

The older titles liked to address a wide spectrum of acceptable hobbies and enthusiasms. 'Badges, caps and colours of our first-class cricket clubs are represented in the coloured plate which forms the frontispiece,' ran a description of a 1906 edition of the *Boy's Own Paper*. 'Anglers, stamp-collectors, cricketers, footballers and lovers of other hobbies are all well catered for.'[73] That was fine up to a point, but it was the fiction that really mattered: tale after tale of plucky lads standing up to school bullies, of boy detectives battling criminal masterminds, of cowboys and sailors, intrepid explorers and strangely gifted eccentrics.

This was an outpouring of words so vast that individual stories were lost in the torrent, leaving the image of a world of excitement, adventure and derring-do, glorious escapism intended to lift a youth from the mundanity of the real world. 'This was to be his life until his days should end. No adventures, no glory, no change, no

---

* The *Girls' Own Paper*, a sister title to the *BOP*, was successful when launched in 1880, but the first story paper aimed exclusively at girls, *School Friend*, did not appear until 1919. The boys' story papers were widely read by girls.

freedom,' mourns Artie Kipps in the days before he comes into his fortune, so he seeks refuge in daydreams, 'his mind far away, fighting the enemies of the Empire'. Ernest Bramah described a typical London street where 'a grocer's errand boy, with basket resourcefully inverted upon his head, had sunk down by the railings to sip the nectar from a few more pages of *Iroquois Ike's Last Hope; or, The Phantom Cow-Puncher's Bride*'.[74]

Such work was still disapproved of in some quarters, and sometimes the line between fantasy and reality was blurred. In 1906 eleven-year-old Frank Burke stole thirty shillings from a neighbour in Bury and was found some days later in Blackpool with just eightpence left, having spent the rest on 'a watch, mouth organ, jacket, vest, belt, collar, sweets &c. and in boating and paying for his lodgings'. When asked why he'd done such a thing, he said he'd been 'reading penny books about Jack, Sam and Pete' and wanted to have the kind of high-spirited fun he'd read about. He apologised for his behaviour and was bound over for six months. 'And you will not read these silly, rubbishy story books?' asked the magistrate. 'No, sir,' he replied, contrite if not wholly truthful.[75]

Jack, Sam and Pete were creations of S. Clarke Hood, first appearing in Alfred Harmsworth's *Marvel* in 1904 – and it wasn't just stuffy old magistrates who objected to them. When the Young Socialist League* launched a paper called the *Young Worker* in 1910, the comrades were clear where the opposition lay. 'Jack, Sam and Pete and Buffalo Bill may be all right for amusement's sake,' said the league. 'They won't develop intellect. They won't make responsible citizens. They will neither encourage the type of mind fit to advocate the glorious ideals of Socialism, nor to enjoy the pleasures of life which Socialism would place within the reach of all.'[76]

That was possibly true, but nonetheless there was a moral

---

* Not to be confused with the Socialist League (which disbanded in 1901 following an anarchist takeover), the Young Socialist League was affiliated to the British Socialist Party.

message in the papers that was more progressive than critics acknowledged. It could be seen most clearly in the work of the most popular boys' writer, Charles Hamilton. Born in Ealing in 1876, the son of a carpenter who also wrote for that self-proclaimed 'anti-Christian organ' *The Freethinker*, Hamilton specialised in tales of public schools. He wrote stories about St Jim's, published in the *Gem* under the pen name Martin Clifford, and about Greyfriars, as Frank Richards in the *Magnet* – two 20,000-word tales each week.*

The best-known of Hamilton's creations was the lower fourth form at Greyfriars, with a cast that included Billy Bunter, overweight, obsessed with food and perpetually penniless. He was the class clown, while its greatest hero was Harry Wharton, a thoroughly decent fifteen-year-old, easily riled, overly proud, yet a natural leader of boys. Arriving a few episodes into the saga was Hurree Jamset Ram Singh, an Indian prince swiftly nicknamed Inky. Some resented his presence at first. 'You confounded nigger!' snarls the bully George Bulstrode, and although the racial epithet is corrected, Singh himself objects to the underlying assumption: 'I have a great respect for negroes, as much esteemfulness as I have for other persons.' When Bulstrode attacks him, he shows that he's capable of looking after himself, physically throwing the bully out of the room. 'I hope you will forgive me for creating the disturbfulness in the sacred apartment of a study,' he says to the others. 'If I have exasperated you, the apologise is very great.'[77]

Singh became a firm favourite with readers, and his language remained that same heavy-handed parody of an Indian voice, complete with mangled metaphors and sayings ('The proof of the pudding is in the boiling'). 'Foreigners are funny,' shrugged Hamilton. 'They lack the sense of humour which is the special gift of our own chosen nation: and people without a sense of humour are

---

* Even that was not the full extent of Hamilton's output, and he went on to become the world's most prolific author, with estimates of his output going up to 100 million words under a couple of dozen pen names.

always unconsciously funny.'[78] Nonetheless, the intention was to break down prejudices.[79] 'I liked the idea of making a coloured boy a friend on equal terms with the other boys,' he said.*

In any event, comic speech-patterns were not reserved for foreigners. There was also the Honourable Arthur Augustus D'Arcy, the monocle-wearing, top-hat-sporting Swell of St Jim's, commonly known as Gussy. 'Bai – bai Jove,' he would exclaim. 'I – I felt wathah queer about the thwoat, deah boys.'[80] For someone so posh, he's a bit of a liberal. At one point he declares himself in favour of votes for women, on the grounds that it would be 'wude to wefuse the deah cweatures anythin' they want,'[81] and when a Jewish boy faces discrimination, he'll have none of it: 'I wegard wace pwejudice as a widiculous thing.'[82] Harry Wharton says the same to an American boy who comes to Greyfriars: 'We don't share your ridiculous prejudice against coloured people.'[83]

Indeed, America generally is seen as an example to be avoided. In 1909 the boys from St Jim's visit the States, where they are singularly unimpressed by the business practices of 'the Chicago meat-king' Hiriam K. Potts. 'Imagine every man employed!' says Potts, outraged by the suggestion. 'We could only get extra labour by paying high wages. Why, if every man were certain of employment, the employers would be at their mercy.' The boys also befriend a hotel pageboy and are shocked to discover that, being black, he's not allowed to travel in the same railway carriage as them. 'It was forty years and more since the great Civil War had abolished slavery in the United States, but the line of cleavage between black and white was as strongly marked as ever.'[84]

vi

One of the standard books given to boys as a Sunday school prize was Frank Mundell's *Stories of the Victoria Cross*. In the revised

---

* Pete, in the Jack, Sam and Pete stories, is a black American who also speaks in an exaggerated accent and has a similarly trenchant response to racial provocation.

edition, published in the summer of 1900 while the Boer War was still in progress, Mundell noted that nearly forty Victoria Crosses had already been awarded in the conflict, and questions were being asked in Parliament about whether this was not too profligate. Were all these VCs justified? After all, wrote Mundell, 'it has been contended that for a man to rescue a wounded comrade left on the field, even though he does so under a deadly rain of bullets, is nothing more than is to be expected of the average Briton'.[85]

The important bit here, and throughout British culture of the period, was the mention of a wounded comrade. The popular song 'When We Were Two Little Boys'* told the story of two friends whose childhood games are replicated later in life on the battlefield, one rescuing the other from certain death. This was the central lesson being taught to boys in the story magazines and in Sunday schools: beyond even patriotism or piousness, there was loyalty to one's chums. Male friendship was the greatest social bond, the constancy of comrades the greatest virtue. In this vision the Empire was seen as a massive, dense network of pals, an essentially human endeavour.

Just as important, though, these were not things to be spoken of, far less flaunted. The fellowship between boys was, as Rudyard Kipling wrote elsewhere of the Union flag, 'a matter shut up, sacred and apart'.[86] In A. E. W. Mason's *The Four Feathers* (1902) Harry Feversham has a comrade in Jack Durrance. 'The friendship between these two men was not one in which affectionate phrases had any part,' we're told early on. 'Both men were securely conscious of it; they estimated it at its true, strong value; it was a helpful instrument, which would not wear out, put into their

---

* Originally an American song, written by Edward Madden and Theodore F. Morse, this was inspired by an incident in the Boer War. It was widely heard in British music halls, sung by both women – Bell Campbell at the Hippodrome, London in 1906 – and by men: Harry Lewis at the Panopticon, Cardiff in 1908. Most famously, it was to be performed by Rolf Harris under the abbreviated title 'Two Little Boys', spending six weeks at number one in the British singles chart in 1969–70.

hands for a hard, lifelong use; but it was not, and never had been, spoken of between them.' Yet this bond is broken when Harry is believed to have acted dishonourably. As Durrance sails for Egypt, he thinks he sees Harry's face in the quayside crowd: 'a haggard, wistful face – a face stamped with an extraordinary misery; the face of a man cast out from among his fellows'. More than nine tenths of the tale remain, yet the two men never meet again.

The inability to articulate emotion was increasingly seen as a failing. John Buchan's *The Half-Hearted* (1900) turns on the hero losing the woman he loves because he cannot tell her how he feels. In despair, he seeks an overseas posting in order to sacrifice himself to duty, and when his best friend, a government minister, entrusts him with a dangerous mission, he's so grateful that he blurts out, 'God bless you, Tommy. I don't deserve to have a man like you troubling himself about me.' But that's all there is. 'It was his one spoken tribute to their friendship; and both, with the nervousness of honest men in the presence of emotion, hastened to change the subject.'

There's an underlying code of honour and behaviour common to both novels, but also a sense of that code being no longer sufficient, an awareness that the buttoned-up ideal of the High Victorian era is lacking in both imagination and humanity.

The emotional silence between friends is seen also between parent and child. Parental neglect is a recurring theme in the fiction of the period, particularly in the work of female novelists; Marie Corelli's *Boy* is a prime example. A more extreme case, Frances Hodgson Burnett's *The Secret Garden* (1911), opens with a ten-year-old British girl, Mary Lennox, being orphaned when both parents die in a cholera epidemic in India. When someone finally notices that she's still alive, they discover that she's not much upset to learn of her loss: 'Mary had liked to look at her mother from a distance, and she had thought her very pretty, but as she knew very little of her she could scarcely have been expected to love her or to miss her very much.'

Even where there is affection between mother and child, its

physical expression is absent. In Frank Danby's *An Incompleat Etonian* (1909)* Vanessa and her son Sebastian are close but display no overt affection. The one exception comes when she rests her hand on his arm and makes him acutely uncomfortable: 'He was embarrassed by her half caress, by the hand on his arm, the intimacy between them had been reached without demonstration.'

Children's lives were poisoned and those of parents were impoverished. John Galsworthy's novel *The Man of Property* (1906)† was set in 1886, and presented a desperately bleak image of the old Victorian order, stripped of all moral authority. Jolyon Forsyte is estranged from his only son and is tortured by the realisation of how hollow his life has become. 'In his great chair with the book-rest sat old Jolyon, the figurehead of his family and class and creed, with his white head and dome-like forehead, the representative of moderation, and order, and love of property. As lonely an old man as there was in London.'

---

* Danby was the pen name of Julia Frankau.
† There was no indication at the time that this was the first volume of a trilogy, the Forsyte Saga. The second book did not appear until 1920.

6

LIBERALS AND LABOUR

Minks hung upon the fringe of that very modern, new-fashioned, but almost freakish army that worships old, old ideals, yet insists upon new-fangled names for them. Christ, doubtless, was his model, but it must be a Christ properly and freshly labelled; his Christianity must somewhere include the prefix 'neo', and the word 'scientific' must also be dragged in if possible before he was satisfied.

Algernon Blackwood, *A Prisoner in Fairyland*, 1913[1]

The Liberal mind is a sour, dour, superior affair, full of kinks and ill-disposed to mankind as a whole.

Lord Alfred Douglas, 1908[2]

"PUT IT THERE."

Caricature of David Lloyd George (1863–1945), chancellor of the
exchequer, demanding money at the time of the People's Budget in 1909.

CHARLES DAVIS WAS A THIRTY-ONE-YEAR-OLD unemployed decorator, 'a clean-shaven, intelligent-looking young man, with curly brown hair', wearing a shabby overcoat and trilby hat.[3] He didn't look like a violent anarchist. Yet when he approached William Smith in Clerkenwell Library, London, in January 1905, that was what he declared himself to be. Smith was organising a demonstration against unemployment, and Davis was keen to do his bit. 'I have a thousand men ready with grenades, pistols and dynamite,' he confided. Smith didn't want to get involved. 'I must be off,' he replied, collecting up his papers. 'I'll see you later, but we must not think of taking blood.'

Davis turned up at the protest, but he was accompanied by just twenty men, and there was no sign of the promised arsenal. Even so, Smith refused to let him speak, and Davis slunk off, returning forty-five minutes later when the crowd was beginning to disperse. There were around 150 people left as Davis launched into a diatribe against the monarchy. 'I want to remove this king, who is pleased to see you starve, from the throne and set up a republican government,' he urged. 'There is enough food thrown into the furnaces at Buckingham Palace every day to feed a thousand families.'

Davis was arrested and charged with using language that might have caused a breach of the peace, though the abuse he received from the crowd suggested that the danger was to no one but himself. In court it turned out that he had previous convictions: fined five pounds for a speech in Hyde Park on one occasion, jailed on another. His behaviour during the trial didn't help his cause; he wept, shouted and demanded to be allowed to cross-examine the police officers giving evidence. 'I don't mind doing time if there's any time to be done, but I want justice!' He did concede that he could be excitable, but he denied using violent language. 'At least, if I did, I am sorry.' He didn't wish to be disrespectful to the king, but if the monarch couldn't help his people, then it was time for a republic.

This focus on the king baffled the court. The prosecuting

counsel wondered whether Davis was of sound mind. After all, 'there was no man in the kingdom who more deeply sympathised with the poor than His Majesty, and there was no one who spent more money upon them'. Anyone who couldn't see that must surely be disturbed. 'Have you ever been in an asylum?' asked the magistrate, more concerned than condemnatory. 'No,' Davis replied, 'but I have a bump on the side of my head which presses on my brain.' He was bound over to be on good behaviour for six months.

The Clerkenwell demonstration was a minor affair, but it was typical of many local protests across the country in 1905. There were also much larger gatherings in London, Glasgow and Manchester, the latter attacked by the police in a way that opened old wounds. 'The spirit of the Peterloo massacre is again upon the authorities,' said Labour MP Keir Hardie. 'As our fathers won then, we shall win now, if only we have their pluck.'[4]

Times were getting hard and there was a growing tone of disquiet. Although some parts of industry were faring well – some ninety-five new mills were opened in Lancashire between 1905 and 1907, increasing spinning capacity by more than a fifth[5] – the economy overall was stagnating. Unemployment had been rising steadily, hitting a peak in 1904 of 9.6 per cent,[6] and although it had then started to fall, there was a serious squeeze on living standards, the loss of jobs pushing working-class wages down just as food prices were going up. In the music halls the likes of Gus Elen were looking ironically on the bright side – 'If you can't get work, you can't get the sack'[7] – but on the streets the mood was less cheerful.

Certainly the authorities were not inclined to laugh. January 1905, the month that Charles Davis preached armed insurrection in Clerkenwell, also saw Bloody Sunday in Russia, when troops opened fire on demonstrators in St Petersburg, killing and wounding hundreds, and sparking an uprising that took two years to crush.

Could such a thing happen in Britain? Probably not, but excitable talk of anarchism and republicanism suddenly looked a little less risible. And there were some incidents that might have proved risky for the royal family, had they gone further. In 1904 the king had helped fund the Labour Tents, an initiative by the Church Army in London that provided food and work for the unemployed; but when the project was repeated the following year, its official opening was disrupted by protestors. 'Banners were carried and a band played the Marseillaise, the demonstrators singing the chorus,' it was reported. 'Each arrival who occupied a carriage was loudly booed and some of the demonstrators shouted "hypocritical religionists", "we don't want charity, but demand work", and similar ejaculations.'[8] The guest of honour was Princess Louise, the king's oldest daughter, and she and her husband 'came in for their share of the hooting'.[9]

On other occasions even the king himself faced protests. When he visited Brighton in 1908, he was met by a group of some fifty local men, 'carrying the usual banners and signs, one of which bore the inscription "Shall Brighton starve?"'[10] The ringleader, thirty-year-old Arthur Hardy, was charged with obstructing the police and remanded for eight days.

It wasn't quite the same as being exiled to Siberia, though. Britain still wasn't Russia, and there never was a great deal of republicanism in evidence. The crowd which had booed Charles Davis was more typical of the country than he was, and even he wasn't really calling for a revolution. Rather his words suggested a desperate wish for the monarch to protect his people in the traditionally approved manner; he wanted intervention not insurrection. The same spirit could be seen in 1908 when plans were made to present a petition on unemployment to the king as he made his way to the opening ceremony of the Olympic Games. Unfortunately, the British weather ruined the occasion; over an inch of rain fell in a torrential ten-hour downpour, and the demonstration was called off.

ii

Those slogans in Hyde Park denouncing charity indicated a decisive departure from Victorian values. Alongside the great legislative changes of the nineteenth century – the abolition of slavery, the

Factories Acts improving the conditions of industrial employment, the Cruelty to Animals Acts and so on – Christian reformers had also established charity as an integral part of society, creating institutions that were intended to be not only transformative but enduring. Some did become entrenched, even if for every YMCA or RSPCA there were a hundred smaller ventures that withered on the vine, many of them the kind of group that Wilkie Collins had decades before satirised as the Mothers'-Small-Clothes-Conversion-Society.[11] And charities remained hugely important; £8.6 million was spent by them in 1913, a rise of a quarter in real terms since the start of the century.

But as all the sociological studies of poverty showed, despite the decades of charitable work there were structural problems in society that demanded a more comprehensive approach, a governmental approach. The realisation of that demand fell to the Liberal government elected in the landslide victory of 1906.

It proved to be one of the most significant governments of all, though few observers had any such expectations at the outset. The new prime minister, Henry Campbell-Bannerman, was not one of the great showmen of British politics. When he became Liberal leader in 1899, *The Times* quoted a group of militant young Liberals predicting that 'he will turn out to be a warming-pan from which neither light nor heat can be expected.' The paper added, a little grudgingly, 'Nevertheless, a warming pan has its uses.'[12] One could say that there are times when a warming-pan prime minister is precisely what the nation needs, supplying calm reassurance at a time of radical change. And the Liberal government was truly radical.

Some of the early work was clearing up outstanding business. The promises from the Boer War were honoured, with the Transvaal and the Orange Free State becoming self-governing colonies.* Similarly, the Trade Disputes Act 1906 ensured that a union could not be sued for damages as a result of a strike, reversing a previous

---

* In 1910, still under the Liberal government, the Union of South Africa was created, bringing together Cape, Natal, Orange River and Transvaal, with dominion status.

House of Lords ruling in the Taff Vale case that had set back the union movement. The intention, said Campbell-Bannerman, was 'to place the two rival powers of Capital and Labour on an equality so that a fight between them, so far as fight is necessary, should be at least a fair fight'.[13] And then there was the question of pensions. Joseph Chamberlain's idea of funding a scheme through tariff reform had failed at the polls, but pensions were high on the agenda of the new government.

By the time a new proposal came before Parliament, however, there had been a change in prime minister. Campbell-Bannerman had a third heart attack in late 1907, and a fourth in February 1908. He resigned the following month, and died three weeks later in Downing Street, having been too ill to move. His last reported words were 'This is not the end of me.'[14]

His replacement was H. H. Asquith, the chancellor of the exchequer. Born in 1852 into a Nonconformist middle-class family in Yorkshire, he had enjoyed a spectacular rise in Liberal politics, appointed home secretary at the age of just thirty-nine by William Gladstone. He was a respected barrister, a good speaker and a politician of considerable intelligence and ability. He also had a fondness for heavy drinking, hence his private nickname Squiff. He'd played his part in the divisions over the Boer War – he'd been one of the leading Liberal Imperialists – but with that dispute having passed, he emerged as a unifying figure, spanning both the party's Gladstonian heritage and its new incarnation. He combined 'social reform and sound finance', enthused the Liberal press; he could be 'an austere type of statesman', but also one with 'the glow and enthusiasm of a great purpose'.[15]

Asquith had already written his budget by the time he became prime minister, and so he presented it himself to the Commons. The key measure was to separate the tax levied on earned and unearned income, and to increase the latter, providing the funds to launch the first national pensions.* These were not overly generous;

---

* State pensions for those in the police, military and civil service already existed.

to qualify for the weekly payment of five shillings – seven shillings and sixpence for a married couple – a person needed to be aged over seventy, to have an annual income of under thirty-one pounds,* to not be in receipt of poor relief, and to have not been in prison in the last ten years.

There were complaints from both sides – those who wanted more and those who wanted none of it. The Trades Union Congress and the Labour Party called for universal pensions at sixty. 'In the agricultural districts seventy years of age will get some people, but in the bulk of the mining and industrial centres it is a mockery of the aged poor,' said Keir Hardie. 'Surely they are entitled to better things.'[16] There were flaws too in the implementation: some eligible for a pension were still working, and found their employers docking their pay. Winston Churchill, now in cabinet as a Liberal, accepted that the provisions were modest: 'We have not pretended to carry the toiler on to dry land; what we have done is to strap a lifebelt around him.'[17]

Meanwhile, there was concern about the bond between master and servant, worry that pensions might spell the end of the loyal old family retainer. John Willis-Bund, formerly law professor at King's College London and now chairman of Worcestershire County Council, predicted that pensions would do immense harm to the country, making 'a large number of persons dependent upon the nation who would never have asked for sixpence in any form, and who would have been maintained by their friends'.[18] And in a similar vein, Lord Lansdowne, foreign secretary during the Boer War, argued that that conflict had been a better investment by the nation, because it had raised 'the moral fibre of the country', whereas pensions would make people less independent.[19] Robert Baden-Powell wasn't convinced either: 'Free feeding and old-age pensions, strike pay, cheap beer and indiscriminate charity

---

* The amount of the benefit was tapered. To get the full five shillings required an income of below twenty-one pounds a year (i.e. ten shillings a week). The large majority of pensioners fell into this category.

do not make for the hardening of the nation or the building up of a self-reliant, energetic manhood. They tend, on the contrary, to produce an army of dependents and wasters.'[20]

Steering a middle course ran the risk of looking like timidity, but Asquith's pension established a key principle, extending the responsibility of the state to provide assistance from the destitute to the poor. It was a decisive moment in the shift away from charity, using current taxation to redistribute wealth on a hitherto unachievable scale: that £8.6 million spent by charity in 1913 was dwarfed by the £12 million paid in pensions the same year. A decisive moment too for the Liberals, no longer the party of laissez-faire economics. Partly from conviction and partly from fear of being outflanked by the growing Labour movement, they had accepted the need for collective state action. The Conservative and Unionist opposition, meanwhile, were wrongfooted. They'd promised pensions and failed to deliver, and now they looked behind the times, still culturally wedded to charity. The fear of sliding into irrelevance was clear when Arthur Balfour felt it necessary to deny that a future Tory government would repeal pensions.

Pensions were first paid on 1 January 1909,* with an estimated £100,000 passing across post-office counters on that day. The significance of the moment was recognised at the time, and the reform was greeted with joy unconfined.[21] According to a postmistress in the East End of London, 'Many of the old women kissed the money,' and one woman didn't even get that far; she fell to her knees at the doorway of the post office and cried out, 'Thank God, thank God, I have lived to see this day.' A policeman helped her back to her feet: 'Come on, mother, you're keeping the rest waiting.'

On White Horse Hill in Wiltshire a giant bonfire was lit to mark the occasion; the town band paraded the streets of Braintree, Essex, playing 'Hail, Smiling Morn'; and there was a civic reception

---

* In Scotland, where New Year's Day was a bank holiday, the first payments were made on 2 January.

in the Drill Hall, Lincoln, for 450 pensioners and guests (the fare included 'ham and tongue, beef, potted beef, white, brown and plum bread and butter, pastry, cakes and jellies'). Many local Liberal Party branches also held celebratory teas for pensioners, reasonably hoping to reap a political reward, and in Tiverton, Devon, the town crier walked the streets reminding people that the local Tory MP, William Walrond, had voted against pensions. Not everyone was suitably grateful, though; a man in Poplar, east London, collected his money and then delivered a verse for the benefit of the press:

> Here's health to Lloyd-George, may his tribe increase,*
> For giving us pensions of five bob apiece.
> But may his lot go, for if we want more,
> We must all look forward to Arthur Balfour.

Altogether, some half a million people benefited from the new system, the majority of them women, and there were some striking variations. In particular, generations of youthful emigration meant that Ireland had 9 per cent of the UK population but 30 per cent of the pensioners. So while only around 1 per cent of Londoners were eligible, in County Fermanagh one in fifteen residents received support. It amounted to a form of regional assistance, providing a boost to local economies; shopkeepers in Enniskillen said it was as if 'the government had started a small factory in the town', and that first pension day saw a boom in public-house trade. In Kingstown, County Dublin,† there was a special delivery, 'a dozen huge wagons laden with Guinness XX'.

There were happy news stories everywhere. A recently married couple in Yarmouth announced that they'd be spending their first week's pension on a honeymoon in Lowestoft. In Glasgow a seventy-three-year-old woman was accompanied by her mother,

---

* David Lloyd George had taken over from Asquith as chancellor of the exchequer.
† Formerly Dunleary, and renamed Dún Laoghaire in 1920.

aged 104, both of them beneficiaries. The first recipient in Kilburn, west London, was seventy-seven-year-old George Hibbard, a veteran of the Crimean War, proudly wearing his medals, while ninety-one-year-old Ed Kemp of Lincoln, formerly of the 1st Life Guards, talked of how he'd been on duty for Victoria's coronation. And as Rebecca Clark of Wood Green, north London, walked briskly to her local post office, her energy belying her 104 years, she shared memories of her brothers going off to fight Napoleon.

Some did particularly well: some post offices paid out in crown pieces, which the enterprising sold on to collectors at a premium. And then there were those who didn't quite make it. There were widespread reports – including from Bishop's Stortford, Blackburn, Glasgow, Horncastle, Kilkenny, Leeds, Maidenhead, Sandwich and Spalding – of pensioners dying just before they were able to claim their money; in some cases it was believed that 'death was due to heart disease, accelerated by the excitement of the occasion'.

Above all, pensions alleviated fear of the workhouse, the shadow of which had long lain heavy in the homes of the poor. Albert Chevalier's best-known song was 'My Old Dutch' (1892), a delicate, maudlin declaration of mature love:

We've been together now for forty years,
An' it don't seem a day too much,
Oh, there ain't a lady livin' in the land
As I'd swop for my dear old Dutch.*

The pathos of his performance was emphasised by the backdrop, which showed the two entrances to a workhouse, one for men and one for women. In a final, cruel blow, this long-loving couple are to be split up – for workhouse accommodation was sex-segregated – and the man prays that 'death may come and take me'.

Now, said a seventy-four-year-old man in Manchester, that shadow had been lifted: 'I have never been in the workhouse, but

---

* Dutch is rhyming slang, short for Duchess of Fife = wife.

saw it in front of me. Thanks to the pension, I can manage to live and my son will give me a shake-down. It's a real godsend.' Harry Hewkin of Nuneaton was moved to verse:

> God bless Lloyd George, and Asquith, too,
> And all who gladly did their parts;
> Here's life and health to all of you,
> For lifting loads from aged hearts.
> Why, laddie, I feel younger, years
> Now, workhouse dreads gone from my mind,
> It's driven right away my fears.
> I never thought folks were so kind.

iii

The praise for David Lloyd George was a little misplaced; pensions had been Asquith's initiative. Beyond him, progress had been driven by sociologists and economists – the likes of Charles Booth, Benjamin Seebohm Rowntree and Beatrice Webb – as well as by the example of Germany, where Otto von Bismarck had introduced pensions in 1889, part of a package of social reforms that were the most advanced in the world.

Nonetheless, the error was understandable. By the time pensions came in, Lloyd George had a higher public profile than any of his colleagues, and as the chancellor he was seen as the key figure in the new creed of social liberalism. His closest ally was Winston Churchill, who when he became president of the board of trade in 1908 was the youngest cabinet minister for over four decades. 'His future is the most interesting problem of personal speculation in English politics,' wrote journalist A. G. Gardiner. 'At thirty-four he stands before the country one of the two most arresting figures in politics.'[22] Between them, Lloyd George and Churchill made a formidable team, the country's best orators committed to selling radical reform.

The defining moment came in April 1909, when Lloyd George

delivered his first budget. There were two big items of expenditure that needed to be funded. First, there was the cost of building dreadnought-class battleships for the Royal Navy; the government was committed to the construction of twelve such ships over the next two years. Second, there was the extension of welfare measures, with the creation of labour exchanges and the proposed introduction of National Insurance; building on the pension scheme, this would add further to the duties of an increasingly interventionist state.

In his four-and-a-half-hour budget speech Lloyd George outlined how he intended to raise the money. There was to be a new, lower rate of income tax, while the standard rate would be increased, and an additional supertax introduced for earnings over £5,000. Offsetting this, there was the innovation of a tax allowance of ten pounds per child, but only for those earning less than £500 – the middle classes. Duties were increased on beer, spirits, tobacco and cars, together with the first petrol tax; at threepence a gallon, it put the price up to around one shilling and fivepence.* And there were new charges on property ownership, most notably a land value tax – essentially a capital gains tax on the sale of land – set at 20 per cent. The combined effect of all the measures was to increase estimated government revenues by nearly 10 per cent in the coming year, and then still further in following years.

It was seen by many as class war. *Punch* caricatured the chancellor as the Giant in *Jack and the Beanstalk*, wielding a cudgel labelled 'Budget':

> Fee, fi, fo, fat,
> I smell the blood of a plutocrat;
> Be he alive or be he dead,

---

* For consumers, the headline figures didn't always reflect reality. The duty on whisky increased, for example, and the distillers responded by putting up the price by a penny a glass. This raised 5s 4d a gallon, of which just 3s 9d went to the Treasury; the other 1s 7d was an agreeable profit.

I'll grind his bones to make my bread.[23]

Lloyd George didn't shy away from the charge. 'This is a War Budget,' he declared. 'It is for raising money to wage implacable warfare against poverty and squalidness.'[24] His epithet didn't catch on, but there were plenty of alternatives for a speech that split the nation – and the press. The *Daily Telegraph* called it the Penal Budget and the *Daily Express* the Red Flag Budget, while the *Daily Chronicle* went with the Democratic Budget and the *Daily Mirror* the Poor Man's Budget. It was the *Daily News* that came up with the phrase that stuck: this was a People's Budget.[25]

The most controversial element was those land taxes, since these would hit estate owners and large landlords hardest, including many members of the House of Lords. And that was where the first battle in Lloyd George's war was destined to be fought.

The Upper House was overwhelmingly Conservative, and it had come into conflict with a Liberal government before, most memorably in 1893 when it rejected Gladstone's second attempt at a Home Rule Bill for Ireland. But such opposition had been relatively rare, a power used sparingly. Now, over the course of the current government, it became almost commonplace. A series of measures – including bills on religious education in state schools, on the licensing of public houses and on removing plural voting – passed the Commons only to be voted down by the Lords. What was once a tactic of last resort had become wilful obstructionism.

This could only be seen as a sign of Tory weakness. The 1906 election had been catastrophic for the Conservative and Liberal Unionists, and there were now just 156 MPs remaining.* Most of them were supporters of Chamberlain, but with his departure from the political stage and with Arthur Balfour still as leader,

---

* Despite the joint billing, the Liberal Unionists were down to no more than a couple of dozen MPs by this stage, and in many parts of the country were indistinguishable from the local Conservatives. The party formally dissolved itself into the Conservative and Unionist Party in 1912.

there was no clear sense of direction. Balfour's return to Parliament, following a by-election, saw him put firmly in his place by Campbell-Bannerman; the new prime minister responded to his predecessor's first speech with a withering assault: 'Enough of this tomfoolery. It might have answered very well in the last Parliament but it is altogether out of place in this.'[26] With no real opposition to the Liberals likely in the Commons, the Tory peers took it upon themselves to fight the good fight. 'Balfour's poodle,' was Lloyd George's contemptuous comment on the House of Lords.

The spoiling tactics of the peers set them against the democratic spirit of the times. 'Is the general election result to go for nothing?' demanded Campbell-Bannerman. 'The present House of Commons was not elected to pass only such bills as commend themselves to the House of Lords.'[27] Lloyd George asked what the point was of the party winning elections 'if the work of Liberalism is to be frustrated by a House which is chosen by nobody, which is representative of nobody and which is accountable to nobody'. The nature of democracy was at stake, he said. 'The whole question resolves itself into this: Do the British people think they are ready for self-government?'[28] And, he might have added, did the Conservative Party think the British people were ready for self-government?

Given what had already been rejected, the People's Budget was inevitably going to lead to a battle with the Upper House. And Lloyd George ensured that it did, gambling that the time had come for a showdown. The land taxes were a minor element of his fiscal plans, estimated to raise just £500,000 (less than a third of the increase on spirits alone), but the chancellor made great play of them, intending to draw a dividing line. The philosopher Bertrand Russell, a member of the Liberal Party, understood the point: 'The excellence of such taxation is to be measured by the hostility it arouses in landlords.'[29] In speeches that summer and autumn Lloyd George ramped up the class-war rhetoric, making the proposals sound more radical than they actually were, with the intention of provoking the peers into open battle. 'Who made 10,000 people owners of the soil and the rest of us trespassers in the land of our birth?' he demanded. He also taunted their lordships themselves, joking that 'A fully equipped duke cost as much to keep up as a couple of Dreadnoughts'.[30]

It was intended to be inflammatory, the peers were duly inflamed, and conservative newspapers lost all sense of proportion. The chancellor was worse than the Jacobins, said the *Scotsman*; his budget was 'the beginning of a socialistic revolution', according to the *London Evening Standard*; he was resolved 'to introduce communism into this country', shuddered the *Western Morning News*.[31] Above all, he was un-British. 'He and his chief colleagues have no real stake in the country,' concluded the *Referee*. 'They are reckless of its future, careless of its permanent interests. They are intent on notoriety and power, and they appeal to the hungry and the unemployed not to change the constitution, but to destroy civilisation.'[32]

On 30 November 1909, the House of Lords rejected the budget, the first time in two centuries it had thrown out a finance bill. This was now a fully fledged constitutional crisis, and the consequence was known in advance: if the budget wasn't passed, Asquith would call a general election to get a specific mandate for the measures. And so, on 2 December Asquith rose to move 'That the action of the House of Lords in refusing to pass into law the financial provision made by this House for the Service of the year is a breach of the Constitution and a usurpation of the rights of the Commons.' The debate on the dissolution was brief. Balfour replied, as did Arthur Henderson, leader of the Labour Party, and then, implausibly, the last word in this historic Parliament went to Liberal maverick and fraudster Horatio Bottomley. He made an inconsequential speech that called for an elected Upper House and ended with a sideswipe at the temperance campaign.*

The results of the January 1910 election were not all that

---

* He should perhaps have taken the opportunity to remind Parliament of his earlier proposal to fund pensions by taxing peerages.

Asquith would have wanted. The Liberals shed over a hundred seats, the Conservatives and Unionists gained around the same, and the parties came out neck and neck: 274 Liberal MPs, 272 Unionists. The Labour Party won 40 seats, and the balance of power lay with the 71 members of the Irish Parliamentary Party, led by John Redmond. Despite the hung parliament, however, there was no doubt about the constitutional outcome: the People's Budget was supported by the Irish and by Labour, and the Lords had to concede. On 29 April 1910, a year to the day since Lloyd George's speech, the budget passed the Upper House.

The way having now been cleared, the National Insurance scheme that had been promised could be implemented. This introduced to Britain the principle of contributory benefits; workers earning less than £160 a year would pay fourpence a week, with their employers paying threepence and the government adding twopence. People were getting ninepence worth of health insurance for just fourpence, said Lloyd George, providing cover for loss of wages when sick. An additional, smaller-scale scheme added insurance against unemployment, with a similar tripartite system of contributions from worker, employer and state. There was also a one-off maternity payment of thirty shillings, available to women whether they were married or not, a symbolic move away from Victorian morality that didn't go unnoticed: 'The Bible says the wages of sin is death,' observed a shepherd in Ettrick, 'and the Act says thirty shillin's.'[33]

But then, just a week after the People's Budget finally passed, King Edward VII died. Although not as traumatic as the death of Victoria, it was still a loss. Edward had been a popular monarch, seen as embodying the good spirit of the nation. 'His qualities were in almost every sense the typical qualities of the average Englishman,' judged the socialist weekly *New Age*. 'No man among his subjects was ever indeed more typically English.'[34] In the public imagination he had presided over the birth of the new century with good humour and an easy-going character.

His son and successor, George V, though respectable and

honest, was a less reassuring prospect. Apart from anything else, he had not been brought up to be king; his older brother, Albert Victor (commonly known as Eddy*), had died in 1892, when George was twenty-seven. The precedents weren't good: both Henry VIII and Charles I were second sons promoted following the death of their elder brothers, and both reigns had seen the country being torn apart. Now George was stepping into a ready-made constitutional crisis that threatened new divisions.

The conflict between the two Houses of Parliament was not over, for the underlying issue remained. The Lords had been defeated this time, but there was no reason to suppose that they wouldn't carry on obstructing the will of the elected house. Something had to change to ensure the smooth running of government. One option was to reform the membership of the Lords, to make it an elected body, or even – as Churchill suggested – to abolish it altogether. Instead, the government resolved to curb its powers, so that it could no longer block a money bill and would be able only to delay the passage of other legislation for two years. This proposal was, inevitably, rejected by the Lords, and the whole process began again: a parliamentary impasse was resolved by consulting the people, with a second general election in December 1910 to legitimise the remaking of the constitution. 'The last election enabled us to carry the budget,' explained Lloyd George. 'This election is going to make it impossible for an hereditary House ever to reject another.'[35]

The result was almost exactly the same as last time. The Conservatives and Liberal Unionists were just one seat behind the Liberals, but they were again outgunned by the combined forces of their opponents, and the case for reform was won.

Some senior Unionists refused to accept that this was so. The

---

* Eddy was rumoured to have been involved in the 1889 Cleveland Street scandal, when a homosexual brothel was discovered and none of its wealthy clients was prosecuted. Some also believed – wrongly – that he was the serial killer known as Jack the Ripper.

so-called Ditchers said they would make a last-ditch stand against the reform (as opposed to the Hedgers, who were prepared to compromise). They made their displeasure known with a noisy protest in the Commons in July 1911. For nearly half an hour Asquith was drowned out by a 'band of insensate rowdies' who were 'lost to all sense of decency', hurling abuse that 'was more foul, perhaps, than any that has ever soiled the ears of the House of Commons'.[36] Conducting this 'orgy of ruffianism' – as Margot Asquith, the prime minister's wife, called it – was Lord Hugh Cecil, shouting and screaming in 'paroxysms of rage'.[37] 'I frankly regret that I have not been able to hear the speech of the prime minister,' said Balfour, when he rose to reply,[38] but it was hardly surprising when the Hughligans had taken over the asylum.

Despite their showy anger, the Ditchers were fighting a lost cause; the government had persuaded the new king to agree that, if necessary, he would raise a battalion of new peers to vote through the legislation.* The threat was sufficient, and in 1911 the Parliament Act was passed, stripping layers of power from the Lords.†

The People's Budget was the most important piece of parliamentary business of the era. It had an impact to a degree that budgets seldom do. It changed the fiscal structure by bringing in different rates of income tax and introducing the child tax allowance. It established the foundations of a welfare state, confirming that this was to be a governmental responsibility. And it provoked constitutional reform: in recognition of the new age of democracy, the elected House now had absolute primacy.

It also confirmed Lloyd George as the dominant political force of the era. He had delivered what his erstwhile hero Joe

---

* Among those on the list to be given peerages were writers Thomas Hardy and J. M. Barrie.

† It also reduced the maximum term of a Parliament from seven years to five. And the preamble promised to introduce an elected Upper House at some future, unspecified, date: 'It is intended to substitute for the House of Lords as it at present exists a second chamber constituted on a popular instead of hereditary basis.'

Chamberlain had failed to achieve: a raft of social reforms that changed the face of Britain and reinvented Liberalism. He was the hero of the hour for some, a villainous hate figure for others, but he was certainly the man setting the political agenda. Music-hall star Billy Williams used to introduce his song 'Poor Old England' (1907) with heavy irony as being 'by kind permission of Lloyd George', though the subject was the old one of immigrant workers:

> Why, the Briton used to boast his homestead was his castle grand
> Until the foreigner came here and swamped this happy land.
> He worked his way into our midst and captured all the trade,
> So everything we use now seems to be all foreign-made.

Many still saw the chancellor as a socialist in liberal clothing, and his party leaders even felt obliged to apologise for him in polite society. 'Lloyd George is essentially a fighting man,' wrote Campbell-Bannerman to Edward VII, 'and has not yet learned that once he gets inside an office his sword and spear should only be used on extreme occasions.'[39] The king was unimpressed, later telling Asquith, 'I shall have no more to do with him than what is absolutely necessary.'[40]

In some circles, though, there was something close to adulation. Socialists deplored the 'blind hero worship' seen in North Wales, and it was a fair description.[41] 'Praise God – and Lloyd George – from whom all blessings flow,' said a woman in Machynlleth, while a man in Llanbrynmair proclaimed, 'Lloyd George for ever, next to Jesus Christ.'[42] In west London the influential Baptist minister John Clifford dubbed him King Lloyd George the First,[43] and at a 1913 baby show in Suffolk, the first prize went to an infant named Lloyd George.[44] The alternative view came from an Anglican vicar who characterised him as the Beast of Revelation, whose number is 666.[45]

iv

In 1905 the publishing house Fisher Unwin ran a competition for a first novel, offering a £100 prize and a book deal. The winner was Margaret Baillie-Saunders, whose *Saints in Society* told the story of a poor printer from a south London slum whose powerful oratory sees him elected as a Labour MP, only for everything to go wrong. Embraced by the establishment, he is seduced by the glamour of publicity and power, losing sight of his roots and his values. Even before he acquires ownership of a newspaper and a morphine habit,* we know he's a wrong 'un because people remark on his physical resemblance to Napoleon.

'I'm a man of the people,' he declares. 'I care nothing for your aristocrats.' But of course he does care, and in particular he cares for female aristocrats, even while putting down his wife. 'Now, my dear, don't be silly,' he tells her; 'there are matters you can't, as a woman, be expected to understand.' Nonetheless, she's the one who remains true to their original ideals, setting up a charitable enterprise to help the children of the poor, while he makes speeches and changes nothing. '*You* are still the Walworth Radical,' she's told by those who know, but he steals the credit for her work and is lauded further by society, becoming a baronet.

As he sinks further into 'his supreme lust of power, grown now to a mania', he finds himself cut himself off from humanity. He has lifted himself into a superior class, only to find the same misery as those born into it; like Jolyon Forsyte, he sits alone in the great country house he's built, a place without soul but perfectly in keeping with the times. 'It said, "Money, money" unceasingly, with a hard gramophone persistency; it glittered money, it blazoned money.'

Saints in Society was far from the only fictional account of a Labour politician trading his principles for status, but it was

---

* This was an occupational hazard for fictional politicians; the title character in Katherine Cecil Thurston's *John Chilcote, MP* (1904) is another who is desperately addicted to morphine.

the first. Indeed, it was so early that it predated even the official naming of the party. For it was only with the 1906 election that a recognisable Labour Party came into existence. The foundations had been laid in February 1900 when a conference called by the Trades Union Congress approved a motion from Keir Hardie to work towards 'a distinct Labour group in Parliament, who shall have their own whips, and agree upon their policy'. To facilitate this, the Labour Representation Committee (LRC) was formed. The need was self-evident, for although the trade unions had a collective membership approaching two million, the political Left was pitifully small. In three successive German elections in the 1890s, the SPD, a Marxist party, won the largest share of the vote; in Britain, by contrast, the Independent Labour Party fielded just twenty-eight candidates at the 1895 election, who between them secured fewer than 35,000 votes, less than 1 per cent of the total.

The composition of the LRC illustrated the broadness of the new church. There were two representatives each from existing parties – the Social Democratic Federation and the Independent Labour Party, one from the Fabian Society and seven trade unionists. They covered a lot of ground: the SDF were Marxist, the ILP mostly democratic socialists, and the Fabians high-born intellectuals and academics. All were dependent on the trade unions, which alone had the membership and money to fund electioneering and to sponsor any MPs who were elected, since parliamentarians were not then paid.* The result was that the LRC was far less concerned with ideology than other British socialist groups had been; its aims were pragmatic from the outset, wedded to industrial politics, committed to class struggle but not class war. When Keir Hardie wrote *From Serfdom to Socialism* (1907), a short book intended 'to put clearly before the public a complete conspectus of the present policy of the English Socialists', he explained that he didn't want to get into too much detail, since a reader might miss the wood for

---

* This was remedied in 1912, when MPs received salaries for the first time, set initially at £400 a year.

the trees; to which a hostile reviewer replied that the book was 'all wood and no trees'.[46] So, to some degree, was the Labour Party – but it proved to be an asset.

The two MPs elected in 1900 were the first return for the new venture, but the key breakthrough came after Ramsay MacDonald, secretary of the LRC, persuaded the Liberals not to field candidates in a number of seats that might be taken from the Conservatives. Of the twenty-nine Labour MPs elected in 1906, twenty-four had stood in seats without a rival anti-Conservative candidate.* Given the size of the gains made by the Liberals that year, this agreement turned out to have been unnecessary, and in later years there were Liberals who regretted opening the door. That was for the future, though. The important thing in 1906 was that there were enough MPs to realise the ambition of being a distinct group, and in recognition of the changed circumstances, the LRC adopted the name of the Labour Party, selecting Hardie as its first leader.

The Labour Party had two core characteristics. First, although it was not the only grouping on the Left, its non-doctrinaire nature meant that it was more stable than, say, the Social Democratic Federation. The SDF had once been able to attract big names – Ramsay MacDonald, Eleanor Marx, William Morris – but had always been prone to ideological splits and, having played its part in creating the LRC, it continued to splinter into irrelevance.† Labour's eschewal of dogma meant that it avoided that fate. It also meant that the party was prepared to work with others, so it could make an impact even when the government had a very substantial majority. The Trade Disputes Act of 1906 was based on Labour's wording, while the Liberals felt obliged to prioritise such measures

---

* A further twenty-four trade union-endorsed candidates were elected as Liberal MPs. Some subsequently made their way into the Labour Party.
† There was a defection of SDF comrades to launch the Socialist Labour Party in 1903 and then the Socialist Party of Great Britain in 1904, before the SDF merged with others to form the British Socialist Party in 1911. The latter split again in 1916, and finally dissolved into the Communist Party of Great Britain in 1920.

as Churchill's Trade Boards Act 1909 – which set minimum wages for some industries – in order to keep their left flank covered.

Second, Labour saw its role as being the political wing of the trade unions. Being attached to a mass movement had an obvious appeal, but there was a noisy minority in the unions that saw no need for parliamentary representation at all. Equally, some on the Left such as Robert Blatchford of the *Clarion* looked forward to a time 'when we have a Socialist Party which does not lean upon the trade unions'.[47] One of Blatchford's followers explained that the union movement protected 'a continuance of the present system of things' and so 'only postpones the revolution'.[48]

Those were the words of Frances 'Daisy' Greville, Countess of Warwick, an ex-lover of Edward VII, whose husband, a former Conservative MP, was the lord lieutenant of Essex. Her journey to the Left was unusual. In 1895 Robert Blatchford wrote about a ball she'd held: 'men and women strutting before each other's envious eyes in mad rivalry of wanton dissipation' while others were 'huddling in their ragged hovels, their meagre, shrunken flesh pierced by the winter's cruel sting'.[49] It was a characteristically overripe diatribe, but Daisy took exception; when she went in person to the *Clarion* offices to remonstrate, she met Blatchford and was converted to the people's cause. She subsequently joined the SDF, probably the only member of the party who ever hired a private train to take her home after a Marxist discussion meeting.

The Countess of Warwick was not typical, of course, but there was room for her in the jostling crowd of radicals, socialists, anarchists, Marxists, cranks and intellectuals who were trying to stake out the ground on the left of the Liberal Party. Room too for the self-proclaimed 'bourgeois, bureaucratic, benevolent' Beatrice Webb,[50] who used to tell herself that she was 'the cleverest member of one of the cleverest families in the cleverest class of the cleverest nation in the world'.[51] She'd once been passionately in love with Joseph Chamberlain, but instead married civil servant Sydney Webb, and the couple began producing research on trade unions, local government and poverty. They also came to dominate the Fabian Society, co-founder of the LRC.

H. G. Wells was in the Fabian Society for a while; a lower-middle-class boy made good, he was flattered to be admitted to such elite circles, though they rather turned his head. In an extraordinary burst of creativity the previous decade, he had mapped out the frontiers of science fiction with a series of seminal works;* now he was still writing novels, but there were also less-interesting essays and pamphlets expounding his technocratic version of socialism. He didn't last long in the Fabians, though, because he fell out with the Webbs. Their personalities, much more than their politics, were too dissimilar to co-exist happily. One of G. K. Chesterton's stories sketched the character types. 'Professor Chadd was, like most of his particular class and type (the class that is at once academic and middle-class), a Radical of a solemn and old-fashioned type.' That was the Webbs. Wells was like Basil Grant in the same tale: 'that more discriminating and not uncommon type of Radical who passes most of his time in abusing the Radical party'.[52]

Wells also fell out with another Fabian, George Bernard Shaw, perhaps the leading public intellectual of the times. GBS, as the papers knew him, was always good for a controversy, whether because of his shocking dramas that coolly analysed social issues, or just because – like Oscar Wilde – he was witty and contrary. Poverty is a crime, he'd argue, and should be treated as such; if there were a jail sentence of twenty years for poverty, 'people would take a great deal more trouble not to be poor'.[53] Shaw described himself as 'an Irishman, a vegetarian, a teetotaller, a fanatic, a humorist, a fluent liar, a social democrat, a lecturer and debater, a fierce opponent of the present status of woman, and an insister on the seriousness of art'.[54] That covered most of the bases, but the socialist-anarchist philosopher Edward Carpenter – an ex-SDF

---

* *The Time Machine* (1895), *The Island of Doctor Moreau* (1896), *The Invisible Man* (1897), *The War of the Worlds* (1898), *When the Sleeper Awakes* (1899)

member of the Fabian Society – added anti-vivisectionism and homosexuality to the list.

These were some of the most important thinkers and campaigners of their age, but they could look to the casual observer like they were somewhat removed from the everyday world, a little peculiar, oddly obsessed. Henry Hyndman of the SDF was clear where he stood: 'I do not want the movement to be a depository of old cranks, humanitarians, vegetarians, anti-vivisectionists and anti-vaccinationists, arty-craftys and all the rest of them.'[55] But that was how it was sometimes seen.

British radicalism had strong roots in the Nonconformist churches, stretching back over a century, but it also intersected with more esoteric faiths. There was Fabian and SDF member Annie Besant, who became president of the occultist Theosophical Society, and Ernest Marklew,* a Grimsby fish merchant and 'well-known Spiritualist and Socialist lecturer, who recently served fourteen days in Preston gaol for street obstruction'.[56] When Thomas Lake Harris, 'America's most famous mystic, the founder of the Brotherhood of the New Life, and a claimant to immortality',[57] visited Britain, he stayed with leading members of the ILP in Scotland. Nor was the radical world immune from the fads of the day: the hopeless cause of Esperanto Socialism was promoted by Comrade Frank Watters of Brixton in south London,[58] and the *Clarion* was one of many papers to advertise free astrological readings by Clay Burton Vance, a notorious conman based in Paris.[59]

Then there was eugenics, the exciting new science that offered a simple solution to the mental, moral and physical deficiencies of the population. This attracted interest from across the political spectrum – Winston Churchill and Arthur Balfour attended the First International Congress of Eugenics in 1909 – though mostly from the Left. Supporters included Sidney Webb, H. G. Wells and George Bernard Shaw, as well as sexologist Havelock Ellis and

---

* Marklew was then a member of the SDF, but was to be elected as a Labour MP in 1935.

Marie Stopes, lecturer in paleobotany at Manchester University.* 'The well-to-do classes in this country are, on average, the finest specimens of humanity which have appeared since the ancient Greeks,' explained William Inge, professor of divinity at Cambridge; but when it came to the lower orders, the 'average physique is exceedingly poor'.[60] Inge was avowedly opposed to democracy, but his perspective wasn't much different to that of Shaw, who believed that 'nothing but a eugenic religion can save our civilisation from the fate that has overtaken all previous civilisations'.[61]

If the appeal was broad, though, it remained shallow, and the eugenicists were mostly unable to persuade their colleagues, let alone the public. In 1904 a Liverpool doctor called Robert Rentoul, much concerned with arresting 'racial decay',[62] proposed a programme of compulsory sterilisation for the unfit, but the British Medical Association rejected it on ethical grounds, while a private member's bill that sought to prevent 'mental defectives' from marrying was defeated in Parliament in 1912.

In this chaotic marketplace of ideas, the Labour Party's twin pillars of Parliament and trade unions lifted the organisation above the throng. Keir Hardie and the other Labour MPs in 1906 were mostly men from heavy industry and manual trades: miners and ironworkers, cobblers and coopers. When a survey asked them for their favourite authors, the top five were John Ruskin, Charles Dickens, Thomas Carlyle, Henry George and Walter Scott.[63] That was a reading list recognisable to normal people: Dickens and Scott were standards, and the others smacked of the autodidact rather than the elite. These men might not look like normal parliamentarians, and they didn't quite look like normal working men, but at least they didn't look like fanatics or monomaniacs either.

---

* Stopes' belief in eugenics informed her promotion of contraception in her best-known book, *Married Love* (written in 1913, though not published till 1918).

V

Perhaps because of its wider image of being a little peculiar, socialism struggled to get a fair hearing in much of popular culture. In
the music halls, the socialist – and the radical, for the boundary
was not clear – was portrayed as something of an outsider. Hugh
E. Wright sang 'A Ballad of Socialism' (1909), in which the narrator identifies the miseries of the working class but finds no takers
for his call to revolution, each chorus ending with a shrug: 'It's a
shame.'* A career in politics elevated you to a different world altogether. In his song 'Poor, Proud and Particular' (1902), Harry Ford
declared that since 'lots of toffs' didn't work, he had no intention
of doing so. And in his list of toffs, along with Lord Rothschild,
Lord Salisbury, Joe Chamberlain and the king, he cites the Liberal
MP John Burns – which seems a little harsh on a self-educated son
of a washerwoman.

The upper-class socialist was an easy target for satirists. Saki's
The Unbearable Bassington (1912) features Lady Caroline Benaresq,
'a professed Socialist in politics, chiefly, it was believed, because she
was thus enabled to disagree with most of the Liberals and Conservatives, and all the Socialists of the day'.[64] 'I am nothing if I am
not a socialist,' declares a countess in Philip Gibbs's *The Street of
Adventure* (1909). 'I do so pity the poor Poor. I have taken them up
as a hobby, and I find it ever so much more elevating and ennobling
than poultry-keeping.'[65]

There was also *The Socialist* (1910),[66] a musical farce staged by
the Cambridge Footlights Dramatic Club in London. This told
the story of Professor Cyrus R. Hank, who arrives at St Botolph's
College in a spaceship from Mars, declaring himself a socialist,
as well as a vegetarian, teetotal anti-vivisectionist who doesn't
approve of gambling; he is assisted in his mission to put 'things
upon a base of absolute equality' by the left-wing Knavian Society.

---

* The song also featured a comic misunderstanding of how the upper classes lived.
'The pampered sons of plutocrats,' sang Wright, 'has their tripe and honions every
evening of the year!'

Chaos ensues, as the undergraduates insist on setting and marking their own papers, and the cooks refuse to work for the college ball, 'being of opinion that, as all are now equal, they should be at the ball too'. A mass meeting is called, Hank is banished, and life returns to how things ought to be – the way they are in Marie Belloc Lowndes' *The Lodger* (1913), in which a waiter at a society function is given a tip of a guinea and is touched by the consideration. This 'confirmed him in his Conservative principles; only gentlefolk ever behaved in that way; quiet, old-fashioned, respectable gentlefolk, the sort of people of whom those nasty Radicals know nothing and care less!'

The violent imagery that was sometimes encountered on the fringes – Charles Davis with his talk of 'a thousand men' and of 'grenades, pistols and dynamite' – was also much mocked. In Charles Hamilton's St Jim's stories, a pupil called Herbert Skimpole discovers politics and turns into 'a real, giddy, red-hot Socialist', directing his abuse at the Honourable Arthur Augustus D'Arcy: 'Here comes the bloated aristocrat. Here comes the oppressor – the roller in wealth – the downtrodder of the toiling millions.'[67] But Gussy wasn't really much of an oppressor. The early cinema likewise viewed left-wing politics as inherently funny, in films such as *Ma Turns Socialist* (1910), *Bobby as a Socialist* (1911) and *Scroggins Gets the Socialist Craze* (1911).

More substantially, the 1906 election and the launch of the Labour Party provoked a spate of novels about the political implications of these events for the future, books such as *The Unknown Tomorrow* (1910) by William Le Queux, only forty-six years old and already author of more than sixty novels.* This was set in 1935 with a violent revolution followed by an even more violent counter-revolution, all of it owing more to accounts of the French Revolution and Reign of Terror than to contemporary Britain. 'Old men, who in their youth recollected the birth of the twentieth

---

* There were another hundred books to come, including five in the year of his death, 1927, and eight published posthumously.

century, the Boer War, and the death of the lamented Queen Victoria, looked back upon what they termed "the good old days" of prosperity under Salisbury and Balfour.'[68] Less sensationally, *The Triumph of Socialism, and How It Succeeded* (1908) was the debut novel of seventy-nine-year-old John Dawson Mayne, former advocate general of Madras and failed Conservative election candidate; he foresaw disaster as early as 1912, with the election of 504 socialist MPs.

Ernest Bramah, author of *The Wallet of Kai Lung*, set his dystopian novel *The Secret of the League* (1909)* in a near-future Britain where the country's first Labour government has been and gone, replaced by a socialist administration. The House of Lords has been abolished, the Church's land has been seized, Ireland has declared independence, and the Empire is largely dismantled. It scarcely needs saying of such a government that 'the word "patriotic" had long been expunged from their vocabulary'. The armed forces have also been run down because 'the Labour Party was definitely pledged to the inauguration of universal peace by declining to go to war on any provocation'. All taxes have increased enormously, and there are demands for workers on boards of companies and a minimum wage or, better yet, 'a full and undocked living wage to every worker in or out of work'.

Against this new establishment is launched the Unity League, headed by the evocatively named Sir John Hampden, and masterminded by George Salt, a naval hero possessed of 'the Elizabethan spirit – the genius of ensuring everything that was possible, and then throwing into the scale a splendid belief in much that seemed impossible'. The political platform of the league can be 'summed up in the single phrase, "As in 1905"', turning back the clock to a time when there was still a Conservative government.

While the analysis is serious, the treatment is not; Bramah

---

* An earlier publication, *What Might Have Been* (1907), had failed to make any impact; *The Secret of the League* was an abridged version of that novel in a cheaper edition and sold well.

was a humorist and couldn't resist mocking the labyrinthine language of the Left, as when Comrade Tintwistle of the railwaymen's union denounces the way that 'the insatiable birds of prey who sucked their blood laughed in their sleeve at the spectacle of the British working men hiding their heads ostrich-like in the shifting quicksand of a fool's paradise'. Equally characteristic of the British humorist are the names he gives to the Labour politicians: Strummery, Guppling, Cadman, Heape, Pennefarthing, Vossit, Chadwing, Stub, Bilch.

The most celebrated of these novels was R. H. Benson's *Lord of the World* (1907), set a hundred years in the future. British history has been changed by the Labour government of 1917 under the inspirational Gustave Herve, whose message was one of uncompromising materialism: 'Patriotism, he said, was a relic of barbarism; and sensual enjoyment was the only certain good.' There have been many reforms over the decades, and secular humanism now has total control – and not just in Britain, for the whole world has evolved into three power blocs: the Eastern Empire, the Americas and Europe (including its African colonies); the latter is pursuing ever closer union, with a proposal for a European parliament.

These three blocs seem to be on the brink of a global conflict, a terrifying prospect in an era of aerial warfare and of devastating new weapons such that 'entire towns would be destroyed with a single shell'. But the world is saved from this nightmare by the emergence of a unifying, charismatic leader, Julian Felsenburgh. 'He was the kind of figure that belonged rather to the age of chivalry: a pure, clean, compelling personality, like a radiant child.' He is 'the greatest orator that the world has ever known', delivering inspirational speeches in fifteen languages across the globe, and in the East he's been 'hailed as Messiah by a Mohammedan mob'. Felsenburgh is also, it emerges, the Antichrist.

Benson was ordained by his father, the Archbishop of Canterbury, and later converted to Catholicism; consequently, *Lord of the World* is more eschatological than dystopian. Rome having been bombed out of existence in an air raid, the only surviving cardinal flees to the relative safety of the Holy Land. 'That place, father,' he asks a Syrian priest, gesturing towards a small settlement, 'what is its name?' And the man replies, 'That is Megiddo. Some call it Armageddon.'

Despite the variation in style and quality, the novels of Le Queux, Mayne, Bramah and Benson share an assessment of what the rise of the Labour Party will mean: attacks on British institutions, a high-tax policy to pacify the working class, the abandonment of patriotism, national defence and a sense of duty to society. Some people saw socialists as 'Mad Mullahs', said Ramsay MacDonald, hell-bent on 'the overthrow of ancient institutions, social organisations and the moral conscience'.[69] As with Margaret Baillie-Saunders' tale of the Labour politician seduced by the establishment, these charges were to become entrenched in British culture.

vi

The general election of 1906, with its great Liberal majority and the creation of the Labour Party, was followed the next year by elections to the London County Council. And there the story was very different.

The LCC had been run since its formation in 1889 by the Progressives, mostly with big majorities. The election in March 1907, however, saw the Municipal Reform Party (replacing the old Moderates, still essentially the Conservatives) secure a clear majority of ninety seats to forty-seven. The Progressives had faced much criticism for economic incompetence – they were the 'Wastrels', said the *Daily Mirror*[70] – but much of the campaign was fought on far less obvious issues, particularly controversies over whether schools should fly the nation's flag and over socialist indoctrination in those schools. The issues were interlinked. 'We cannot with one hand hoist the Union Jack in our schools and with the other open the door and welcome the Socialist,' insisted the *Islington Gazette*. 'The two things are a contradiction.'[71]

The idea of schools flying the flag came from a post-Boer

War drive to inculcate patriotism and imperial pride in children's hearts. The Boy Scouts were the most notable manifestation of this, but there was also Empire Day, which had been celebrated in Canada and South Africa since the late 1890s and was introduced to Britain in 1905. Held on 24 May, the birthday of the late Queen Victoria, this was chiefly marked in schools,* and a typical programme was that seen in Wordsley, Staffordshire in 1906: special lessons were given on 'The Empire and our duties as citizens to it', after which the teachers and children assembled in the playground, gathered around a Union Jack, and sang the national anthem and other patriotic songs, accompanied by a string band. It wasn't hugely inspiring, but it was popular with pupils, accompanied as it was by a half-day holiday.

It was with the same intention of motivating the young that some newspapers – the *Daily Telegraph* and the *Referee* prominent among them – began calling in January 1907 for every London school to fly the Union flag. The Progressives at the LCC, however, refused to authorise this. Yet this was the council, noted the same papers, that allowed its premises to be used for holding socialist Sunday schools, and surely that fact gave the game away: this administration put radical politics before love of country.†

There wasn't much in this. The socialist Sunday school movement had grown slowly and patchily since the 1880s: at the time of the 1907 controversy, only five London schools were being used to house such groups. The inspiration came directly from faith-based institutions, and the proceedings were rooted heavily in Christian practice. Songs were sung from *The Socialist Hymn Book*‡

---

* In 1907 it was noted that no government buildings flew the Union flag.

† Around the same time, in further proof of its lack of patriotism, the LCC also refused the offer of two field guns, captured from the Boers, to be used for ornamental display.

‡ In her memoir of her husband, Vladimir Lenin, Nadezhda Krupskaya remembered when they visited a socialist church in London in 1902, where the congregation sang, 'Lead us, O Lord, from the Kingdom of Capitalism into the Kingdom of Socialism'.

and later from *The Socialist Sunday School Hymn Book*, and the Ten Socialist Precepts were recited, starting with a thoroughly recognisable sentiment: 'Love your schoolfellows, who will be your fellow-workmen in life.'[72]

None of it was particularly shocking, but some of the press took vehemently against socialist Sunday schools: 'We do not want the minds of young children to be poisoned by the religion of hate.'[73] And ratepayers were reminded that this was happening on publicly owned property: 'The schools for which they pay through the nose are being used for the purpose of teaching the children that landlords are thieves, that employers of labour are rascals, that shopkeepers are swindlers.'[74] The issue was raised in Parliament by Liberal Unionist MP William Anson, who had served as an education minister. He objected to the irreligious hymns, which taught children 'to look for no help from any other source, except such as was to be found in this world, and entirely through themselves'. Further, he said, these schools used a catechism that included overt propaganda, with exchanges such as 'If the masters had their way, to what level do you think they would reduce your father's wages?' 'To the level of the Chinaman's.' 'Has this been attempted?' 'Yes; in South Africa, where they employ Chinamen instead of white men.'[75]

The complaints were such that when the Municipal Reform Party won power in London, one of its first actions was to ban the use of its premises for socialist Sunday schools. A demonstration in Trafalgar Square against the decision attracted 5,000 people – including hundreds of children, who, 'led by the band, sang several songs objected to by the LCC' – but there was to be no backtracking by the council.[76]

It was a setback for the Left in its drive to win the next generation for socialism, but the movement continued. The National Council of British Socialist Sunday Schools Union was founded in 1909, and by 1912 was said to represent over 120 schools, attended by 7,000 children and 1,600 adults. They were hardly a threat to the Christian Sunday schools, but then they had never really been the target of the press campaign. The point of attacking the schools was to paint the Liberals as enablers of socialism, to suggest that they had drifted so far to the left as to be indistinguishable from 'the red menace to property, family and the state'.[77] As the *Oxford Times* said during the People's Budget crisis, 'What Keir Hardie would have no chance of doing, it is possible that Mr Winston Churchill and Mr Lloyd George may do.'[78]

This was a time when the Conservative Party was at a desperately low ebb, while the Liberals were overflowing with new policies and new thinking. The tone of the moment, said John Buchan, himself a Unionist, was one of moral superiority, the Liberals believing that they 'alone understood and sympathised with the poor; a working man who was not a Liberal was inaccessible to reason, or morally corrupt, or intimidated by laird or employer'.[79] It might be unfair, but right now this was how it was. And so, losing the economic argument, the Conservatives focused on cultural issues, aiming at their opponents' alleged lack of patriotism.

As for the flags, they never did appear – the new LCC had no objection to them being flown but had no wish to pay for them.* The *Daily Telegraph* launched an appeal to provide a flag and flagstaff for every elementary school in London, but once the election was past, interest waned. By the end of 1907 the paper's attention had turned to an initiative to get schoolchildren from the Dominions to donate flags to appropriately named places in Britain – the children of Waterloo, Sydney sent a twelve-foot-long Union Jack to Waterloo Road School in Lambeth, London. 'Needless to say, the children at that school are heartily delighted with the idea,' reported the *Telegraph*. 'If they were not they would not be English children, or there would have been something radically wrong with their upbringing and teaching.'[80] They were, though, expected to send a flag in return.

---

* In 1907 a school trustee in Hastings appealed for donations to erect a flagpole on the roof. He estimated the work would cost five pounds, and if there was any money left over, he proposed 'to apply it to the purchase of Empire maps to hang on the walls of our schools'.

7

WOMEN AND MEN

'But, Lady Blakeney,' said the young man, touched by the gentle earnestness of this exquisitely beautiful woman, 'do you know that what you propose doing is man's work?'

Baroness Orczy, *The Scarlet Pimpernel*, 1905[1]

Women everywhere – many women at any rate – were turning indiscriminately against the old bonds, the old yokes, affections, servitudes, demanding 'self-realisation', freedom for the individuality and the personal will; rebelling against motherhood, and life-long marriage; clamouring for easy divorce, and denouncing their own fathers, brothers and husbands, as either tyrants or fools.

Mrs Humphry Ward, *Delia Blanchflower*, 1914[2]

Cartoon from *Punch* magazine, published 1 January 1908 and titled 'Leap Year, or The Irrepressible Ski', depicting the women's suffrage campaign taking off on skis labelled 'Agitation'.

FOLKESTONE IN KENT ADVERTISED ITSELF as 'the most fashionable summer resort on the South Coast', offering 'all the advantages of a cross-Channel port and the attractions and gaieties of a first-class watering place'.[3] And in the late summer of 1907 the hottest ticket in the seaside town was for a one-off show on the Victoria Pier, so popular that hours before it started 'there was a tremendous crowd outside, and standing room only was announced'; still 1,200 people had to be turned away. The event was billed as a Beauty Show for Gentlemen.[4]

It wasn't an original idea. A male beauty show had been held in Berlin in 1901, 'a very serious affair', according to the British press, in which the entrants were judged by 'sculptors, painters, and professors of physiology and the fine arts'.[5] Equally earnest was the 1903 contest in Vienna, set up by the Austrian United Athletic Societies, which were 'anxious to discover whether athletic training of the past ten years in Austria has had any appreciable effect on the development of the human body'.[6] The British, on the other hand, saw such events as a splendid opportunity for knockabout seaside fun; there were contests in Lowestoft in 1904 and Southend in 1906. At the latter a forty-three-year-old grey-bearded brake conductor won the top prize – a walnut clock – in the ugliest-man category, which illustrated the somewhat less elevated tone.

Folkestone in 1907 was the largest such competition yet staged, with more than sixty entrants, though some got last-minute fits of nerves, whittling the field down to 'about fifty young men of all shapes and sizes'. Most were British, though there were also French, Italians, Germans, a Hungarian, a Turk and a Japanese. The focus was on the face, so the stage was dominated by 'an immense gilt frame hung with black silk, through a slit in which they were to push their beautiful heads', and unlike the continental versions, the judges were the female members of the audience. ('Fancy the nerve of a man who boldly claims to be beautiful, and submits himself to the ordeal of scrutiny by a giggling jury of girls!' marvelled the papers.[7]) The winner was Sergeant W. T. Hodgetts of the 7th School of Musketry, who received 200 votes and the top prizes of an eight-guinea bicycle, a four-guinea suit of clothes, and a silver watch.[*]

The contest was sufficiently popular that it became an annual event. The use of the frame was discontinued, which gave more scope to stylish dressers; in 1909, John Ojijatekha Brant-Sero, a forty-year-old Canadian of mixed Mohawk and English parentage, sporting long black hair and full native dress, came second to a member of the local lifeboat crew.[†] The following year there was an additional prize on offer when a thirty-year-old widow, 'tall and handsome', announced that as long as the winner was 'good looking, of good disposition, and in receipt of £100 per year', she would marry him. 'I am anxious for my family's sake that my name should not be revealed for the present,' she told the press, 'but you may say that I was born in India, where I have spent most of my life, and my husband was in the Civil Service out there. My only income is a pension of £75. I am musical, and speak French, German and Hindustani.' Regrettably, the winner, Bert Harris of Hampstead, was already engaged so couldn't take her up on the offer.[8]

There was a spate of such shows across England and the tone remained resolutely jocular. In 1910 the women's beauty contest at New Brighton on the Wirral saw over 500 entrants and the victory of Hettie Gale of Plymouth, an aspiring actress who had just secured a leading role in a play with the title *The Right Mr Wrong*; she won a purse of gold, a silver fruit-and-flower stand and a gold pendant. The men's contest, however, was notable for the inclusion in the supposedly all-female judging panel of a man in

---

[*] The appeal of the military man was evident elsewhere. At another contest in 1907, the Kursaal, Southend, had two categories, for fair and dark men; both were won by serving artillerymen.

[†] Brant-Sero had toured extensively in Canada, America and Britain, lecturing on the Mohawk people.

drag, and for 'the appearance as a contestant of a beautiful and well-groomed donkey'.[9]

These were boisterous affairs, with women comprising much of the audience. At Sadler's Wells Theatre in London they 'expressed their opinion by applause, laughter and, indeed, groans',[10] while there was 'loud laughter and facetious remarks' at the Corn Exchange in Hertford.[11] 'The struggle to get into the Kursaal for the male beauty show reminded one of an autumn sale,' it was reported of Southend-on-Sea, and onstage the competitors tried their best 'to appear calm and beautiful and undisturbed under the storm of execration that greeted them'.[12]

Predictably, some derided the contests. 'Fancy any self-respecting Englishman deliberately curling his hair, waxing his face-moss, and exposing his dial through a frame for the delectation of village idiots!' mocked Horatio Bottomley's newspaper, *John Bull*.[13] But there were others who saw it as a sign of the times. 'Men are the vainer sex,' said a London photographer; 'coxcombs outnumber coquettes.' He thought it revealed a vigorous culture: 'A national male beauty show would dispel the impression, entertained by some, that the race of Englishmen is degenerating.'[14]

It was striking, though, that the most serious 'man show', as the papers dubbed it, was the inspiration of a German. Eugen Sandow was a professional strongman who moved to Britain in 1889 and became a successful music-hall act, before finding even greater acclaim in America. Beyond his theatrical career, his real interest was in muscle development; he coined the word bodybuilding to describe his approach to what was then more generally called physical culture. At the Albert Hall in 1901 he staged the world's first bodybuilding competition, with Arthur Conan Doyle and sculptor Charles Lawes as his co-judges, and the winner – from the ranks of 'almost perfect specimens of developed manhood' – was W. L. Murray from Nottingham, 'his development and symmetry being as nearly perfect as could be wished'. He received a gold statuette of Sandow, said to be worth 500 guineas, and the proceeds from the evening were donated to the Transvaal War Relief Fund.[15]

ii

Eugen Sandow having popularised muscular semi-naked male bodies in the music halls, there arose an appetite for wrestling, but again it needed a foreigner – George Hackenschmidt – to elevate the sport to top billing. Born in Dorpat, then in the Russian Empire, Hackenschmidt had won wrestling tournaments in Vienna and Paris before coming to Britain in early 1902, hoping to make money in the halls. He succeeded in his ambition, but it took a while for his career to blossom.

His problem was that he was too good. He was a serious sportsman working in the entertainment business and he didn't really put on much of a show, polishing off even experienced opponents within a couple of minutes. Also, he wrestled in the Graeco-Roman style, which permits holds only above the waist, and tends to interest the connoisseur rather than the casual spectator. His manager, an aspiring young hustler named C. B. Cochran,* persuaded him to switch to catch-as-catch-can, a more entertaining discipline popular at funfairs in which all holds are permitted, and to delay his victories a little, allowing his opponent to gain the upper hand before defeating him. The result was a 'wrestling boom'[16] that was one of the features of the time.†

The high point came in January 1904, when Hackenschmidt, the Russian Lion, fought Ahmed Madrali, the Terrible Turk, at Olympia in West Kensington. 'Seldom, if ever, has any athletic event been looked forward to with greater interest,'[17] frothed the

---

* Cochran would later become a respectable theatrical impresario; he was knighted in 1948.

† When 'an eminent medical man' suggested in 1904 that British manliness was being undermined by too much tea-drinking, P. G. Wodehouse lamented in the *Daily Chronicle*:

'I might,' he added, bitterly,
'Have got my muscle up,
And wrestled Hackenschmidtily,
Had I but shunned the cup.'

papers; it was 'the sole topic of conversation in sporting circles'.[18] There were breathless stories that the seating at Olympia had to be replaced 'in order to cope adequately with the great demand for tickets to witness the most important wrestling match of modern times',[19] and the vast numbers who gathered, both inside and outside the venue, caused what was said to be the worst traffic jam ever seen, stretching back to Piccadilly in the West End. For the *Daily Mirror*, it was the story of the day, with its front page filled with drawings of the two men.

The combatants – Hackenschmidt in a 'gorgeous purple gown', Madrali in 'a dull-coloured fur-lined cloak' – entered through a sell-out crowd ('it was remarkable how numerous were "the gentler sex"'[20]) and took their places on a stage in the centre of the hall, illuminated by thirty carbon-arc lights to ensure clear pictures for filming. This was sport as spectacle, a triumph of promotion and a world away from the Corinthian spirit. There was a £2,000 purse. 'I shall win, or I shall die in the ring,' declared Madrali melodramatically.[21]

He did neither, for the reality did not live up to the hype. The match was fought according to Graeco-Roman rules, to be decided by the best of three falls, and a two-hour time limit was set. It lasted less than one minute. Hackenschmidt got a hold on Madrali, threw him 'like a sack of flour' without releasing his grip, and fell on top of his opponent. He secured the first fall but in the process dislocated the Turk's arm, leaving him unable to continue. It was all deeply disappointing. 'I could sooner understand if I fell down dead than for a thing like this to happen,' lamented Madrali, before seeking comfort in his Islamic faith: 'It is Kismet.'[22]

The following year, Hackenschmidt departed for America, but the wrestling craze endured, and England continued to be, said the press, 'invaded by wrestlers, men of muscle and skill, from all parts of the Continent'.[23] There were more and more over-promoted bouts until, in late 1905, there came the first allegations of corruption. An exposé in the *Daily Record and Mail* headlined FAKED WRESTLING MATCHES sensationally claimed that agreements were made in advance, determining who would win a contest and how it would be won; these arrangements had become so common that 'genuine wrestling is fast becoming a thing of the past'.[24] When asked in New York about such practices, Hackenschmidt denied any involvement, though he did say he was offered $100,000 to throw the Madrali fight, which didn't exactly refute the allegations of match-fixing.

This was unashamed entertainment, and it was absorbed into wider cultural life. Hal Forde's song 'The Wrestling Wife' (1904) told the tale of a man who 'used to boss his wife' until she goes to the music hall and catches 'the wrestling craze'; now she rules the house, adorning the walls with pictures 'of gentlemen with nothing on worth mentioning'.*

In the race for novelty, the pack was led by the man who'd managed Madrali, Antonio Pierri. A former wrestler himself ('one of the best in the business', according to the *Sporting Life*[25]), Pierri had been billed as the Terrible Greek[†] and was one of Hackenschmidt's early victims. That defeat was enough to prompt a move into management and promotion, at which he excelled; cross-eyed and with a tendency to refer to himself in the third person – 'Pierri is a very straight man,' he'd reassure doubters[26] – he was a master of puffery and dubious business practices.

In 1906, deciding that male wrestlers were old hat, Pierri launched the career of Juno May, a twenty-two-year-old from Brockley, south-east London, who stood six feet two inches tall and weighed eighteen stone, with a bust measurement of fifty inches and a waist of thirty-three inches.[27] 'There is nothing coarse or excessively muscular about this very Juno-esque British girl,' readers of the *Newcastle Evening Chronicle* were told. 'She is, indeed, extremely handsome with dark brown hair, a clear

---

* The previous year Forde had played the Duke of Brum, a parody of Joseph Chamberlain, in the London Hippodrome pantomime *Dick Whittington and His Cat*.

† He was Italian.

complexion, and refined features. Moreover, she is perfectly proportioned and her hands and feet are beautifully shaped.'[28]

Described by Pierri as 'the Champion Wrestler of the World' even before her first bout,[29] she was booked to appear twice a night at the Royal Cambridge Music Hall in Commercial Street, east London, for a week (plus a matinee on Thursday), with a challenge to all-comers: a prize of five pounds to any gentleman who could last fifteen minutes on the mat with her, £100 to any lady wrestler who could defeat her. None succeeded. Dressed in a loose, sleeveless blouse, knickerbockers and boots, May made short work of her opponents. That wasn't entirely surprising, since the referee was Pierri himself and her opponents paid stooges; May fought and beat a woman named Belle Mackenzie five times in four days. When a serious challenger presented herself, excuses were made. A Welsh wrestler called Connie Mathias – who'd worked the circuit for some years and, billing herself as 'the Undefeated', had her own 'celebrated troupe of international lady wrestlers'[30] – was turned away by Pierri, denied a shot at the prize.

Juno May's wrestling career lasted just four months, but it was characteristic of the times: not just in that it was built entirely on money and advertising, but also in that it saw the intrusion of women into traditionally male territory. She was exceptional, but more generally there was a vogue for athletic pursuits among young women. 'What with improved calisthenics and gymnasiums during school days, and golf, lawn tennis, archery, bicycling and riding,' read one report, 'the female physique has undergone a wonderful alteration for the better.' It was, though, as ever, a question of class. These activities required time and money that was not available to all; it was noted that 'owing to various causes, the average workgirl of the poorer class is too frequently a stunted ill-formed person'.[31]

Moreover, little women's sport was competitive. Of the 2,008 participants in the 1908 Olympic Games, just thirty-seven were women, mostly competing in archery, figure skating and tennis. Indeed the latter sport was the major exception, particularly at

Wimbledon, where the ladies' singles tournament had been an annual fixture since 1884. Unlike wrestling, this was a graceful game of suburban gentility; the first Wimbledon final saw Maud Watson, a vicar's daughter from Harrow, triumph over her older sister, Lilian, in three sets.

Perceptions changed in 1905 when May Sutton became the first foreigner to win the title (though she was at least born in Britain, her family moving to California when she was six).* Sutton was just eighteen, had already won the US Open and hit the ball very hard. Described in the press as 'not at all pretty', she was 'magnificently muscular' – nothing like the elegant, willowy ideal, as represented by defending champion twenty-six-year-old Dorothea Douglass (another vicar's daughter, this time from Ealing). Sutton dressed differently, too, wearing a skirt that was, depending on one's point of view, either scandalous – 'so very short as to reach the knee, but by no means to shroud it' – or practical, meaning she was 'costumed for the work before her'. She celebrated her victory 'in a self-assertive manner not usual among English girls, who consider it better taste to be modest under success'.† The physical and cultural differences were striking, but Sutton was well received by the British public: 'There is something very refreshing about her confident, smiling manner and she has made herself very popular during her short stay in this country.'[32]

iii

The language of the papers was quietly revealing: there was 'nothing offensively masculine'[33] about May Sutton, Juno May had 'refined features'.[34] Ladies were expected still to be ladylike, even though there was a greater tendency to appropriate masculine style than

---

* The first overseas winner of the gentlemen's singles at Wimbledon was Australian Norman Brookes in 1907. The same year, French golfer Arnaud Massy became the first foreign winner of the Open.
† Sutton and Douglass met again in the next two finals, winning one apiece.

there had been a generation earlier. The heroine of John Strange Winter's novel *A Blaze of Glory* (1902),* for example, finds herself admiring 'handsome Maud, who had the broadest shoulders and the tiniest little waist she had ever seen, who played the banjo and did skirt dances at penny readings, who wore stiff collars and gentlemanly ties, and smoked a cigarette like a young man'. In real life, while the male art students known as the Slade Coster Gang were adopting working-class dress, female students at the same college – Dorothy Brett, Dora Carrington, Barbara Hiles – were cutting their hair short into a boyish bob, becoming known as the Slade cropheads.[35]

These were also the peak years of the male impersonator in music halls. The act had been pioneered by Annie Hindle, the first to specialise as an 'impersonator of male characters',[36] back in the mid-1860s. She then moved to America, where she married an English comic singer, Charles Vivian, though his violent behaviour ensured that the union didn't last. They separated and, after his death, she remarried; this time her partner was her dresser, Annie Ryan. Hindle wore male clothing for the ceremony, but the officiating clergyman wasn't fooled. 'The groom gave me her – I mean his – name as Charles Hindle,' he said. 'I believe they love each other, and that they will be happy.'[37] And so they were, living together until Ryan's death, after which Annie Hindle married a third time, another woman.

The best-known of all the male impersonators started on stage not long after Hindle's British success. By the end of the 1860s, five-year-old Vesta Tilley was donning a fake moustache and a three-piece suit; her routine as the Pocket Sims Reeves involved singing the work of the country's most popular tenor. It was only in her late teens, though, that Tilley turned her entire act over to male impersonation. Her reasoning was much the same as many of those who adopted blackface: it was an act of liberation. 'Young as I was, I had, in song, run through the whole gamut of female

---

* John Strange Winter was the pseudonym of Henrietta Stannard.

characters, from baby songs to old maid's ditties, and I concluded that female costume was rather a drag,' she wrote. 'I felt that I could express myself better if I were dressed as a boy.'[38]

In her new guise Tilley rose steadily to the top, helped by a good marriage in 1890 to Walter de Frece, the son of a theatre manager, who promptly gave up his architectural apprenticeship to manage her career and went on to have his own theatres, building a circuit of eighteen venues. By the turn of the century, she was one of the biggest stars in the country, soon to be billed as 'The World's Greatest Artiste',[39] and indisputably the leading male impersonator.* She played a variety of characters, some more convincingly than others: she didn't really have the bulk to make a policeman, but she looked impeccable when dressed in frock coat, top hat and monocle, satirising the young fop about town in 'The Piccadilly Johnny with the Little Glass Eye' (1895) or 'Burlington Bertie' (1900).†

This was a slick, professional act that required serious investment to keep Tilley clear of the competition. Her tailor's bill was £250 a year, and that didn't include the accessories, the hats, sticks, gloves and jewellery; the amount spent on her wardrobe, said the papers, 'rivals that of a cabinet minister'.[40] When appearing in New York, her clothes – intended as a parody – 'were so approved of by the American dudes that she was prevailed upon to give a series of lectures on How to Dress, to men only'.[41]

It was also a thoroughly respectable act; there were no saucy

---

* Her biggest rival was Hetty King, daughter of a blackface comedian, who was acclaimed as 'a second Vesta Tilley' in 1905, and was still recording into the 1960s. Others included Nina Bainbridge, 'the Tyneside Vesta Tilley', and Rhoda Paul, 'the smallest male impersonator in the world', as well as (among many others): Lilian Bishop, Aggie Flanagan, Katie Florence, Flo Hilton, Millie Hylton, Florence May, Effie Morton, Constance Moxon, Maggie Rimmer, Eva Rudell, Evelyn Taylor, Mabel Toney, Louie Tracey, Winifred Ward and Flo Windsor. There were also child male-impersonators: Little Millie Burton, Madge Osmonde, Lily Shaw, Lena Snaith.
† Not to be confused with the later 'Burlington Bertie from Bow' (1914), sung by another male impersonator, American-born Ella Shields.

winks as there were with Marie Lloyd, let alone the sexual ambiguity of Annie Hindle. Even in character, Tilley was clearly a woman – she didn't adopt a masculine singing voice – and she never wore drag in real life; she appeared in the gossip pages wearing white muslin frocks, with matching hat and parasol, the very model of a modern English gentlewoman. However clean the material and the delivery, though, it had an undeniable frisson; there was still something titillating about a pretty woman dressing up as a young man. Playing with accepted gender conventions implied an interest in sex, and at the very least there was something to be said for a woman in tight trousers.*

The music hall also had female impersonators, but they were not such big names and they tended to deal in comedy. Malcolm Scott (the Woman Who Knows) was successful with historical sketches of Boadicea, Queen Elizabeth and Nell Gwynn, but he didn't attempt to disguise his big, masculine face; consequently, said the critics, he was 'screamingly funny as a lady'.[42] There was less of a sexual charge here, the audience not wishing to be tricked into finding a man attractive. The most convincing female impersonator was Bert Errol, who was 'quite indistinguishable on the stage from a lady'[43] and had a beautiful singing voice, such that 'he might be taken for a versatile soprano'.[44] But he knew not to overdo it: 'His few male mannerisms dispel the illusion and cause a good deal of laughter.'[45] For the avoidance of doubt, he revealed he was a man at the end of the act, and brought his wife on stage.

The most commonly encountered type of female impersonator was the pantomime dame, a role that had been popularised by the double act of Dan Leno and Herbert Campbell in more than a dozen productions at the Theatre Royal, Drury Lane at the end of the last century. In pantomime, as in the halls, women impersonated men, men impersonated women, and – in the case of Fred

---

* This was a truth that had been discovered in earlier generations. In 1829 the *Morning Chronicle* deplored the sight of opera singer Madame Vestris appearing on stage 'in the very tightest buckskins she could obtain, to fit her shape'.

Barnes – the lines became ever more blurred: he was the only male to take the role of principal boy in pantomime, a man acting as a woman acting as a man.

But then Barnes always was a law unto himself. The son of a Birmingham butcher, he was inspired to go on stage after seeing Vesta Tilley perform. He had a pleasant tenor voice and enjoyed a modest career until he hit big with what became his signature song, 'The Black Sheep of the Family' (1907), written by himself:

> It's a queer, queer world that we live in
> And Dame Fortune plays a funny game.
> Some get all the sunshine,
> Others get the shame.

He was soon being billed as the Prince of Light Comedians,[46] though the press sometimes referred to him as 'the male Vesta Tilley',[47] a nudging reference to the fact that he made no secret of being homosexual. He was a friend of Marie Lloyd, who pulled him up when his offstage make-up overstepped the mark. 'What have you done to your lashes?' she'd exclaim. 'They look like bloody park railings.'[48]

In this regard at least, the complaints from liberals that music hall was conservative, jingoist and reactionary were wide of the mark, and overlooked the fact that it was a place of liberation and licence, a safe space for images and concepts that subverted social standards. When Vesta Tilley dressed as an Eton schoolboy to sing her most disingenuous song, 'Following in Father's Footsteps' (1903), she was not only playing with gender roles, but gently guying the loose morality of the upper classes – in this case a supposedly upright businessman who sets a drinking, womanising example to his impressionable son.

Indeed the patriarch of the family was a frequent target of humour. 'Father Did Look Funny,' sang Harry Champion in 1906, and it was a running theme, whether for his incompetence around the house in Billy Williams's 'When Father Papered the Parlour'

(1910), or his refusal to find a job in Maidie Scott's 'Everybody Works but Father' (1905). Dan Crawley's 'Father Keeps on Doing It' (1905) reveals him to be so inept he can't even boil a chicken properly: 'The poor old cock's as hard as rock, and Father keeps on doing it.' The Victorian veneration of the family was routinely ridiculed in the halls.

Nonetheless, music hall was edging ever closer towards being accepted in polite society. In 1911 the new king, George V, agreed to attend a special performance at Edward Moss's flagship theatre, the Edinburgh Empire, as part of the coronation celebrations. No monarch had visited a hall before – though when he was prince of Wales, the future Edward VII had invited Dan Leno, Vesta Tilley and others to Windsor for private performances – so this was an opportunity for a huge breakthrough.

Unfortunately, two months before the scheduled date, the Edinburgh Empire burned to the ground after a fire broke out on stage during the act of the world's most celebrated magician, the Great Lafayette (born Sigmund Neuberger in Munich). There was much mourning when the body of Lafayette was discovered in the rubble – and then much marvelling when he was found again a couple of days later, and it turned out that the first corpse had been that of a body double used in one of his illusions. It was said that a quarter of a million people witnessed the funeral cortège that took his ashes to be interred in Piershill Cemetery alongside his beloved dog Beauty, on whom he'd doted and who'd been laid to rest just four days before his own death.*

All of which meant that the first-ever Royal Command Performance – as it became known – was delayed by a year and relocated to the Palace Theatre in London. But when it did finally happen in 1912, it fulfilled all the hopes of the industry, bestowing the great seal of propriety, marking a new era of clean, inoffensive entertainment that was appreciated by the highest in the land. 'Vulgar display is by no means a characteristic of the modern music hall,'

---

* Beauty had been a gift from American escapologist Harry Houdini.

approved *The Times*.[49] 'The day of the naughty music hall is gone,' agreed the *Sporting Life*; anyone who desired 'the full limit of naughtiness' would now have to 'spend a holiday in Budapest or some of the Spanish and Italian cities'.[50] Vesta Tilley, who appeared at the performance, expressed her pride: 'It has been a tremendous struggle, but gradually the halls have risen, superior, and now there are no better or cleaner entertainments in the world.'[51] Sir Edward Moss was to die less than six months later, but he had lived long enough to see his dream of respectability achieved.

The Command Performance boasted an impressive bill, including George Chirgwin, Harry Lauder, Billy Williams, Little Tich, Wilkie Bard and George Robey.* Conspicuously absent, though, was Marie Lloyd, her innuendo-laden act deemed inappropriate for the king and queen; she wasn't even among the 150 artists invited to a garden party to mark the event. It was, said the *Tatler*, 'the Great Omission'.[52] With stylish bravado, she responded by appearing the same night at the Shaftesbury Theatre, with billboards reading, 'Every performance by Marie Lloyd is a Command Performance by Order of the British Public'. She still resented the snub, though. But perhaps the promoters were right to be cautious; even one of the acts who'd been considered safe proved controversial, the ladies of the royal party shielding their faces with fans at the sight of a woman in trousers. QUEEN MARY FROWNS ON VESTA TILLEY, read a headline in the *New York Times*. 'Shows plainly that she does not approve of actresses wearing male costume.'[53] Standards had relaxed a little, but the subversive fluidity of male impersonation was still not quite acceptable in the highest circles.†

---

* 'The restrained melancholy of Mr Wilkie Bard,' wrote P. G. Wodehouse; 'the joyous abandon of Mr George Robey.'

† Acceptance into high society did eventually come to Vesta Tilley. In 1919 Walter de Frece was knighted for his contribution to the war effort, and the following year was elected as a Conservative MP, at which point his wife retired from the stage, settling into her role as Lady de Frece. She was presented at court in 1923, and died, an elderly and thoroughly respectable widow, in Monte Carlo in 1952.

iv

The stock themes of music-hall songs continued to be what comedian Will Evans described as 'the old story: love, courtship, marriage, kids, rows, mother-in-laws etc.'[54] Marriage might look attractive from the outside, but a legion of male singers asserted that appearances could be deceptive. In Mark Sheridan's 'I Wanted a Wife' (1911) he advertises for a spouse and finds himself besieged by two hundred men wanting to give him theirs. Women were regularly portrayed as tricking or coercing men into marriage: 'She pushed me to church,' lamented Ernie Mayne.

Once the knot had been tied, things got worse; the home was a female-dominated arena, where women bankrupted men – Tom Costello's 'At Trinity Church I Met My Doom' (1893) – or bullied them, as in Gus Elen's 'It's a Great Big Shame' (1895). Both these old favourites were still to be heard throughout the period,* and others followed to drive home the point. George Robey's 'Archibald, Certainly Not' (1909) opened with a frank admission: 'It's no use me denying facts, I'm henpecked, you can see.' All a man could do was accept that this was how things were. 'I've got a large house and I've also a wife,' sang Wilkie Bard in 1902, adding with a resigned shrug, 'We've all got our troubles.'

The female perspective was, of course, somewhat different.

Vesta Victoria was born in 1873, the child of music-hall performers; her mother, Marie Nelson, was a singer, and her father Joe Lawrence was billed as the Upside Down Comedian because he performed his act standing on his head. Vesta appeared on stage from infancy; billed as Baby Victoria until she was ten, she made her name with 'Daddy Wouldn't Buy Me a Bow Wow' in 1892.

Thereafter, celebrated as the Queen of Domestic Comedy,[55] Vesta became best known for her songs of thwarted courtship. In her most famous song, 'Waiting at the Church' (1905), she makes it as far as the altar, only to be handed a note sent by her intended:

---

* With the arrival of sound film in the 1930s, Pathé News filmed Tom Costello and Gus Elen, and they were still singing these songs.

'Can't get away to marry you today – my wife won't let me!' The last five words, shouted out by the audience, was one of the great comic punchlines of the day. 'The words are inane,' complained a critic, 'and yet at the Tivoli on Monday night, a full house riotously demanded a fifteenth repetition of the chorus.' But the song is darker than it sounds. Though the chorus is comic, the verses reveal the man to be not just an adulterer but a freeloader and swindler: when they were courting, it was 'me that used to pay', and she 'lent him all my money so that he could buy a house'.

In 'Now I Have to Call Him Father' (1908) her beloved has at least paid for his own house, and all seemed to be going well:

> He used to call me 'Dreamy-eyes' and take me on his knee,
> Kiss my little ruby lips and make a fuss of me.

But then she takes him home to meet her mother, and the man transfers his affections to the older woman: 'It broke my heart to see William cuddling Mother as he used to cuddle me.' The mother is also the problem in 'Don't Get Married Any More, Ma' (1907), which predates 'I'm Henery the Eighth, I Am' (1910), Harry Champion's better-known tale of a much-married woman.* Again there's a note of quiet pain under the comedy:

> Four times in my time a bride you've been,
> And more before I came upon the scene.
> I don't like so many changes,
> Makes me sort of wonder where we are.
> Soon as I get used to one, another comes along –

---

* Harry Champion sang of being the eighth husband of 'the widow Burch', all of whom were named Henry. What happened to the previous seven is not spelled out, but there are suspicions when the undertaker arrives in the fourth verse to measure up the current spouse. The best-known version of the song, by Manchester band Herman's Hermits, reached number one in the American singles chart in 1965, but omitted the verses.

Can't I have a permanent papa?

Even when achieved, married life isn't always blissful, as Vesta noted in 'It Ain't All Honey and It Ain't All Jam' (1905):

When I wed my husband, I thought it jolly fine,
Told me all my life that I should have the best of wine,
But on me, for champagne, he's never spent a quid,
The only wine that I get is the whining of the kid.

Vesta Victoria's real-life experience was no better. In 1897 she married Fred McAvoy, the manager of the South London Palace of Varieties, but it wasn't a happy relationship. He felt insecure in the face of her stardom and emasculated by her greater earning power, though he readily borrowed money from her that he never repaid. At their divorce proceedings six years later, she said that he had been intensely jealous from the start of their marriage. On their wedding night he had shaken her violently and the next day insisted upon a medical examination because he claimed to have heard a rumour that she had previously had 'at least six children'. She had not, but the belief that he was a cuckold continued to consume him; his baseless accusations of infidelity culminated in him alleging that he was not the father of their daughter. 'The cruelty complained of was a long series of abominable treatment,' the court heard, 'not only consisting of physical violence, but also such treatment as was deleterious to health.' She said of his behaviour, 'It made me very weak. I had attacks of crying, and at times I had to give up my engagements.'[56]

The 'one touch of humour' in the proceedings, said the *Daily Mirror*, came when the judge revealed how out of touch he was with popular culture. 'It may be my ignorance,' he asked of Vesta, 'but what do you do?'[57] Other than that, the case revealed a tale of abject misery, one that was far from uncommon in Edwardian homes.

Most famously there was Marie Lloyd, who married Percy

Courtenay in 1887, when she was seventeen, their daughter being born six months later.* A racecourse tout who drank and gambled heavily, Courtenay used his wife's money to do so – and resented her for the fact. By 1894 she'd moved out of the marital home, and they'd formally separated. He took the split badly and in a drunken rage tracked her down to the stage door of the Empire in Leicester Square, shouting and swearing, threatening to kill her and causing enough disturbance for her booking there to be cancelled. All this emerged in Marlborough Street Police Court, where Courtenay was bound over to keep the peace.

Ten years later he petitioned for divorce on the grounds of her adultery. Lloyd put up no defence, but Courtenay still had to see his sorry story paraded in the press, his subservient position contrasted with his wife's independence.† Even ending the marriage almost defeated him; he'd filed for divorce once before but had lacked the funds to pursue it. Similarly, he had made no contribution to the support of their child, now sixteen years old. 'If I had had means to do so, I should have done,' he protested.[58]

The man named by Courtenay as co-respondent was Alec Hurley, with whom Marie Lloyd had been living for some time. The London-born son of an Irish sea captain, Hurley was a coster comedian, with songs including 'My Old Barrer' and 'I Ain't Nobody in Particular'. He had a strong, expressive voice and a local following in London, but he wasn't in the same league as Marie. When they finally got married in 1906, the *Daily Mirror* spelled out the pecking order: 'The wedding of Miss Marie Lloyd, one of the most popular music-hall favourites, and Mr Alec Hurley has just taken place.' The reception was held at the Gaiety Restaurant, where Marie was prevailed upon to speak. 'I am proud of my

---

* As an infant, the daughter appeared on stage with her mother as Little Maudie Courtenay, but became better known as an adult singer, billed as Marie Lloyd Junior.
† In a similar case novelist Katherine Cecil Thurston was divorced in 1910, and her husband, the far less successful writer Ernest Temple Thurston, 'complained that she was making more money than he was'.

husband,' she declared. 'I hope for a few years more to amuse the public on the music-hall stage; then me and my old man will settle down at one of those roadside hostelries where the motor-cars pass by and never stop, and I shall say to my husband, "Come on, Alec, put up the shutters and let's be off on 'ossback."'[59]

This cockney idyll was never realised, again poisoned by her husband's inability to accept inferior status. The couple separated; Hurley began drinking and gambling heavily and was declared bankrupt in 1911. In December 1913 he died of pneumonia; he was forty-two years old. Marie wasn't at the funeral, she was on a tour of America, accompanied by the new man in her life, Derby-winning jockey Bernard Dillon. There was a suggestion that the two had secretly married just a fortnight after Hurley's death, but they had the decency to delay the public ceremony for two months.

The unhappy marriages of Vesta Victoria and Marie Lloyd were extraordinary only in that these were women with the resources to free themselves. For the vast majority, legal remedy was not an option; between 1900 and 1913 there were an average of just 585 divorces a year in England and Wales. On the other hand, courts could be understanding of the realities of abusive family life. When seventeen-year-old John Peters of Illogan in Cornwall was charged in 1907 with murdering his father with a hammer, a grand jury reduced the charge to manslaughter. 'The evidence showed that the father was a lazy, worthless man, who was often cruel to his wife and children,' it was reported, and the defendant received a lenient sentence of three years' penal servitude.[60]

Even among the upper-middle class, marital unhappiness was mostly something to be endured. It was a common theme in literature. 'Oh, how dull it was!' exclaims Mrs Adair in *The Four Feathers*. 'There are women, heaps of them, no doubt, to whom the management of a big house, the season in London, the ordinary round of visits, are sufficient. I, worse luck, was not one of them. Dull!'[61] In a more extreme case, much of John Galsworthy's *A Man of Property* hinges on the loveless marriage of desiccated, money-obsessed

Soames Forsyte and his semi-detached wife, Irene. Enraged by her aloof remoteness, Soames finally snaps. 'A good beating is the only thing that would bring you to your senses,' he tells her. It's only words – he's too cold-blooded to act upon his threat – but a few nights later he rapes her. And eventually even he recognises what lies behind the inscrutable mask she wears: 'He understood nearly all there was to understand – understood that she loathed him, that she had loathed him for years, that for all intents and purposes they were like people living in different worlds.'[62]

The depiction of domestic anguish was increasingly common, but there were subjects that remained inappropriate for artistic expression. When H. G. Wells wrote of a young woman's passion for an older married man in *Ann Veronica* (1909), the novel was turned down by his usual publishers because it 'would be exceedingly distasteful to the public'.[63] Hubert Wales's novel *The Yoke* (1907) depicted a middle-aged woman in a quasi-incestuous sexual relationship with a younger man – he's her ward, and she wishes to protect him from the prostitutes he encounters in music halls. Originally priced at six shillings, it sold well enough to warrant a cheap reprint priced at one shilling, at which point the publisher, John Long, was summonsed under the Obscene Publications Act and a destruction order was issued. (British obscenity prosecutions have always tended to target cheap editions.)

Those novels were at least published. Drama fared less well, since the theatre – though not the music hall – was subject to censorship by the Lord Chamberlain's Office. Scripts had to be submitted in advance for a licence; changes and deletions could be ordered and, in extreme cases, a production could be banned outright. A vigorous campaign to abolish this requirement proved unsuccessful, and playwrights who sought to explore controversial subjects continued to be silenced. Henrik Ibsen's *Ghosts*, which included themes of venereal disease and incest, would only receive its first public performance in Britain in 1914, more than thirty years after it was written. Similarly, George Bernard Shaw's *Mrs Warren's Profession* (her profession was prostitution) was written in 1893, but had only a single, private performance in 1902.* And the plays *Waste* (1906) by Harley Granville-Barker and *The Breaking Point* (1907) by Edward Garnett dealt with abortion and were both refused a licence.

Although these plays depicted genuine issues, the prevailing attitude was that there was no need for writers to thrust depravity in the public's face. But this was now the newspaper age and such censorship was increasingly ineffective, particularly as the press displayed far less reticence when such subjects turned up in real life.

In Stone, Staffordshire, in 1903 a sixty-seven-year-old woman and her forty-year-old daughter were sentenced to four and seven years in prison respectively, having been convicted of supplying pills containing diachylon with intent to procure an abortion. Diachylon was a mixture of lead oxide and olive oil widely available in chemists, and was used to help plasters stick to the skin. When taken internally, it was potentially lethal, since it caused lead poisoning. It could also, however, terminate a pregnancy, which is why it was sometimes consumed. 'Lead is frequently taken by women to prevent conception or to procure abortion,' explained Dr Mason of Darnall, Yorkshire, in another court case, 'and diachylon was the most convenient form in which to take it.'[64] It was unclear how widespread the practice was – the case in Stone was the first in the area – but, said the prosecuting counsel, subsequent investigation had revealed that the product 'was used extensively' for that purpose. Now 'the authorities were particularly anxious the public should know the danger of diachylon – that it was not only an abortive but a terrible lead poisoner.'[65]

The problem was that any such warning would simply spread information about the product, and those who were desperate enough might still be prepared to take the risk. In 1906 there were similar prosecutions for supplying the drug in Blackpool, Nottingham and Sheffield; in the latter case, the convicted woman was

---

* The first public performance came in 1925.

a midwife. There were also inquests into women who'd died as a result of taking diachylon. Typical was Annie Fitzhugh, 'a young married woman' from Chaddesden in Derbyshire. The inquest was told that 'if the child had been allowed to live, it would have been the woman's sixth in five years'.[66] It was the second such death in Derby Infirmary inside a week.

The fact that Fitzhugh was married was not unusual; the same was true of the women in all of these cases. Abortion was often associated with unmarried women seeking to avoid the social stigma of having an illegitimate child, but it was also seen as a last resort by the despairing working-class mother.*

v

Back in the mid-1880s, the Salvation Army had been low on funds. It was expanding its operations faster than its resources allowed, and at a meeting in London's Exeter Hall General William Booth appealed for donations. One of his officers in the hall, Major John Carleton, responded that he had little to give, but did have a suggestion: 'By going without my pudding every day for a year, I calculate I shall save fifty shillings. This I will do.' The simplicity of the proposal had something of the Widow's Mite[†] about it, and Booth was inspired. While a year-long commitment seemed a bit steep, he concluded, the idea of asking members 'to unite in going without something every day for a week and to give the proceeds to the work' was plausible.[67] And thus, in 1886, was born Self-Denial Week, raising £5,000 and repeated every year thereafter.

When, a generation later, the Women's Social and Political Union found itself in similar need of funds, the organisation's treasurer Emmeline Pethick Lawrence, who'd been brought up in

---

* Diachylon was added to the Poisons Register in 1917.

† 'Verily I say unto you, That this poor widow hath cast more in than all they which have cast into the treasury. For all they did cast in of their abundance; but she of her want did cast in all that she had.' (Mark 12:41–44)

a strict Methodist family, adopted the Salvation Army's concept. The first WSPU Self-Denial Week was held in March 1908, raising £7,000 and doubling the organisation's income for that financial year.* More importantly, observed Pethick Lawrence in the journal *Votes for Women*, it was a moment of moral reinvigoration that brought 'a new consciousness of self-mastery and power, a new zeal and burning enthusiasm, a new spirit of glad surrender'.[68] It also illustrated the fact that the fight for women's suffrage was firmly rooted in Christian tradition. 'Let there be no mistake about it,' wrote campaigner and journalist Helena Swanwick in her memoir of the period, 'this movement was not primarily political; it was social, moral, psychological and profoundly religious.'[69]

Swanwick was not actually a member of the WSPU, but of the National Union of Women's Suffrage Societies, an older organisation founded in 1897 from the merger of seventeen existing groups and under the leadership of Millicent Fawcett. It was committed to constitutional change, to securing the vote for women through parliamentary lobbying, petitions and political meetings. Its members were known as suffragists; it was the largest body campaigning for change, and it was making some headway in persuading politicians.

In terms of public attention, however, it was to be entirely eclipsed by the smaller WSPU, founded in Manchester in 1903 by Emmeline Pankhurst, a former member of the Independent Labour Party and an early ally of Keir Hardie. Initially, this organisation also used constitutional means, but following the failure of yet another suffrage bill in Parliament in 1905, it relocated to London and turned to more radical tactics. 'We adopted Salvation Army methods and went out into the highways and the byways after converts,' Emmeline Pankhurst wrote later. 'Just as the Booths and their followers took religion to the street crowds in such fashion that the church people were horrified, so we took suffrage

---

* The Salvation Army's Self-Denial Week, held the same month, raised £72,670.

to the general public in a manner that amazed and scandalised the other suffragists.'[70]

Derisively referred to in the *Daily Mail* as suffragettes – a name they swiftly adopted – the WSPU courted newspaper coverage by disrupting political meetings, demonstrating in Westminster and staging street protests that were intended to provoke a police response. 'Deeds, not words' was their slogan, and the aim was to gain publicity for the cause. The first arrests came in October 1905, when mill worker Annie Kenney and Christabel Pankhurst (daughter of Emmeline) attended a Liberal meeting in Manchester and interrupted a speech by Edward Grey, soon to become foreign secretary. The two were convicted of obstruction and, refusing to pay their fines, were jailed for a week.

Thereafter, the number of arrests rose rapidly. So too did the profile of the campaign. Horse-drawn carts were hired to carry placards, released prisoners were paraded through the streets in triumph, and protestors chained themselves to the fixtures in Parliament and elsewhere. In 1909 Marion Dunlop was sentenced to a month in jail for graffitiing a wall of the House of Commons, and announced that she would refuse to eat until her demand to be treated as a political prisoner was met. This new tactic wrong-footed the authorities – she was released within four days – and was soon adopted by others. The WSPU awarded its Hunger Strike Medal to imprisoned suffragettes who refused to eat. As well as the politics, there was a sense of excitement about cocking a snook at authority. 'I didn't enjoy anything until militancy began,' remembered Mary Phillips, who joined the WSPU in 1907; 'when I was just a suffragist it was boring.'[71]

As the scale and intensity of the action grew, so the police response became more heavy-handed, and the behaviour of officers shocked and further radicalised many middle-class campaigners. Conversely, the sight of seemingly respectable women behaving in such an unladylike manner scandalised many more, the king among them. 'The conduct of those so-called suffragettes has really been so outrageous,' Edward VII complained in 1907; it had 'done that cause (for which I have no sympathy) such harm'.[72] The argument that change would come only if the WSPU behaved better was to follow it for the whole of its existence. 'While these tactics of silly disorder and petty violence continue, there is not the slightest chance of any government or any House of Commons giving them reform,' said Winston Churchill.[73] In other words, mocked F. E. Smith – a newly elected Tory MP and himself no friend of women's suffrage – the Liberals' position was heads I win, tails you lose: 'Having promised votes to women because they are women, they withhold them because they are suffragettes.'[74]

However self-serving it might be for politicians to cite suffragette militancy as an excuse to maintain the status quo, there was no doubt that goodwill was being lost, among women as well as men. An internal NUWSS document concluded that the WSPU aimed 'not so much to educate the public on the question of Women's Suffrage as to harass the government'.[75] This was not propaganda in the sense of persuasion and presenting arguments, it was simply disruption, pursued in the hope that politicians would give up and accept change for the sake of a quieter life.

The Liberal Party in particular was targeted, since it was in power and the suffragettes reasonably believed that its huge parliamentary majority from the 1906 election provided the opportunity for legislation. So, for example, a 1908 meeting of Liberal women in the Albert Hall degenerated into chaos as soon as David Lloyd George rose to speak. A seemingly endless succession of protestors sprang up around the hall, shouting abuse and repeatedly chanting 'Deeds, not words! Deeds, not words!' Some chained themselves to pillars, others attempted to rush the stage, and there were confrontations with stewards, some of whom responded aggressively to cries of 'Shame!' It was, said Lloyd George, 'lunacy and hysteria'. He was a supporter of women's suffrage, yet even his patience was being tried. 'A man is amenable to reason, but he won't be bullied,' he declared.[76]

When Annie Kenney heckled Edward Grey in Manchester in 1905, he had refused to reply, later justifying his silence by maintaining that female suffrage wasn't a party issue. That was true: politicians of all stripes were divided on the question. Many simply opposed the idea on principle, but there were also calculations to be made. There was, for example, a widely held belief that women tended towards the traditional rather than the progressive; having a greater emotional stake in their children's future, it was argued, made women cautious about radical change, inclined towards stability.

Evidence for this could be seen in the existence of the Primrose League, a social and political group founded in 1883 to propagate the Conservative message in the country.* By the start of the century it was claiming a membership of one and a half million, and though that was almost certainly exaggerated, this was a genuine mass movement; a more reliable figure showed 800,000 members in 1914, split almost equally between the sexes.[77] Certainly it included more women than any other organisation save for the churches, giving the Conservatives a huge head start in mobilising their support. The involvement of women in grass-roots politics also helped shape the party's thinking. Prior to the league's founding, Tory MPs had opposed by a very large majority all the women's suffrage bills that came before Parliament; thereafter they tended to vote in favour, until the radicalism of the suffragettes began to drive away support from 1909 onwards.[78]

Not all the women in the Primrose League supported the extension of the franchise, and there was no single position even among those who did. There was no consensus – either in the league or more widely – on what change should be introduced, what 'Votes for Women' meant in practice. One interpretation was that it should entail universal suffrage, removing all the existing property qualifications as well as the barrier of sex, thereby enfranchising the entire adult population. That would have instantly made women the majority of the electorate. It would also have made the working class the majority, a fact that worried some Liberals, looking over

---

* It was named after the favourite flower of Benjamin Disraeli, who had died in 1881.

their shoulders at the growing Labour movement. Anyway this clashed with the suffragettes' own demand, which was for equality of voting based on the criteria currently applied to men: 'Votes for Ladies,' as the Social Democratic Federation called it, for 'well-to-do women only'.[79] The Parliamentary Labour Party, on Keir Hardie's initiative, initially supported this proposal against the wishes of its rank-and-file membership, which provoked the first of many conflicts about internal democracy. The question, said veteran socialist Edward Hartley, was 'Are the members of the Party to rule, or are the members to be ruled by their elected representatives?'[80]

A third option was that approved by the Conservative Conference in 1907, of extending the parliamentary franchise to those women already eligible to vote in local elections – a million or so of them at the start of the century.* All three of these positions could reasonably be justified by the slogan 'Votes for women', but they represented very different concepts of democracy.†

Further, there were women who opposed not just the tactics of the suffragettes, but the very idea of parliamentary suffrage itself, including some of the most popular female writers of the time. Beatrix Potter had no interest in the issue, while Edith Nesbit, a member of the Fabian Society and a staunch defender of women's rights in her work – 'Girls are just as clever as boys, and don't you forget it!' a father tells his son in *The Railway Children* – tended to defer to her husband's views. ('Votes for women? Votes for dogs!' he said.[81]) And Marie Corelli had no sympathy with the suffragettes because 'politics are no longer dignified; they have become

---

* In 1908 Elizabeth Garrett Anderson in Aldeburgh, Suffolk became the first woman to be elected as a mayor in Britain.

† Horatio Bottomley supported women's suffrage using another male perspective. 'Why should we have to do all the voting? Why should we have to neglect our work, our business, our pleasures, to go and elect a House of Commons, while the wife goes to the theatre or sits at home?' It would have made a good subject for a music-hall song.

vulgar' – consequently, a woman in politics 'is utterly out of her sphere'.[82] Then there was the Women's National Anti-Suffrage League, founded in 1908, with members including the novelist Mrs Humphry Ward, as well as the explorer and mountaineer Gertrude Bell and Beatrice Chamberlain, daughter of Joseph. This league argued that it was perfectly appropriate for women to vote in local elections, since councils dealt with social issues, with public health, education and the like, but that national government was concerned with defence, diplomacy and strategic industry – areas in which women played no part.*

The arguments – and the disruptions – continued fruitlessly through the Parliament of 1906–10. There was no extension of the franchise and no sign of progress in the near future. Instead, the opposing positions were becoming more entrenched. Increasingly, there was criticism of the more militant forms of campaigning, as people pointed out that there was something incongruous about a fight for democratic rights being pursued 'with the organised violence of the suffragettes, which is the very negation of democracy'.[83] But this was also the time when the House of Lords was endeavouring to thwart the will of the elected government over the People's Budget. If those at the very heart of the political establishment showed no inclination to be constrained by the democratic process, it was hard to see why those who were excluded should do so.

More tellingly, there were complaints from inside the WSPU about the organisation's lack of internal democracy, specifically the fact that no one voted for the leadership or was consulted on operational matters. Emmeline and Christabel Pankhurst countered that what was needed was strong, unchallenged authority; that was why a central committee, appointed by them, exercised complete control. 'We have no constitution and by-laws,' said Emmeline, 'no annual meeting, no business sessions, no elections of officers. The

---

* The wrestler Juno May was also not a supporter of women voting. 'Please don't ask me if I'm a woman suffragist,' she told the press. 'But if you must know – I'm not.'

WSPU is simply a suffrage army in the field.'[84] The imagery again echoed that of the Salvation Army, though some reached for other comparisons: 'Mrs Pankhurst is as truly a general as Napoleon, and is said to be almost as autocratic,' said the *Women's Journal*, an American suffrage paper in Boston, Massachusetts.[85]

The autocracy became too much for some; in 1907 a group split from the WSPU to form the Women's Freedom League and began to develop new forms of campaigning. They called for women to refuse to pay taxes; they mounted vigils outside Parliament and Downing Street; they sent caravans on educational tours of towns and villages, and – in the manner of Joseph Chamberlain in his tariff-reform days – they made gramophone records to take the message further still.

There was also a brief venture into the London music halls, with week-long engagements at the Islington Empire and the Grand Theatre in Clapham.[86] Two WFL members, Irene Miller and Dorothy Molony, accompanied by supporters carrying banners, came on stage after the main bill to deliver a speech. 'The uproar on the first night resembled pandemonium!' said the press. 'Neither of the speakers could get a word in edgeways, and the management was not a little alarmed lest a free fight should ensue in both pit and gallery.' But they stuck to their task, and by the end of the week they'd won over the crowds. They 'might have been speaking to a gathering of our own members, for all the interruption there was', concluded the League. 'It is difficult to gauge the results in a move of this kind, but I think we may say that it has been a valuable, as well as a novel, form of propaganda.'[87]

vi

There were other cultural manifestations of the campaign for women's suffrage. American-born actress Elizabeth Robins – who had played the title character in the British premiere of Ibsen's *Hedda Gabler* in 1891 – wrote the first suffragette play, *Votes for Women*, directed by Harley Granville-Barker at the Court Theatre in Sloane Square in 1907, and there were novels such as Gertrude Colmore's *Suffragette Sally* and Constance Maud's *No Surrender* (both 1911).

The most striking work, though, came in the visual arts, with a rich series of posters, postcards, leaflets and, above all, banners. The latter were, as Mary Lowndes, chairman of the Artists' Suffrage League, pointed out, a long-standing tradition, though there was now one crucial difference: in the past, she wrote, 'it has been women's part to make the banners, if not carry them.'[88] Lowndes was primarily a stained-glass artist, and the pieces she designed for the NUWSS echoed the style of the Arts and Crafts Movement, with clean lines and blocks of colour depicting women's history from Elizabeth Fry and Jane Austen to Queen Victoria and Marie Curie.* Meanwhile the WSPU, in one of the most enduring examples of Edwardian advertising, branded itself with distinctive colours. 'The White means purity in private and in public life,' explained Annie Kenney; 'the Green, hope for the cause and for the human race; the Purple, the royal blood flowing within the veins of every man and woman loving freedom, and prepared to fight against oppression and tyranny.'[89] The impact of this palette was powerful enough to horrify the fashion houses. 'Suffragette colours would never be offered in combination to the customers of a first-class firm,' declared the manager of a Regent Street establishment. 'The really charming, well-bred and well-dressed woman would speedily resent it, and we should suffer considerable damage to our trade.'[90]

The propaganda produced for the suffrage campaigns was impressive, but the movement was always going to be outgunned in the cultural battle. Even in the rarefied and radical world of socially committed drama, there was a certain cynicism. In Harley Granville-Barker's play *The Madras House* (1909) an American

---

* The Polish-born Marie Curie was one of the most famous women and scientists in the world, winning the Nobel Prizes in physics in 1903 (with her husband, Pierre) and in chemistry in 1911.

financier visits Britain to buy a London fashion house and becomes tremendously excited by the 'Great Modern Women's Movement'. His eyes are fixed on the commercial possibilities that will come with more independence. 'The middle-class women of England,' he enthuses, are 'one of the Greatest Money Spending Machines the world has ever seen.' In the mainstream theatre J. M. Barrie's *What Every Woman Knows* (1908) told the story of John Shand, a railway porter who goes to college, takes up politics and becomes an MP without ever realising that his rise has been driven from behind the scenes by his fiancée, and later wife, Maggie. 'He loves to think he does it all himself,' she shrugs; 'that's the way of men.' He becomes known as the Ladies' Champion, advocating votes for women, though again it's Maggie who engineers this career move. Women, it is implied, already wield considerable political power.

More broadly, the suffragette was portrayed as a caricature. Like the socialist, she was seen in early films as a stock figure of fun. Typical was *She Would Be a Suffragette* (1908), in which a middle-aged woman leaves her husband at home while she goes to speak at a rally. He thereupon disguises himself with a false beard and buys eggs, flour and other missiles, which he distributes to bored members of the crowd at the meeting. The final scene sees a bedraggled wife returning home in tears and vowing to give up campaigning. The same year came *My Suffragette Wife, A Day in the Life of a Suffragette, The Suffering Suffragettes* ('screamingly funny throughout'[91]), *The Woman Who Was Not a Suffragist* and *Votes for Women*. All were comedies.

Even less respect was shown to the suffragettes in the music halls. An early entry in the field came in a song from Wilkie Bard:

> Put me upon an island where the girls are few,
> Put me amongst the most ferocious lions in the Zoo;
> Put me upon a treadmill and I'll never fret,
> But for pity's sake don't put me near a suffragette.

The comic character of the suffragette was irresistible to female impersonators such as Tom Conway, Russell Wallet (The Lady in Black) and Freddy French. The latter had a sketch of a protestor in a confrontation with a policeman, a situation depicted in dozens of routines, normally with the star playing the officer. 'A lady suffragette chained herself to me,' sang Harry Champion in 'P.C. Green' (1910), 'and she's going to do the same tomorrow night.' In similar vein, there was J. W. Rickaby's 'P.C. 49' (1913):

> How those women mauled me when they caught me by the
>   throat!
> They tore the clothes right off my back, to try and get the vote,
> For all they left me wearing was the collar of my coat,
> With 'P.C. Forty-Nine'.

On a larger scale were the Six Brothers Luck, a comedy troupe who staged short plays with several scenes and a large cast of extras. In October 1908 they dressed up as suffragettes and took an open-top motor bus into a big demonstration in Parliament Square in a publicity stunt to advertise their new production *HMS Perhaps*. Set on board a battleship, this was a simple comedy of mistaken identity, but it did include a subplot involving a suffragette who gets thrown overboard. At the end, said the reviews, 'She bobs up serenely for the finale with her colours nailed to the mast.'[92]

The suffragette was only a minor character in *HMS Perhaps*, but her inclusion was apparently controversial enough to cause street demonstrations when the show was staged in Leeds in 1909, and elsewhere as it travelled around the country. Representatives of the Women's Political Freedom League held meetings outside the theatres where the Six Brothers Luck were appearing in order 'to protest against the way in which the performance ridicules the suffragist movement'. They were sometimes met by members of the ensemble; the actress who played the part of the suffragette told them that this was how she made her living. 'Would the Women's Political Freedom League compensate her for her loss of work if the sketch were dropped?'[93] And then there were demonstrations inside the music halls. Individual women stood up in the audience to denounce the performance and were ejected from the theatre by the management, much to the delight of the audiences, for whom it was part of the entertainment.

The publicity engendered by these protests was sufficient to ensure the success of the act. *HMS Perhaps* was still topping the bill at places like the Empire in Leeds and the Palace in Leicester in 1913, five years on from its debut. The controversy was, however, entirely manufactured. The demonstrators – both inside and outside the venues – were part of the act. There was no such organisation as the Women's Political Freedom League, though the similarity of the name to the Women's Freedom League was close enough to confuse the casual observer – and the casual journalist.

In short, there was from 1908 a surfeit of songs and sketches, revues and routines that made fun of suffragettes in music halls and theatres across the land.* This was testament to just how newsworthy the suffragettes had become, but it also acted as a counterweight to the momentum of the movement. A rare exception could be found with Happy Fanny Fields, 'the jolly little American-Dutch girl',[94] whose song 'The Suffragette' (1909) was intended as parody but got some cheers with her patter between the choruses. 'The point is, girls, stand up for your rights,' she suggested. 'If you can't stand up, sit down, but don't let them catch you bending. Why should a woman play second fiddle to a man? And when it comes to this, why should a woman play second fiddle at all, if she's got her old man's bald head for a drum?' The humour was gentle enough for Fields to be invited to perform the piece at the Royal Command Performance.

It's not that there was no support for women's suffrage among performers. Most notably, Marie Lloyd performed at benefits for

---

* Even the boy's story papers joined the fun. In one of the stories of Sexton Blake, a low-budget Sherlock Holmes, the detective's cockney housekeeper, Mrs Bardell, declares, 'I am proud to state that I 'ave become an 'umble decipher of the great Mrs Spankhard.'

the Women's Freedom League and was a member of the Actresses' Franchise League, a group mostly comprising stars from legitimate theatre including Ellen Terry, Sybil Thorndike and Lillie Langtry. But despite the large number of female performers, power in the industry rested almost entirely in the hands of men – proprietors, managers and agents – and they were disinclined to encourage dissent.

That in itself was sufficient to politicise some. Katherina Schafer was born in Germany and came to Britain as a fifteen-year-old in 1886, where under the name Kitty Marion she made a modest living as an actress and then as a comedienne in the music halls. In 1910 she was arrested for throwing bricks at the windows of the offices of the Moss Empires headquarters in London, though she insisted in court that she had no grievance against that circuit in particular; she just wanted to draw the public's attention to 'the disgraceful state of the theatrical and music-hall profession'. It was, she said, 'almost impossible for a woman to earn her living respectably on the stage', and in her (unpublished) autobiography she would detail the casting-couch culture that prevailed. She'd written to newspapers and given evidence to the London County Council, but nothing had changed, which was why she'd resorted to throwing bricks. She was bound over to keep the peace for two months.[95]

Speaking out on such issues did Kitty Marion's career no good at all, and nor did her membership of the WSPU. By 1912 she was finding stage work so hard to come by that she had to take employment as a domestic servant.

8

ALIENS AND REVOLUTIONARIES

If we put a stop to alien immigration,
What a very great improvement it would be.
If we didn't get the scum of every nation,
What a very great improvement it would be.

H. G. Pélissier, 'What a Very Great Improvement', *c.* 1904[1]

Since I've been an anarchist, sad to relate,
My missis has turned very strange.

Jack Pleasants, 'I Shall Be a Bad Lad, Liza Ann!', 1910[2]

Home secretary Winston Churchill (1874–1965), pictured in the *Illustrated London News* directing the police operation at the Sidney Street siege in 1911.

THE FOUR JUST MEN (1905), the self-financed, self-promoted debut novel that almost ended the writing career of Edgar Wallace before it properly began, was a curious book. At first it looks like another tale of an international criminal enterprise with enormous, secretive power, but unlike most who came in the wake of Professor Moriarty, this was not a single, charismatic figure leading a large organisation, but a small self-contained team of lawbreakers. And we are invited to support, not condemn, their illegal activities.

The Just Men of the title are international vigilantes, executing wrongdoers who have evaded the law. 'We kill for justice,' they explain; 'we are the indispensable instruments of a divine providence.' Among their victims thus far have been a priest who raped a girl, the owner of a London sweatshop who abused his female employees, an embezzling Belgian prefect and a corrupt city treasurer in New York. Now they have their sights trained on the British home secretary, Sir Philip Ramon.

Ramon's offence is to be pushing through Parliament the Aliens Extradition (Political Offences) Bill, which will allow the government to deport foreigners who use Britain as a safe haven for engaging in political agitation against their own countries. This is, Ramon insists, 'a law that will remove from this country colonies of dangerously intelligent criminals', but the Just Men beg to differ. 'The Bill that you are about to pass into law is an unjust one,' they write to him. 'It is calculated to hand over to a corrupt and vengeful government men who now in England find an asylum from the persecutions of despots and tyrants.' Unless Ramon withdraws the bill, they conclude, they will kill him.

Faced with such a threat, cabinet colleagues try to persuade Ramon to back down, but he refuses. Similar legislation has already been adopted in other countries, and to change course now would risk the British government being seen as bad Europeans: 'We are breaking faith with the Cortes, we are breaking faith with France, we are breaking faith with every country in the Union.'

And so he is killed, at the precise time that the Just Men say that he will be, despite being guarded by hundreds of policemen. Unusually for a thriller, the terrorists win.

If, that is, we are meant to think of them as terrorists. They do, after all, excite admiration in some unexpected places. 'Think of the enormous power for good or evil often vested in one man,' reflects the British prime minister. 'And then think of the four men, known to none; vague, shadowy figures stalking tragically through the world, condemning and executing the capitalist, the corner maker, the tyrant – evil forces all, and all beyond reach of the law.' In the second volume in the series, *The Council of Justice* (1908), Wallace himself concurs; 'my sympathies are with them,' he acknowledges.

It's still strange, though. Breaking the law in pursuit of a higher justice is one thing; murdering the home secretary is quite another. And that's even before we come to the chosen cause. Because the fictional Aliens Extradition (Political Offences) Bill was intended to echo the recently passed Aliens Act, for which there was assumed to be widespread popular support.

The issue of immigration had recently become more contentious. There being no restrictions on people coming into the country, figures were imprecise, but it was believed that at the start of the new century around 80,000 people a year were arriving in Britain.* Concern was centred particularly on the wave of Jewish migration from Eastern Europe. In the aftermath of the assassination of Tsar Alexander II in 1881, increased Russian repression had included a ban on Jews owning property, and over the next quarter-century there was an exodus from Russia and neighbouring lands. Around 100,000 Jews settled in Britain, though not all intended this as their destination. Representative of many was a tailor named Moshe (later anglicised to Morris), who came from Łódź; unable to read or write and speaking only Yiddish, it was

---

* More than twice as many were leaving, half of them to the Dominions, most of the rest to the USA.

four months before he realised he was in the East End of London and not New York as promised by the people he'd paid to arrange his passage.*

Most of the immigrants remained in the impoverished, over-crowded districts around the London docks, and the local papers were quick to note the changes taking place in the area. 'Year by year, the English population has been driven out, by underselling in the labour market and by the filthy and insanitary conditions under which these people live, until it is a rare thing to find an English family in certain streets.'³ Politicians began to demand greater control of the borders. 'We have criminals and paupers of our own,' said Sir Henry Seton-Karr, Conservative MP for St Helens; 'we do not want all the rubbish of the world dumped on our shores.'⁴ Sir Arthur Fell, Conservative candidate and future MP for Great Yarmouth, was blunter still: 'These foreigners were the very scum that other countries would not admit.'⁵

In response to this pressure, the government brought forward the Aliens Bill in 1904, seeking powers to exclude undesirable would-be immigrants. It met with determined opposition, most notably from Winston Churchill, still a Tory but already distancing himself from the tariff-reforming mainstream in his party. As a free trader, Churchill's objection to immigration controls was intellectually coherent, but he insisted that it was deeper than this, a commitment to 'those ancient traditions of freedom and hospitality for which Britain has been so long renowned'. He pointed out that the number of aliens in Britain was much lower than in Germany or France and said the bill was 'an attempt on the part of the government to gratify a small but noisy section of their own supporters, and to purchase a little popularity in the constituencies by dealing harshly with a number of unfortunate aliens who have no votes'. It was the kind of policy that appealed 'to those who like patriotism at other people's expense'.⁶

---

* Morris's son, Ian Mikardo, would later become Labour MP for the East End constituency of Poplar.

It was during the debate on the bill that Churchill crossed the floor to join the Liberals; he and others then put down so many amendments that the legislation became hopelessly bogged down in its committee stage. After seven full days of consideration, just three lines had been agreed of a 240-line bill, and the government gave it up as a bad job.

The following year, however, another attempt was made. This time it was successful, the Aliens Act passing into law in 1905, the first time there had been controls on immigration since the threat from Revolutionary and Napoleonic France had receded. It applied only to those who were not British subjects – there remained free movement within the Empire – and everyone understood that it was aimed at Jews, even if that wasn't specified in the legislation. Henceforth, any ship landing in Britain with more than twenty alien passengers in steerage was to be inspected, and entry was to be denied to anyone unable to show they had the means to support themselves and their dependants, anybody who was 'a lunatic or an idiot', and those who had a criminal record in another country. Further, any alien who committed an imprisonable offence while resident in Britain could be deported at the conclusion of their sentence.

Provision was made to admit those fleeing religious or political persecution, but in practice this rarely happened. There was an exceptional year in 1906, as a result of pogroms in Russia, but even then just 500 such refugees were admitted. Some radicals argued that many who should have benefited were being turned away. Typical was the case of one David Rabinowitz, a deserter from the Russian army who said that he'd been at Kiev during the 1905 massacres and was arrested when he refused to fire at Jews; he managed to escape and reached London, only to be refused entry and sent back to his port of departure.

The Liberals had opposed the Aliens Act, but it remained in operation when they took office, and it had the desired effect: there was a decline in immigration, particularly of Jews. In 1911 a government report marking the first five years of the act said that the numbers admitted from inspected ships had fallen from nearly 34,000 in 1906 to just over 19,000, with the greatest reduction being in Russians. Over that time permission to land had been denied to around 5,000 people, of whom half appealed, a third of them successfully. There had also been 1,793 expulsion orders against aliens convicted of criminal offences, though how effective these were was uncertain: in the previous twelve months seventy-five people who should have been expelled were found to be still in the country; presumably there were many others who remained undetected.

There was support for the Aliens Act, but the success of *The Four Just Men* also indicated a reluctance to relinquish those 'ancient traditions' of which Churchill spoke. And while the Jews of the East End attracted no particular compassion, victims of the Russian state had long been viewed with sympathy. As music-hall star the Great MacDermott sang in 1891:

The English people have the right
To fight for those who are
Being oppressed and trodden down
By Order of the Czar.

ii

The Reverend Arthur Baker did not take a traditional path to the pulpit, though his background was conventional enough.[7] His father had been a general in the Royal Engineers and under-secretary of state for the Presidency of Bombay, and an uncle had been a Liberal MP. Arthur himself was educated at Clifton College and Balliol, Oxford, and came third in the exam for the Indian Civil Service when aged just seventeen (the minimum age was meant to be eighteen). He showed considerable linguistic flair – 'He has passed examinations in eleven different languages, and taught a twelfth,' it was later said, he was a talented chess player, and he seemed destined for a high-flying career in imperial administration.

However, the prospect failed to inspire him. He lasted just two years as a civil servant, before giving it all up and joining the Salvation Army, going to work in the slums of Salford. Later he became a member of the Social Democratic Federation and began preaching a radical gospel of Tolstoyan asceticism and social reform. As the classics master at the Independent College, Taunton,* he wrote textbooks such as *Latin Prose for London Students*, but there were also pamphlets including 'A Plea for Communism'. And then in 1902 he was appointed minister of the Brotherhood Church in Hackney, east London, a Congregationalist chapel with strong socialist leanings. Baker was evidently no normal priest, but even so he wasn't the obvious host for a gathering of hundreds of Russian revolutionaries. Yet it was he who, in 1907, welcomed into his church the delegates to the Fifth Congress of the Russian Social Democratic Labour Party.

The Congress wasn't meant to be in Britain at all, let alone in a Hackney church, but the original plans to hold it in Copenhagen fell through when the Danish government threatened to hand the delegates over to the Russian police. Norway and Sweden proved equally hostile. Britain might have been less convenient than Denmark – it took one revolutionary, a man who called himself Koba, nearly a month to reach London, travelling on a false passport from Georgia† – but it did at least offer tolerance and a safe return to their homes. 'The contrast between the hostile reception in Copenhagen and their friendly reception in London,' reported the British press, 'has made a powerful impression on the minds of the Russian Socialists.'[8]

Some of the 300 or so who 'filled the pews of the dingy but hospitable Brotherhood Church'[9] for the three weeks of the congress were rising stars in European socialism – Angelika Balabanoff, Alexander Bogdanov, Rosa Luxemburg, Julius Martov, Georgi

---

* Founded in 1847 to educate the sons of dissenters and later renamed Taunton School.
† In 1912 Koba was to adopt a new pseudonym: Stalin.

Plekhanov, Grigory Zinoviev. There was even a splash of glamour when the celebrated Russian writer Maxim Gorky turned up from Italy, and was seen one evening dining in a German restaurant near the Angel, Islington. His later account spoke of 'the ridiculously shabby wooden church in the suburbs of London, the lancet windows of a small narrow hall much like the classroom of an impoverished school'.[10]

The key players, though, seemed to be Vladimir Lenin and Leon Trotsky, the latter 'a man of strong character and remarkable will power', according to the press.[11] They were associated with, respectively, the Bolshevik and Menshevik factions of the party, and the former won all the important votes, rejecting the Menshevik programme of working with Russian liberals and building a proletarian movement, in favour of developing a revolutionary party.* As the *Daily Mirror* put it, 'History is now being made in London.'[12] That paper also displayed an excitable fascination with these sanguinary socialists. 'You can take my word for it that if terrorism is inevitable, and I am certain it is, we shall resort to it without fear of the consequences,' one delegate told a reporter.[13] The women were especially captivating, with tales of their daily firearms training. One young woman said they sought 'war at any price' and declared, 'Free Russia can only evolve out of a stream of blood.'[14]

Given such pronouncements, it wasn't unreasonable to suppose the British authorities were keeping an eye on proceedings. Even so, when Labour MP Ramsay MacDonald attended a session of the congress, he was shocked to learn that British police officers were monitoring the comings and goings at the Brotherhood church, along with a couple of Russian detectives. 'It is proper that Scotland Yard should keep militant anarchists under observation,' said the *Daily News*, which was in one of its more radical

---

* Koba didn't speak at the congress, but wrote afterwards that the Mensheviks were mostly Jews, so 'it would not be a bad idea for us Bolsheviks to organise a pogrom of the Party'.

moods. 'But these men are socialists, bitterly opposed to terrorism in all its forms.'[15] That wasn't really true, as the *Mirror* stories had shown, but Herbert Gladstone, the home secretary (and son of William), denied there was intrusive policing: 'The government never interfered with political freedom, nor was it doing so in this case.'[16] Despite his reassurance, the delegates – many of them with first-hand experience of the Russian secret police – were taking no chances. Admission to the church was heavily restricted, with a password and secret handshake required; names were not used, and, it was said, delegates 'arrive early in the morning and do not leave till nightfall, in order to evade observation, taking their meals in the church,'[17] though on Sundays the sessions had to start at two o'clock in the morning in order to fit around divine service.

There were different perceptions of these enigmatic visitors to London. On the Left, the attitude was one of near hero-worship. The delegates had 'chins and cheekbones that denoted determined enthusiasm, eyes that glowed with strange fires, foreheads almost Grecian in their intellectual strength', rhapsodised *Justice*, the voice of the SDF. They were 'inspired with the same spirit of self-abnegation and martyrdom as those who, long ago, were swayed by the Essenic dreams of that bold young revolutionist who preached by the blue waters of Galilee.'[18] *Justice* was edited by Harry Quelch, former publisher of Lenin's own paper *Iskra*, so the adulation was to be expected, but the same imagery turned up elsewhere. 'There can have been nothing quite like it since stealthy gatherings of primitive Christians under the persecuting emperors,' opined the *Daily News*. 'Some of them are workmen, but the majority are educated men, whose zeal for the working classes is pure altruism.'[19]

On the other hand, there were the crowds of layabouts and sightseers who gathered on the other side of the street to the church, hooting and laughing and shouting their derision. Some delegates wondered whether the 'Islington hooligans' were being directed by Russian agents – 'The method of stage-managing crowds by agents provocateurs is well known on the Continent,' they argued[20] – but this was nothing so sinister, nor so political;

the idlers and urchins of north London were just amused by these strangely serious foreigners, trying to shield their bearded faces with hats and umbrellas as they slunk into church. There was also some suspicion, as articulated by a woman whose house backed on to the yard behind the church: 'Them foreigners comes out into the yard and gabbles away something dreadful. They aren't here for no good, I'm sure, and I don't like it.'[21]

But there were no disturbances, no arrests, and at the end of the proceedings the delegates duly left Britain to return home or to their places of exile. Just as the congress was wrapping up, the Reverend Arthur Baker was making his own departure, 'having accepted a call to the pastorate of Truro Congregational Church'. For the Cornish press his arrival was something of a coup: 'Under the lead of a man who never spares himself, it is believed that Congregationalism in Truro has a bright future.'[22]

iii

The first recurring character to appear in comic-strip form was Ally Sloper, a good-for-nothing cockney with a deplorable tendency towards pocket-picking and petty swindles. Created by Charles H. Ross, he had a drinker's nose and wore a top hat and tails that had seen better decades – 'the urban John Bull', H. G. Wells called him.[23] He first appeared in 1867 in *Judy* magazine (a rival to *Punch*, as the title suggests), becoming popular enough to warrant his own publication, *Ally Sloper's Half-Holiday*, launched in 1884 and lasting for over three decades.

An 1870 strip, 'Anarchy in Islington', saw him standing on a barrel, haranguing the 'lawless and demoralised' people of 'this ferocious suburb' in 'a highly inflammatory style'.* A supporter is pictured, waving a banner that proclaims, 'Down with

---

* Back then, according to the *Sporting Times*, Islington was 'the filthiest suburb outside civilisation' with 'its unswept roads, its slimy pavements, its bands of hooligans in undisputed possession of its main thoroughfares'.

Everything'.[24] This was good, knockabout stuff, not to be taken too seriously; the anarchist was a fanciful role that a comic character could adopt in the same way that he might, in another week, be a park keeper or a lion tamer. That levity didn't last. In 1894 a bomb exploded outside the Royal Observatory in Greenwich, detonating prematurely and killing the bomber, a French anarchist named Martial Bourdin.* In response, Ally Sloper dropped the jokes. 'The country is to a man set dead against anarchy,' declared the *Half-Holiday* sternly; anarchists 'should be swept from Great Britain like so many vermin'.[25]

The Greenwich bomb was the only serious manifestation in Britain of an international fashion for 'propaganda of the deed', the idea that targeted acts of violence could provide a focus for turning popular discontent into revolutionary action. The tactic had been approved by the International Anarchist Congress, held in London in 1881. That was the year Tsar Alexander II was assassinated, and there followed a series of outrages around the Western world, including the killings of the French president (in 1894), the Spanish prime minister (1897) and the kings of Italy and Portugal (1900 and 1908 respectively). There was also an attempt on the life of the Prince of Wales in 1900 when, in protest at the Boer War, a Belgian anarchist fired two shots into the railway carriage occupied by the future king.† The assassination that made the biggest impact in Britain was the shooting dead of American president William McKinley in 1901. In tribute to him, his picture was shown in music halls, with orchestras playing 'The Star-Spangled Banner' and 'Rule Britannia' to rousing cheers. Eugen Sandow's bodybuilding competition at the Albert Hall was preceded by the band of the Irish Guards playing the Dead March in *Saul*, while the audience stood in silence.

Still, this was not really a British problem. There was no sequel

---

* The episode inspired Joseph Conrad's novel *The Secret Agent* (1907).

† Jean Baptiste Sipido was acquitted by a Belgian court on the grounds of his age: he was just fifteen.

to the incident in Greenwich, and when it became clear that the wave of violence wasn't going to spill over from Europe, the jokes began to return. The image of the anarchist as a black-cloaked foreigner carrying a bomb became familiar in early film comedies. In *The Wishbone* (1908), for example, a tramp is given a talisman that makes his wishes come true; he wishes himself a king, is transformed into one, and is promptly blown up by an anarchist. Similarly, *The Anarchist and His Dog* and *The Anarchist's Mother-in-Law* (both 1907) see bombs aimed at, respectively, a rival in love and the wife's mother, to comic effect; both were popular enough to be still playing several years after release.

The imagery was sufficiently vague that, in the public mind, anarchism – insofar as it registered at all – merged into the more radical manifestations of socialism, and none of it was much understood.* 'They learn about anarchists from sixpenny novels,' complained Lucian Gregory, a suburban anarchist poet in G. K. Chesterton's novel *The Man Who Was Thursday* (1908), and 'from *Ally Sloper's Half-Holiday* and the *Sporting Times*.' Chesterton's novel didn't make things any clearer: it tells the story of the central council of European anarchism, which is directing the political violence – but it turns out that all the members are actually undercover government agents.†

Again, though, the humour was to be overtaken by events. A new phenomenon emerged of political extremists raising funds for their cause by theft, and it brought revolutionaries on to British streets in a way that hadn't been seen before. In January 1909 two armed robbers, members of the Latvian Socialist Party, staged a heist at a factory in Tottenham, north London. Police gave chase, and in a running battle that lasted some hours an officer and a

---

* There were also occasional mentions of nihilism, said to be popular in Russia and the subject of a novel by William Le Queux, *Strange Tales of a Nihilist* (1892).
† The head of this organisation is compared at one point to Pan. 'Pan again!' says one of the characters. 'You seem to think Pan is everything.' To which another replies, 'So he is in Greek. He means everything.'

ten-year-old boy were shot dead, twenty-one others were injured, and the two criminals committed suicide.

The Tottenham Outrage, as it was dubbed,[26] was only the curtain raiser. The main event came in December 1910, when police interrupted the attempted robbery of a jeweller's shop in Hounds-ditch, a largely Jewish part of the East End, by a group of Latvian revolutionaries. Three officers were shot dead and another two seriously wounded in the worst incident for police casualties since the force was founded.* The gang leader was also killed, and others were subsequently apprehended in a massive manhunt. Much of the press and public attention was focused on a man known as Peter the Painter, believed to be one of the robbers; a picture of him was circulated by the police, looking very much like one of those 'dangerously intelligent criminals' that Sir Philip Ramon wanted to deport in *The Four Just Men*. The sobriquet was sufficiently memorable that he came to embody in the popular imagination the violent revolutionaries lurking in East End shadows.

On 3 January 1911 the last two members of the gang still at large were tracked down to a tenement house in Sidney Street, Stepney. Armed police surrounded the building and a firefight ensued. Finding themselves outgunned, the Metropolitan Police requested the support of the army – for the first time in the force's history – and a detachment from the Scots Guards duly arrived. So too did Winston Churchill, now home secretary and cutting a photogenic figure in top hat and astrakhan-collared overcoat (it was a very cold day). For nearly six hours a 'quiet and supposedly respectable little street in the heart of the most civilised city of the world'[27] was the setting for a gun battle. Word spread rapidly. Beyond the immediate area of fire, the pavements were packed with the curious, and householders in the vicinity rented out their windows to specta-tors, while pickpockets worked their way through the crowds.

The shooting was dramatic, but despite the absurd imbal-ance of forces – two men against a thousand or so policemen and

---

* It remains the worst such incident.

soldiers – it showed no signs of resolution, one way or another. In an attempt to break the deadlock, a Maxim gun and field-artillery pieces were called up, but they proved unnecessary. In the early afternoon smoke began to billow from the building, and it became clear that a fire had broken out in the second-floor rooms where the gunmen were holed up; by the time it was extinguished, both men were dead. Neither of them was Peter the Painter; indeed, he was never seen or heard of again, which only served to make him more notorious and glamorous.*

The Houndsditch robbery and the Sidney Street Siege saw the deaths of three police officers, three criminals and a fireman. Britain wasn't used to this kind of thing. 'Londoners saw new and evil sights,' reported the *Standard*. 'They saw war in their midst; ruthless, bloodthirsty, desperate anarchy.'[28] Nonetheless, it was tremendously exciting and plenty of sightseers visited Sidney Street over the following days, including 'the leisured ones of the West – elegant ladies and well-dressed gentlemen, who never journey eastwards of the Bank'.[29] Souvenir postcards did a roaring trade as well, several of them featuring Churchill.

In the aftermath of the episode, there was much criticism across Europe of Britain's apparent readiness to accommodate foreign revolutionaries. The country was too lax in its attitude to political asylum, according to France's *La Liberté*: 'Anarchists from the four quarters of the globe have been allowed to establish their arsenals in London.' The Viennese police agreed: 'For these criminals London is a veritable paradise.' A Hamburg paper hoped for 'the abolition of right of asylum for anarchists in Great Britain'.[30] As Sir Philip Ramon had worried in *The Four Just Men*, Britain was out of step with Europe.

At home, there were similar calls on the government to follow the more hostile policies in place on the Continent. Churchill,

---

* In 2008, amid some controversy, Tower Hamlets Council named two residential blocks in his honour – Peter House and Painter House – with plaques describing him as 'the anti-hero of the nearby Sidney Street Siege'.

who had earlier denounced the Aliens Act as 'patriotism at other people's expense', was now convinced that further legislation was necessary, and in April 1911 he introduced the Aliens (Prevention of Crime) Bill in the Commons. The previous year, he said, some 2,271 aliens had been convicted in British courts, but only 405 were recommended for expulsion; under his plan the courts would be obliged to explain their reasoning if they chose *not* to expel. He also proposed greater control of gun ownership by aliens. The bill failed to make it on to the statute book, but it was an indication that the tide was turning. Lenin, Trotsky and their comrades would not have found such a ready welcome in this new atmosphere, nor would the Four Just Men be so easily presented as heroes.*

One corner of British society took a particular interest in these events. In the small world of British anarchism there was serious concern that repression was coming. Police and press alike had portrayed the Houndsditch gang as anarchists, and in vain did *Freedom*, the leading anarchist paper, try to set the record straight: 'No evidence has been forthcoming as to the political opinions of the persons engaged in the crime.' Nonetheless, there were political points to be made. The ruling classes were hypocrites, mourning the three policemen while happy to condone the slaughter of thousands in war. Similarly, the press didn't really care about human life, otherwise horrific industrial accidents – such as the deaths of 344 men and boys in the 1910 explosion at the Pretoria Pit in Lancashire – would merit more column inches than Sidney Street. And when it came to theft, the Houndsditch raid was as nothing compared to the Enclosure Acts that had stolen the common land from the people. 'Do you know,' demanded *Freedom*, 'that more than half the area of the United Kingdom is owned by only 2,500 people?'[31]

---

* The first post-Sidney Street appearance of the Just Men is in the story 'The Poisoners' (1912), where they kill a fraudulent financier who's committed multiple murders, a far less controversial choice of victim. Indeed it's not clear that their services are needed at all since the police are on the killer's trail.

iv

The Sidney Street Siege was captured on film by the cameras of Pathé News, with the footage screened at the Alhambra, Leicester Square and the Palace Theatre of Varieties, Cambridge Circus, the following night. Within three days the pictures had got as far as Aberdeen. It was the first time a major news story in Britain had appeared on screen almost as rapidly as in print. This was a harbinger of a new world.

The immediacy of the pictures helped produce a change in public attitudes. It could be seen in the movies, which were becoming less facetious than in the days of *The Anarchist's Mother-in-Law*. At one end of the market was the melodrama of *The Anarchist's Son* (1910), in which a bomber accidentally kills himself, while his young son is blinded when he unknowingly plays with his father's chemicals. At the other was the spectacular *The Aerial Anarchists* (1911), directed by Walter R. Booth, which climaxed with St Paul's Cathedral being bombed by an aeroplane.

There were a lot of these films, including *The Anarchist's Plot* (1910), *The Bitten Hand* (1911), *The Baby and the Bomb* (1911), *Lieutenant Rose and the Royal Visit* (1911),* *The Anarchist's Wife* (1912), *The Anarchist's Sweetheart* (1912), *The Anarchist's Doom* (1913) and *Retribution* (1913). Cornish novelist the Reverend Silas K. Hocking – he who had earlier lamented the lack of manliness in the younger generation – wrote the script of *The Great Anarchist Mystery* (1912), which ended with the death of a would-be assassin; the studio, the B. & C. Company, followed Edgar Wallace's lead by offering a cash prize for the first person to work out how he died.

None of these pictures, of course, bore any more resemblance to reality than had the comedies. Instead, they drew heavily on old stereotypes of Italian secret societies, with clandestine meetings, love versus the law and the drawing of lots to determine which of the conspirators will do whatever dastardly deed needs

---

* Lieutenant Rose, played by P. G. Norgate, was a popular character in early British cinema, featuring in seventeen films between 1910 and 1915.

to be done.* The one departure from the established formula was the addition of a science-fiction element, the invention of a new weapon or explosive, sought by government agents and anarchists alike, a plot device used in several films, including the wonderfully titled *Demonyte* (1913).†

However inaccurate, these pictures shaped public perceptions, for the British film industry was enjoying remarkably rapid growth. It was also aspiring to be taken seriously as a business. In 1912, amid claims that moving pictures were 'the most popular form of amusement, as well as the most popular educator, in the world',[32] the Cinematograph Exhibitors' Association of Great Britain and Ireland (CEA) was launched. An early meeting heard that there were 5,000 film theatres in the country, with seven million admissions each week, and that the industry employed 120,000 people.[33] Things had come a long way in the fifteen years since the mutoscope had seemed such an exciting technology.

The first item on the CEA's agenda was censorship. The Cinematograph Act of 1909 had imposed strict fire regulations on venues that showed films and given local councils the responsibility of licensing such places. There were no objections to this, but a subsequent court ruling established the principle that the granting of licences could also be subject to the content of the films shown. So councils began imposing their own requirements. In Darlington, for example, licences were issued with conditions attached: 'No picture, to which reasonable exception can be taken on the ground of morality or religion, shall be exhibited.' This caveat was tested when William Lancaster, manager of the Alhambra Picture Palace, was prosecuted for showing *Sapho* (1912), a French film

---

* The latter element turned up in George Robey's song 'I Shouldn't Be at All Surprised', in which he becomes an anarchist 'in a fit of peevishness' and draws the short straw when it comes to executing a traitor.
† The secret weapon was becoming a common fictional theme, from the revolutionary new submarine design in the Sherlock Holmes story 'The Bruce-Partington Plans' (1908) to the aero-torpedo in *The Mystery of Dr Fu-Manchu*.

based on Alphonse Daudet's novel. 'It was not what one actually saw but what the mind was led up to,' said the prosecution; it was 'suggestive of immorality' even if it wasn't 'actually immoral at any given juncture'. Lancaster had put up a notice saying 'Children under sixteen not allowed', which it was claimed was proof that he knew it was indecent. But Lancaster shrugged: it was just smart advertising, intended to 'draw the public'.[34]

In this instance the magistrates ruled that the film wasn't objectionable, but the episode illustrated the danger of differing standards across the country: if each local authority adopted its own regulations, it would jeopardise national distribution. What was required was a uniform system, and since the government had no wish to get involved, the CEA resolved to create its own body, the British Board of Film Censors (BBFC). To make sure things were as respectable as possible, George A. Redford, until recently the examiner of plays in the Lord Chamberlain's Office, was appointed the first president of the board.

And so, at a time when the stage was desperately trying to free itself of censorship, the cinema actively embraced the same system. Films would be submitted for the BBFC's approval prior to exhibition, and would be certified as either Universal, for viewing by everyone, or Adult, for those aged sixteen or above. As with the theatre, cuts could be ordered or a certificate refused altogether. These certificates had no statutory authority, and the BBFC was an entirely private body, but the Home Office signalled its approval of the arrangement, and the system was generally accepted. The BBFC commenced operations on 1 January 1913 and in its first year examined 7,488 films, of which 6,861 passed with a U certificate. Cuts were required of 166 films, with just 22 rejected outright.

The numbers are a little misleading, for most of the releases were one-reel films of no more than fifteen minutes in duration. But 1913 was also the year that British cinema began to take itself seriously as a cultural form, rather than simply a pleasing novelty. A version of *David Copperfield*, written and directed by Thomas Bentley, ran for sixty-seven minutes and is credited as the first feature-length British film.* A similar level of ambition was evident in other films released that year, with a string of prestige projects rooted in literary adaptations: *The Cloister and the Hearth*, *Dante's Inferno*, *East Lynne*, *Hamlet*, *The Old Curiosity Shop*, *Shylock*, *Sixty Years a Queen*. Despite the more sophisticated – if overfamiliar – source material, however, these were still not great works. They tended to be studio-bound, with a single static camera, and dominated by caption cards and overacting. Compared to, say, the German film *The Student of Prague*, or the French *Fantômas*, or the American *Traffic in Souls*, all made in 1913, British cinema was labouring in the shadow of the stage. There were, though, some exceptions, including George Pearson's *Heroes of the Mine*.

Pearson was a headmaster in Essex who first became interested in film for its educational possibilities and then fell in love with the medium. He was thirty-six years old when he resigned from teaching, becoming a full-time writer and director at the start of 1913, and *Heroes of the Mine* was his fourth film that year. Made with a budget of £400 and with a thirty-seven-minute running time, it was a slightly hackneyed tale of two miners in love with the same woman, who overcome their enmity when they're trapped underground after an explosion. What lifted it above the mundane was the fact that it looked so convincing, filmed in a real iron-ore mine, set both on the surface and underground with, said the reviews, 'remarkably realistic and extraordinary scenes in the bowels of the earth'.[35] Many of those appearing on screen were amateurs, miners and their wives and children, which added to the verisimilitude.

The film was released the same month as the Senghenydd colliery disaster in South Wales, when an underground explosion killed 439 men in Britain's worst-ever pit accident; the publicity did Pearson no harm at the box office. 'The price paid for coal is dramatically portrayed in *Heroes of the Mine*,' boasted the adverts.

---

* Albert Capellani's French adaptation of Victor Hugo's *Les Misérables*, also released in 1913, ran to 163 minutes.

'The terrors of a pit explosion vividly illustrated. See what a colliery disaster really means.'[36] If that seemed a little cynical, it should also be noted that the picture did good business in the coalfields; when it played in the mining village of Six Bells, the *South Wales Gazette* called it 'the great pit drama'.[37]

Heroes of the Mine was ground-breaking. In the studio Pearson had been told that actors were not to cross the white line chalked down the middle of the room, otherwise 'their feet would be cut off in the camera view, an unforgiveable sin',[38] and he'd been reprimanded for using a close-up. But liberated by location shooting, he began to find a distinctively British voice for cinema that was not chained to the stage.

v

Heroes of the Mine was a compassionate portrayal of working men, but it was one without a political dimension. More pertinent to the times, if also less sympathetic, was John Galsworthy's play *Strife* (1909).

The piece is set in a tin works that has been shut down for several months by a strike. As the drama opens, management and workers are weary of the conflict, but they are kept from settling by the eloquence of the chairman of the board on one side and the leader of the strike on the other. Both men have political agendas. The strike leader is determined to stand up against the power of capital, while the chairman claims the historical high ground. 'I am thinking of the future of this country,' he says, 'threatened with the black waters of confusion, threatened with mob government, threatened with what I cannot see.' Neither has much time for the men below him.

The play wasn't actually about capital and labour, Galsworthy explained; it was about 'extremism or fanaticism'.[39] Which is what made it so contemporary, for there was a good deal of talk of extremism and fanaticism as a rash of industrial unrest spread across the country. Between 1901 and 1907, an average of

2.7 million days were lost to strikes each year; in the ensuing seven-year period, the average was 13.4 million days. That latter figure, however, is distorted by the five-week national strike called by the Miners' Federation in 1912; a million men withdrew their labour, and 30 million days were lost in this single dispute. Even before that, though, the trend towards militancy was becoming clear: in 1908 there was a series of stoppages in shipyards, coalfields, docks and mills that cost 10 million working days.

In late 1910 things took a turn for the worse when strikes in the South Wales coalfield saw increasingly violent clashes between police and miners, and indeed between striking miners and those still at work. By early November the authorities were losing control of the situation and the chief constable requested the assistance of the army. Winston Churchill, as home secretary, approved the request, but asked for the troops to be held in reserve; instead he sent in men from the Metropolitan Police and promised that the soldiers would not be used if calm was restored.

His words had no effect, and the violence escalated into a full-scale riot in the centre of Tonypandy. One man was killed, with hundreds injured. The town 'looked as if it had sustained a mighty siege' said one report of the aftermath. 'Houses had been raided, shops wrecked, and the goods of unoffending shopkeepers scattered about the street.' It was noted that drapers and chemists were targeted, and xenophobia was suspected since 'Messrs Bracchi, sellers of ice-cream and general confectionery, lost the contents of three shops.' Even more unforgivably, 'some journalists came in for rough treatment'.[40]

The army arrived too late to deal with the riot, but its presence was sufficient to ensure there was no repeat of the violence. Nonetheless, the involvement of the military was deeply resented. 'The presence of troops is regarded as an insult,' said Keir Hardie in Parliament, 'and in itself might lead to disorder.' He added, a little threateningly, that many miners had served in the Boer War, where the destruction of enemy property was a patriotic duty; since they were now at war with the colliery owners, they might well apply 'to the present enemy the principles they were taught to apply to the enemy in South Africa.'[41]

Churchill in particular was vilified as the man who had sent in the army to quell a strike, an image that would linger. More importantly, he faced accusations of being too soft on the rioters. 'He would not hurt their sensitive feelings by sending soldiers,' scorned the right-wing press with heavy sarcasm. 'He was forwarding some nice London policemen, and hoped the strikers would appreciate his kind intentions.'[42] Some in his own party made the same criticism, including D. A. Thomas, Liberal MP for Cardiff, though he did have a dog in the fight, being head of the mining conglomerate that owned the pit at the heart of the dispute. Two months later, during the Sidney Street Siege, there would be no such hesitation.

Tonypandy was not the end of the story. The summer of 1911 was the hottest since 1868, with temperatures peaking at 98 degrees Fahrenheit.* It saw strikes by sailors and firemen, dockers, railwaymen, miners and cotton workers, a relentless barrage of industrial disputes that could be violent and in some cases turned into full-scale battles, as when mounted police with drawn swords were called upon to clear rioters off the streets of Salford. In Liverpool the riots were so serious that the battlecruiser HMS *Antrim* was sent in to protect the docks.

It was the action on the railways that worried the government most, since they were integral to British industry and to food supply chains. So when the first-ever national rail strike was called in July 1911, 58,000 troops were made available, and the country was divided up into districts, with the soldiers in each commanded by an officer charged with liaising with the civilian authorities. 'So far as I know,' said Viscount Haldane, the war secretary, in August, 'only five people have been killed by the rifles of the troops.'[43] Among them were two men in Llanelli, Carmarthenshire, where Churchill authorised the use of troops; three more died in the riot that ensued.

To the disruption of the strikes was thus added a disturbance

---

* 37 degrees Celsius. This British record was not to be beaten until 1990.

in the nation's sense of propriety. Sentimental affection for the military in wartime did not extend to the presence of troops in British towns, and the use of the army in industrial affairs was deeply troubling. Compounding his offence, Churchill suspended the Army Regulations during the rail strike, leaving commanding officers to act on their own initiative, rather than wait for calls from local magistrates. 'The military were brought into play without any request from the civil authorities,' protested some quarters of the press. 'At Manchester it was done even after the end of the strike, and the Lord Mayor and citizens are rightly indignant at this unnecessary and uncalled for intervention.'[44]

In October 1911 the Trades Union Congress (TUC) debated a motion from John Stokes of the Glassblowers' Union that called for the abolition of the regular army, to be replaced by a citizen force with elected officers and 'to be used for defensive purposes only'.[45] He didn't convince his comrades – the proposal was rejected by 1,500,000 votes to 93,000* – but the fact that the motion was debated at all was noteworthy.

Industrial unrest was increasingly a political matter. Strikes were mostly sparked by employment issues – wages, working hours, conditions – but the violence raised questions of whether the country's social and political structures were able to keep the peace. Trade unionists confronted by police and troops were becoming more receptive to socialist arguments. William Anderson of the Independent Labour Party said the militancy was 'due to labourers' subjection, to capitalism and to the growth of social consciousness'.[46] On the other side there were those who feared that society would not be able to contain the ever-growing union movement: in 1901 there were around two million members of trade unions, by 1914 that had more than doubled. Organised labour was becoming a force strong enough to challenge the state itself, if it could only co-ordinate across industries.

---

* Unions affiliated to the TUC exercised a block vote, based on their declared membership, hence the large figures.

Did it wish to do so? Some thought that it did. In search of an explanation for what had caused this descent into industrial conflict, there was much talk of syndicalism, a political creed that was said to be spreading rapidly through the unions. The press explained that whereas socialists aimed to win control of the state and conventional trade unionists sought better pay and conditions, syndicalists didn't believe in a centralised state at all and wanted to take over their industries entirely. The workers would seize the means of production, rather than the levers of government. 'In the syndicalist state each industry would be independent; there would be no central control, no unifying influence,' said the *Scotsman*; the *Shoreditch Observer* added sardonically, 'the mines for the miners, the railways for the railwaymen, the mills for the mills operatives and, we suppose, the dustheaps for the dustmen'.[47] Syndicalists wanted to destroy capitalism, and therefore had no qualms about violence.

It hardly needed to be said – though it was said, and often – that syndicalism was a foreign business. Like anarchism, with which there was a certain overlap of philosophy and personnel, it had been imported into Britain, associated primarily with France. Its best-known British adherent was Tom Mann, one of the great nineteenth-century pioneers of trade unionism; he had been a Marxist, a member of the SDF, but he converted to syndicalism after meetings in Paris with French trade unionists. He launched the Industrial Syndicalist Education League in 1910, which rather enjoyed playing up to the lurid expectations of the press. In its response to the Sidney Street siege, the league's paper, the *Syndicalist*, set its readers a problem: 'If two men can keep 2,000 men employed and keep them at bay in one street, how many men would be required to defeat two or three million men spread over the area of Great Britain?' A prize of two guineas was offered for the best solution.[48]

In reality, syndicalism didn't ever gain much of a foothold in British trade unions, and the TUC, which represented more than half of union members, remained committed to political change through the Labour Party. 'We must respect the dignity of Parliament, because it is the only machinery we have to realise the will of the democracy,' argued Ramsay MacDonald. 'If we have no respect for its dignity, how can we expect the country to respect it when we control it.'[49]

The greatest challenge to this orthodoxy came with the spectacular by-election victory in Colne Valley, West Yorkshire in 1907 that saw the arrival in Westminster of socialist Victor Grayson. Just twenty-five years old, he remained independent of the Labour Party and rapidly lost patience with parliamentary protocol. When, in October 1908, the speaker refused his demand for an emergency debate on unemployment, he was furious. 'I shall not keep order,' he exclaimed. 'I am alone in this House, but I am going to fight.' Not even the personal intervention of semi-detached Liberal MP Horatio Bottomley, crossing the floor to have a quiet word, could calm him down, and he was suspended for nine weeks, shouting as he was led out of the chamber, 'This House is a House of murderers.'[50]

Grayson had a large following, and a reputation as one of the Left's best orators.* Nonetheless, he lost his seat in the January 1910 general election, his enormous potential already dissolving in alcohol. He drifted towards syndicalism, and on a trip to America endorsed the Industrial Workers of the World, a syndicalist union commonly known as the Wobblies. He was also prepared to back violent tactics. While he didn't wish to 'encourage or propagate the idea of wholesale murder to win a strike', he told the *New York Times*: 'Anything is defensible which is necessary to win the cause.'[51]

---

* Lenin was unimpressed, though. 'Given to mere phrases,' was his dismissive view. And sometimes Grayson's words caught up with him. Horatio Bottomley's paper *John Bull* had a regular column 'John Bull's Biscuits' that – like *Private Eye*'s 'Colemanballs' – mocked misspeaking and absurdities, and Grayson got an entry in 1907 for his comment to a students' meeting in Glasgow: 'I do not really think that socialism will ever be as successful as I think it will.'

Grayson wasn't the only loser in that 1910 election; only forty Labour MPs were returned, and it was clear that progress had slowed a little. Nonetheless, there had been achievements, and there was no great appetite to abandon the parliamentary road to socialism. At its conference in 1912 the TUC overwhelmingly rejected a syndicalist proposal to amalgamate unions within industries rather than organising by trade, to 'approving cheers' in the hall.[52] There were further such cheers in the press. 'The truth is that the average worker will have nothing to do with syndicalism,' the papers sighed in relief. It was different on the Continent, but in Britain the unions had 'responsible leaders'.[53]

Most socialists agreed. 'The working man is not opposed to parliamentary action,' opined the *Labour Leader*; 'he is not in the least impressed by the idea of a succession of strikes culminating in a general strike with a view to a complete overthrow of capitalist society.'[54] William Anderson of the ILP said syndicalism was 'a counsel of despair which had no real appeal to the British workman', insisting that it was a bogeyman conjured up by the press.[55]

That didn't altogether stop people worrying, though. The recent industrial disruption seemed so alien that it made sense to see it as foreign in spirit. The national miners' strike of 1912 was the biggest dispute Britain had ever seen, and some discerned in it an augury of bad times. 'This coal strike is the beginning of a revolution,' warned Edward Grey, the foreign secretary; 'power is passing from the House of Commons to the trade unions.'[56]

vi

Aliens, Russian revolutionaries, foreign anarchists, imported political creeds – they all contributed to a feeling that Britain was somehow being infiltrated by those who were not friends of the country. And that feeling in turn fed into the rise in popularity of invasion novels.

The genre had been around since Colonel George Chesney's

The Battle of Dorking (1871) and had reached its artistic peak with H. G. Wells's *The War of the Worlds* (1898), but it was in the Edwardian years that invasion fiction truly flourished. The most significant of the hundreds of novels was *The Riddle of the Sands* (1903) by Boer War veteran Erskine Childers. In literary terms, the book's importance lies in the influence it had on the evolution of the spy thriller, but its immediate social impact was the change it caused in the British public's perception of Germany, seen here as a military, not just an economic, threat.

The story is set off the German coast, between the mainland and the East Frisian Islands. These are very shallow waters, and when the tide goes out, large expanses of sand are uncovered, with treacherous and largely uncharted channels running through them, a maritime maze through which only the most confident would attempt to sail. One such is our hero, Arthur Davies, a man whose life is shaped by 'devotion to the sea, wedded to a fire of pent-up patriotism'. He's an expert sailor whose attempts to explore the sands are thwarted by outside forces because, he comes to believe, he is about to stumble upon some great military secret.

Childers meant his book to serve as a warning to Britain that its North Sea flank was dangerously exposed. As Davies puts it, 'We're a maritime nation – we've grown by the sea and live by it; if we lose command of it we starve.' We've forgotten these truths, though, grown complacent and apathetic. 'It's not the people's fault. We've been safe so long, and grown so rich, that we've forgotten what we owe it to. But there's no excuse for those blockheads of statesmen, as they call themselves.' Meanwhile, as the British lion sleeps, the Prussian eagle is spreading its wings. Germany has expansionist, bellicose ambitions but is frustrated by its lack of naval options: its coast, split by Denmark, is severely restricted compared to those of Britain or France, so it will have to be more creative. Hence the significance of the sands, from where an invasion of Britain might be mounted.

What was striking was the way Childers took it for granted that military conflict with Germany was inevitable. Up to this point popular culture had assumed that Britain's chief enemy was France. Typical was *The Great War in England in 1897* (1894) by William Le Queux, in which the country is invaded by French and Russian troops, repelled only when Germany joins the conflict on Britain's side.*

After *The Riddle of the Sands*, though, those attitudes changed, and Germany became the default foe. 'We all know they are coming some day,' observes a schoolboy in one of Charles Hamilton's St Jim's stories.[57] When Le Queux returned to the theme a decade later with *The Invasion of 1910* (1906), the Germans were the aggressors. This 166,000-word epic was serialised in the *Daily Mail* over several months. Launched with a stunt that saw men in Prussian uniforms carrying placards and goose-stepping through London, the progress of the invading forces made no military sense, but it did ensure that they visited a great many towns and cities, enabling the *Mail* to do special promotions around the country.

As with Childers, Le Queux's underlying theme is political failure: 'The real criminals were the British ministers, who neglected precautions, permitted the British fleet to be surprised.' Unlike Childers, though, he sees the issue as being not complacency so much as the degeneration of political and moral values: 'Socialism, with its creed of "Thou shalt have no other god but Thyself," and its doctrine, "Let us eat and drink, for to-morrow we die," had replaced the religious beliefs of a generation of Englishmen taught to suffer and to die sooner than surrender to wrong.'

That twinning of British socialism and German aggression was not uncommon, and it echoed the message of the novels that envisaged a future Labour government. Horace Newte's *The Master Beast* (1907) again depicted Britain being invaded by Germany, and again the country that succumbed had sunk into a

---

* There were alternative visions. M. P. Shiel's *The Yellow Danger* (1898) saw Dr Ye How, 'the son of a Japanese father by a Chinese woman', set the Western powers at each other's throats and take advantage of the disruption to lead a Chinese invasion of Europe.

squalid socialist mire. Similarly, though more subtly, Saki's version in *When William Came* (1913) – the title refers to the Kaiser – saw British cultural decline as the reason for Germany's easy victory. 'They were tired of their faith, but they were not virile enough to become real Pagans,' reflects a visiting Hungarian; 'good young men who tripped Morris dances and ate health foods and believed in a sort of socialism which made for the greatest dullness of the greatest number.' The political class has failed, of course, but it's not solely their fault, as a young clergyman explains: 'the voters and householders do not realise, still less admit, that it was they who called the tune to which the politicians danced. They had to choose between the vote-mongers and the so-called "scare-mongers", and their verdict was for the vote-mongers all the time.'

For the most part Edwardian invasion literature sees the ultimate triumph of Britain, once the nation has rediscovered its true nature – often inspired by a single hero who tends to emerge from the ranks. Guy du Maurier's play *An Englishman's Home* (1909) centres on the perfectly normal Brown family during an invasion. When Mr Brown is told that, as a civilian, he can't fight, he retorts, 'Bah! What does that matter? I'm an Englishman.' This was the still, small voice of hope running through the period, the belief that the Briton remains at heart the stout yeoman of old. 'To an outsider we must appear on the brink of incapacity,' one of John Buchan's heroes says, 'but then it is not the first time we have produced that impression. You will still find men who in all their spiritual sickness have kept something of that restless, hard-bitten northern energy, and that fierce hunger for righteousness.'[58]

When Edgar Wallace ventured into the territory with *Private Selby* (1912), he told the story of a poor orphan from Deptford, south-east London, who discovers his destiny in a thrilling adventure. Richard Selby's actions ensure that an invading force is beaten back, leaving the royal family of the defeated attackers regretting that they've lost the support of their own people. 'This is the twentieth century, when kingly and queenly power is delegated to parliaments,' laments the invaders' Prince Charles. In a splendidly implausible sequence, Selby meets the enemy empress and takes the opportunity to speak for the peaceful British people. 'I have no ambitions that need make me sin against humanity,' he declares. 'I do not desire to walk to power over dead bodies. But you – you – so long as you can broaden your empire, it is nothing to you that war runs like a blight though the country.'

It fell to P. G. Wodehouse to satirise the genre. In *The Swoop* (1909) the Germans land in Essex on the same day that, coincidentally, several other countries – from Russia to Monaco – also invade Britain. None of them meets with any resistance because the British army has been abolished by a socialist government in the name of equality: 'They demanded that every man in the army should be a general.' The consequence is instant capitulation. 'England was not merely beneath the heel of the invader. It was beneath the heels of nine invaders. There was barely standing-room.'

Happily, one power remains capable of resisting this occupation. The Boy Scouts are still a force to be reckoned with,* especially with the rapid promotion to chief Scout of fourteen-year-old Clarence Chugwater. Learning that the German and Russian generals have been employed as freak turns to tell their stories on the music-hall stage, he sparks professional jealousy between them, splitting their alliance. In any event, the foreign troops are growing restless, unable to cope with either the attitude of the conquered – 'the cold, contemptuous, patronising gaze of the Englishman' – or the weather: 'The late English summer had set in with all its usual severity, and the Cossacks, reared in the kindlier climate of Siberia, were feeling it terribly.'

The result is a huge, mutually destructive battle between the occupiers, fought on Hampstead Heath 'in the densest, yellowest London particular that had been experienced for years'. Those who survive are easy prey for the Boy Scouts, armed with hockey sticks and catapults. 'I am England,' Clarence declaims to the German general, in triumph. 'I am the Chief Scout, and the Scouts are

---

* It's the Boy Scouts who give hope at the end of *When William Came* as well.

England. Prince Otto, you thought this England of ours lay prone and helpless. You were wrong.'

vii

Why was there this obsession with the theme of invasion? Britain prided itself on having avoided that fate for over eight centuries. If there was to be conflict with Germany, the logical assumption was that it would follow the old pattern of a British expeditionary force being sent into Europe, but the overwhelming imagery was of German troops landing here. It feels psychological, rather than political.

Maybe it was that the protective barrier of the sea wasn't quite so secure as it had been. 'Don't you realise what this means?' *Daily Mail* proprietor Alfred Harmsworth said following the invention of heavier-than-air flight. 'Britain is no longer an island.'[59] Perhaps it was the disturbing truth of that realisation that explained the strange panic of 1913, sparked by rumours about 'nocturnal visits of aerial craft of a more or less formidable appearance'.[60]

These stories started in January that year with reports of mysterious aircraft that came in from the sea over Aberdeen, Bristol, Cardiff, Dover, Liverpool and elsewhere. The following month the sightings moved further inland, with strange lights in the skies over Leeds and Selby in Yorkshire, and Preston, Lancashire, among others, and in March they reached London, with a 'mysterious flashing searchlight' seen high above St Paul's Cathedral.[61] It was all nonsense, harrumphed doubters, a shared and contagious delusion. The government didn't seem so sure, though, and took the opportunity to rush the Aerial Navigation Act through Parliament, giving new powers to shoot down aircraft that entered prohibited territory. And whatever the truth of the spate of sightings, there was a genuine threat from the skies for the first time. In 1914 a French aeroplane landed on Brighton beach, and the local press speculated gloomily that, if a Frenchman could fly here, 'why not a German?'[62]

The other common element in the invasion stories, the belief that British culture was in decline, had long been a defining feature of the culture itself. In recent times we had become 'a sneaking poor race, half-begotten and tame', as Henry Fielding wrote in his song 'The Roast Beef of Old England'. That was back in 1731, and even then he put the blame on foreign culture: we'd adopted French customs. And perhaps that was an element of the fear in Edwardian literature too – that the invasion had already started, albeit in cultural rather than military form.

Fielding, of course, hadn't been speaking about the whole country when he wrote that 'we have learnt from all-vapouring France to eat their ragouts as well as to dance'. He was a twenty-four-year-old Londoner, educated at Eton and at Leiden University in Holland, and the world he'd been satirising was fashionable London society. That was still the case. In Saki's *When William Came* it is noted that London has taken to the German occupation with greater ease than the rest of the country as a result of its cultural cosmopolitanism. 'Many things in modern life, especially in the big cities, are not national but international,' explains one of the characters. 'Some of our British devotees of such arts are more acclimatised to the ways of Munich or Moscow than they are familiar with the life, say, of Stirling or York.'[63] There were murmurings of a cultural divide, a feeling that the nation's elite was drifting away, seduced by the fads and follies of Europe.

If that were the case, then it derived from a nagging suspicion in sophisticated society that Britain was being left behind culturally, as well as politically, economically and militarily. Not that British culture was in the doldrums. The pastoral escapism that dominated so much of the cultural landscape might have been in thrall to the past, but it also allowed Ralph Vaughan Williams, Edwin Lutyens, Arthur Machen and others to create some magnificent work; Thomas Hardy was using the rhythms of folk ballads to fashion a unique poetic expression;* in Newlyn, Cornwall, an art commu-

---

* Hardy was still being routinely described in the press as Britain's greatest living novelist, two decades after his last novel *Jude the Obscure* (1895) was published.

nity centred on Stanhope Forbes was depicting the rustic world and, said the *Illustrated London News*, maintaining standards against 'the wilful and childish lawlessness of much recent painting'.[64] And there was so much else. Edward Elgar was at the peak of his powers with his two symphonies (1908, 1911) and his violin concerto (1910). There was Charles Rennie Mackintosh, blending Scottish and Japanese influences into art nouveau design and architecture. There were new visions of Midlands life in the novels of Arnold Bennett and D. H. Lawrence, while Rudyard Kipling was playing with the emerging conventions of the short-story collection in *Puck of Pook's Hill* (1906) and *Rewards and Fairies* (1910).

It was, in short, a good time for serious art in Britain. And much of it reached a very wide audience; Elgar might have been the most revered composer in the nation's history, but he also had a big popular hit with 'Land of Hope and Glory', with words written by A. C. Benson* for the Coronation of Edward VII. Elgar also wrote a football anthem, 'He Banged the Leather for Goal', for Wolverhampton Wanderers, the club he rightly supported.

Yet by the end of the Edwardian period there was a growing belief that Britain and Europe were going down very different paths. Stories began to circulate, for example, of Arnold Schoenberg, the 'super-ultra-modern Viennese composer'.[65] His music went beyond even that of Richard Strauss and Gustav Mahler, it was said, with 'no definite rhythm, no traceable melodic outline or scheme of climax'.[66] So complex was his work that even experienced musicians struggled to play it – which all sounded thrillingly dangerous. In January 1912 London finally got a chance to hear some of this strange new noise, when American pianist Richard Buhlig included 'Three Piano Pieces' (1909) in a concert at the Steinway Hall. There was 'derision' from the audience and the critics were unimpressed: 'If there were a prize to be given to the most nonsensical and ugly harmonic progression I should unhesitatingly plump for Mr Schoenberg's pieces.'[67]

---

* The older brother of E. F. Benson and R. H. Benson.

That was just an amuse-bouche. The main course came later that year, when the eighteenth season of Sir Henry Wood's promenade concerts at the Queen's Hall featured the world premiere of Schoenberg's *Five Orchestral Pieces* (1909). There were neither riots nor acclaim. Instead, reported the papers, there was 'loud laughter' and at the end 'a great deal of hissing and booing.'[68] The reviewers went on to hiss and boo in print. 'It was like a poem in Tibetan,' said *The Times*; 'literally shocking,' according to the *Daily Telegraph*; 'little short of a nightmare,' in the *Daily Express*'s view.[69] The *Referee*'s critic thought the work 'formless, incoherent, disjointed and utterly defiant of all preconceived ideas of what constitutes music' and concluded: 'I feel sorry for Mr Schoenberg.'[70]

Praise was not noticeably forthcoming, though some felt that public taste would adapt eventually, as it had so often before. 'Up to the present he appears merely to have frightened audiences by horrible cacophony. That, however, is perhaps because they have not been educated up to it. Many of us can well recall the reception which Wagner got when he first introduced "the music of the future".'[71] That prospect horrified many. If this was the music of the future, declared the *Illustrated London News*, 'the elderly among us may find some compensation for the rapid march of the years'.[72] The *Daily Chronicle* felt safe for the time being: 'one can only say that the composer is about a thousand years ahead of his time'.[73]

The response was understandable, for this was genuinely difficult music. Schoenberg seemed to have jettisoned the essential elements of the European tradition, eschewing melody in favour of mood, and using harmonies that teetered on the brink of dissonance. Sometimes harsh, sometimes haunted, always nebulous, there was nothing to grasp hold of, no clear logic to the composition. It was deeply unsettling. It was made more so by the impressive quality of the orchestration, which suggested Schoenberg wasn't a charlatan but a serious musician who had, for reasons unknown, taken a very strange turn. 'If he chose his present walks,' wrote composer Ethel Smyth in the *Suffragette*, 'it was not because others were not open to him.' Perhaps, she concluded, 'he is at present going through a mad phase'.[74]

Much the same response greeted the work of painters Pablo Picasso and Georges Braque when it was exhibited in 1912. This was Britain's first sighting of cubism, an artistic style more interested in shapes and planes than in depth of vision. Shockingly, it ignored the conventions of perspective that had dominated European painting for centuries and instead allowed for multiple viewpoints within the same canvas. Like Schoenberg's work, this seemed a deliberate attempt to subvert complacency, for perspective was as integral to Europe's painting as melody and harmony were to its music. It allowed people, objects and landscapes to be seen from a fixed point, a place occupied simultaneously by artist and viewer. Cubism removed that reassurance; this was a vision that existed independently of the human gaze, and it was deeply disorientating to many.

Again, Picasso's talent was undeniable – he was 'one of the greatest but most bewildering draughtsmen of modern times', acknowledged the critics.[75] He clearly meant what he painted; it was just that even those who admired him couldn't always identify what that meaning was. 'Since his capacity to draw in an academic manner is undoubted,' noted one critic, 'his apparent eccentricity must be put down to the sincere desire to express something deeper than reasoned statements.'[76] Others were less indulgent. 'To express oneself, as children do, with a series of coloured bricks – to return, as it were, to the language of the nursery – seems to put an unnecessary handicap upon one's message.'[77] His works were 'jigsaw puzzles with the pieces in hopeless confusion. It may be possible to rearrange them, and one might welcome the task as a pleasant recreation for winter evenings, but they are only distantly related to art.'[78]

There were many such puzzles on the Continent. One could point to the violent rhetoric of the Italian art movement Futurism. Or, beyond the arts, to the scandalous Austrian psychiatrist Sigmund Freud, who wrote about the sexual urges lurking in the deep reaches of our subconscious; English translations of his work were becoming available with the publication of *Three Essays on the Theory of Sexuality* in 1910 and *The Interpretation of Dreams* in 1913. And at the outer fringe of knowledge were the frankly incomprehensible theories of German physicist Albert Einstein, which seemed to undermine what Isaac Newton had told us of the world, the science we had accepted as gospel for two hundred years.

Wherever one looked in Europe, in whichever field of human endeavour, there were old certainties being overturned. Perhaps this was to be the future. If so, it was almost entirely alien to Britain, though there were some in fashionable circles who embraced the new, particularly when it came to the visual arts.

Among them was painter Roger Fry, who in 1912 organised an exhibition titled 'Manet and the Post-Impressionists' and introduced London to the work of Paul Gauguin, Henri Matisse and Vincent Van Gogh.* Not all visitors were convinced – not even the most civilised ones. 'Gauguin and Van Gogh were too much for me,' said E. M. Forster, and Robert Ross, Oscar Wilde's literary executor, thought the work 'of no interest except to the student of pathology'.[79]

On the other hand, Arnold Bennett – who had only recently returned to England after a decade in Paris – took the cosmopolitan high ground. He loftily dismissed criticism of the show as 'humiliating to any Englishman who has made an effort to cure himself of insularity'.[80] He had in mind the likes of the art critic of *The Times*, a man who drew a parallel between this wilful embrace of primitivism and the dangerous and destructive political influences also coming from Europe: 'Like anarchism in politics, it is the rejection of all that civilisation has done, the good with the bad.'[81]

---

* The term post-impressionism was Fry's own.

9

ALARMS AND EXCURSIONS

'People don't know how to dance nowadays,' grumbled
Major Shirley in response. 'I can't stand these American
antics.'

Ethel M. Dell, The Knave of Diamonds, 1913[1]

That ragtime suffragette, that ragtime suffragette,
Ragging with bombshells and ragging with bricks,
Haggling and naggling in politics.
That ragtime suffragette, she's no household pet.

Ethel Levey, 'Ragtime Suffragette', 1913[2]

REDMOND'S CONCESSION.

Mr. John Redmond. "AND SOON WE'LL BE FREE FROM THE DEGRADING TYRANNY OF THE SAXON."
Irish Peasant. "AN' WHERE WILL WE BE AFTHER GETTIN' OUR OULD AGE PINSIONS FROM?"
Mr. John Redmond. "OH, WE'LL STILL TAKE THEIR MONEY!"

Cartoon from *Punch* magazine in 1909, showing the leader of the
Irish Parliamentary Party John Redmond (1856–1918) demanding
Home Rule for Ireland while still wishing to keep British pensions.

HALL CAINE, THE BEST-SELLING BRITISH NOVELIST,* was visiting New York in 1903 when he first heard ragtime, a new form of dance music or, as he saw it, 'a revolting device for tempting human passions which has recently been created in east-side saloons and dance-halls'. On encountering it in the Bowery, he was horrified. 'This ragtime dance is beyond all comparison the most offensive I have ever witnessed. It can only be likened to a possession of devils.'[3]

Other early accounts making their way across the Atlantic were no more reassuring. 'Two thousand negro servants held a dance in New York City on Monday,' reported the British press. 'Under the influence of the wild ragtime music hundreds reverted to savagery, and disorderly scenes resulted.'[4] This was, it appeared, music that whipped its disciples into hysteria, lost in the thrill of the moment, with no thought of the hereafter. And it was surely destined to come to these shores.

Ragtime first emerged from black bars and clubs in America in the 1890s. It was originally played on the piano, and the structure of the pieces owed more to the work of military bandleader John Philip Sousa – then the country's favourite musician – than to the simple verse-chorus-verse-chorus of popular song. It wasn't the compositional sophistication that attracted the most attention, though, so much as the oddly accented, insistent rhythms. The left hand was orthodox, mimicking the metronomic regularity of a military band, while the right hand slurred a melody across the strict 4/4 marching beat, pushing and pulling against the pulse. Syncopation it was called, this off-beat style, and the swinging, swaying, rolling result allowed for dancing that was more lascivious and lewd than anything that had gone before, dances whose bestial nature was revealed in their very names: the Bunny Hug, the Dog Bite, the Grizzly Bear, the Turkey Trot. Ragtime blended European and African musics, and the result was uniquely American. In

---

* He'd sold a million copies of *The Eternal City* (1901).

The Sport of the Gods, a 1902 novel by black writer Paul Lawrence Dunbar,* a couple dance in a New York club to the sounds of a rag pianist. 'Dancing is the poetry of motion,' he says, and she replies, 'Yes, and dancing in ragtime is the dialect poetry.'

The version that reached Britain was not quite as thrilling as the phenomenon described by Hall Caine. It had been tamed a little by the music industry of New York's Tin Pan Alley, where white writers incorporated what had been a black style into the existing conventions of song writing, with simplified melodies and silly words. This was what Britain experienced, not the piano instrumentals,† and it didn't really live up to its billing. There was a steady trickle of songs – 'The Ragtime Oysterman' (1906), 'The Ragtime Milkman' (1907), 'My Ragtime Girl' (1908) – but they were innocuous enough; the whole thing was initially treated as a minor novelty, so that the Five Olracs, who'd been touring British music halls for years with an act of acrobatics and comedy, changed their billing in 1908 to declare themselves 'ragtime acrobats'.

The real breakthrough came with Irving Berlin's song 'Alexander's Ragtime Band' (1911), which swept America, selling two million copies of the sheet music, and then hit Britain with equal force. It was more of a march than a rag, but it was irresistibly jaunty and turned the novelty into a craze. 'This is going to be the ragtime pantomime season,' announced the press in 1912.[5] And indeed London's most prestigious pantomime-house, the Theatre Royal Drury Lane, which was staging *Sleeping Beauty* that year, featured three of the biggest hits: 'Hitchy Koo' ('the ragtime sensation of

---

* Published in Britain as *The Jest of Fate*, the novel was mostly well received by critics. 'The book has dignity and humour,' said the *St James's Gazette*, and the *Daily News* was effusive: Dunbar is as 'powerful in prose as he is delightful in verse. He is a man of genius.' The *Evening Standard*, however, had reservations: 'The plot becomes almost ludicrous in its attempts to blacken the white man.'

† The most celebrated piano piece was 'Maple Leaf Rag' (1899), written by Scott Joplin, dubbed the King of Ragtime. Its first release on disc in Britain, though, was by American banjoist Vess Ossman in 1907, played at breakneck speed and entirely losing the swing.

the year', according to the adverts[6]), 'That Mysterious Rag' and 'Alexander's Ragtime Band'. The latter was particularly hard to avoid that Christmas, shoehorned into productions all around the country, including *Cinderella* at the Nottingham Royal, *Dick Whittington* at the Leeds Royal, *Little Red Riding Hood* at the Hull Grand, *Robinson Crusoe* at Cheltenham Opera House and *The House that Jack Built* at the Royal in Glasgow.* 'We used to see Cinderella in rags, now we see her in ragtime!' joked the press.[7] For those who needed more, once the pantomime season was over, the variety theatres of London could offer shows such as *Hello Ragtime* at the Hippodrome, *Ragmania* at the Oxford, and *Ragtime Revue* at the Surrey.

Yet even in this emasculated, trivialised form, ragtime was excoriated in some quarters. 'This American music is to real music as Yankee slang is to ordinary English speech,' complained one critic.[8] It wasn't as though we didn't have enough cheap music of our own, pointed out educationalist A. T. Davies; he was concerned by the loss of 'the old Welsh songs and lullabies', now that 'taste was rapidly being depraved by ragtime and music-hall ditties'.[9] Martin Anderson, better known as the political cartoonist Cynicus, had the same thought: 'Britain has lost any claim that it may have towards originality and is rapidly becoming Americanised.'[10]

The younger generation, of course, took to this latest cultural import with enthusiasm and, wrote Irish poet Teresa Beatrice O'Hare, assumed their parents were ignorant of such modernity. They were wrong. 'We know a great deal about ragtime,' she insisted. 'The good honest fathers and mothers had the rag-times and the half-fed times, that their sons and daughters might go to colleges and wear broadcloth and red neckties and learn "nigger" dialect and slang and then come home to crush the heart out of them with their ignorance and selfishness.'[11]

As that suggested, some were disturbed that ragtime was not

---

* In the Glasgow production it was sung by Fred Barnes in the female role of the Prince.

merely American but black, that it was primitive and primal in its physicality. Critics compared the music to 'an aboriginal first effort at utterance,'[12] and there was a fear for civilisation itself: those who fell under the spell were 'taking part in some of the most blood stained orgies of barbarism', frothed the *World*.* 'Ragtime is only a primitive form of negro dancing, an American memory of Darkest Africa's hideous rituals.'[13] Lionel Monckton, composer of some of the biggest hit musicals of the time, was despondent:[14] 'If this is what they call "music", then I write no more!'†

Despite all of which, the public couldn't get enough of the craze. 'Blackpool has got the ragtime fever,' enthused the local press, as the summer season started in 1913. 'We shall w-alk in ragtime, t-alk in ragtime, and we're wr-iting this in syncopated time.'[15] At the other end of the social spectrum, a band from the Brigade of Guards played arrangements of ragtime hits at that year's state opening of Parliament: 'Hitchy Koo', 'Waiting for the Robert E. Lee' and – inevitably – 'Alexander's Ragtime Band'. No 'blood stained orgies' were reported.

Nonetheless, like the chaotic music and painting making its way across the Channel, the ragtime invasion from America subverted what had hitherto been considered right and proper, introducing new and unsettling rhythms. The realisation was dawning that the upheavals of the new century would be every bit as disruptive as those of the old. 'There is a wave of unrest passing all over the world,' observed the *Tatler* in 1913. 'It is not confined merely to capital and labour, but has infected art, music and the drama, even the home. Everything and everybody is restless with the spirit of revolution.'[16]

ii

Fergus Hume's novel *The Blue Talisman* (1912) centres on Fodio, a Cambridge-educated Nigerian chief, fiercely proud of his heritage:

---

* Founded in 1883, the *World* had been bought in 1905 by Alfred Harmsworth.
† He did write more, with one last major success, *The Boy* (1917).

'My people come of a stock which attained to civilisation when all Europe was barbaric.' He has some odd fancies ('Atlantis really existed,' he says, 'Nigeria formed a portion of it'), but nonetheless he's the hero of the story. The villain is a monocle-wearing Englishman with 'the aspect of a Mayfair dandy', who has a secret identity as a rogue warlord, causing terror on the fringes of British rule in west Africa. This bizarre twist on the theme of double lives implausibly requires him to use blackface make-up in Africa ('he simply darkened his skin and changed his dress'), but the evil is real. 'The man's a Congo beast,' says a British Army officer. 'He's a slaver too, and keeps up the traffic with the Arabs. By George, I have heard stories of his doings; theft on a large and comprehensive scale, murder in the form of massacres . . .'

The allusion to the Congo was characteristic of the time. The Congo Free State had come under the direct rule of King Leopold II of Belgium in the 1880s, and there had been warnings early on that things were going very wrong indeed. An investigative campaign led by British journalist E. D. Morel,* culminating in his book *Red Rubber* (1906), exposed an industrial level of brutality, with countless dead and more mutilated. As the stories began to emerge, the image that made the most impact was of baskets full of hands; hands that had been chopped off both corpses and those still living, to encourage others to work faster on the rubber plantations. Some Africans were forced to work as overseers: 'They kill us if we do not bring rubber. The Commissary has promised us if we bring plenty of hands he will shorten our service,' one explained.[17]

Whatever charges could be laid against Britain's conduct of the Boer War, this was barbarity of a different order entirely, and the country was outraged. In Arthur Conan Doyle's non-fiction book *The Crime of the Congo* (1909) he wrote that it was humanity's worst atrocity. 'Other great crimes in history have been caused either by fanatical religion, which is in itself just an exaggeration

---

* Morel was jailed in 1917 for his pacifist campaigning, and later still elected as a Labour MP.

of a respectable emotion,' he said, 'or by racial hatred, which is a perverted and exaggerated patriotism. But in the case of Belgium's criminal misrule on the Congo it has been cold-blooded, and actuated by the lowest and most sordid motive of gain.'[18]

One of the journalists sent in 1906 to report on the allegations was Edgar Wallace, writing for the *Daily Mail*. No articles were published, however, for what he later claimed were political reasons: his job had been to discredit the stories of atrocities, but instead he found ample evidence, and Alfred Harmsworth chose to suppress his reports. Nonetheless, the experience prompted the creation of one of Wallace's most popular characters, *Sanders of the River* (1911).*

Commissioner Sanders is responsible for the administration of a large chunk of west Africa. Officially, he's the representative of the British government, for this is part of the Empire, but in reality he rules the territory in his own fashion. His subjects understand this; as far as they are concerned, his word is law – particularly when he turns up in their villages on his riverboat, complete with a couple of Maxim guns. 'You may say of Sanders that he was a statesman, which means that he had no exaggerated opinion of the value of individual human life,' explains Wallace.

This isn't the Belgian Congo, but even so it's a negative image of the Empire, depicted in terms of simple power and greed. In one episode Sanders tries to persuade his superiors to authorise a military expedition to suppress a rebellious village and is refused on grounds of cost; when he discovers gold deposits in the area, expense suddenly proves to be no object. There is nothing here to reassure readers in Britain that imperialism is a civilising enterprise. Sanders has no belief that the people he rules can be reformed, let alone converted to Christianity; his only aim is to prevent – or, failing that, to punish – the most extreme behaviour: murder, child sacrifice, cannibalism and above all war. All he really wants is as

---

* A further eleven volumes followed, up to *Again Sanders* (1928), as well as three films.

quiet a life as possible. There's no desire to use his great personal gifts actually to *do* anything, not even to feather his own nest.

Saki's *The Unbearable Bassington* (1912) was even more loftily dismissive of colonial administrators. Having made a mess of his life and prospects in England, Comus Bassington is sent by his family to west Africa. He isn't pleased at the prospect. 'He would be in some unheard-of sun-blistered wilderness, where natives and pariah dogs and raucous-throated crows fringed round mockingly on one's loneliness,' he feared. The reality is even more soul-crushing: 'Here a man simply made a unit in an unnumbered population, an inconsequent dot in a loosely-compiled deathroll.'

A new tone was emerging in the popular depiction of Empire. In the wake of the South African concentration camps and the atrocities in the Congo, it was harder to see the colonies as a stage set for action-loving adventurers. It was perhaps significant that the greatest real-life hero of the times was Captain Robert Scott, the man who lost the race to be first to the South Pole, and who died in March 1912 together with the other four members of his expedition as they struggled to return from the frozen emptiness of Antarctica. Here there were no commercial opportunities, no mineral rights, no lands to colonise; nor were there natives to fight and to conquer. It was a story of courageous men pitting themselves against a hostile, unrelenting environment, living and dying at the very extremity of existence. This was what inspired the folk back home; it was the essence of the imperial adventure, stripped of all the fripperies of wealth and power. Scott was seen as the embodiment of the national spirit. The final entry in his diary read, 'For God's sake look after our people.'[19] He was referring to the men's families, but he could have been speaking of Britain.

Scott was an exception, though. More generally, a note of cynicism was creeping in to undercut the romance. Edgar Wallace mocked missionaries, do-gooders, progressive administrators and capitalists alike, yet the wild popularity of the Sanders stories showed that this was a vision of the Empire that the public were ready to accept. The moral high ground felt less solid now, perhaps threatening the imperial structure built upon it. Barry Pain, chronicler of suburban life in the Eliza books, contributed a satire, *The Exiles of Faloo* (1910), in which a British MP – the beautifully named Wilberforce Lechworthy – visits missionaries in the South Seas and returns unimpressed: 'He had found that the teaching of Christianity had involved too often the teaching of much that was worthless in European civilization and positively dangerous when transported to these islands.'

Even in novels that relied still on adventuring, there was a sense of impending doom. John Buchan's *Prester John* (1910) was set in an uneasy present-day South Africa. If 'the Kaffirs have been quiet for the better part of half a century', observes a British intelligence officer, 'It is no credit to us. They have had plenty of grievances, and we are no nearer understanding them than our fathers were.' What has been lacking is an African leader who can unite the various factions and give them direction. But now just such a leader has emerged, in the shape of the charismatic, American-educated Reverend John Laputa. 'What have ye gained from the white man?' he demands of his followers. 'Ye, the old masters of the land, are now the servants of the oppressor. And yet the oppressors are few, and the fear of you is in their hearts.' He invokes 'the God of Israel' and identifies Africans with the Jews. 'He pled with God to forget the sins of his people, to recall the bondage of Zion.' In describing Laputa, Buchan reaches for a familiar image: 'If he had been white he might have been a second Napoleon.'

The subsequent clash of cultures clarifies for our young hero, David Crawfurd, what it means to be a white man. 'He has to take all risks, recking nothing of his life or his fortunes, and well content to find his reward in the fulfilment of his task,' he concludes. 'That is the difference between white and black, the gift of responsibility, the power of being in a little way a king; and so long as we know this and practise it, we will rule not in Africa alone but wherever there are dark men who live only for the day and their own bellies.'

The book ends with a benevolent imperialism bringing the modern world to Africa. A training college is set up with 'playing-fields and baths and reading-rooms and libraries just as in a school at home'. This is 'no factory for making missionaries and black teachers, but an institution for giving the Kaffirs the kind of training which fits them to be good citizens of the state'. The result is that the land is now worked scientifically and the area has found prosperity. Even so, the memory lingers of Crawfurd's fear of 'the Armageddon which I saw approaching'.

'Many clever men like you have trusted to civilisation,' says a character in G. K. Chesterton's *The Napoleon of Notting Hill*. 'Many clever Babylonians, many clever Egyptians, many clever men at the end of Rome. Can you tell me, in a world that is flagrant with the failures of civilisation, what there is particularly immortal about yours?'

iii

Just as invasion novels were implausible as accounts of how a coming conflict with Germany might play out, so these whispers of imperial collapse were similarly insubstantial. The Empire was not really under threat from within. The Boer War might have been more troublesome than anyone had anticipated, but British military power had ultimately proved successful, and it had never truly seemed that the Boers would win. Nor was there a real-life Laputa ready to lead the colonised peoples of Africa in a crusade of liberation; a Zulu rising in 1907 was easily crushed.*

These weren't rational fears based on evidence or probability, but vague expressions of the insecurity that loomed ever larger in the national psyche, a sense that, however solid and entrenched British society might seem, it was not destined to last. And for all

---

* Serving as a medical auxiliary with British forces in this conflict, as he had in the Boer War, was the man who would later prove to be the real nemesis of the Empire, the Indian lawyer Mohandas Gandhi.

the emphasis on external forces, from Germans and Americans to Chinese and Zulus, the real concern was what was happening at home. Because society was growing dangerously unstable.

This could be seen in the new mood of militancy in the campaign for women's suffrage. We last heard of Kitty Marion, 'the music hall suffragette',[20] in January 1910, when she was up in court for throwing bricks at the windows of the Moss Empires offices. In December 1912 she was back in the dock, charged this time with setting off a fire alarm in central London by smashing the glass with a hammer. 'I intended to set fire to a valuable public building, which would have been far more serious than a false alarm,' she warned the court. 'Unless we get votes for women very speedily I shall do something very desperate.'[21] She was fined twenty-five pounds and, refusing to pay, was sentenced to a month in jail. The following year she made good on her threat. She was charged with setting fire to a grandstand at Hurst Park Racecourse, Surrey, and this time received a three-year sentence.

The escalation of Marion's crimes was not an isolated case, for her desperation was shared by others. Hope that the Liberal government might introduce female suffrage if sufficient pressure were brought to bear was dealt a major blow by the two general elections of 1910. The Liberals' inability to win a majority meant that the arithmetic was now more complicated, since the Irish Parliamentary Party held the balance of power and its leader, John Redmond, was opposed to votes for women. Bills came and went, and when Millicent Fawcett led a deputation to a meeting in Downing Street in 1913, Herbert Asquith 'frankly declared that he had undergone no change of heart in the matter and that there could be no question of the government undertaking the desired measure during the present Parliament'.[22] Fawcett increasingly looked to the Labour Party rather than the Liberals in her search for allies.

There were hopes here for progress. The Labour conference of 1913 voted to oppose any bill that extended the franchise for men alone, committing itself to universal suffrage, and the same year the Trades Union Congress called for 'the immediate enfranchisement of women'. The causes of socialism and women's rights were beginning to align. The Women's Social and Political Union, led by Emmeline and Christabel Pankhurst, remained above the fray, telling its members not to support any political candidates or parties until women had the vote, but not everyone agreed, even within the Pankhurst family. Sylvia, Emmeline's second daughter, had been a leading member of the WSPU, but she began to drift from the official line, advocating universal suffrage and campaigning in the East End of London with working-class women and with the Labour MP George Lansbury.

Beyond constitutional politics, maverick figures were also pushing at the boundaries of the space opened by the suffrage groups. Born in 1882 and brought up in poverty in Yorkshire, Dora Marsden was a beneficiary of the schooling reforms of the late nineteenth century, and went on to graduate from Owens College.* She joined the WSPU and became a senior figure in the organisation, then split with others to found the Women's Freedom League, but she proved too awkward a figure to fit in there either. 'You know nothing of the spirit of the League,' one of her erstwhile colleagues reprimanded her as she was leaving the WFL, 'but you evidently never had the least intention of adjusting yourself to it.'[23]

The problem was that Marsden's thinking had moved on so far that the vote alone no longer seemed of such overwhelming significance. In 1911 she helped launch a weekly paper, the *Freewoman*, billed as a 'feminist review'. 'Feminism has yet no definite creed,' the paper admitted,[24] but it was more than the 'externals of freedom'; what was needed was personal, not just political, change. 'Our journal will differ from all existing weekly journals devoted to the freedom of women,' announced the editorial in the first issue. 'They deal with something which women acquire. We find our chief concern in what they become.'[25] Quite what this entailed

---

* Later the University of Manchester.

was never fully resolved, and there is a sense of a radical philosophy born too early and struggling to find words to express itself. The *Freewoman* was short-lived and had only a small circulation, but it exerted an influence, attracting contributions from the likes of H. G. Wells and Edward Carpenter, and it pointed the way to future developments.*

All other activity, however, by suffragists from Fawcett to Marsden, counted for little in the eyes of the public and press. The only story that mattered was that of the suffragettes in the WSPU, particularly when the Pankhursts' impatience with the lack of legislative progress turned to violence in 1912.

The existing tactics of vandalism – smashing windows, cutting telegraph wires and so on – were ratcheted up. Phosphorus and sulphuric acid were poured into pillar boxes; the aim was still to destroy property, but there were also injuries to postal workers.† An arson campaign was launched, with houses belonging to government ministers burnt down, spreading later to seemingly random attacks on non-political targets including football grounds, timber yards, schools and the refreshment pavilion at Kew Gardens. There was a spate of letter-bombs, again more of a risk to postal workers than to their intended recipients, and of more substantial explosive devices, increasingly sophisticated weapons using nitroglycerine, dynamite and shrapnel. The intentions and implications were more serious now. The pipe supplying Glasgow with water was bombed, as was Northfield Free Library in Birmingham, and there were attempts to flood villages by blowing up Stratford-upon-Avon Canal in Worcestershire and Penistone Reservoir in South Yorkshire. Bombs were planted on trains and at railway stations, outside the Bank of England, and in churches, including Westminster Abbey and St Paul's Cathedral. Many of

---

* It was followed by the *New Freewoman* (1913) and by the *Egoist* (1914).
† It is just such an attack in one of Charles Hamilton's St Jim's stories that finally persuades the Honourable Arthur Augustus D'Arcy to abandon the 'Suffwagist' cause; one of the letters destroyed contained a five-pound note from his father.

these devices were discovered or failed to detonate, but substantial damage was done, people were injured and some were killed. Meanwhile politicians found not only their meetings disrupted, but their lives threatened: when Asquith visited Dublin in 1913, a hatchet was thrown at his head (it missed, though it cut the ear of John Redmond), and an attempt was made to burn down the Theatre Royal while he was attending a lunchtime matinee.

The attacks continued through 1913 and into 1914, and represented something shockingly new in British life. There had been terrorist campaigns before, most often by Irish groups, but nothing so widespread, nor so sustained. This was the anarchist tactic of propaganda by deed, adopted by middle-class Englishwomen and on a far greater scale than any dissident Russians had ever attempted. It was, proclaimed the *Suffragette*, a 'reign of terror'.[26]

It was also, many argued, counter-productive; it was hard to see how burning down David Lloyd George's house was going to bring about votes for women, and the consensus was that the campaign was doing great harm to the cause. Nor did it stir others to action; recruitment to the WSPU fell dramatically, while membership of the much more moderate NUWSS passed 50,000, and opposition grew to the violence. 'When a fire has once been lit it is not easy to set a limit to the conflagration,' warned Millicent Fawcett.[27] 'Secretly planned militancy was a method of desperation,' reflected Sylvia Pankhurst, which 'retarded a wonderful movement.'[28] But the WSPU were now far beyond any conventional politics.

Indeed, they were beyond politics of any clear description. Emmeline Pankhurst still used the rhetoric of the Salvation Army – 'We are soldiers engaged in a holy war, and we mean to go on until victory is won'[29] – but the WSPU more closely resembled a millennial cult, fuelled by publicity, righteousness and the visceral thrill of destruction, by what Christabel Pankhurst called 'the rapture of battle'.[30] The deliberately anti-democratic structure of the organisation led to the expulsion of those deemed disloyal to the leadership, including Emmeline and Frederick Pethick Lawrence, the married couple who had edited *Votes for Women*. Even Sylvia Pankhurst was ultimately cast out, family counting for less than blind loyalty. 'You have your own ideas,' Christabel reproved her younger sister as she severed contact: 'We want women to take their instructions, and march in step like an army.'[31]

Along with this came unquestioning veneration of the leader. In 1914 Mary Richardson slashed the *Rokeby Venus* by Diego Velázquez, which hung in the National Gallery, with a meat cleaver; she explained that this was a protest at the arrest of Emmeline Pankhurst: 'I have tried to destroy the picture of the most beautiful woman in mythological history as a protest against the government for destroying Mrs Pankhurst, who is the most beautiful character in modern history.'[32]

There was also a growing desire within the WSPU to control sexual behaviour. Woman is 'the priestess of humanity', wrote Christabel,[33] while men 'want to resort to practices which a wife would not tolerate'.[34] In her pamphlet *The Great Scourge* (1913) she claimed that three in four men were infected with gonorrhoea, and that the only cure was, in an expansion of the familiar slogan: 'Votes for Women and Purity for Men'. She added, with an echo of eugenics, that it might prove necessary for the state to enforce this commandment: 'Self-control for men who can exert it! Medical aid for those who cannot!'[35]

And there was an idealisation of martyrdom. In the dock at the Old Bailey on conspiracy charges, Annie Kenney invoked the examples of Socrates, Joan of Arc, Galileo and the early Christians. Martyrdom, though, was precisely what the state sought to deny the group. The prison authorities' answer to the tactic of the hunger strike was to force-feed the women, an ugly process requiring the prisoner to be restrained while a tube was inserted down her throat and liquid food poured in. The practice ensured that none died on hunger strike, but it was denounced as a form of torture, and the effects could be terrible. Kitty Marion was released eight months into her three-year sentence, too weak to keep imprisoned; she'd been force-fed on 232 separate occasions, had lost thirty-six pounds in weight, and – at the age of forty-three – looked 'like a woman of seventy'.[36]

Marion had in fact already been released once to allow her to recover, before being rearrested to continue her sentence. This procedure was made possible by the Prisoners (Temporary Discharge for Ill Health) Act 1913, commonly known as the Cat and Mouse Act, and the clumsy inhumanity of the legislation was an indication of the government's helplessness in the face of the campaign. So too were the futile attempts to ban public meetings and to suppress the WSPU's newspaper. All of it was both illiberal and inadequate, and none of it was capable of stopping the bombs. The government, the police and the courts seemed increasingly impotent.

iv

In general, it was not a good time for the political system, which was weakened by allegations of corruption. The most damaging of these related to the announcement in 1912 by Herbert Samuel, the postmaster general, that a valuable government contract was being awarded to Marconi's Wireless Telegraph Company. It later transpired that, shortly before the contract was made public, the attorney general, Sir Rufus Isaacs, had bought a block of shares in the firm, some of which he sold on to his cabinet colleagues David Lloyd George and Alexander Murray. These shares were in Marconi's American subsidiary and were not directly relevant to the contract, but they rose very substantially in value, allowing them to be sold for a handsome profit. It looked murky.

The waters were further muddied by the fact that Rufus Isaacs' brother Godfrey was the managing director of Marconi. And then there were anti-Semitic insinuations. Herbert Samuel and the Isaacs brothers were all Jewish (while Lloyd George, joked the *Sporting Times*, 'is a Welshman, and worse than a Jew'[37]). 'I have nothing to say about the Jewish race,' declared Cecil Chesterton (brother of G. K.), whose paper the *Eye Witness* exposed the story, 'but I do think that Jewish finance is a dangerous thing.'[38]

Chesterton was speaking in court in June 1913, facing a charge of criminal libel brought by Godfrey Isaacs. He failed to win over the jury, though they awarded the plaintiff only nominal damages of £100. Earlier a parliamentary enquiry had seen a Liberal-dominated committee exonerate the ministers of any wrongdoing. Despite the verdicts of court and committee, though, the affair left a distinctly unpleasant odour. There was no clear proof of corruption, but it was not difficult to imagine that there was a connection between the awarding of the contract and the purchase of shares. The British political system, said Lord Robert Cecil, a Tory member of the committee, was based on 'respect for our public men and their personal integrity'; without that, 'we are done for absolutely'.[39]

There were also suggestions that the government was selling honours and titles. William Pirrie, chairman of Belfast shipbuilders Harland & Wolff, was ennobled in 1906, and *John Bull*[40] gleefully reported rumours that he'd given £150,000 to the Liberal Party on the condition that he 'should be made a peer'.* It was Lord Pirrie who would later tell the press that Harland & Wolff's *Olympic*-class ocean liners were 'practically unsinkable',[41] a comment that came back to haunt him in April 1912, when the second of those liners, the *Titanic*, sank on its maiden voyage. Some 1,500 people died, two thirds of those aboard, the worst death toll ever from the loss of a single ship.† As a symbol of national insecurity, it could hardly be bettered. This was the largest vessel in the world, 'the latest thing in marine architecture and marine engineering',[42] and it failed to complete its first crossing of the Atlantic.

One cause for governmental concern, at least, was less pressing

---

* *John Bull*'s proprietor, Horatio Bottomley, was in no position to lecture on financial morals. In 1911 his past finally caught up with him when he lost a major court case, sued by the estate of an investor for £50,000. The following year he was declared bankrupt and obliged to resign as an MP.

† One of those who died was journalist W. T. Stead, who spent his last hours, as the ship sank, in his cabin, reading.

than it had been. The mood of industrial militancy had abated a little, and there was nothing to match the massive miners' strike of 1912. When the National Transport Workers' Federation called for a national walkout in support of London dockers later that year, the appeal fell on mostly deaf ears, and the anticipated chaos failed to materialise.

But there were still disputes, and they could still be divisive and disruptive. In December 1913, for example, council workers in Leeds withdrew their labour. ANARCHY IN LEEDS, read the headlines, as conservative papers wondered 'whether a body of municipal workers has any right to make an attempt to improve its own position at the expense of the whole community'.[43] Utilities were largely the responsibility of councils, so there was a reduced gas supply to homes, though the electricity stayed on and the trams were kept running, albeit with police riding on every car. And although the council held firm and the strike was defeated, it still had to be paid for: the five-week action cost the city £112,000 in lost revenue and policing, around half its annual education budget. Worse yet, there was further evidence of the bitterness and violence that had crept into industrial disputes. There were prosecutions for assault, for criminal damage and for intimidation of non-strikers. A bomb exploded outside the municipal power station at Crown Point, and another at the Territorial Army barracks in Woodhouse Lane, where police drafted in from Liverpool and Huddersfield were being housed. Henry Wilson, the Conservative leader of the council, was given armed police protection after a murder attempt on a councillor.

More broadly, while the number of days lost to strikes had fallen, there lurked the fear that one day there might be concerted action across industries. In 1914 that came a decisive step closer to reality when the miners joined up with the National Transport Workers' Federation and the National Union of Railwaymen to create what was dubbed the Triple Alliance. Between them, should they choose to flex their muscles, these three were capable of shutting down most of British industry.

But beyond the Marconi scandal and the sale of peerages, beyond even the suffragettes and the trade unionists, the anarchists and the revolutionaries, the most pressing issue for the stability of civil society was the position of Ireland.

It was a long-standing issue. The first Home Rule Bill in 1886 had split the Liberals and been rejected by the House of Commons. The second, in 1893, had been thrown out by the Lords. But things were different now. John Redmond's Irish Parliamentary Party (IPP) was propping up the Liberal government, and the price for its support was new legislation. This time there was a strong majority in the Commons for Irish Home Rule, and the 1911 Parliament Act, curbing the veto power of the upper chamber, meant that a bill could not be sabotaged by the Lords.

And so came the third Home Rule Bill. It was essentially a federalist project, based on the model adopted by Australia and Canada. Much domestic policy would be passed to an Irish legislature in Dublin, while imperial, foreign and military policy would remain the responsibility of Westminster; so too would policing, with the Royal Irish Constabulary under the control of the imperial Parliament. It was a compromise, and while the IPP accepted the proposed settlement, there were others for whom partial devolution of power was no longer sufficient; concurrent with the clamour for Home Rule, there had been a revival of Irish cultural nationalism that fed dreams of independence from Britain.

In 1884 – on 1 November, the day of the Celtic festival of Samhain – the Gaelic Athletic Association for the Cultivation and Preservation of National Pastimes (GAA) had been founded. To a degree this was part of the late-Victorian drive to codify the rules of sports, and in 1887 the first All-Ireland Championships were staged, with counties competing in hurling and Gaelic football, but this was also an attempt to revive an old, vanishing culture, analogous to the work of the Folk Song Society in England. There was, though, a crucial difference: where the English initiatives were a reaction to industrialisation, the GAA was consciously rejecting Britishness. It was a turn away from what Thomas Croke,

Archbishop of Cashel* called 'such foreign and fantastic field sports as lawn tennis, polo, cricket and the like'. This was a nationalistic enterprise. It was also, said Croke, an assertion of masculinity, in opposition to England's 'masher habits and such other effeminate follies'.[44]

A further parallel with English cultural revivalism came with the foundation of the Gaelic League in 1893, which aimed to promote the Irish language. Douglas Hyde, its founder, explained that this was very much a partner to the GAA, 'both tending to de-Anglicisation'.[45] And that in turn fed into a literary movement that saw early flowerings with W. B. Yeats's volumes *Fairy and Folk Tales of the Irish Peasantry* (1888) and *The Celtic Twilight* (1893), and was to reach fruition with the opening of the Abbey Theatre, Dublin, in 1904; the Abbey's first productions were plays by Yeats, J. M. Synge and Lady Gregory.†

The political manifestation of this nationalist impulse emerged with the founding by Arthur Griffith, a newspaper editor from Dublin, of Sinn Féin (Ourselves) in 1905. The fledgling party scored a propaganda victory in 1908 when the sitting MP for North Leitrim defected to its ranks in protest at the lack of progress by the IPP; when he resigned to fight a by-election, however, he was outpolled three to one by the IPP candidate, who was subsequently returned unopposed in both 1910 elections. But if Sinn Féin was not yet a major political force, it at least represented a shift in the debate. Independence was being talked about in the Irish press as a possibility.

The most immediate threat to the prospect of Home Rule came from the north of Ireland, where four of the nine counties of Ulster had Protestant majorities, and where there was resistance to the idea of power passing to what would inevitably be a

---

* Croke became a patron of the GAA and the Croke Park stadium in Dublin was named after him.
† The Abbey also staged George Bernard Shaw's *The Shewing-Up of Blanco Posnet* (1909), which had been banned from the London stage for blasphemy.

Catholic-dominated assembly. Belfast in particular, responsible for some 90 per cent of Ireland's manufactured exports, was a larger, and far wealthier, city than Dublin, and it had little desire to be ruled from there. Quite apart from questions of faith and identity, there was no wish to see the riches of Ulster commandeered by a government in the south. Most Belfast businessmen were against Home Rule for precisely this reason, though there were exceptions. William Pirrie, having bought his peerage, was now committed to the Liberal Party and supported government policy. It didn't make him popular. Travelling to London in 1912, he was greeted in Larne by a 600-strong mob, 'who pelted him with rotten eggs, herring and small bags of flour' and denounced him as 'a traitor and a turncoat'.[46]

The principal vehicle for northern disaffection was the Ulster Unionist Council, founded in 1905, which in 1910 chose as its leader Edward Carson, Unionist MP for Dublin University and formerly solicitor general for England and Wales. He was – as Oscar Wilde, Edgar Wallace and others had found to their cost – one of the most formidable barristers of his generation, an unimaginative, tenacious man with strongly held convictions of right and wrong and a shrewd eye for his opponents' weaknesses. These attributes he now brought to bear on Ireland.

The aims of the Ulster Unionists were, first, to prevent Home Rule from happening at all; second, if that were not possible, to secure a settlement that kept Ulster, or some part of it, separate from the rest of Ireland; and third, if necessary, to set up their own independent state. If this brought conflict with the government in Westminster, then so be it. In September 1912 a document was drawn up, the Ulster Covenant, declaring opposition to Home Rule. Men were invited to sign this commitment to use 'all means which may be found necessary to defeat the present conspiracy to set up a Home Rule Parliament' and, should such a body be set up, 'to refuse to recognise its authority'. There was also a declaration for women to sign, expressing their 'uncompromising opposition' to the proposal. Carson was the first to put his name to the covenant, followed by nearly 500,000 others across the two lists, with an almost equal balance between the sexes. There were lurid reports of some 'signing with pens dipped in their blood'.[47]

The involvement of a senior Unionist MP in what was effectively a call to break the law was startling. Even more so was the position taken by Andrew Bonar Law, who'd succeeded Arthur Balfour as Conservative leader the previous year. In 1912 he declared that, in the event of a Home Rule Bill being passed by Parliament, 'I can imagine no length of resistance to which Ulster will go, in which I shall not be ready to support them.'[48] That commitment took on a new menace in January 1913, with the formation of the Ulster Volunteers, a body dedicated to fighting for the covenant. They were initially unarmed, confining their activities to drilling, but the intention was clear; in due course 30,000 rifles and bayonets, together with three million rounds of ammunition, were purchased in Germany and landed at Larne for their use.

In response came the creation of the Irish Volunteers, a nationalist militia backed by, among others, the Gaelic League and Sinn Féin. The ranks of each of these forces grew rapidly to number some 100,000 men. Right across the island preparations were being made for armed conflict. 'Even in Limavady, a sleepy town of about 3,000 persons, seventeen miles from Derry, I found the Protestants training and arming for war,' reported the *Derry Journal*. A drill hall had been built and there was 'a volunteer force of 200 infantry and 100 cavalry, one soldier to every ten inhabitants'.[49]

Meanwhile the Home Rule Bill was slowly making its way through Parliament. The House of Lords was unable to block its passage, but it delayed its progress, so that the whole process took two years to complete. Along the way there were amendments and compromises, such that neither side was going to get what it wanted, and the principle of separation, of excluding some of the Ulster counties, either for an interim period or indefinitely, became part of the discussions.

As the critical moment approached, it became clear that the army might have to be deployed to assist the police in keeping order when Home Rule was passed. This would be, though, controversial, even dangerous. 'If the government dares to order the army to march upon Ulster,' warned F. E. Smith, another supportive Tory MP, 'they will be lynched upon the lampposts of London.'[50] If there had been some disquiet about fighting the Boers – 'a race akin to our own, a Christian people, a Protestant people,' as Henry Campbell-Bannerman had said – then this was all of that and more. Indeed the Ulsterman, more likely to be Calvinist than Anglican and with his commemorations of William of Orange, had much in common with the Boer, and could be expected to fight his corner with similarly stubborn determination.

Further, it was clear that the army itself did not wish to be used to enforce Home Rule; many of those serving came from Ulster and there was a good deal of sympathy with Carson's cause. The government's hope, as in the Tonypandy miners' strike, was that a show of strength would be sufficient; as a precautionary move, it was proposed to send troops to barracks in the north. Even that proved impossible. In March 1914 news of a possible deployment was received at the Curragh, County Kildare, the principal base of the army in Ireland, and sixty cavalry officers immediately tendered their resignations, with around a hundred from the infantry declaring that they too would resign. The government backed down.

It was dubbed the Curragh Mutiny,[51] and although no orders were disobeyed this was a startling development. It suggested that the government could not count on the co-operation of the army and called into question the integrity of the entire political system. Was Parliament still master of the country's destiny? The incident also emboldened extremists on both sides. The Ulster Volunteers now knew they were unlikely to face the full force of the state, while those who supported independence doubted Britain's ability to implement Home Rule.

Through it all ran the extraordinary behaviour of the Conservative leadership, which actively encouraged dissent and attended mass parades of the Ulster Volunteers. 'We have to consider,' said

Balfour in the Commons, 'what the result of civil war would be.' And he answered his own question: 'It would ruin Ulster. It would ruin a great deal more than Ulster.'[52] But the Tories pressed on regardless with their support. And with their preparations: the Primrose League took on responsibility for housing the women and children who were expected to flee the coming conflict. Nor was violence likely to be confined to Ireland. Other British cities, most notably Glasgow, Liverpool and Manchester, had large Irish populations, and would be disinclined to sit idly by as spectators to the conflagration. Speaking in Glasgow, Bonar Law said that there were 'in Ireland all the elements of an explosion which might take place at any moment', and he urged the Scottish people to join him in trying to get the government to back down.[53] The argument, supported in certain sections of the press, was that this was entirely the fault of the Liberal administration, 'bringing the country nearer to anarchy, civil war and bloodshed'.[54]

It had become a game of brinkmanship, with the integrity and safety of the realm at stake. Having spent years pushing the constitution to its limits with deliberately obstructive parliamentary tactics, the principal opposition party was now prepared to threaten, even risk, an actual armed uprising within the United Kingdom. As Asquith said, it was a 'declaration of war against constitutional government'.[55] And yet he, as prime minister, seemed powerless to prevent the slide towards violence.

v

The first film made by the pioneering French director Georges Méliès was *Playing Cards* (1896), which lasted for sixty-seven seconds and showed three men at a table in a garden, playing a card game and drinking wine. It wasn't much, but these were the earliest days of cinema when it was sufficient for audiences that the pictures moved at all. Méliès went on to do more than anyone else to explore what this new art form might achieve; within six years he was making the first science-fiction picture with *A Trip to the*

Moon (1902), a film that proved 'phenomenally successful' in Britain.[56] 'The pictures have been contrived with great ingenuity and much beauty,' said the critics, 'and the whole fantastic adventure is followed with the closest interest by the audience.'[57]

Even more fantastical was his fifteen-minute-long *Tunnelling the English Channel* (1907),* in which Edward VII and the French president Armand Fallières simultaneously dream of a rail tunnel being built to link Britain and France. The two men – remarkably alike: portly, bearded, born within three days of each other – meet in Britain to great rejoicing and the accompaniment of an all-female Salvation Army band, before the dream ends with a rail crash under the sea. Despite the unhappy ending, the depiction of the two leaders in an embrace was a cinematic symbol of a new era opening in international relations.

As the old century ended, Britain was still pursuing its long-held policy of avoiding permanent commitments in Europe; 'alliances, especially continental alliances, are not in accordance with our traditions', said Liberal Edward Grey.[58] But the situation in Europe was changing, the old Franco-German rivalry amplified by the creation of two blocs. In 1882 the Triple Alliance brought together Germany, Austria-Hungary and Italy, prompting a counter-move in the form of the Franco-Russian Alliance, signed in 1894. Britain remained aloof from these alignments, its attention focused on the Empire, but could do so only while there was rough parity between the two groupings. 'The whole of Europe is an armed camp,' the prime minister explained to Sherlock Holmes in a story set in 1888. 'There is a double league which makes a fair balance of military power. Great Britain holds the scales.'[59]

Those scales were now tipping, and to rebalance them would require Britain to add its weight to the French side – neither the obvious nor the first choice. 'The natural alliance is between ourselves and the great German empire,' argued Joseph Chamberlain.[60]

---

* In reality, the Moon landings ended up pre-dating the Channel Tunnel by twenty-five years.

His attempts to build such an alliance foundered in 1901, not least because of the vociferous support offered by the Germans to the Boers in the South African war. The main problem, though, was that Germany's rapid economic growth meant it increasingly saw itself as Britain's chief rival as an imperial power. There was, said the British press, an emerging Anglophobia in Germany, the message of which was 'that England is the enemy, and that to deal with England, to lay hands upon the world's inheritance of which she has acquired too large a share, Germany must have a fleet'.[61] This was what underlay Erskine Childers's thriller *The Riddle of the Sands*: the conviction that German imperial aspirations and naval expansion were heading inexorably towards conflict.

France too had been hostile to Britain over South Africa, but its overriding concern was that, since defeat in the Franco-Prussian War in 1871, it had slipped far behind Germany. Its economy was lagging and its population was stagnant while those of its rival continued to grow. There was a willingness to find new allies – hence the treaty with Russia – and in 1903 a highly successful visit by Edward VII to Paris created the conditions for some kind of rapprochement across the Channel, an Entente Cordiale, as it was dubbed. Negotiations were opened and were given added urgency by the outbreak of war between Russia and Japan in February 1904; there was a danger that France and Britain – as the respective European allies of those countries – might be dragged into the fighting. And so in April 1904 the Anglo-French Treaty was signed, resolving a string of outstanding colonial disputes between the two nations and promising closer co-operation in the future.

The deal got a good press. 'It allays fears about intervention in the war now raging in the East, and makes generally for the peace of Europe and of the world,' said the *Scotsman*.[62] The *St James's Gazette* was equally sanguine: it 'gives to an anxious world a strong guarantee of peace at a moment when such a guarantee is most earnestly desired'.[63] The king was much praised for his contribution – including in the French press – and his stock rose still further at home. Even so, Lottie Lennox's music-hall song 'There'll Be No War (While We've Got a King Like Good King Edward)' (1908) seemed to be setting the bar unreasonably high.

The political expediency behind the alliance was clear, but it was hardly a love match. The Entente Cordiale was like 'a prosy, middle-aged French marriage', teased the *Westminster Gazette*, 'not a trace of romance on either side, material interests having been minutely guarded, no loophole being left for nagging, much less litigation, stolid bridegroom and sprightly partner jogging comfortably along'.[64] The upper classes and the intelligentsia – those who used the 'jargon of denationalised culture', in Saki's phrase – saw the alliance as affirmation of a modern Britain, confident in its relations with Europe, but the wider public remained suspicious. 'We have a firm belief in the immorality of the French people,' journalist Philip Gibbs pointed out in 1911, adding that it was 'in the English music-halls where the popular idea is most clearly expressed'.[65] He was thinking of songs such as Billy Williams's 'Oh! Oh! Oh!' (1909), in which a vicar visits Paris without his wife and is corrupted by its loose morals: 'With a lady he was pally, quite entente-cordi-ally.'

There was one step further that could be taken. Should Britain also work with France's other partner, Russia? While in London for the 1907 Congress of the Russian Social Democratic Labour Party, Leon Trotsky spoke passionately (in French) at a public meeting against such a development; it would be not an entente cordiale, he said, but 'an entente liberticide'.[66] His advice went unheeded, and later that year the Anglo-Russian Convention was signed. Now there was a Triple Entente – Britain, France, Russia – to balance the Triple Alliance of Germany, Austria and Italy. The balance of power had been restored in Europe, though only by dramatically raising the stakes in the event that there was armed conflict.

Many in Britain found this new partnership an even more difficult pill to swallow. Russia had been despised for its despotism for so long that it was hard to readjust, to think of the country now as a friend and ally.* Again, though, there was a class divide, with Russian culture embraced in elevated circles. Pianist and composer Sergei Rachmaninoff toured Britain, and prima ballerina Anna Pavlova moved from St Petersburg to Golders Green in north London. Sergei Diaghilev's Ballet Russe performed at Covent Garden in a 1911 season that 'revived the taste for a form of art which it was generally supposed had fallen permanently into disregard';[67] the company returned in 1913 to London with Igor Stravinsky's *The Rite of Spring* shortly after its French premiere, and it was received without the hostility seen in Paris. The plays of Anton Chekhov were belatedly staged in public for the first time in London – *The Cherry Orchard* (written 1904) in 1911, *The Seagull* (1896) in 1912, *Uncle Vanya* (1900) in 1914 – while the publisher William Heinemann made the novels of Fyodor Dostoyevsky available in a new set of translations: *The Brothers Karamazov* (1912), *The Idiot* (1913), *Crime and Punishment* (1914). And the second post-Impressionist exhibition in 1912 took care to include some minor Russian painters (though no Germans).

Balalaika orchestras also visited Britain and performed at the more upmarket music halls of the West End. One of these ensembles was even invited to play for the king and queen at Windsor Castle, and their popularity inspired the creation of home-grown balalaika bands – the Coldstream Guards debuted theirs in 1910. It was noticeable, however, that these groups didn't appear at working-class halls, and nor did the Russian dancers, for whom there was a fad among the fashionable. Much more characteristic was Wilkie Bard's 'You Are My Girl-ski' (1910), which sang the praises of his girl, named Vodka Popoff, but came with a sting in its tail:

I think about your face, I can't forget it.

---

* It was also feared as a threat to India. A character in Buchan's *The Half-Hearted* sees Russia as the Empire's greatest enemy. 'Britain is getting sick, and when she is sick enough, some people who are less sick will overwhelm her. My own opinion is that Russia will be the people.'

I've often heard of faces causing pain.
But when I think of your face I thank heaven you're in Russia,
And I'm in England singing this refrain.

Meanwhile the film *The Russian Peasant* (1912) was billed as 'depicting Russian inhumanity to man'.[68] There were many others with the same theme, including *The White Terror, Innocently Condemned to Siberia* and *The Convict's Song* (all 1911).

But despite what some saw as the unsavoury nature of Britain's new allies, the value of the new European order seemed to be proved in the First Balkan War of 1912–13. All the members of the Triple Alliance and the Triple Entente had interests in this clash between the Balkan League and the Ottoman Empire, but hostilities didn't spill over into a wider conflict because the most bellicose nations – Russia and Austria-Hungary – were restrained by their allies.

The war was far from insignificant – over half a million were killed, wounded or captured – and nor was it the end of disputes in the region; in May 1913 the Treaty of Rome brought a cessation of hostilities, but within a month the Second Balkan War broke out. Nonetheless, the violence was contained, and most of Europe remained at peace. 'All that we have to bear in connection with the Triple Entente,' reasoned the *Spectator*, 'is borne for the single end of keeping peace.'[69] And as the Second Balkan War came to a close in August 1913, Stephen Pichon, the French foreign minister, expressed his relief: 'Everything leads to the belief that we are reaching the end of the crisis which has so often brought about the danger of war between the Great Powers.'[70]

Or perhaps it was more the case that neither France nor Germany, whose rivalry lay at the heart of European instability, was yet ready for open confrontation. The signs, though, were ominous. In early 1913 the German government introduced a swathe of one-off taxes intended to fund further military spending; these raised in a single year more than three times the monies announced in Lloyd George's People's Budget. 'The Germans in themselves do not want war,' journalist Bart Kennedy had written in his popular book *The German Danger* (1907). 'But the idea of discipline is so ingrained in them that all the military party would have to do would be to say the word, and Europe would be ablaze.'[71]

And all the while the invasion stories continued and the popular newspapers, particularly Alfred Harmsworth's *Daily Mail*, continued to thunder against the German threat. As E. M. Forster wrote in *Howards End* (1910), 'the remark "England and Germany are bound to fight" renders war a little more likely each time that it is made, and is therefore made the more readily by the gutter press of either nation'.

vi

The Britain that existed between the death of Queen Victoria in January 1901 and the assassination of Archduke Franz Ferdinand in Sarajevo in June 1914 has inevitably been seen in retrospect as a transitional period. That, of course, was not how it felt at the time. The Empire still stood and, despite the increasing competition from America and Germany, the economy remained strong. A sense of being post-Victorian was emerging: a turn away from suppressed emotions, a new emphasis on the humble as well as the exalted, a recognition that charity was not enough and that the state needed to address poverty, to provide for the very young and the very old. Leisure had become ever more important: music halls, cinemas and ice rinks and, for the middle classes, gramophones, motor cars, bridge-parties and golf.* For most people life was better than it had been a generation ago.

And yet there was also a growing sense of insecurity and instability, a vulnerability, a fear that the nation stood on the brink of a precipice. Over the course of a decade or so the country tried to reassure itself that all would be well, that it could remain apart,

---

* It was reported in 1908 that 80,000 people were employed in Britain as golf caddies.

amused rather than alarmed by the outside world, gloriously isolated in a state of artificially induced arcadia. For all the vastness of the Empire, the mood was essentially parochial, inward-looking. Culturally, politically, even intellectually, most of Britain was content to be an island entire of itself. If sufficient trade barriers were built, if alien doctrines and alien revolutionaries could be kept out, if the distinction between British and foreign were maintained, if the pageants and folk revivals continued to be staged, then perhaps storms might yet be avoided.

It was not enough. It could never be enough. With seemingly insoluble problems mounting up at home, and with wars and rumours of wars abroad, it came to seem as though the very fabric of society was unravelling, and there was much trepidation about what might lie ahead.

Towards the end of the period Arthur Conan Doyle's novel *The Poison Belt* reintroduced the great scientist Professor Challenger, who had earlier found dinosaurs on a remote South American plateau in *The Lost World* (1912). There had been peril then, but nothing like now; Challenger has discovered that the Earth is about to pass through a cloud of poisonous gas that will end all life on the planet. Nothing can be done to save us, but he believes that for some the end might be delayed a little. He summons his comrades from the previous adventure to his house, high on the Sussex Weald, where, having equipped themselves with oxygen cylinders, they seal off a room. And here the little band settle down 'in four front seats of the stalls at the last act of the drama of the world', knowing that when their supply of oxygen runs out, they too will die.

Through a great bow window, they look out upon 'the vast stretch of the Weald to where the gentle curves of the South Downs formed an undulating horizon'. As the invisible gas cloud passes, it leaves behind a landscape of death, no birds in flight, no human or animal moving, and in the foreground Challenger's dead chauffeur: 'Down in the yard lies Austin with sprawling limbs, his face glimmering white in the dawn, and the hose nozzle still projecting from his dead hand. The whole of human kind is typified in that one half-ludicrous and half-pathetic figure, lying so helpless beside the machine which it used to control.'

John Buchan's *The Power House* was being serialised in *Blackwood's Magazine* at the same time that *The Poison Belt* was appearing in the *Strand*. 'You think that a wall as solid as the earth separates civilisation from barbarism,' says the supervillain Andrew Lumley in Buchan's best-known passage. 'I tell you the division is a thread, a sheet of glass.' Conan Doyle takes that fragile pane and turns it into a literal window, the only barrier separating the survivors in Challenger's living room from the desolate world outside: 'There brooded over it all the stillness and the silence of universal death – a death in which we were so soon to join. At the present instant that one frail sheet of glass, by holding in the extra oxygen which counteracted the poisoned ether, shut us off from the fate of all our kind.'

The Poison Belt was published in August 1913, twelve months before the glass shattered and the nation was changed for ever. During the First Balkan War Winston Churchill had spoken of the consequences of the conflict spreading into a general European war. 'All might be cast into the abyss,' he warned, 'plunging us back almost into the desolation and barbarism of the Middle Ages. The only epitaph which history could write upon such a catastrophe would be that "This whole generation of men went mad and tore themselves to pieces."'[72]

TWO KILLERS

In 1910 this great country will have very much trouble and sickness, and for seven years afterwards there will be many trials and difficulties to face. These will come in great part through the aliens admitted from other European countries. After seven years, however, the great times will come. England and France will become united under a British ruler, and Canada and the United States will be one also under the British flag.

> The predictions of Golab Shah, proprietor of the Bombay Indian restaurant, High Holborn, London, 1909[1]

Even in the orgy of diabolism to which the world is at present being treated, we can still spare a thought of contempt and loathing for an individual murderer.

> *Edinburgh Evening News*, 1915[2]

Music-hall singer Belle Elmore (1873–1910), born
Kunigunde Mackamotski in New York.

S HE WENT BY VARIOUS NAMES in her thirty-six years on earth. She was born in Brooklyn, New York, in 1873 as Kunigunde Mackamotski, of German, Polish and Russian heritage. In due course she started to go by the more American-sounding Corrine Turner, but she became best known in her stage incarnation as singer and dancer Belle Elmore. She left home at the age of sixteen, and at nineteen met the man she would go on to marry in 1894, a somewhat diffident homeopath originally from Coldwater, Michigan. He was ten years her senior and a widower, with one child, a son. Three years later, the couple emigrated to London, leaving the young boy in Los Angeles with his paternal grandparents.

Now known in everyday life as Cora, she returned to her stage name when Belle Elmore, 'the Belle of New York', made her debut British appearance at the Bijou Theatre of Varieties, Teddington, in 1900. 'Her forte is coon songs and dances,' said the press,[3] and she sang numbers such as 'The Pally Girl' and 'She Never Went Further than That'. For the next four years, while her husband remained in London as manager of the Drouet Institution for the Deaf (a place that fraudulently advertised itself as curing deafness), she toured the country. She went down well with audiences and got decent reviews – she was called 'a comely comedienne,'[4] 'a spark from the Land of the Stars and Stripes'[5] and 'a dainty soubrette'[6] – but she wasn't playing the major halls, nor was she appearing alongside the biggest acts. Good enough to make a living, not special enough to become a star, she left the stage in 1904 and settled down to married life.

Cora and her husband took a lease on 39 Hilldrop Crescent in north London at an annual rent of £52 10s. It was a three-storey, semi-detached villa with ten rooms and a basement, some mature trees in the front and a decent-sized garden at the back. It looked and felt like the very epitome of suburban respectability, though it wasn't really in the suburbs. Rather, Hilldrop Crescent was an enclave off the Camden Road, a major thoroughfare that stretched from the retail bustle of the Holloway Road at one end to the disreputable grubbiness of Camden Town at the other, where Belle had often appeared at the New Bedford Music Hall. A couple of minutes' walk away was His Majesty's Prison Holloway, the largest women's gaol in Europe, where suffragettes including Emmeline and Christabel Pankhurst would soon be incarcerated. The peaceful haven of the Crescent seemed many miles from all such distractions; it 'nestles serenely in a backwash of the whirling waters of the modern Babylon', said one local newspaper.[7] It was no substitute for the stage, though, and in 1907 Cora once again donned the identity of Belle Elmore, enticed back during one of the less likely industrial disputes of the time.

Over the last few years, ever since the Moss Empires had introduced twice-nightly performances, with additional matinees becoming ever more frequent, there had been demands from the acts for higher wages. It wasn't a problem for the stars, who had sufficient leverage to negotiate lucrative contracts, but for the lesser performers things were getting desperate. And in January 1907 there was a walkout by artists appearing at the Holborn Empire and then a London-wide strike in support.

With the halls struggling to find acts to stay open, Belle Elmore was among those prepared to take the company shilling. Apart from anything, money was getting tight in Hilldrop Crescent; her husband's work at the Drouet Institution had ended – the place having been exposed as the quack establishment it was – and they'd had to take in lodgers. She returned to the halls, only to be stopped, it was said, at a picket line that included Marie Lloyd – always a supporter of the underdog, Lloyd had given her full backing to the action. But the Queen of the Halls[8] was too contemptuous to argue with the likes of Elmore: 'Let her go in – she'll do more for the strike by playing than she will by stopping out.'[9]

The dispute ended after two weeks, with the introduction of a minimum wage and a cap on the number of hours that could be worked, but for a few months Belle Elmore continued her revived career. Her husband travelled with her now, employed as her manager, though the title over-dignified his role. 'There was a sort of idea that she supplied her husband with pocket-money,' remembered another of the acts. 'In fact he was looked upon as what they call in the business a music-carrier – taking the band-parts to and from the hall and otherwise looking after his wife generally.'[10]

They were a comically mismatched couple: he stood just five foot three inches, slight of frame and bespectacled, with a heavy moustache to compensate for his thinning hair; she was taller and bigger built, starting to run to stoutness in middle age. He was retiring, she extrovert. She was also believed to be cuckolding him with one of their lodgers. There was something here of the stock music-hall marriage, both the stage image of the henpecked husband and domineering wife, and the real-life relationships of Vesta Victoria and Marie Lloyd with men who felt emasculated by their lower status.

The return to the stage didn't last. In 1908 Belle Elmore retired once more and found a new role as treasurer of the newly formed Music Hall Ladies' Guild, a charitable concern that paid the medical bills of ill or pregnant members of the profession and encouraged its members to sew baby clothes for donation to new mothers. In September 1909 she was formally thanked for all her work, though she insisted she did it just for love. And she promised to keep on going 'so long as I am permitted to'.[11] It wasn't long. Barely three months later the guild committee received a resignation letter, saying that family illness compelled a sudden return to America.

And then came a notice in trade paper the *Era*. The death in California on 23 March 1910 was announced of 'Miss Elmore (Mrs H. H. Crippen)'.[12] Of all her names, this was the one by which she would be remembered: Cora Crippen.

Her husband, Dr Hawley Harvey Crippen, told anyone who asked that she'd gone to stay with his son from his first marriage in Los Angeles, California, and had died of pneumonia. But when friends got in touch with Crippen Junior he said he'd only heard of her death through his father. Something didn't ring true. There

were further suspicions when a younger woman, Ethel Le Neve
– who'd been Dr Crippen's secretary for a decade, moved into
Hilldrop Crescent and was seen wearing his late wife's clothes and
jewellery. And finally it was suggested that the resignation letter
was a forgery: the signature was misspelled 'Ellmore'. The police
were informed and, under questioning, Crippen admitted that
he'd lied; the truth was that he and his wife had had a falling-out
and she'd left him, so he'd concocted the story of her death in
America to avoid social humiliation.

The house was searched, nothing was found, and the police
were initially satisfied, but when Crippen and Le Neve suddenly
disappeared, suspicions were aroused once more. The house
was searched again, and buried in the cellar were found human
remains, pieces of torso from a filleted body. The police patholo-
gist identified these as Belle from a scar she was said to have had.
Poison was also discovered – hyoscine, otherwise known as devil's
breath – and it was established that Crippen had recently bought
a quantity of the drug.

The case was an instant sensation. 'No crime that has occurred
in London of recent years has stirred public feeling so deeply,'
said the *Daily Telegraph* the day after the discoveries were made
public.[13] Largely, it was the incongruity of this happening in Hilldrop Crescent, the last place one would expect to find the glamour
of the music hall, let alone horrific murder. 'In the placid atmosphere of well-to-do suburbia the tokens of the grim deed seized the
heart with a greater shock than they would have done in the denser
and darker neighbourhood that lies not far away,' proclaimed
the press.[14] The public were hooked. Large crowds from all over
London gathered in the Crescent. 'The women were especially
hostile to Crippen,' reported the *Daily Mirror*, 'the men inclined
to be jocular'.[15]

Meanwhile, a national and international alert was issued for
Crippen and Le Neve. For a few days there was silence, for they
had covered their tracks. They fled to the Continent, first to Brus-
sels, and then to Amsterdam where, posing as father and son, with

Le Neve in boy's clothing, they took passage to Quebec on the SS *Montrose*. It was the cross-dressing that first alerted crew members: Le Neve was unconvincing as a boy – the clothes didn't fit, and the couple seemed overly affectionate with each other. Convinced this was the missing couple, the captain made use of the onboard Marconi telegraph, sending a message to Scotland Yard just as the ship was passing south of Land's End. The fugitives had a two-day head start, but Chief Inspector Walter Dew embarked on the SS *Laurentic*, a faster ship sailing from Liverpool, and managed to arrive in Canada a day before the *Montrose*, arresting the pair on the St Lawrence River.

There were incongruities about the case. Generally, poison is used as a murder weapon in order to make the death look natural; poisoners don't tend to draw attention to their crimes by chopping up their victims. And when a murderer does dismember a body, it is in order to dispose of the pieces. In this case, it seemed, Crippen had managed to get rid of the head, limbs and bones so effectively that they were never found, before deciding to bury parts of the torso in his own cellar. If he were the killer, and these really were the remains of Belle Elmore, then the crime was a strange mix of expertise and incompetence.* But the jury were convinced, and took less than half an hour to find him guilty of murder. He was hanged on 23 November 1910 by John Ellis, a shopkeeper from Rochdale ('Hairdresser, Wholesale Newsagent, Umbrella Repairer,' read the sign over his premises[16]) who doubled as the public executioner.

In essence it was a conventional domestic murder, the story of a quiet, unassuming man who poisoned his overbearing wife so that he might be with his lover. But the hue and cry, the international manhunt, was such that by the time he was captured Crippen had been recast as 'one of the most dangerous and remarkable men of the century'. Those were the words of F. E. Smith, who defended Le Neve at her trial, held immediately after Crippen's conviction. He

---

* Nearly a century later DNA tests suggested that the remains in the cellar were not those of Belle Elmore.

was 'a compelling and masterful personality', said Smith; 'imperturbable, unscrupulous, dominating, fearing neither God nor man'.[17] Clearly, Smith was just doing his job by portraying Crippen as the evil manipulator and Le Neve as his helpless dupe, but the narrative fitted well with established perceptions.* There was, said the press, 'no more horrible story in the annals of crime'[18] than the tale of this 'brutal monster',[19] this 'phenomenally cold-blooded and clever criminal'.[20]

The murder of Belle Elmore captured the popular imagination and was the most notorious crime of the era. 'This is the spot where we'll put Crippen', the night porter at Madame Tussaud's told reporters the day after the arrest, and a wax effigy was on display even before the man was hanged.[21] The whole episode was so perfectly Edwardian, so much of its time. This was a story of the music hall, of strikes and strike-breaking; of hidden lives, multiple identities and a woman in boy's clothing; of medical charlatans, poison, the American invasion and the violence of foreigners. It relied on new technology, for Crippen was the first murderer to be caught using wireless telegraphy. It involved Marie Lloyd – and Edgar Wallace, whose *Four Just Men* was the last book Crippen had read before his arrest.† Keen to be in on the act, Horatio Bottomley offered to pay Crippen's legal fees in exchange for his story, to be published in *John Bull*.‡ As home secretary, Winston Churchill signed the death warrant. The killer was even known by the same initials as the prime minister himself: while H. H. Asquith was vainly struggling to contain the disruption of the suffragettes, H. H. Crippen was murdering his wife. Above all, this

---

* Smith's oratory was enough to see Le Neve acquitted as an accomplice to the killing.

† The publishers promptly sold serialisation rights for *The Four Just Men* to various local papers, who advertised it as 'The book Crippen read'. This time it had Wallace's final chapter, giving the solution.

‡ *John Bull* did publish a message from the condemned cell, but Bottomley never made good on his promise to pay. In any event, the message was almost certainly written by Bottomley himself, safe in the knowledge that Crippen could hardly sue.

was a story about a normal suburban house that concealed a dark secret, the corpse in the cellar literally rotting into the foundations of respectability.

And then there was the fact that it all played out in the pages of the popular press. It was the hunt for the fake heiress Violet Charlesworth writ large. This time the police made their contribution. So anxious were they to find Crippen that they released far more information than was usual, and did so in phrasing that was tailor-made for the papers. The police description of the wanted man was full of delightful detail: 'wears hat on back of his head; is plausible and quiet-spoken; rather slovenly appearance; throws his feet out when walking; he carries firearms; and shows his teeth much when talking'.[22] This was, wrote novelist Arthur Machen admiringly, 'a precise and studied description' such as the police had never given before, 'reminding one of the portraits drawn by Balzac'.[23]

There were seventeen days between the revelation of the find in the Camden cellar and the arrest in Canada, and every one of them saw page after page of detail. Much of it was the same as that which had been printed the previous day, but the public didn't seem to mind. And for the last week there was the most delicious situation of all, what the papers called the 'Great Ocean Chase'.[24] Everyone – save the suspects themselves – knew that Chief Inspector Dew was in hot pursuit across the Atlantic and that – if all went according to plan – he would be waiting for Crippen and Le Neve. As they sailed unaware into the trap that had been set for them, this was dramatic irony on a grand scale; newspaper readers at home were both thrilled by the chase and satisfied by the result. There was a sigh of contentment that justice had been done and stability restored. If there was something rotten in the state of post-Victorian Britain, there was at least a calling to account.

ii

A society reveals something of itself in the crimes that it chooses to elevate above the common herd. If Crippen was sometimes painted as a monster, it was only because that was easier to accept than the reality of the mundane suburban murderer, the kind of man a respectable office worker might see in his mahogany-framed hall-mirror. When the contents of Hilldrop Crescent were auctioned by Messrs Tooth & Tooth of Oxford Street to raise money for his legal costs, it was the sheer ordinariness of the items that stood out. A cottage piano went for fourteen guineas, his gramophone and record collection for £2 12s 6d. An agent for Madame Tussaud's picked up a few items for its display: 'an old armchair, a shawl which was worn by Mrs Crippen, and an oak dinner waiter'. The entire sale raised less than £150.[25] This was not the lair of evil incarnate.

A generation earlier things had been different. Back in 1888, when six women were murdered in Whitechapel by the serial killer known as Jack the Ripper, there had been much speculation that the pseudonym might conceal a gentleman, a figure in upper-class society. 'The murderer is a man living a dual life, one respectable and even religious, and the other lawless and brutal,' deduced one commentator.[26] Neither the murderer nor a motive were ever identified, but the idea of a real-life Jekyll and Hyde took root. There was an evil glamour to the mystery of the Whitechapel killer, a depraved allure to the sheer scale of the wickedness. But that was then, and these were more prosaic times.

On 26 August 1910, the day before the handcuffed Hawley Crippen and Ethel Le Neve landed back in Britain, a man calling himself Henry Williams married Bessie Mundy in Clifton, a suburb of Bristol. It wasn't his real name. He had been born George Joseph Smith in Bethnal Green, London, in 1872, and he posed variously as an artist, a writer of music-hall songs and an antique dealer. Really he was a small-time criminal who'd served several jail terms, starting with a spell in a reformatory at the age of nine. He had come to specialise in the manipulation of women. Some were servants, who he induced to steal from their employers; others were courted and robbed. Bessie Mundy was marked out as one of the latter, and soon after their marriage Smith disappeared, taking with him around £140.

Thus far this was the normal pattern. For she wasn't his first wife; there had been at least four before her, as well as abandoned fiancées. What Bessie had that the others lacked was a legacy of some £2,500. This was tied up in investments and had escaped Smith's clutches, but when he encountered her again in 1912, he effected a reconciliation, determined to get his hands on the big money. The couple rented rooms in Weston-super-Mare, where – having persuaded her to rewrite her will – he murdered her, drowning her in a bath that he'd bought for this purpose. An inquest found she'd died of natural causes.

Two other murderous marriages followed: in Blackpool – under his real name – in 1913, and in London the following year, as John Lloyd. Each time he took out life insurance on his wife, for £500 and £700 respectively, and each time he drowned her in the bath. There were inquest verdicts of natural causes in both instances. When the latter case received national coverage in the *News of the World,* a boarding-house owner in Blackpool noticed the similarities with the previous death there. He sent newspaper cuttings of both cases to the police and in February 1915 Smith was arrested.

That spring London suffered its first air raid, when a Zeppelin dropped incendiary bombs on the eastern suburbs; the ocean liner the *Lusitania* was sunk by a U-boat, with the deaths of 1,198 passengers and crew; German forces used poison gas for the first time during the Second Battle of Ypres; and Winston Churchill initiated what turned out to be a disastrous offensive on the Gallipoli Peninsula. But for nine days in June 1915 the big story in Britain was the so-called Brides in the Bath trial. The papers vied with each other to denounce Smith in the strongest terms. 'Foully clever, utterly mean and utterly callous', he was 'the most heartless and the most callous murderer of all time'.[27] He was referred to as 'Bluebeard Smith' and as 'the Man of Many Brides', and the consensus was that 'No death sentence was ever more thoroughly deserved.'[28]

The press struggled to comprehend his success with women.

Again, the image of an arch manipulator was invoked. 'He had a hypnotic personality that gave him a strange influence over girls and women,' it was claimed.[29] One of the most celebrated lawyers of the age, Edward Marshall Hall (the Great Defender) represented Smith, and even he came to the same conclusion: 'I am convinced that he was a hypnotist. Once accept this theory and the whole thing is to my mind satisfactorily explained.'[30]

The truth was probably more straightforward. Smith was plausible and presentable. 'He is much better-looking than in the photograph published of him,' wrote novelist William Le Queux, employed by the *Daily Sketch* to report on the trial. 'He certainly carried himself with a somewhat dandified air. About forty-three, his hair rather long, though well brushed, is slightly tinted with grey while his dark eyes are deep set beneath a rather receding brow, with a fair moustache above a somewhat prominent well-shaven chin.'[31] For an unmarried Edwardian woman of the respectable but insecure lower-middle class, quietly desperate at the passing of her youth, he appeared, if not quite the catch, then at least an accept-able substitute for one. The deception worked because there was a readiness to be deceived.

But it was all so pathetically tawdry. There was no crime of passion here, not even domestic tragedy, just the banal cruelty of a petty conman, a third-rate villain whose luck ran out because he lacked the imagination to vary his modus operandi. Smith was a shabby failure, even as a criminal; with the exception of Bessie Mundy's inheritance, the sums he gained were not great. His small-minded avarice was such that he removed the wedding ring from one of his victims as she lay in her coffin; such that, having killed Bessie, he took the bath back to the shop he'd bought it from, demanding a refund. If W. T. Stead was correct that 'Money is the coming king,' then the Brides in the Bath murderer was the petty, amoral product of that new kingdom.

Conversely, Smith's trial was a reaffirmation that even now there were standards to be upheld, a civilisation to defend. 'Since last August, all over Europe, sometimes in England, sometimes on the sea, thousands of lives of combatants have been taken daily,' said Mr Justice Scrutton in his summing-up. 'Yet while this wholescale destruction of human life is going on, for nine days, with all the apparatus of justice in England, we have been considering whether the prosecution are right in saying one man should die.' It might seem disproportionate, absurd even, to expend so much time and energy on Smith, but it mattered, it really mattered. This trial symbolised what was being fought for: values of stability and order, the rule of law that underpinned society, the normality that must one day return. 'In England, in this national crisis, we have tried to carry on business as usual,' said Scrutton.[32] As with Crippen, it took the jury under half an hour to return a guilty verdict.

Smith was executed at Maidstone Prison on 13 August 1915, again by John Ellis, making the long trip down from Rochdale. There were no reporters present, and only a small crowd gathered outside, 'principally of working people'.[33] No photographs were taken because it was a proscribed area under the Defence of the Realm Act. The same day, in the southern Aegean Sea, the British troopship *Royal Edward* was torpedoed by a German submarine, with the loss of 935 men. They had been destined for Gallipoli.

Appendix

STORIES AND SONGS

Fiction

The following titles were read in the preparation of this book.

Harold Avery, *Under Padlock and Key* (Thomas Nelson and Sons, 1905).

Margaret Baillie-Saunders, *Saints in Society* (Fisher Unwin, 1905).

Robert Barr, *The Triumphs of Eugène Valmont* (Hurst and Blackett, 1906).

J. M. Barrie, *The Admirable Crichton* (staged 1902 – published Hodder & Stoughton, 1914).

——, *What Every Woman Knows* (staged 1908 – published Hodder & Stoughton, 1918).

——, *Peter and Wendy* (Hodder & Stoughton, 1911).

Hilaire Belloc, *Mr Clutterbuck's Election* (Eveleigh Nash, 1908).

Arnold Bennett, *The Card* (Methuen, 1911).

E. F. Benson, *The Room in the Tower and Other Stories* (Mills & Boon, 1912).

Robert Hugh Benson, *Lord of the World* (Dodd, Mead, 1907).

E. C. Bentley, *Trent's Last Case* (Nelson, 1913).

John Davys Beresford, *The Hampdenshire Wonder* (Sidgwick & Jackson, 1911).

Algernon Blackwood, *John Silence: Physician Extraordinary* (Eveleigh Nash, 1908).

——, *A Prisoner in Fairyland* (Macmillan & Co., 1913).

Ernest Bramah, *The Wallet of Kai Lung* (Grant Richards, 1900).

——, *The Secret of the League* (Thomas Nelson, 1909 – adapted from *What Might Have Been*, John Murray, 1907).

John Buchan, *The Half-Hearted* (Isbister, 1900).

——, *Prester John* (Thomas Nelson & Sons, 1910).

——, *The Power-House* (*Blackwood's Magazine*, 1913 – volume form: William Blackwood, 1916).

Frances Hodgson Burnett, *The Secret Garden* (Charles Robinson, 1911).

G. K. Chesterton, *The Napoleon of Notting Hill* (Bodley Head, 1904).

——, *The Club of Queer Trades* (Harper & Brothers, 1905).

——, *The Man Who Was Thursday: A Nightmare* (J. W. Arrowsmith, 1908).

——, *The Flying Inn* (Methuen, 1914).

Erskine Childers, *The Riddle of the Sands: A Record of Secret Service* (Smith, Elder & Co., 1903).

Winston Churchill, *Savrola* (*Macmillan's Magazine* 1898 – volume form: Longman, Green & Co., 1900).

Joseph Conrad, *Heart of Darkness* (*Blackwood's Magazine* 1899 – volume form: William Blackwood, 1902).

Joseph Conrad & Ford M. Hueffer (Ford Madox Ford), *The Inheritors: An Extravagant Story* (William Heinemann, 1901).

Marie Corelli, *Boy* (Hutchinson, 1900).

Frank Danby (Julia Frankau), *An Incompleat Etonian* (William Heinemann, 1909).

Richard Harding Davis, *In the Fog* (R. H. Russell, 1901).

Ethel M. Dell, *The Knave of Diamonds* (Unwin, 1913).

Arthur Conan Doyle, *The Adventures of Sherlock Holmes* (George Newnes, 1892).

——, *The Great Shadow* (J. W. Arrowsmith, 1892).

——, *The Memoirs of Sherlock Holmes* (George Newnes, 1893).

——, *The Return of Sherlock Holmes* (George Newnes, 1905).

——, *The Poison Belt* (Hodder & Stoughton, 1913).

——, *His Last Bow* (John Murray, 1917).

Guy du Maurier, *An Englishman's Home* (Harper & Brothers, 1909).

Paul Lawrence Dunbar, *The Sport of the Gods* (Dodd, Mead & Co., 1902).

John Finnemore, *The Wolf Patrol: A Tale of Baden-Powell's Boy Scouts* (Adam & Charles Black, 1908).

E. M. Forster, 'The Story of a Panic' (1904, collected in *The Celestial Omnibus and Other Stories*, Sidgwick & Jackson, 1911).

——, *The Longest Journey* (Edward Arnold, 1907).

——, 'The Machine Stops' (1909, collected in *The Eternal Moment*, Sidgwick & Jackson, 1928).

——, *Howards End* (Edward Arnold, 1910).

John Galsworthy, *The Man of Property* (Heinemann, 1906).

Philip Gibbs, *The Street of Adventure* (Heinemann, 1909).

Edmund Gosse, *Father and Son* (Heinemann, 1907).

Kenneth Grahame, *The Wind in the Willows* (Methuen, 1908).

Harley Granville-Barker, *The Madras House* (staged 1909 – published Methuen, 1977).

Thomas Hardy, *The Dynasts* (Macmillan & Co., 1904–8).

——, *Satires of Circumstance: Lyrics and Reveries* (Macmillan & Co., 1914).

E. W. Hornung, *The Amateur Cracksman* (Methuen & Co, 1899).

——, *The Black Mask* (Grant Richards, 1901).

Fergus Hume, *The Blue Talisman* (Werner Laurie, 1912).

Violet Hunt, *Tales of the Uneasy* (William Heinemann, 1911).

M. R. James, *More Ghost Stories* (Edward Arnold, 1911).

Jerome K. Jerome, *Three Men in a Boat (To Say Nothing of the Dog)* (J. W. Arrowsmith, 1889).

Rudyard Kipling, *Stalky & Co.* (Macmillan, 1899).

William Le Queux, *The Invasion of 1910: With a Full Account of the Siege of London* (E. Nash, 1906).

——, *The Unknown Tomorrow: How the Rich Fared at the Hands of the Poor, Together with a Full Account of the Social Revolution in England* (F. V. White, 1910).

Arthur Machen, *The Great God Pan* (John Lane, 1894).

——, 'The White People'(*Horlick's Magazine* 1904 – collected in *The House of Souls*, Grant Richards, 1906).

A. E. W. Mason, *The Four Feathers* (Macmillan & Co., 1902).

——, *At the Villa Rose* (Hodder & Stoughton, 1910).

Alice Maud Meadows, *A Million of Money* (Sisley's Ltd, 1903).

Edith Nesbit, *The Story of the Treasure Seekers* (T. Fisher Unwin, 1899).

——, *The Railway Children* (Wells Gardner, 1906).

Sydney H. Nicholson (ed.), *British Songs for British Boys* (Macmillan & Co., 1903).

Baroness Orczy, *The Scarlet Pimpernel* (Greening & Co., 1905).

Barry Pain, *Eliza* (S. H. Bousfield and Co., 1900).

——, *The One Before* (Grant Richards, 1902).

——, *The Exiles of Faloo* (Methuen & Co., 1910).

——, *Eliza's Son* (Cassell, 1913).

Eden Phillpotts, *The Human Boy Again* (Chapman and Hall, 1908).

Plutarch (trans. Frank Cole Babbitt), *Moralia* (William Heinemann, 1936).

Beatrix Potter, *The Tale of Squirrel Nutkin* (Frederick Warne & Co., 1903).

Sax Rohmer, *The Mystery of Dr Fu-Manchu* (Methuen & Co., 1913).

Saki (H. H. Munro), 'The Chronicles of Clovis' (Bodley Head, 1912).

——, *The Unbearable Bassington* (John Lane, 1912).

——, *When William Came* (John Lane, 1913).

Evelyn Sharp, *The Other Side of the Sun* (Bodley Head, 1900).

Siegfried Sassoon, *Memoirs of a Fox-Hunting Man* (Faber & Faber, 1928).

James Stephens, *The Crock of Gold* (Macmillan & Co., 1912).

Bram Stoker, *The Lair of the White Worm* (William Rider & Son Ltd, 1911).

Katherine Cecil Thurston, *John Chilcote, MP* (W. Blackwood & Sons, 1904).

Louis Tracy, *The King of Diamonds* (F. V. White & Co., 1904).

Robert Tressell, *The Ragged-Trousered Philanthropists* (Grant Richards, 1914).

Hubert Wales, *The Yoke* (John Long, 1907).

Edgar Wallace, *Writ in Barracks* (Methuen and Co., 1900).

——, *The Four Just Men* (Tallis Press, 1905).

——, *The Council of Justice* (Ward, Lock & Co., 1908).

——, *Sanders of the River* (Ward, Lock & Co., 1911).

——, 'The Poisoners' (*Novel Magazine*, 1912).

——, *Private Selby* (Ward, Lock & Co., 1912).

Mrs Humphry Ward, *Delia Blanchflower* (Ward, Lock & Co., 1914).

H. G. Wells, *The Food of the Gods and How It Came to Earth* (Macmillan & Co., 1904).

——, *Kipps: The Story of a Simple Soul* (Macmillan & Co., 1905).

——, *Tono-Bungay* (Macmillan & Co., 1909).

——, *Ann Veronica* (T. Fisher Unwin, 1909).

——. *The New Machiavelli* (John Lane, 1911).

——, *The Wife of Sir Isaac Harman* (Macmillan & Co., 1914).

John Strange Winter (Henrietta Stannard), *A Blaze of Glory* (Lippincott, 1902).

P. G. Wodehouse, *The Swoop: or How Clarence Saved England* (Alston Rivers, 1909).

——, *Psmith in the City* (A. & C. Black, 1910).

Songs

These are the songs that are referred to in the text, listed by performer, with writers given in parentheses.

Wilkie Bard, 'Has Anyone Been Asking for Me?' (Frank Leo, 1902).

——, 'Limerick Mad' (Frank Leo, 1907).

——, 'Put Me on an Island' (Will Letters, 1908).

——, 'You Are My Girl-ski' (George Arthurs & Worton David, 1910).

Fred Barnes, 'The Black Sheep of the Family' (Fred Barnes, 1907).

Harry Bedford, 'A Second-Hand Aristocrat' (E. J. Hillary, F. J. Barnes & R. P. Weston, 1906).

Herbert Campbell, 'I Don't Want to Fight' (Henry Pettitt & T. Vincent Davies, 1878).

Pat Carey, 'The Irish Are Always in Front' (J. F. Lambe & George Le Brunn, 1900).

Harry Champion, 'I'm Henery the Eighth, I Am' (Fred Murray & R. P. Weston, 1910).

——, 'P.C. Green' (Fred Murray, C. Hilbury & Percy Ford, 1910).

——, 'Any Old Iron' (Charles Collins, Fred Terry & E. A. Sheppard, 1911).

Albert Chevalier, 'My Old Dutch' (Albert Chevalier & Charles Ingle, 1892).

——, 'Cosmopolitan Courtship' (Albert Chevalier & Alfred H. West, 1896).

——, 'Hif Not, Why Not?' (Albert Chevalier & Alfred H. West, 1904).

George Chirgwin, 'The Cockney Coon' (Charles Osborne, 1899).

Lottie Collins, 'Ta-ra-ra Boom-de-ay' (words by Richard Morton, tune unknown, 1891).

Tom Collins, 'Fly Away Peter, Come Back Paul' (Harry Leighton & George Everard, 1906).

Dan Crawley, 'Father Keeps on Doing It' (T. W. Connor, 1905).

Harry Dacre, 'Oh Flo' (Harry Dacre, 1901).

T. E. Dunville, 'The Wide, Wide World Man' (Charles Osborne & T. E. Dunville, 1898).

Gus Elen, 'The Cockney's Garden' (Edgar Bateman & George Le Brunn, 1894).

——, 'The Coster's Mansion' (W. Fieldhouse & George Le Brunn, 1899).

——, 'Arf a Pint of Ale' (Charles Tempest, 1905).

——, 'Wait Till the Work Comes Round' (Gus Elen & Charles Cornell, 1906).

Will Evans, 'You Don't Know, They Don't Know and I Don't Know' (Sam Richards, 1900).

——, 'The Mermaid's Lament' (Alisse & Evans, 1911).

Happy Fanny Fields, 'The Suffragette' (writers unknown, 1909).

Harry Ford, 'Poor, Proud and Particular' (Harry Boden & Bert Brantford, 1902).

Florrie Forde, 'Girls, Study Your Cookery Books' (Joe Burley & Bennett Scott, 1908).

——, 'Hold Your Hand Out, Naughty Boy' (C. W. Murphy & Worton David, 1913).

Hal Forde, 'The Wrestling Wife' (Chas H. Taylor & Hartley Milburn, 1904).

George Formby, 'One of the Boys' (Fred J. Barnes, R. P. Weston & Bennett Scott, 1907).

——, 'It Must Be the Clothes I'm Wearing' (Paul Pelham & J. P. Long, *c.* 1912).

Lottie Lennox, 'Look Out Boys! There's a Girl About' (Fred Murray & Charles Hilbury, 1906).

Ethel Levey, 'Ragtime Suffragette' (Nat Ayer & Charles Williams, 1913).

Marie Lloyd, 'Oh, Mr Porter' (George Le Brunn, 1892).

——, 'She Wore a Little Safety-Pin Behind' (W. T. Lytton & Denham Harrison, 1896).

——, 'What Did She Know About Railways?' (C. G. Coates & Bennett Scott, 1897).

——, 'The Red and the White and the Blue' (E. W. Rogers, 1900).

G. H. MacDermott, 'MacDermott's War Song' (G. W. Hunt, 1877).

——, 'By Order of the Czar' (C. Deane & Leo Dryden, 1891).

Ernie Mayne, 'She Pushed Me into the Parlour' (Alf Ellerton & Will Mayne, 1912).

Sam Mayo, 'Kind Friends' (Sam Mayo, George Davenport & Ted Cowan, 1902).

——, 'The Chinaman' (Worton David & Sam Mayo, 1906).

——, 'Wallah, Wallah, Wallaperoo' (Worton David & Sam Mayo, 1910).

H. G. Pélissier, 'What a Very Great Improvement' (Arthur Wimperis & Harry G. Pélissier, c. 1904).

Jack Pleasants, 'I Shall Be a Bad Lad, Liza Ann!' (C. W. Murphy, 1910).

Pat Rafferty, 'What Do You Think of the Irish Now?' (Albert Hall & Harry Castling, 1899).

Ella Retford, 'Have You Seen My Chinee-Man?' (Bennett Scott & A. J. Mills, 1908).

J. W. Rickaby, 'P.C. 49' (William Hargreaves, 1913).

George Robey, 'My Hat's a Brown 'Un' (E. W. Rogers, 1891).

——, 'The Chinese Laundry Man' (writers unknown, 1900).

——, 'I Shouldn't Be at All Surprised' (writers unknown, c. 1907).

——, 'Archibald, Certainly Not' (John L. St John & Alfred Glover, 1909).

Mark Sheridan, 'It's Very, Very Warm Round There' (A. J. Mills & Frank W. Carter, 1899).

——, 'We'll March to Trafalgar Square' (A. J. Mills & Bennett Scott, 1913).

Ella Shields, 'Burlington Bertie from Bow' (William Hargreaves, 1914).

Leo Stormont, 'Sons of Our Empire' (John Bradford & B. M. Ramsay, 1899).

——, 'No Fear' (Robert Martin & François Cellier, 1903).

Vesta Tilley, 'In the Days of the Cavalier' (John S. Baker & Charles Wilmott, 1897).

——, 'I Want to Have a Chinese Honeymoon' (J. P. Harrington & George Le Brunn, 1904).

George Whitehead, 'The John Bull Store' (B. Fletcher Robinson & Robert Eden, 1903).

Billy Williams, 'Poor Old England' (Fred Godfrey & Harry Castling, 1907).

——, 'Serves You Right' (R. P. Weston & Fred J. Barnes, 1908).

——, 'Oh! Oh! Oh! (A Tale of Paris)' (Fred Godfrey & Fred E. D'Albert, 1909).

Hugh E. Wright, 'A Ballad of Socialism' (Hugh E. Wright & Wolseley Charles, 1909).

REFERENCES

Note on Currency and Income

1 Peter Wilshire, *The Pound in Your Pocket 1870–1970* (Cassell & Company, 1970) pp. 94–7.

Prologue

1 *Wigan Observer and District Advertiser* 6 February 1901.
2 Wallace, *Private Shelby* Chap. 22.
3 Oscar Wilde, *De Profundis* (written 1897, first published in expurgated form 1905, and in full in *Collected Letters of Oscar Wilde*, Rupert Hart-Davis, 1962).
4 Joseph Pearce, *The Unmasking of Oscar Wilde* (HarperCollins, 2000) p. 277.
5 Hesketh Pearson, *The Life of Oscar Wilde* (Methuen, 1946) p. 364.
6 Ibid. p. 357.
7 Richard Ellman, *Oscar Wilde* (Hamish Hamilton, 1987) p. 545.
8 *Greenock Telegraph and Clyde Shipping Gazette* 1 December 1900.
9 *Evening News* (London) 1 December 1900.
10 *Sheffield Independent* 3 December 1900.
11 *Times* 1 December 1900.
12 *Evening News* (London) 1 December 1900.
13 Barrie, *The Admirable Crichton* Act 1.
14 David Cecil, *Max: A Biography* (Constable & Company, 1964) p. 246.
15 *Cheltenham Examiner* 18 January 1905.
16 *Western Morning News* 23 January 1901.
17 Hansard 25 January 1901.
18 *Isle of Wight County Press and South of England Reporter* 26 January 1901.
19 *Henley Advertiser* 2 February 1901.
20 A. N. Wilson, *After the Victorians* (Hutchinson, 2005) p. 6.
21 *Illustrated London News* 1 July 1899; *London Evening Standard* 3 July 1899; *Illustrated Sporting and Dramatic News* 5 August 1899.

22 John Buchan, *Memory Hold-the-Door* (Hodder & Stoughton, 1949) p. 126.

23 Asa Briggs, *A Social History of England* (Weidenfeld & Nicolson, 1983) pp. 286–7

24 Peter Wilshire, *The Pound in Your Pocket 1870–1970* (Cassell & Company, 1970) p. 93.

25 Briggs, *A Social History of England* p. 267.

26 *Tatler* 25 September 1912.

27 *Bystander* 15 March 1905.

28 *London Daily News* 25 July 1908.

29 Simon Heffer, *The Age of Decadence: Britain 1880 to 1914* (Windmill, 2017) p. 544.

30 Charles Wintour, *The Rise and Fall of Fleet Street* (Hutchinson, 1989) p. 11.

31 *Elgin Courant, and Morayshire Advertiser* 6 November 1903.

32 Heffer, *The Age of Decadence* p. 547.

33 Frank Harris, *Oscar Wilde: His Life and Confessions* (published by the author, 1916) pp. 151–2.

34 *Reynolds's Newspaper* 27 August 1905.

35 *Oxfordshire Weekly News* 4 April 1906.

36 *Leeds Mercury* 11 November 1905.

37 *Leek Times* 9 March 1912.

38 *Belfast Telegraph* 2 October 1912.

1: Money and Music Hall

1 Meadows, *A Million of Money* Chap. 72.

2 Pamela J. Walker, *Pulling the Devil's Kingdom Down: The Salvation Army in Victorian Britain* (University of California Press, 2001) p. 201.

3 *Buckingham Advertiser and Free Press* 9 January 1909.

4 *Paisley & Renfrewshire Gazette* 10 August 1901.

5 Buchan, *The Half-Hearted* Chap. 16.

6 Chesterton, 'The Secret People' (1907, collected in *Poems*, Burns & Oates, 1915).

7 *Globe* 22 April 1898.

8 *Windsor* magazine 27 June 1903.

9 *Sporting Life* 20 July 1908.

10 *Bolton Evening News* 14 July 1908.

11 *Belfast Telegraph* 30 January 1906.

12 *Sporting Times* 27 January 1912.

13 *Illustrated London News* 29 December 1900.

14 *Labour Leader* 2 October 1908.
15 *Suffragette* 17 October 1913.
16 *Pearson's Weekly* 6 September 1913.
17 Wodehouse, *The Swoop* Part 2 Chap. 2.
18 *Era* 25 January 1913.
19 J. A. Hobson, *The Psychology of Jingoism* (Grant Richards, 1901) 'Introductory'.
20 Sam Beale, *The Comedy and Legacy of Music-Hall Women 1880–1920: Brazen Impudence and Boisterous Vulgarity* (Palgrave Macmillan, 2020) p. 2.
21 *Sheffield Weekly Telegraph* 7 June 1902.
22 *Lyttelton Times* 27 February 1904.
23 *Western Mail* 7 February 1900.
24 *Daily News* (London) 15 November 1922.
25 *Music Hall and Theatre Review* 27 September 1907.
26 James Harding, *George Robey & the Music Hall* (Hodder & Stoughton, 1990) p. 25.
27 Peter Brent, *The Edwardians* (BBC, 1972) p. 108.
28 Daniel Farson, *Marie Lloyd & Music Hall* (Tom Stacey, 1972) p. 57.
29 Arthur Roberts, *Fifty Years of Spoof* (John Lane/The Bodley Head, 1927) p. 138.
30 Walker, *Pulling the Devil's Kingdom Down* p. 190.
31 Ibid. p. 191.
32 *Western Daily Press* 7 July 1879.
33 *London Daily News* 22 September 1882.
34 Pain, *The One Before* p. 44.
35 *Tottenham and Edmonton Weekly Herald* 24 April 1914.
36 *Ealing Gazette and West Middlesex Observer* 27 September 1913.
37 *West London Observer* 15 May 1914.
38 *Bradford Daily Telegraph* 23 October 1909.
39 *Era* 8 February 1913.
40 *Clarion* 10 October 1902.
41 *Stage* 17 May 1900.
42 *Manchester Evening News* 26 January 1909.
43 *Truth* 8 May 1907.
44 *Music Hall and Theatre Review* 21 December 1906; *Leicester Daily Post* 29 December 1906.
45 *Lloyd's Weekly Newspaper* 30 June 1907.
46 *Daily Mirror* 21 June 1907.
47 Quoted *Edinburgh Evening News* 3 July 1900.

48 *Southend Standard and Essex Weekly Advertiser* 13 September 1906.

49 *Bournemouth Graphic* 24 October 1907.

50 *Music Hall and Theatre Review* 6 July 1900.

51 Roberts, *Fifty Years of Spoof* p. 58.

52 Margaret Lane, *Edgar Wallace: A Biography* (William Heinemann, 1938) p. 97.

53 *Newcastle Daily Chronicle* 9 May 1898.

54 Lane, *Edgar Wallace* p. 146.

55 Quoted *Derry Journal* 31 July 1901.

56 Lane, *Edgar Wallace* p. 54.

57 Ibid. p. 187.

58 *Evening News* 2 November 1905.

59 *Daily Mirror* 10 November 1905.

60 Lane, *Edgar Wallace* p. 190.

61 Ibid. p. 103.

62 *St Stephen's Review* July 1887.

63 *Shipley Times and Express* 26 March 1909.

64 Wodehouse, *Psmith in the City* Chap. 13.

65 *Gloucestershire Echo* 13 March 1909.

66 Julian Symons, *Horatio Bottomley: A Biography* (Cresset Press, 1955) p. 58.

67 *Tatler* 28 March 1906.

68 Symons, *Horatio Bottomley* pp. 60, 119.

69 Ibid. p. 64.

70 Ibid. p. 143.

71 *Aberdeen Press and Journal* 29 March 1909.

72 Symons, *Horatio Bottomley* p. 15.

73 *Gloucestershire Echo* 13 March 1909.

74 *Batley News* 23 February 1906.

75 *Manchester Courier and Lancashire General Advertiser* 14 February 1907.

76 *Milngavie and Bearsden Herald* 2 April 1909.

77 *Exeter and Plymouth Gazette* 7 April 1906.

78 *Sheffield Independent* 9 June 1909.

79 *Weekly Dispatch* 24 October 1909.

80 *John Bull* 16 June 1910.

81 Peter Green, *Kenneth Grahame 1859–1932* (John Murray, 1959) p. 243.

2: War and Imperialism

1 Written by John Bradford & B. M. Ramsay, dedicated to the New South Wales Lancers.

2 Tressell, *The Ragged-Trousered Philanthropists* Chap. 2.

3   *Edinburgh Evening News* 23 June 1899; *South Wales Daily News* 22 June 1899; *Western Times* 21 June 1899.

4   Jock Macleod, *Literature, Journalism and the Vocabularies of Liberalism: Politics and Letters 1886–1916* (Palgrave Macmillan, 2013).

5   *Aberdeen Press and Journal* 18 October 1899.

6   Robert Gittings, *The Older Hardy* (Heinemann Educational Books, 1978 – revised paperback edition: Penguin, 1980) p. 140.

7   *Hampshire Advertiser* 18 November 1899.

8   *Liverpool Daily Post* 21 December 1899.

9   *York Herald* 1 January 1900.

10 *Dundee Evening Post* 5 February 1900.

11 *Abergavenny Chronicle* 31 August 1900.

12 Ian Knight, *Marching to the Drums: From the Kabul Massacre to the Siege of Mafeking* (Greenhill Books, 1999) p. 286.

13 *Liverpool Mercury* 19 May 1900; *London Evening Standard* 21 May 1900; *Scotsman* 21 May 1900; *Taunton Courier and Western Advertiser* 23 May 1900; *Reading Mercury* 26 May 1900; *Western Gazette* 25 May 1900; *Hastings and St Leonards Observer* 26 May 1900.

14 Hansard 18 October 1899.

15 *Irish Times* 29 September 1900.

16 *Jersey Independent and Daily Telegraph* 21 November 1874.

17 *Carmarthen Journal* 15 November 1878.

18 *Birmingham Daily Post* 20 January 1973.

19 *Yorkshire Evening Post* 9 December 1898.

20 *Dundee Evening Telegraph* 24 July 1903.

21 *John Bull* 16 June 1906.

22 *Kirkintilloch Herald* 27 September 1899.

23 Stephen J. Lee, *British Political History 1815–1914* (Routledge, 1994) p. 212.

24 Michael W. Doyle, *Empires* (Cornell University Press, 1986) p. 293.

25 *Clarion* 21 October 1899.

26 *Justice* 28 October 1899.

27 *Clarion* 4 November 1899.

28 Roy Hattersley, *The Edwardians* (Little, Brown, 2004) p. 95.

29 *Sheffield Daily Telegraph* 24 September 1900.

30 *St James's Gazette* 11 February 1904; *Salisbury and Winchester Journal* 13 February 1904: *Hants and Sussex News* 25 March 1908.

31 *Burnley Gazette* 15 September 1906.

32 *Yorkshire Evening Post* 21 April 1924.

33 Ibid.

34 Knight, *Marching to the Drums* p. 293.

35 Quoted *Lincolnshire Echo* 24 June 1901.

36 Gary Sheffield, *The Chief: Douglas Haig and the British Army* (Aurum Press, 2011) p. 50.

37 *Scotsman* 18 June 1901; *Evening Mail* 19 June 1901.

38 *Edinburgh Evening News* 19 June 1901.

39 *Bradford Observer* 1 July 1901.

40 *Scotsman* 20 June 1901.

41 *East Anglian Daily Times* 18 June 1901.

42 *Times* 22 October 1901.

43 Roy Hattersley, *Campbell-Bannerman* (Haus, 2006) p. 79.

44 *Bradford Observer* 15 June 1901.

45 *Leinster Reporter* 6 September 1902.

46 Quoted *Cambrian News* 27 December 1901.

47 A. G. Gardiner, *Prophets, Priests and Kings* (Alston Rivers, 1908).

48 Wells, *The Wife of Sir Isaac Harman* Chap. 9.

49 Belloc, *Mr Clutterbuck's Election* Chap. 1.

50 *Herts & Cambs Reporter & Royston Crow* 5 April 1901.

51 Cecil Rhodes (ed. W. T. Stead), *The Last Will and Testament of Cecil John Rhodes* (Review of Reviews, 1902) Part 2 Chap. 1.

52 John Buchan, *Memory Hold-the-Door* (Hodder & Stoughton, 1949) p. 113.

53 *Berkshire Chronicle* 22 March 1902.

54 Quoted *St James's Gazette* 27 March 1902.

55 *Queen* 22 March 1902.

56 *London Daily News* 27 March 1902.

57 Rhodes, *Last Will and Testament* Part 2 Chap. 1.

58 *St James's Gazette* 27 March 1902.

59 *Coventry Evening Telegraph* 27 March 1902; *Edinburgh Evening News* 28 March 1902; *Dundee Evening Post* 27 March 1902.

60 *Gloucestershire Echo* 27 March 1902.

61 Quoted *London Evening Standard* 27 March 1902.

62 Quoted *St James's Gazette* 27 March 1902.

63 Chesterton, *The Flying Inn* Chap. 21.

64 Hardy, *The Dynasts* Part First, Act Sixth, Scene VI.

65 Buchan, *The Power-House* Chap. 3.

66 *Belfast News-Letter* 9 April; *Irish Independent* 27 April 1893, *John Bull* 22 July 1911; *Berks and Oxon Advertiser* 8 December 1903; *Sketch* 24 June 1903, *Tatler* 4 May 1904.

67 *Lisburn Standard* 24 August 1907; see also *Eastbourne Gazette* 2 May 1906.
68 Wells, *Tono-Bungay* Book 3 Chap. 2 Section 9.
69 Doyle, *The Great Shadow* Chap. 1.
70 Rhodes, *Last Will and Testament* Part 2 Chap. 2.
71 *Dundee Courier* 12 September 1903.
72 Quoted *Dundee Evening Post* 27 March 1902.

3: Past and Future
1 Vesta Tilley, 'In the Days of the Cavalier' (John S. Baker & Charles Wilmott, 1897).
2 Gosse, *Father and Son* Chap. 12.
3 *Edinburgh Evening News* 18 December 1897.
4 *Northern Whig* 19 February 1897.
5 *Northants Evening Telegraph* 30 December 1902; *Dublin Evening Mail* 31 December 1902.
6 *Yarmouth Independent* 10 August 1901.
7 *Western Mail* 18 April 1899.
8 *Sheffield Evening Telegraph* 16 August 1899.
9 *Hampstead & Highgate Express* 10 August 1901.
10 *Worcestershire Chronicle* 15 April 1899.
11 *Rhyl Record and Advertiser* 21 July 1900.
12 *Folkestone, Hythe, Sandgate & Cheriton Herald* 1 December 1900.
13 *Cork Weekly News* 7 October 1899.
14 *Hull Daily Mail* 1 February 1912.
15 *Surrey Advertiser* 13 April 1912.
16 Saki, *The Unbearable Bassington* Chap. 5.
17 *Burnley Express* 5 December 1900.
18 *Lincolnshire Chronicle* 12 July 1895.
19 *Cheltenham Examiner* 23 August 1905.
20 *Nottingham Evening Post* 1 October 1902.
21 Bennett, *The Card* Chap. 10 Section 1.
22 *Tablet* 13 July 1895.
23 Danby, *An Incompleat Etonian* Chap. 27.
24 Clifford Musgrave, *Life in Brighton: From the Earliest Times to the Present* (Faber & Faber, 1970 – revised edition: John Hallewell Publications, 1981) p. 357.
25 William Booth, *In Darkest England and the Way Out* (Salvation Army, 1890) p. 23.

26 *Morning Post* 29 September 1900.

27 *Leeds Mercury* 16 April 1909.

28 *St James's Gazette* 13 December 1901.

29 *Irish News and Belfast Morning News* 28 January 1908.

30 *Pall Mall Gazette* 4 June 1901.

31 Figures quoted in Lawrence James, *The Middle Class: A History* (Little, Brown, 2006) p. 254.

32 Thomas A. Welton, 'Occupations in England and Wales, 1881 and 1901', *Journal of the Royal Statistical Society* Vol. 73, No. 2 (1910) p. 164.

33 Ford Madox Hueffer, *The Soul of London: A Survey of the Modern City* (Alston Rivers, 1905) p. xv.

34 *Middlesex & Surrey Express* 29 January 1909.

35 James Hilton, *To You, Mr Chips* (Hodder & Stoughton, 1939) Chap. 1.

36 *Walthamstow and Leyton Guardian* 3 December 1909.

37 Hilton, *To You, Mr Chips* Chap. 1.

38 Quoted in advertisement, *Westminster Gazette* 8 April 1904.

39 *Bromsgrove & Droitwich Messenger* 18 January 1908; Robert Withington, 'Louis Napoleon Parker', *The New England Quarterly* Vol. 12, No. 3 (1939) p. 518.

40 Louis N. Parker, *Several of My Lives* (Chapman & Hall, 1928) p. 279.

41 Michael Shallcross, 'The Pomp of Obliteration: G. K. Chesterton and the Edwardian Pageant', in Angela Bartie et al. (ed.), *Restaging the Past: Historical Pageants, Culture and Society in Modern Britain* (UCL Press, 2020) p. 81.

42 *Forres Elgin and Nairn Gazette, Northern Review and Advertiser* 20 February 1907.

43 *Hull Daily Mail* 16 June 1905.

44 *Labour Leader* 19 July 1907.

45 *Clarion* 7 February 1908.

46 *Globe* 3 April 1902.

47 *Middlesex Gazette* 2 June 1900.

48 *Totnes Weekly Times* 21 April 1900.

49 *Diss Express* 26 December 1902.

50 *Longford Journal* 18 October 1902.

51 Roger Savage, *Masques, Mayings and Music-Dramas: Vaughan Williams and the Early Twentieth-Century Stage* (Boydell Press, 2014) pp. 300–301.

52 *Pall Mall Gazette* 10 February 1914.

53 *Talking Machine News* 2 November 1908.

54 Ibid.

55 *Times* 15 January 1912.

56 *Globe* 18 June 1914.

57 Sassoon, *Memoirs of a Fox-Hunting Man* Part 1.

58 Plutarch, *Moralia*, Book 5 Chap. 29.

59 G. K. Chesterton, *The Everlasting Man* (Hodder & Stoughton, 1925) Part 1 Chap. 8.

60 Wilde, 'Pan – Double Villanelle' (1880, collected in *Charmides and other Poems*, Methuen, 1913).

61 Saki, 'The Music on the Hill', *The Chronicles of Clovis*.

62 Benson, 'The Man Who Went Too Far', *The Room in the Tower*.

63 Barrie, *Peter and Wendy* Chap. 10.

64 *Sheffield Daily Telegraph* 14 March 1907.

65 *Scotsman* 23 June 1909.

66 *Manchester Evening News* 4 February 1909.

67 *Bingley Chronicle* 12 February 1909.

68 *Hampshire Post and Southsea Observer* 12 March 1909.

69 *Nottingham Journal* 25 January 1904.

70 *Daily Mirror* 12 February 1909.

71 *Walsall Advertiser* 4 December 1909.

72 *St James's Gazette* 26 July 1901.

73 *Illustrated London News* 3 August 1901.

4: Home and Abroad

1 Saki, *The Unbearable Bassington* Chap. 7.

2 *Evening News* (London) 23 November 1901.

3 *Illustrated London News* 24 January 1846.

4 *Central Somerset Gazette* 19 January 1884.

5 *Graphic* 16 April 1904.

6 *Luton Times and Advertiser* 30 November 1906.

7 *Music Hall and Theatre Review* 25 May 1900.

8 Edward Lear, 'The Owl and the Pussy-Cat', *Nonsense Songs, Stories, Botany and Alphabets* (R. J. Bush, 1871).

9 Introduction to 1923 edition.

10 Nadezhda Krupskaya, *Memories of Lenin* (International Publishers, 1930) Part 1, 'Life in London 1902–1903'.

11 Barr, 'The Absent-Minded Coterie', *The Triumphs of Eugène Valmont*.

12 Mason, *At the Villa Rose* Chap. 10.

13 Galsworthy, *The Man of Property* Part I Chap. 7.

14 Bennett, *The Card* Chap. 11 Section 2.

15 Saki, *The Unbearable Bassington* Chap. 9.

16 *Referee* 27 October 1907.

17 *Truth* 8 May 1907.

18 *Kinematograph Weekly* 6 October 1910.

19 *Graphic* 28 October 1911.

20 John Buchan, *Memory Hold-the-Door* (Hodder & Stoughton, 1949) p. 96.

21 *London and China Express* 14 September 1900.

22 *St James's Gazette* 2 October 1900.

23 Ibid. 26 September 1900.

24 *Wrexham Advertiser* 20 October 1900.

25 *St James's Gazette* 2 October 1900.

26 *Western Daily Press* 16 October 1900.

27 *Eastbourne Chronicle* 24 November 1900.

28 *Londonderry Sentinel* 20 February 1906.

29 *Nottingham Evening Post* 22 November 1906; *Daily Mirror* 23 November
    1906; *Leominster News and North West Herefordshire & Radnorshire
    Advertiser* 30 November 1906.

30 *Cornubian and Redruth Times* 29 September 1910.

31 *John Bull* 16 January 1909.

32 City of Liverpool, 'Report of the Commission' p. 6.

33 *Daily Mirror* 23 November 1906.

34 *Pearson's Weekly* 21 March 1907; *Dundee Evening Telegraph* 19 July 1911.

35 *Belfast Telegraph* 6 December 1902.

36 *Queen* 6 January 1906.

37 *Dublin Evening Mail* 18 June 1904.

38 *Graphic* 30 November 1907.

39 *Illustrated Sporting and Dramatic News* 4 November 1899.

40 *Tatler* 16 October 1901; *Illustrated Sporting and Dramatic News* 7 July
    1906.

41 *Sporting Gazette* 19 May 1900.

42 *Pall Mall Gazette* 22 March 1900.

43 Rudyard Kipling, 'The Ballad of East and West' (1889, collected in
    Rudyard Kipling's Verse: Definitive Edition, Hodder & Stoughton, 1940).

44 *St James's Gazette* 2 October 1900.

45 *Daily News* (London) 7 April 1904.

46 *Highland News* 7 October 1905.

47 *Blackburn Standard* 29 December 1900.

48 *John Bull* 16 June 1906.

49 Buchan, *Memory Hold-the-Door* pp. 158 & 163.

50 *John Bull* 16 June 1906.

51 *Spalding Guardian* 17 October 1903.

52 *Dundee Courier* 6 November 1903.

53 *Graphic* 6 June 1903.
54 *Dundee Courier* 25 November 1901.
55 *Reynolds's Newspaper* 5 June 1904.
56 Hansard 28 May 1903.
57 *Evening News* quoted in *Westminster Gazette* 19 June 1903.
58 *Preston Herald* 14 October 1903.
59 *Cork Examiner* 18 May 1904.
60 *Leigh Chronicle and Weekly District Advertiser* 5 February 1904.
61 *Edinburgh Evening News* 16 May 1903.
62 *Hampshire Advertiser* 21 January 1899.
63 *Scotsman* 16 May 1903.
64 *Burnley Express* 3 July 1901.
65 *Graphic* 6 June 1903.
66 *Northern Whig* 21 October 1903.
67 *Daily Mirror* 27 November 1903.
68 *Manchester Evening News* 27 November 1903.
69 *Scottish Referee* 30 October 1903.
70 *Evesham Standard & West Midland Observer* 17 October 1903.
71 *Northern Constitution* 19 December 1903.
72 *Northern Whig* 28 December 1903.
73 *Sussex Agricultural Express* 12 December 1903.
74 *Northampton Mercury* 25 December 1903.
75 *Dundee Courier* 28 January 1904.
76 *Edinburgh Evening News* 9 January 1904.
77 *London Evening Standard* 5 December 1905.
78 *London Daily News* 19 November 1903.
79 *Faringdon Advertiser and Vale of the White Horse Gazette* 13 January 1906.
80 *Manchester Evening News* 27 November 1903.

5: Children and Youths

1 *Alcester Chronicle* 24 November 1906.
2 *Nuneaton Observer* 12 July 1901.
3 *St James's Gazette* 20 November 1903; *Oxfordshire Weekly News* 25 November 1903; *Framlingham Weekly News* 28 November 1903; *Eastern Evening News* 10 December 1903; *Aberdeen People's Journal* 2 January 1904.
4 *Halifax Evening Courier* 1 December 1903; *Sunderland Daily Echo and Shipping Gazette* 9 December 1903; *Aberdeen People's Journal* 2 January 1904.
5 *Daily Mirror* 10 December 1903.

6   *Daily Telegraph & Courier* (London) 23 December 1903.

7   *Eastern Daily Press* 10 June 1905.

8   *Socialist* 1 June 1905.

9   Robert Ensor, *England 1870–1914* (Oxford University Press, 1936) p. 361.

10 *Alloa Advertiser* 24 October 1903.

11 *Brecon County Times* 19 January 1906.

12 *Stockton Herald, South Durham and Cleveland Advertiser* 24 September 1904.

13 *Daily News* (London) 4 April 1906.

14 *Daily Telegraph & Courier* (London) 21 March 1907.

15 *Leigh Chronicle and Weekly District Advertiser* 5 May 1905; *Workington Star* 8 September 1905.

16 *Shoreditch Observer* 19 February 1910.

17 *Daily News* (London) 4 April 1906.

18 *Northern Whig* 21 May 1904.

19 *Dundee Evening Telegraph* 4 March 1901.

20 *Sheffield Evening Telegraph* 3 August 1907.

21 *Luton Times and Advertiser* 13 July 1906.

22 George Smithson, *Raffles in Real Life: The Confessions of George Smithson alias 'Gentleman George'* (Hutchinson, 1930) pp. 44–51.

23 *East London Observer* 20 August 1881.

24 Wells, *The New Machiavelli* Book 1 Chap. 3 Section 4.

25 *Daily Citizen* (Manchester) 10 March 1914.

26 *Brighton Gazette* 15 August 1901.

27 *Daily Mirror* 4 December 1903.

28 *Weekly Dispatch* (London) 15 February 1903.

29 Simon Heffer, *The Age of Decadence: Britain 1880 to 1914* (Windmill, 2017) p. 121.

30 Alan Ereira, *The People's England* (Routledge & Kegan Paul, 1981) p. 217.

31 *Coventry Evening Telegraph* 7 November 1905.

32 *Western Daily Press* 1 February 1908.

33 Charles Dickens, *Sketches by Boz* (John Macrone, 1836) 'Scenes' Chap. 7.

34 *Kirkintilloch Herald* 28 November 1900.

35 *Coventry Evening Telegraph* 7 November 1905.

36 Charlie Chaplin, *My Autobiography* (Bodley Head, 1964) p. 114.

37 *Leominster News and North West Herefordshire & Radnorshire Advertiser* 20 October 1905.

38 *Daily Graphic* 16 November 1900.

39 *Wigan Observer and District Advertiser* 1 August 1907.

40 *Dundee Courier* 24 March 1906.

41 *South Wales Daily News* 26 October 1900.

42 *Gloucestershire Echo* 14 December 1901.

43 *Uttoxeter Advertiser and Ashbourne Times* 19 March 1902.

44 *Portsmouth Evening News* 25 June 1904.

45 *Dundee Courier* 24 March 1906.

46 *Shields Daily News* 20 November 1900.

47 *County Advertiser & Herald for Staffordshire and Worcestershire* 24 March 1906.

48 *Western Daily Press* 29 October 1900.

49 *Walsall Advertiser* 8 December 1900.

50 *Sheffield Daily Telegraph* 21 August 1902.

51 *Leominster News and North West Herefordshire & Radnorshire Advertiser* 26 October 1900.

52 *Greenock Telegraph and Clyde Shipping Gazette* 4 August 1906.

53 *St James's Gazette* 13 December 1901.

54 Naomi Stanton, 'A Culture of Blame: Sunday School Teachers, Youth Workers and the Decline of Young People in Churches', *Crucible: The Christian Journal of Social Ethics* (2014).

55 Katriona McCartney, 'British Sunday Schools: An Educational Arm of the Churches, 1900–39', *Studies in Church History* Vol. 55 (2019).

56 *Leicester Daily Post* 7 October 1910.

57 *Sunday School Chronicle* 10 May 1923.

58 *London Daily News* 4 November 1902.

59 *Army and Navy Gazette* 18 January 1908.

60 *Birmingham Daily Gazette* 7 September 1908.

61 *Volunteer Service Gazette* 22 January 1908.

62 David Boyd Haycock, *A Crisis of Brilliance: Five Young British Artists and the Great War* (Old Street Publishing, 2009) p. 53.

63 *Liverpool Daily Post* 19 August 1901.

64 *Gloucester Journal* 14 December 1901.

65 Haycock, *A Crisis of Brilliance* p. 54.

66 *Eastbourne Gazette* 2 April 1902.

67 *South Wales Echo* 17 October 1900.

68 *Linlithgowshire Gazette* 11 August 1905.

69 Joseph McAleer, *Popular Reading and Publishing in Britain 1914–1950* (Clarendon Press, 1992) p. 21.

70 E. S. Turner, *Boys Will Be Boys: The Story of Sweeney Todd, Deadwood Dick, Sexton Blake, Billy Bunter, Dick Barton et al.* (Michael Joseph Ltd, 1948 – revised edition 1975) p. 111.

71 *The Boys' Friend* 8 October 1910.

72 Turner, *Boys Will Be Boys* p. 101.

73 *Stamford Mercury* 30 March 1906.

74 Bramah, *The Secret of the League* Chap. 9.

75 *Lancashire Evening Post* 16 August 1906.

76 *Justice* 17 September 1910.

77 Frank Richards, 'Aliens at Greyfriars', *Magnet* 6 (1908).

78 Mary Cadogan, *Frank Richards: The Chap Behind the Chums* (Penguin Books, 1988) pp. 71–2

79 Ibid. p. 82.

80 Martin Clifford, 'Darryl's Secret', *Gem* 37 (1908).

81 Martin Clifford, 'D'Arcy the Suffragist!', *Gem* 274 (1913).

82 Martin Clifford, 'The Jew of St Jim's', *Gem* 394 (1915).

83 Frank Richards, 'The Yankee Schoolboy', *Magnet* 150 (1910).

84 Martin Clifford, 'Tom Merry in Chicago', *Gem* 48 (1909).

85 Frank Mundell, *Stories of the Victoria Cross and the Humane Society* (National Sunday School Union, *c.* 1899 – revised edition 1900) p. 160.

86 Kipling, *Stalky & Co.*, 'The Flag of Their Country'.

6: Liberals and Labour

1 Blackwood, *A Prisoner in Fairyland* Chap. 2.

2 *Academy* 20 June 1908.

3 *Dundee Evening Post* 5 January 1905; *Daily Mirror* 13 January 1905; *Daily Telegraph & Courier* 13 January 1905; *Globe* 13 January 1905; *St James's Gazette* 13 January 1905; *Fifeshire Advertiser* 28 January 1905.

4 *East Anglian Daily Times* 2 August 1905.

5 Peter Wilshire, *The Pound in Your Pocket 1870–1970* (Cassell & Company, 1970) p. 107.

6 George R. Boyer & Timothy J. Hatton, 'New Estimates of British Unemployment, 1870–1913', *Journal of Economic History* (Vol. 62 No. 3, September 2002).

7 Gus Elen, 'Wait Till the Work Comes Round'.

8 *Peterhead Sentinel and General Advertiser for Buchan District* 25 November 1905; *Nottingham Journal* 30 November 1905.

9 *Dundee Courier* 30 November 1905; *Nottingham Journal* 30 November 1905.

10 *Globe* 11 February 1908.

11 Wilkie Collins, *The Moonstone* (Tinsley Brothers, 1868) Part 2 Chap. 1.

12 *Times* 17 January 1899.

13 *Morning Post* 31 March 1906.

14 Simon Heffer, *The Age of Decadence: Britain 1880 to 1914* (Windmill, 2017) p. 597.

15 *Westminster Gazette* 19 April 1907.

16 *Fifeshire Advertiser* 6 June 1908.

17 Stephen J. Lee, *British Political History 1815–1914* (Routledge, 1994) p. 228.

18 *Manchester Courier and Lancashire General Advertiser* 4 January 1909.

19 Peter Brent, *The Edwardians* (BBC, 1972) p. 130.

20 Lawrence James, *The Middle Class: A History* (Little, Brown, 2006) p. 308.

21 *Belfast News-Letter* 2 January 1909; *Derby Daily Telegraph* 2 January 1909; *Eastern Evening News* 2 January 1909; *Hampstead & Highgate Express* 2 January 1909; *Irish Times* 2 January 1909; *Sheffield Evening Telegraph* 2 January 1909; *Eastern Daily Press* 4 January 1909; *Retford and Worksop Herald and North Notts Advertiser* 5 January 1909; *Nuneaton Observer* 7 January 1910.

22 A. G. Gardiner, *Prophets, Priests and Kings* (Alston Rivers, 1908) 'Winston Churchill'.

23 *Punch* 28 April 1909.

24 Lee, *British Political History 1815–1914* p. 229.

25 *Westminster Gazette* 30 April 1909.

26 *Times* 16 March 1906.

27 Roy Hattersley, *Campbell-Bannerman* (Haus, 2006) pp. 123–4.

28 *Greenock Telegraph and Clyde Shipping Gazette* 24 January 1907.

29 Alan Ryan, *Bertrand Russell: A Political Life* (Allen Lane, 1988) p. 38.

30 *Referee* 10 October 1909; *Dublin Daily Express* 11 October 1909.

31 *Scotsman* 27 August 1909; *London Evening Standard* 5 October 1909; *Western Morning News* 5 August 1909.

32 *Referee* 17 October 1909.

33 John Buchan, *Memory Hold-the-Door* (Hodder & Stoughton, 1949) p. 149.

34 *New Age* 12 May 1910.

35 *Times* 22 November 1910.

36 *Irish News and Belfast Morning News* 25 July 1911; *Westminster Gazette* 25 July 1911.

37 J. B. Priestley, *The Edwardians* (William Heinemann, 1970) p. 195; *Dundee Courier* 25 July 1911.

38 Hansard 24 July 1911.

39 Hattersley, *Campbell-Bannerman* p. 121.

40 Heffer, *The Age of Decadence* p. 598.

41 *Labour Leader* 19 August 1910.

42 *Aberystwyth Observer* 21 January 1909.

43 *Barrow Herald and Furness Advertiser* 6 January 1912.

44 *Sheffield Evening Telegraph* 19 August 1913.

45 *Runcorn Examiner* 26 April 1913.

46 *Economic Journal* Vol. 17 No. 68 (1907).

47 Harry Taylor, *Victor Grayson: In Search of Britain's Lost Revolutionary* (Pluto Press, 2021) p. 86.

48 *Wigton Advertiser* 13 October 1906.

49 *Clarion* 16 February 1895.

50 Samuel Hynes, *The Edwardian Turn of Mind* (Princeton University Press, 1968) p. 90.

51 Ibid. p. 97.

52 Chesterton, *The Club of Queer Trades* Chap. 5.

53 *Justice* 14 May 1904.

54 *Framlingham Weekly News* 10 March 1906.

55 A. J. Davies, *To Build a New Jerusalem: The British Labour Movement from the 1880s to the 1990s* (Michael Joseph, 1992) p. 56.

56 *Todmorden Advertiser and Hebden Bridge Newsletter* 14 December 1906.

57 *Westminster Gazette* 28 July 1906.

58 *Clarion* 28 May 1909.

59 *Clarion* 16 February 1912.

60 James, *The Middle Class* p. 310.

61 *St James's Gazette* 17 May 1904.

62 *Irish Independent* 12 August 1907.

63 Jonathan Rose, *The Intellectual Life of the British Working Classes* (Yale University Press, 2001) p. 42.

64 Saki, *The Unbearable Bassington* Chap. 4.

65 Gibbs, *The Street of Adventure* Chap. 5.

66 *Evening News* (London) 18 November 1910; *Westminster Gazette* 19 November 1910; *Era* 26 November 1910; *Stage* 1 December 1910.

67 Martin Clifford, 'Skimpole's Little Scheme', *Gem* 41 (1907).

68 *Scotsman* 20 October 1910; *Midlothian Advertiser* 21 October 1910; *Overland China Mail* 24 December 1910.

69 *Dundee Courier* 21 April 1908.

70 *Daily Mirror* 21 February 1907.

71 *Islington Gazette* 11 June 1907.

72 Jessica Gerrard, '"Little Soldiers" for Socialism: Childhood and Socialist Politics in the British Socialist Sunday School Movement', *International Review of Social History* Vol. 58 No. 1 (2013) p. 87.

73 *Islington Gazette* 11 June 1907.

74 *Referee* 27 January 1907.

75 Hansard 13 March 1907.

76 *Justice* 3 August 1907.

77 *Westminster Gazette* 3 November 1909.

78 *Oxford Times* 11 September 1909.

79 Buchan, *Memory Hold-the-Door* p. 146.

80 *Daily Telegraph & Courier* (London) 19 November 1907.

7: Women and Men

1 Orczy, *The Scarlet Pimpernel* Chap. 20.

2 Ward, *Delia Blanchflower* Chap. 1.

3 *Manchester Courier and Lancashire General Advertiser* 2 August 1907.

4 *Manchester Evening News* 7 September 1907; *Irish News and Belfast Morning News* 10 September 1907; *Hampstead & Highgate Express* 14 September 1907.

5 *St James's Gazette* 2 September 1901.

6 *Westminster Gazette* 11 May 1903.

7 *Weekly Dispatch* (London) 23 August 1908.

8 *Liverpool Daily Post* 23 August 1909; *Dover Express* 27 August 1909.

9 *Aberdeen Evening Express* 3 October 1910.

10 *Islington Gazette* 28 September 1909.

11 *Reynolds's Newspaper* 8 November 1908.

12 *Weekly Irish Times* 12 September 1908.

13 *John Bull* 28 September 1907.

14 *Londonderry Sentinel* 17 October 1903.

15 *St James's Gazette* 16 September 1901; *Illustrated Sporting and Dramatic News* 21 September 1901; *Paisley & Renfrewshire Gazette* 28 September 1901.

16 *Showman* 28 March 1902.

17 *St James's Gazette* 30 January 1904.

18 *Music Hall and Theatre Review* 29 January 1904.

19 *Illustrated Police News* 30 January 1904.

20 *Daily Telegraph & Courier* (London) 1 February 1904.

21 *Bolton Evening News* 30 January 1904.

22 *St James's Gazette* 1 February 1904.

23 *Sportsman* 1 October 1907.

24 *Daily Record* 27 October 1905.

25 *Sporting Life* 1 January 1907.

26 Graeme Kent, *A Pictorial History of Wrestling* (Spring Books, 1968) p. 153.

27 *Lancashire Evening Post* 29 October 1906.

28 *Newcastle Evening Chronicle* 8 November 1906.

29 *Music Hall and Theatre Review* 28 December 1906.

30 *Croydon Guardian and Surrey County Gazette* 30 December 1905.

31 *Illustrated Sporting and Dramatic News* 21 September 1901.

32 *Western Mail* 1 July 1905; *Cheltenham Looker-On* 8 July 1905; *Herts & Cambs Reporter & Royston Crow* 14 July 1905; *Daily Chronicle* quoted in *Ottawa Free Press* 23 August 1905.

33 *Daily Chronicle* quoted in *Ottawa Free Press* 23 August 1905.

34 *Penny Illustrated Paper* 10 November 1906.

35 David Boyd Haycock, *A Crisis of Brilliance: Five Young British Artists and the Great War* (Old Street Publishing, 2009) p. 95.

36 *Era* 6 March 1864.

37 Lisa Duggan, *Sapphic Slashers: Sex, Violence and American Modernity* (Duke University Press, 2000) p. 147.

38 Lady Matilda Alice Powles de Frece, *Recollections of Vesta Tilley* (Hutchinson, 1934) p. 25.

39 *Fleetwood Chronicle* 17 July 1906.

40 *Sheffield Evening Telegraph* 7 November 1902.

41 *Music Hall and Theatre Review* 4 January 1907.

42 *Referee* 16 May 1909.

43 *Sporting Times* 3 October 1908.

44 *Gloucester Citizen* 13 June 1906.

45 *Hull Daily Mail* 22 February 1910.

46 *Evening Star* 7 December 1908.

47 *Era* 5 August 1914.

48 Daniel Farson, *Marie Lloyd & Music Hall* (Tom Stacey, 1972) p. 73.

49 *Times* 2 July 1912.

50 *Sporting Life* 5 July 1912.

51 *Music Hall and Theatre Review* 4 July 1912.

52 *Tatler* 10 July 1912.

53 *New York Times* 2 July 1912.

54 Will Evans, 'The Mermaid's Lament'.

55 *Era* 3 April 1909.

56 *Evening News* (London) 6 November 1903.

57 *Daily Mirror* 7 November 1903.

58 *Globe* 4 November 1904.

59 Ibid.

60 *Leicester Daily Post* 11 June 1907.

61 Mason, *The Four Feathers* Chap. 23.

62 Galsworthy, *The Man of Property* Part III Chap. 6.

63 Paul Ferris, *Sex and the British: A Twentieth-Century History* (Michael Joseph, 1993) p. 23.

64 *Sheffield Independent* 4 April 1906.

65 *Newcastle Guardian and Silverdale, Chesterton and Audley Chronicle* 1 August 1903.

66 *Aberdeen Press & Journal* 3 December 1906.

67 *Kensington News and West London Times* 1 October 1937.

68 *Votes for Women* March 1908.

69 Helena Swanwick, *I Have Been Young* (Victor Gollancz, 1935) p. 187.

70 Emmeline Pankhurst, *My Own Story* (Eveleigh Nash, 1914) p. 62.

71 Diane Atkinson, *Rise Up, Women! The Remarkable Lives of the Suffragettes* (Bloomsbury, 2018) p. 107.

72 Roy Hattersley, *Campbell-Bannerman* (Haus, 2006) p. 119.

73 *Irish Times* 19 October 1909.

74 *Votes for Women* 6 December 1907.

75 Simon Heffer, *The Age of Decadence: Britain 1880 to 1914* (Windmill, 2017) p. 724.

76 *South Wales Daily News* 7 December 1908.

77 Martin Pugh, *The Tories and the People 1880–1935* (Basil Blackwood Ltd, 1985) pp. 27 & 168.

78 Ibid. p. 61.

79 *Justice* 11 June 1914.

80 *Clarion* 18 January 1907.

81 *London Review of Books* 18 February 1988.

82 Quoted in *Bradford Daily Telegraph* 23 October 1909.

83 *Portadown News* 10 July 1909.

84 Pankhurst, *My Own Story* p. 59.

85 Quoted in *Votes for Women* 27 August 1909.

86 *Referee* 12 July 1908; *Clarion* 17 July 1908; *John Bull* 8 August 1908.

87 *Women's Franchise* 16 July 1908.

88 Jane Beckett & Deborah Cherry (ed.), *The Edwardian Era* (Phaidon Press & Barbican Art Gallery, 1987) p. 106.

89 *Votes for Women* 31 December 1908.

90 *Daily Mirror* 1 December 1909.

91 *Kinematograph Weekly* 15 October 1908.

92 *Croydon Chronicle and East Surrey Advertiser* 20 November 1909.

93 *Yorkshire Evening Post* 12 November 1909.

94 *Era* 21 August 1909.

95 *Westminster Gazette* 5 January 1910; *Empire News & The Umpire* 9 January 1910; *Bristol Magpie* 13 January 1910.

8: Aliens and Revolutionaries

1 H. G. Pélissier, 'What a Very Great Improvement' (Arthur Wimperis & Harry G. Pélissier, *c.* 1904).
2 Jack Pleasants, 'I Shall Be a Bad Lad, Liza Ann!' (C. W. Murphy, 1910).
3 *Tower Hamlets Independent and East End Local Advertiser* 16 April 1904.
4 *Manchester Courier and Lancashire General Advertiser* 8 December 1904.
5 *Eastern Daily Press* 24 September 1904.
6 *Manchester Courier and Lancashire General Advertiser* 31 May 1904.
7 *Gloucester Citizen* 30 May 1902; *Islington Gazette* 19 June 1902; *Justice* 7 March 1903; *Royal Cornwall Gazette* 4 July 1907.
8 *Reynolds's Newspaper* 9 June 1907.
9 *London Daily News* 4 June 1907.
10 Maxim Gorky, *Collected Works Volume 9: Literary Portraits* (Progress, 1982) p. 280.
11 *Daily Mirror* 10 May 1907.
12 Ibid. 15 May 1907.
13 Ibid. 10 May 1907.
14 Ibid. 15 May 1907.
15 *London Daily News* 23 May 1907.
16 *Aberdeen Press and Journal* 28 May 1907.
17 *Hackney and Kingsland Gazette* 17 May 1907.
18 *Justice* 1 June 1907.
19 *London Daily News* 4 June 1907.
20 Ibid. 25 May 1907.
21 *Daily Mirror* 15 May 1907.
22 *Royal Cornwall Gazette* 4 July 1907.
23 Wells, *Tono-Bungay* Book 1 Chap. 2 Section 1.
24 *Judy* 23 November 1870.
25 *Ally Sloper's Half-Holiday* 10 March 1894.
26 *Westminster Gazette* 23 January 1909.
27 *Dundee Courier* 4 January 1912.
28 *London Evening Standard* 4 January 1911.
29 *Daily News* (London) 5 January 1911.
30 *Evening Irish Times* 5 January 1911; *Daily Telegraph & Courier* (London) 6 January 1911; *Scotsman* 6 January 1911.
31 *Freedom* 1 February 1911.
32 *Bioscope* 8 February 1912.

33 *Times* 4 March 1914.

34 *Leeds Mercury* 22 July 1913; *Yorkshire Post and Leeds Intelligencer* 22 July 1913; *Bioscope* 24 July 1913; *Kinematograph Weekly* 25 September 1913.

35 *Evening News* (London) 16 October 1913.

36 *Kinematograph Weekly* 30 October 1913.

37 *South Wales Gazette* 28 November 1913.

38 George Pearson, *Flashback: An Autobiography of a British Film Maker* (George Allen & Unwin, 1957) p. 29.

39 Jan McDonald, *The New Drama 1900–1914* (Methuen, 1986) p. 122.

40 *New Ross Standard* 11 November 1910; *Grantham Journal* 12 November 1910; *Wicklow People* 12 November 1910; *Referee* 13 November 1910.

41 *Labour Leader* 18 November 1910.

42 *Referee* 13 November 1910.

43 Hansard 22 August 1911.

44 *Northampton Chronicle and Echo* 22 August 1911.

45 *Evening Mail* 13 October 1911.

46 *Freeman's Journal* 28 May 1912.

47 *Scotsman* 1 January 1913; *Shoreditch Observer* 7 September 1912.

48 John Quail, *The Slow Burning Fuse: The Lost History of the British Anarchists* (Paladin, 1978) pp. 267–8.

49 *Evening News* (London) 23 April 1909.

50 Harry Taylor, *Victor Grayson: In Search of Britain's Lost Revolutionary* (Pluto Press, 2021) p. 119.

51 Ibid. p. 188.

52 *Shoreditch Observer* 7 September 1912.

53 *Luton Times and Advertiser* 6 September 1912.

54 *Labour Leader* 5 September 1912.

55 *Freeman's Journal* 28 May 1912.

56 Peter Hain, *Political Strikes: The State and Trade Unionism in Britain* (Viking, 1986) p. 12.

57 E. S. Turner, *Boys Will Be Boys: The Story of Sweeney Todd, Deadwood Dick, Sexton Blake, Billy Bunter, Dick Barton et al.* (Michael Joseph Ltd, 1948 – revised edition 1975) p. 195.

58 Buchan, *The Half-Hearted* Chap. 23.

59 Matthew Engel, *Tickle the Public: One Hundred Years of the Popular Press* (Victor Gollancz, 1996) p. 72.

60 *Overland China Mail* 1 March 1913.

61 *Dundee Courier* 8 March 1913.

62 Clifford Musgrave, *Life in Brighton: From the Earliest Times to the Present*

(Faber & Faber, 1970 – revised edition: John Hallewell Publications, 1981) p. 368.

63 Saki, *When William Came* Chap. 3.

64 *Illustrated London News* 23 December 1911.

65 *Truth* 8 February 1911.

66 *Pall Mall Gazette* 24 January 1912.

67 *Dublin Daily Express* 5 September 1912; *Referee* 28 January 1912.

68 *Daily News* (London) 4 September 1912; *Dublin Daily Express* 5 September 1912.

69 Quoted in *Pall Mall Gazette* 4 September 1912.

70 *Referee* 8 September 1912.

71 *Newcastle Daily Chronicle* 5 September 1912.

72 *Illustrated London News* 11 January 1913.

73 Quoted in *Pall Mall Gazette* 4 September 1912.

74 *Suffragette* 14 March 1913.

75 *Illustrated London News* 9 December 1911.

76 *London Evening Standard* 29 April 1912.

77 *Pall Mall Gazette* 12 September 1912.

78 *Pall Mall Gazette* 4 October 1912.

79 Samuel Hynes, *The Edwardian Turn of Mind* (Princeton University Press, 1968) p. 328; *Morning Post* 7 November 1910.

80 *New Age* 8 December 1910.

81 *Times* 7 November 1910.

9: Alarms and Excursions

1 Dell, *The Knave of Diamonds* Part 1 Chap. 2.

2 Ethel Levey, 'Ragtime Suffragette' (written by Nat Ayer & Charles Williams, 1913).

3 *Household Words*, quoted in *Oxfordshire Weekly News* 18 February 1903.

4 *Lancashire Evening Post* 13 September 1906.

5 *Cannock Chase Courier* 26 October 1912.

6 *Referee* 22 December 1912.

7 *Bystander* 15 January 1913.

8 *Cannock Chase Courier* 26 October 1912.

9 *Liverpool Daily Post* 7 August 1913.

10 *Todmorden Advertiser and Hebden Bridge Newsletter* 31 January 1913.

11 *Irish News and Belfast Morning News* 4 April 1901.

12 *Hamilton Daily Times* 10 June 1913.

13 Quoted in *Cheltenham Looker-On* 10 January 1913.

14 Jack Read, *Empires, Hippodromes & Palaces* (Alderman Press, 1985) p. 35.

15 *Fleetwood Chronicle* 8 July 1913.

16 *Tatler* 30 April 1913.

17 Arthur Conan Doyle, *The Crime of the Congo* (Hutchinson, 1909) p. 37.

18 *Daily News* (London) 16 September 1909.

19 J. B. Priestley, *The Edwardians* (William Heinemann, 1970) p. 252.

20 *Bristol Magpie* 13 January 1910.

21 *Yorkshire Evening Post* 18 December 1912.

22 *Ottawa Free Press* 8 August 1913.

23 Les Garner, *A Brave and Beautiful Spirit: Dora Marsden 1882–1960* (Avebury Gower, 1990) p. 52.

24 *The Vote* 18 November 1911.

25 *Freewoman* 23 November 1911.

26 *Suffragette* 31 January 1913.

27 *Central Somerset Gazette* 2 August 1912.

28 Mary Davis, *Sylvia Pankhurst: A Life in Radical Politics* (Pluto Press, 1999) p. 32.

29 *Suffragette* 30 May 1913.

30 Ibid. 29 May 1914.

31 George Dangerfield, *The Strange Death of Liberal England* (Harrison Smith & Robert Haas, 1935) p. 325.

32 Simon Webb, *The Suffragette Bombers: Britain's Forgotten Terrorists* (Pen & Sword, 2014) p. 38.

33 *Suffragette* 21 November 1913.

34 Paul Ferris, *Sex and the British: A Twentieth-Century History* (Michael Joseph, 1993) p. 44.

35 Ibid. p. 43.

36 *Suffragette* 24 April 1914.

37 *Sporting Times* 5 April 1913.

38 *Irish Independent* 6 June 1913.

39 A. N. Wilson, *After the Victorians* (Hutchinson, 2005) p. 120.

40 *John Bull* 19 December 1908.

41 *Brechin Review, and Forfar and Kincardineshire Advertiser* 21 October 1910.

42 *Londonderry Sentinel* 1 June 1911.

43 *Kilmarnock Herald and North Ayrshire Gazette* 19 December 1913.

44 John Connolly & Paddy Dolan, *Gaelic Games in Society: Civilising Processes, Players, Administrators and Spectators* (Palgrave Macmillan, 2020) p. 24.

45 *Reynolds's Newspaper* 2 August 1896.

46 *Dundee Evening Telegraph* 12 February 1912.

47 *North Down Herald and County Down Independent* 4 October 1912.

48 Stephen J. Lee, *British Political History 1815–1914* (Routledge, 1994) p. 238.

49 *Derry Journal* 6 May 1914.

50 *Westminster Gazette* 1 October 1912.

51 *Liverpool Daily Post* 25 March 1914.

52 *Scotsman* 30 April 1914.

53 *Aberdeen Press and Journal* 13 June 1914.

54 *Belfast Weekly News* 18 June 1914.

55 David Reed, *Ireland: The Key to the British Revolution* (Larkin Publications, 1984) p. 40.

56 *Music Hall and Theatre Review* 14 October 1904.

57 *Dundee Evening Telegraph* 25 September 1902.

58 Lee, *British Political History 1815–1914* p. 263.

59 Doyle, 'The Second Stain', *The Return of Sherlock Holmes*.

60 Lee, *British Political History 1815–1914* p. 260.

61 *Evening Mail* 15 January 1902.

62 *Scotsman* 12 April 1904.

63 *St James's Gazette* 9 April 1904.

64 *Westminster Gazette* 20 April 1904.

65 *Graphic* 28 October 1911.

66 *London Daily News* 25 May 1907.

67 *Westminster Gazette* 28 December 1911.

68 *Kinematograph Weekly* 1 February 1912.

69 Quoted in *Dartmouth & South Hams Chronicle* 4 July 1913.

70 *Westminster Gazette* 25 August 1913.

71 *East Anglian Daily Times* 27 December 1907.

72 *Scotsman* 30 November 1912.

Epilogue: Two Killers

1 *Evening News* (London) 8 March 1909.

2 *Edinburgh Evening News* 2 July 1915.

3 *Surrey Comet* 8 September 1900.

4 *Era* 29 September 1900.

5 *Grimsby Daily Telegraph* 6 November 1900.

6 *Ealing Gazette and West Middlesex Observer* 11 October 1902.

7 *Islington Gazette* 15 July 1910.

8 *Wolverhampton Express and Star* 9 March 1905.

9 Peter Brent, *The Edwardians* (BBC, 1972) p. 113.

10 *Daily Mirror* 3 August 1910.

11 *Music Hall and Theatre Review* 30 September 1909.

12 *Era* 26 March 1910.

13 *Daily Telegraph & Courier* (London) 15 July 1910.

14 *Islington Gazette* 15 July 1910.

15 *Daily Mirror* 2 August 1910.

16 *Dundee Evening Telegraph* 24 November 1910.

17 *Ballymena Weekly Telegraph* 29 October 1910.

18 *Northampton Chronicle and Echo* 24 October 1910.

19 *Reynolds's Newspaper* 13 November 1910.

20 *Birmingham Weekly Post* 24 December 1910.

21 *Daily Mirror* 2 August 1910.

22 *Westminster Gazette* 14 July 1910.

23 *Evening News* (London) 16 July 1910.

24 *Daily Mirror* 1 August 1910.

25 *Daily News* (London) 21 September 1910.

26 *Leicester Daily Post* 12 October 1888.

27 *Sheffield Evening Telegraph* 30 July 1915; *Dundee People's Journal* 7 August 1915.

28 *Dundee People's Journal* 7 August 1915; *Daily Sketch* 23 June 1915; *Edinburgh Evening News* 2 July 1915.

29 *Ballymena Weekly Telegraph* 21 August 1915.

30 *People* 23 June 1929.

31 *Daily Sketch* 23 June 1915.

32 *Falkirk Herald* 3 July 1915.

33 *Ballymena Weekly Telegraph* 21 August 1915.

ACKNOWLEDGEMENTS

First, my thanks to Euan Thorneycroft at A. M. Heath for helping shape the original proposal for this book.

Then to all the good people in Profile and related territories: Andrew Franklin, whose early enthusiasm was much appreciated; Nick Humphrey, who's a terrific editor; copy editor Hugh Davis (also terrific); managing editor Georgina Difford; cover designer Pete Dyer; typesetter Jonathan Harley; editorial assistant Jon Petre; proofreader Rachel Wright; Clare Beaumont and Sian Gibson in sales; Dahmicca Wright and Rosie Parnham in marketing; publicist Valentina Zanca; audio editors Louisa Dunnigan and Audrey Kerr. They're all wonderful, and are collectively responsible for the good things about this book.

After a decade at the University of Chichester, I'm still grateful to Hugo Frey for allowing me to teach there. And for allowing me to learn there: I'm indebted to three post-graduate students – Ben Blackwood, Nicola Buckley and Maxine Harcourt-Kelly – for introducing me to Lord Pirrie, Dora Marsden and Fred 'Pimple' Evans respectively. (Sorry, Maxine, that Pimple didn't make the cut.)

Many people have offered comments or suggestions of themes, books or ideas, much of which I've cheerfully stolen for my own purposes: Dan Atkinson, Jennie Bird, Anthony Broxton, Ben Finlay, Brian Freeborn, Michael Glasper, Ted Goodman, Will Lloyd, Simon Matthews, York Membery, George Owers, John Radford, Harry Taylor. As pompous headmasters used to say, it would be invidious to single out any individuals in particular, so my apologies to Adenike Deane-Pratt, John Flaxman and Anthony Teague for not doing so.

My granddad, James Turner, was born in 1900 and attended the Salvation Army Sunday school in Willenhall, Staffordshire, where he was presented with copies of T. W. Jamieson's *A Boy's Book of Heroes* and Frank Mundell's *Stories of the Victoria Cross*, books that I now own. I hope that some of the influence has survived, and that the present work repays some of my debt to my family.

As ever, my greatest thanks are to Sam Harrison, to whom this book is dedicated. And to Thamasin Marsh, whose love and support continues to be invaluable (and whose great-granddad, George Pearson, turns up in the story).

INDEX

Note: page numbers in **bold** refer to information contained in captions.